creating emotion in games

in games

The Craft and Art of Emotioneering™

by David Freeman
www.freemangames.com

New Riders

800 East 96th Street, 3rd Floor, Indianapolis, Indiana 46240
An Imprint of Pearson Education
Boston • Indianapolis • London • Munich • New York • San Francisco

creating emotion in games

The Craft and Art of Emotioneering™

Contents at a Glance

Creating Emotion in Games: The Craft and Art of Emotioneering™

International Standard Book Number: 1-5927-3007-8

Library of Congress Catalog Card Number: 2002111250

Printed in the United States of America

First printing: September, 2003

08 07 06 05 04 03   7 6 5 4 3 2 1

Interpretation of the printing code: The rightmost double-digit number is the year of the book's printing; the rightmost single-digit number is the number of the book's printing. For example, the printing code 03-1 shows that the first printing of the book occurred in 2003.

Trademarks

Warning and Disclaimer

Publisher
Stephanie Wall

Production Manager
Gina Kanouse

Executive Development Editor
Lisa Thibault

Senior Project Editor
Sarah Kearns

Copy Editor
Linda Laflamme

Indexer/Proofreader
Lisa Stumpf

Composition
Kim Scott

Manufacturing Coordinator
Dan Uhrig

Interior Designer
Kim Scott

Cover Designer
Aren Howell

Marketing
Scott Cowlin
Tammy Detrich
Hannah Onstad Latham

Publicity Manager
Susan Nixon

Acknowledgments

Whenever I'd read the acknowledgment page in a book, I'd see a list of "thank you's" and have no idea what all those thanked people actually did. Now that I've actually written a book, I still have no idea.

But I do have an idea what the people thanked below did. As this book was being written, I'd shoot the chapters off to them, and they'd grace me with their comments and suggestions. Just about every suggestion any of them made has been used. You, the reader, and I, the writer, are better off for these people being so generous with their time and insights, and for their knowing how to type.

This book is dedicated to David Perry. David gave me my first job in the game industry. That was just the first of a long list of doors he has opened for me.

For feedback on the chapters, I sincerely thank Warren Spector, Richard Ham, Jason Della Rocca, Jeff Barnhart, Anand Rajan, Chris Klug, Tommy Tallarico, Gordon Walton, Kenneth Holm, and Tyrone Rodriguez.

There has been a core group of people who saw where I was going and who continuously encouraged me to keep pressing on. Their support has meant so much. They are Jason Bell, Chris Klug, Troy Dunniway, and Martin Spiess.

From day one, I've relied heavily on my research associate, Stephane Dreyfus, and rely on him still.

I had no idea, when I began, if anyone really cared about creating emotion in games. The affirmative answer came soon and came loudly. And so I'd like to thank everyone on the publishing side, and the teams at the great development studios, who brought me on board for the games I've been working on at Electronic Arts, Activision, Vivendi Universal Games, Microsoft, Atari, Ubi Soft, Midway Games, 3D Realms, and numerous others.

Finally I'd like to thank my publisher, Stephanie Wall, and my editor, Lisa Thibault. Every author should be as fortunate as I to have their kind of support.

About the Author

david@freemangames.com ◆ www.freemangames.com ◆ www.beyondstructure.com

David Freeman not only operates in the worlds of both games and film, but is a leading teacher in both media.

As this book is being written, David, along with his game design and writing consultancy The Freeman Group, is currently working as either a designer/writer or writer on three games for Vivendi Universal Games, three games for Activision, two games for Atari, two games for 3D Realms, and games for Electronic Arts, Ubi Soft, and others. Only a few of these games have been announced and thus can be named. They are *Command and Conquer 3* (working title) for Electronic Arts, *Van Helsing* for Vivendi Universal Games, both *Duke Nuken Forever* and *Prey* for 3D Realms, *Terminator: Redemption* for Atari (the working title for their game that goes to and then beyond Judgment Day), dialogue for *Mission Impossible: Operation Surma* for Atari, and work on both *Shark Slayer* and *Pitfall* for Activision. David also contributed to the script for Atari's and Shiny Entertainment's *Enter the Matrix*. He has worked in the past on game projects for Microsoft and Midway Games. No doubt, by the time you're reading this, this list will be long out of date. For David's current activities, please see: **www.freemangames.com**

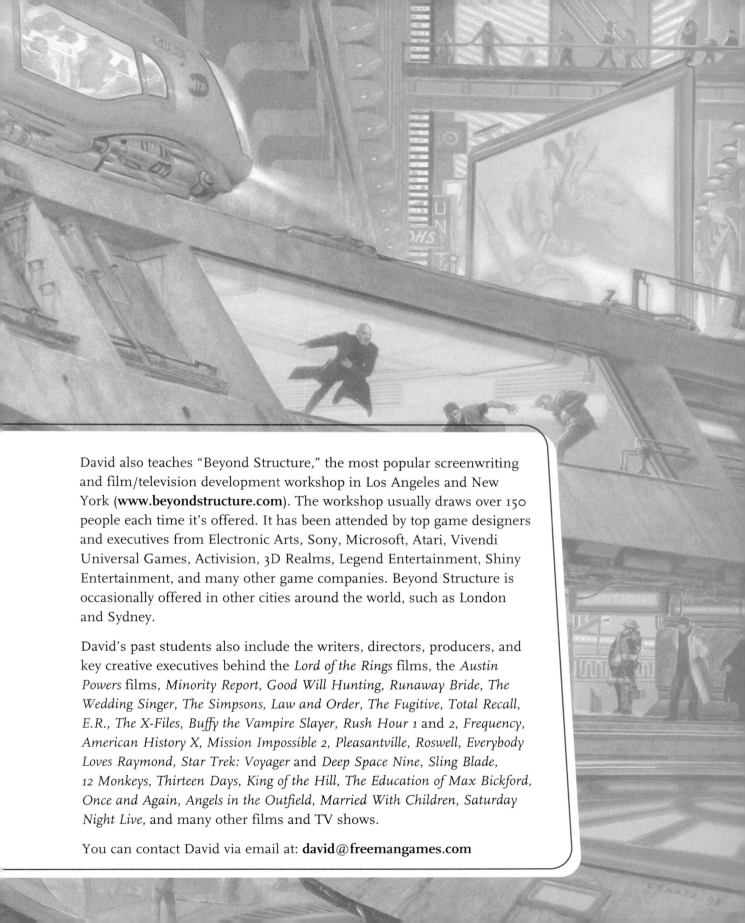

David also teaches "Beyond Structure," the most popular screenwriting and film/television development workshop in Los Angeles and New York (**www.beyondstructure.com**). The workshop usually draws over 150 people each time it's offered. It has been attended by top game designers and executives from Electronic Arts, Sony, Microsoft, Atari, Vivendi Universal Games, Activision, 3D Realms, Legend Entertainment, Shiny Entertainment, and many other game companies. Beyond Structure is occasionally offered in other cities around the world, such as London and Sydney.

David's past students also include the writers, directors, producers, and key creative executives behind the *Lord of the Rings* films, the *Austin Powers* films, *Minority Report, Good Will Hunting, Runaway Bride, The Wedding Singer, The Simpsons, Law and Order, The Fugitive, Total Recall, E.R., The X-Files, Buffy the Vampire Slayer, Rush Hour 1* and *2, Frequency, American History X, Mission Impossible 2, Pleasantville, Roswell, Everybody Loves Raymond, Star Trek: Voyager* and *Deep Space Nine, Sling Blade, 12 Monkeys, Thirteen Days, King of the Hill, The Education of Max Bickford, Once and Again, Angels in the Outfield, Married With Children, Saturday Night Live,* and many other films and TV shows.

You can contact David via email at: **david@freemangames.com**

About the Technical Reviewer

This reviewer contributed his considerable hands-on expertise to the entire development process for *Creating Emotion in Games*. As the book was being written, this dedicated professional reviewed all the material for technical content, organization, and flow. His feedback was critical to ensuring that *Creating Emotion in Games* fits our reader's need for the highest-quality technical information.

Jason Della Rocca oversees the day-to-day running of the International Game Developers Association (IGDA)—giving particular focus to outreach efforts and member programs, and working to build the sense of a unified game development community and provide a common voice for the game development industry. Jason and the IGDA deal with such diverse topics as the education of the next generation of game developers, dealing with the concern over violence in games, diminishing the impact of exploitative software patents, and working to attract more women and diverse cultures to game development. Jason also oversees the running of the Game Developers Choice Awards, an annual industry event that recognizes and rewards outstanding achievement within the game development community.

Jason has been a member of the game development community for many years, spending several as the Developer Relations Group Manager at Matrox Graphics, a leading supplier of consumer graphics hardware. Jason also enjoyed short stints at Quazal, evangelizing its online game networking middleware, and Silicon Graphics, where he worked with 3D and web technologies.

Jason can be reached at **jason@igda.org**.

REGISTER YOUR PRODUCT!

Congratulations!

You have just become the owner of ___1___ emotional interactive reality generation system, ___Creating Emotions in Games___ Edition ___1.0___ .

Please go to our web site, **www.freemangames.com**, and register your product. Click on the button called **Participate**.

As a Registered User, your name and address will never be sold or given to any other party, even if that party has some kind of weapon. However, Registered Users may get periodic updates, announcements, musings, insights, and other communications from the author. Or, if the author gets really busy, maybe not. But you never know.

The author also welcomes your feedback at: **david@freemangames.com** As Registered Users tend to be fairly communicative, it may not be possible for the author to answer every email. But every single email will be read by the author, and that's a promise.

Tell Us What You Think

As the reader of this book, you are the most important critic and commentator. We value your opinion and want to know what we're doing right, what we could do better, what areas you'd like to see us publish in, and any other words of wisdom you're willing to pass our way.

As the Publisher for New Riders Publishing, I welcome your comments. You can fax, email, or write me directly to let me know what you did or didn't like about this book—as well as what we can do to make our books stronger. When you write, please be sure to include this book's title, ISBN, and author, as well as your name and phone or fax number. I will carefully review your comments and share them with the author and editors who worked on the book.

Please note that I cannot help you with technical problems related to the topic of this book, and that due to the high volume of email I receive, I might not be able to reply to every message.

Fax: 317-428-3280
Email: **stephanie.wall@newriders.com**
Mail: Stephanie Wall
          Publisher
          New Riders Publishing
          800 East 96th Street, 3rd Floor
          Indianapolis, IN 46240 USA

Table of Contents

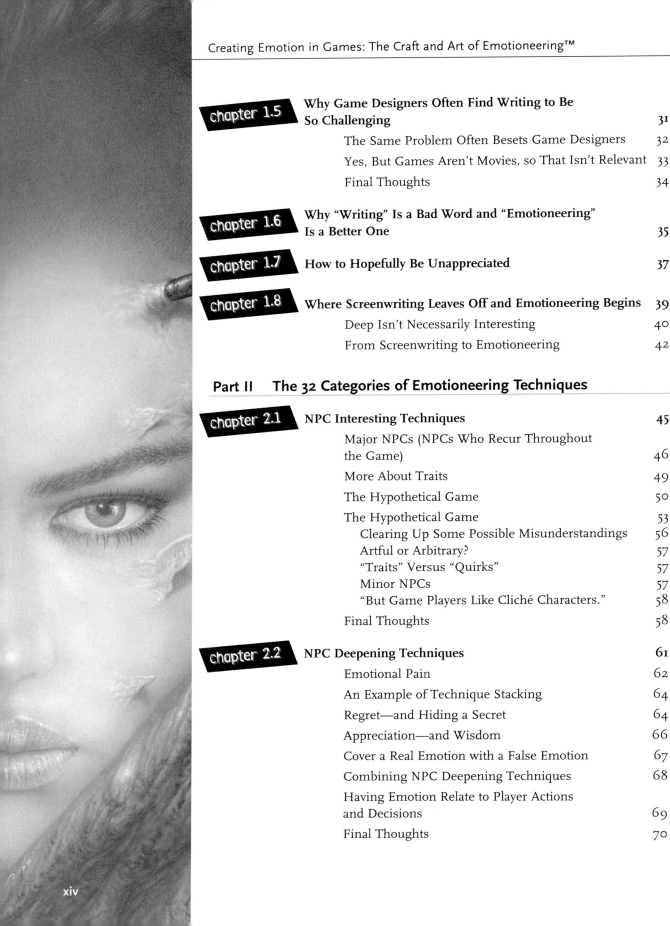

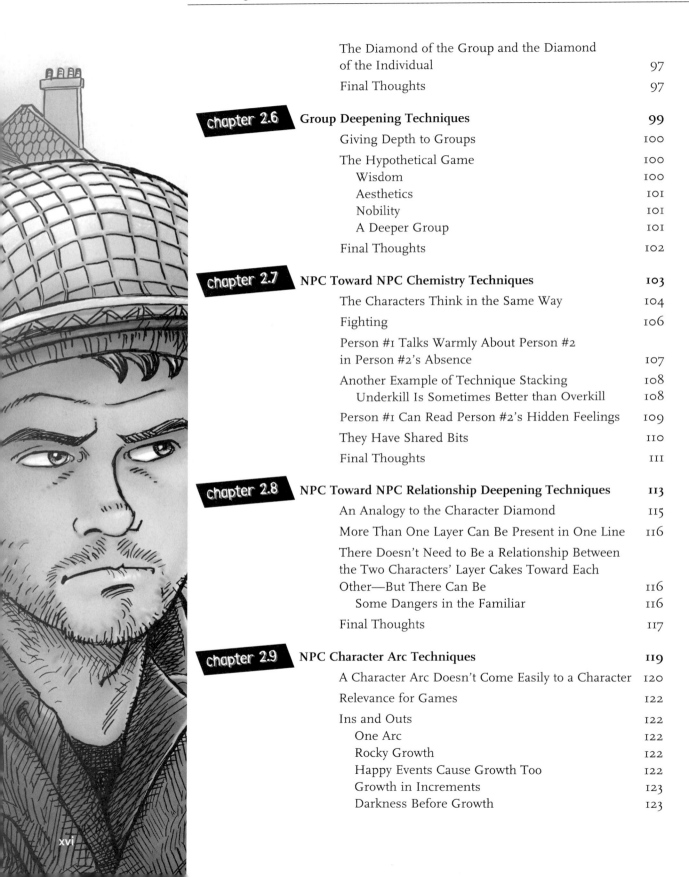

chapter 2.24   Self-Created Story Techniques (a.k.a. Agency Techniques)   327

chapter 2.25   Motivation Techniques   333

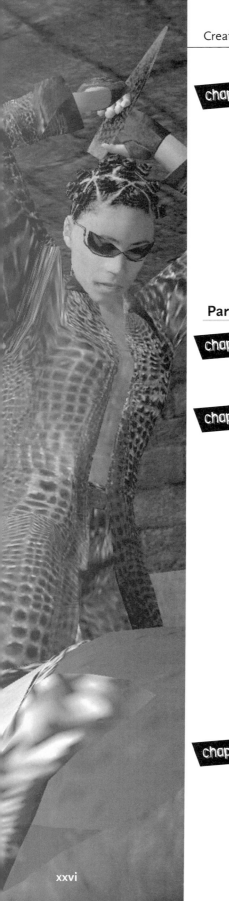

chapter 3.4   **Rough Trade**   **439**

Part IV   Magic

chapter 4   **Magic**   **449**

Foreword

by Will Wright, Creator of "The Sims"

There's an old saying in biology: "Ontogeny Recapitulates Phylogeny."[1] This is really more of a myth, but what it means is that the developing embryo of an organism roughly replays it's own evolutionary history. The human embryo, for instance, goes through successive stages that closely resemble fish, reptiles, small mammals, then man. Interesting, you might say (or maybe not), but what does that have to do with this book?

I've been involved with creating computer games for about 20 years. It seems to me that games are mirroring the emotional development of humanity in a similar way. The earliest games appealed primarily to our more primitive instincts. These instincts originate in the central portion of our brain, our so-called "reptilian" brain stem. Over time, the emotional

---

1. ontogeny— *def*: The physical development of an *individual* into maturity.
   recapitulates—*def* (as used here): An embryo repeats human evolutionary stages.
   phylogeny—*def*: The development over time of a *species*.

   "Ontogeny recapitulates phylogeny" refers to the theory that an embryo's growth and development (ontogeny) repeats the stages of (recapitulates) evolution from amoeba up to modern man (phylogeny).

palette of games has broadened beyond instinctive issues of survival and aggression to include the more subtle mechanisms of empathy, nurturing, and creativity. We still have a long way to go, however, to reach the outer cerebral cortex. Compared to other forms of media (books, films, music), games are still stuck somewhere around the "small rodent" phase.

Comparing games to previous forms of media (which are, for the most part, linear experiences) can be both useful and dangerous. Useful, because by studying other forms, we can get a good sense of what games are missing and how far they have yet to go in this important direction. Dangerous, because interactive entertainment is a fundamentally different proposition than its linear cousins, involving quite different psychological mechanisms.

As pre-humans (and other social animals) began to live in groups, their survival was determined more and more by their ability to understand and predict the other members of their groups (which they became increasingly dependent on). It became as important for Ugg the caveman to predict what his tribe members were thinking and likely to do as it was for him to understand the rest of the world around him. This would seem to be the evolutionary basis for empathy, the almost magical ability we have to put ourselves in someone else's shoes; to feel what they feel; to relive their experiences from their point of view. In essence, we can simulate the thought and experiences of other people in our imagination and insert ourselves into this model.

This is important to us because this empathic ability we seem to exercise so seamlessly is also the psychological engine that drives the thing we call "story." Story (in its many forms) seems to be an "educational technology" of sorts that we have developed over millennia that allows us to share experiences with one another across great distances of time and space. We can learn to avoid failures or achieve successes from people who are long dead across the world or who never existed at all. It's a technology that's entirely dependent on our ability to empathize with other beings.

Games, on the other hand, are most directly dependent on something else entirely: the concept of agency. Agency is our ability to alter the world around us, or our situation in it. We are able to act, and that action has effects. This is probably the first thing we learn as babies. This is the crucial distinction between interactive and linear entertainment.

Interactive works demand that the player has the ability to act; to affect the situation; to make a difference at every possible turn. When a player loses control of the joystick or mouse, it's similar to watching a movie when the screen goes blank. You've just closed down the primary feedback loop.

So what place does empathy have in interactive works, where the player is driving the experience rather than just going along for the ride? The answer is that we really need both, perhaps in equal measures. We need agency to engage the volition and creativity of the player; we need empathy to engage the outer region of our brain that wants to simulate and predict complex, emotional beings around us.

One of the main reasons games have been so emotionally shallow up to this point is that there hasn't really been anything in them worth empathizing with. We find it rather difficult to empathize with one-dimensional game characters that only have the ability to regurgitate canned speech and perform predictable actions. We know that they have no emotional depth, so we basically disengage that circuit in our brain and treat them more like appliances than as people. Our ability to fully simulate human thoughts, behavior, and emotions is still a long way off, but we are making progress toward that goal in bits and pieces. I don't know when we'll get as far as C-3PO, but I think we're rather close to R2D2 right now.

This book contains an important piece of that puzzle. David Freeman is one of the few people I know who has successfully bridged the emotionally rich world of linear media and story with the structurally demanding world of interactive games. He has found ways to utilize empathy as an emotional draw, even within the widely varying structures of games.

But beyond this, he also lays out techniques to make agency an emotionally rich experience. To mention but a few, these include taking the player on both an external and internal journey...enticing the player into becoming involved in rich game worlds...allowing the player to explore new identities as well as new ways of feeling and acting...and placing the player in emotionally complex situations.

It's a long hill we're climbing, but efforts like this will ensure that games will one day realize their full potential.

—Will Wright

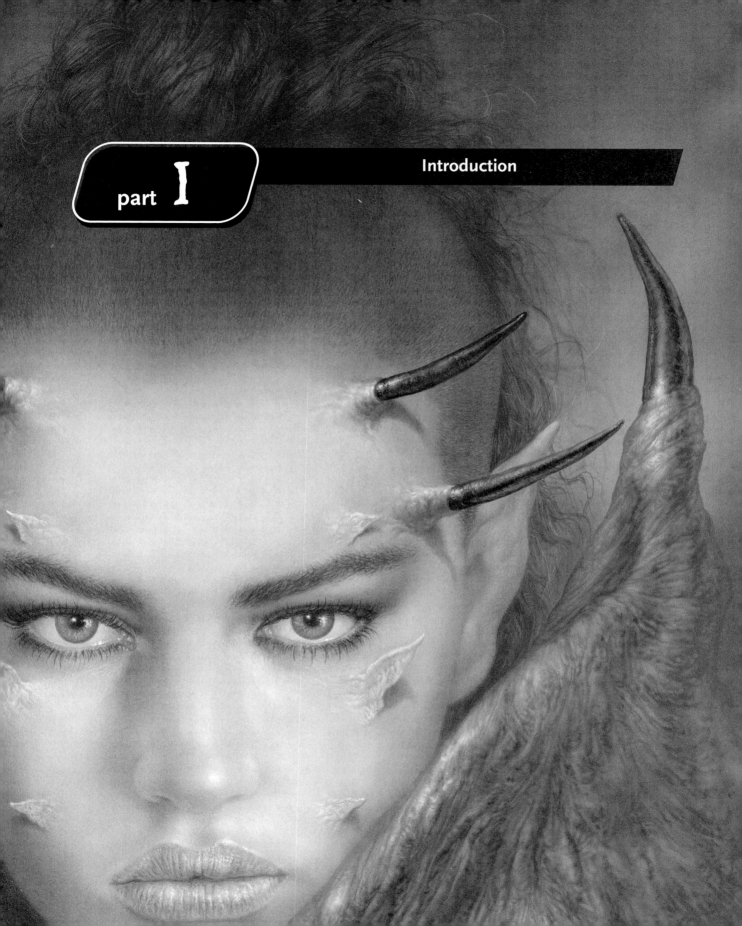

Communicate...
Explore...
Help...
Words...
Edge...

First things first.

Every freeway

needs an onramp. Some books do too. So let's put the pedal to the metal....

Communicate

Because the game industry evolves so fast, we who are creating the future of this entertainment and art form must have easy and frequent communication.

Feel free to email me at:

david@freemangames.com

Explore

You also might want to take a look at my two websites: **www.freemangames.com** and **www.beyondstructure.com**

The **www.freemangames.com** site describes my game design and game writing activities, as well as those of The Freeman Group.[1] It also provides information about my teaching, as well as articles on the subjects of emotionally engaging game design and game writing.

Several times a year, I teach "Beyond Structure," the most popular screenwriting and fiction workshop in Los Angeles and New York. I occasionally offer the workshop outside the United States as well. The **www.beyondstructure.com** site provides detailed information about "Beyond Structure."

Help

As you read this book, you might have ideas on how to improve or expand the book for future updates. I welcome your feedback and suggestions.

Words

The key to understanding a subject is knowing the meaning of every single word, without exception. This book uses a number of specialized words and phrases—some commonly used in the game industry and some that I invented. Each one is defined when first used in the book and later in the Glossary.

---

1. The Freeman Group is a group of WGA (Writers Guild of America) writers trained in my techniques, and with whom I often work on game projects.

Edge

There are some critical ways of creating emotion in games that aren't discussed in this book, such as music, art, animation, and level design. All of these important and immense subjects deserve books in their own right (and many such books already exist). The line had to be drawn somewhere; a subject needs to have a border or an edge.

Even if you work in these other areas of game creation, you may very well find tools in this book that are applicable to your own art. Sparks have a way of spreading.

An Introduction to Emotioneering

Don't become an accidental Buddhist.

Emotioneering™ is

the vast body of techniques created and/or distilled by David that can create, for a player or participant, a breadth and depth of emotions in a game or other interactive experience, or that can immerse a game player or interactive participant in a world or a role. It also means the application of these techniques. "Emotioneering"™ is the trademarked property of David Freeman.

The goal of Emotioneering is to move the player through an interlocking sequence of emotional experiences.

Has something like this ever happened to you?

I was sitting in at a "round table"—a moderated group discussion—at the Game Developers Conference.[1] The focus was how to put emotion into games.

In the room where this session was held, 32 people crowded around a number of tables arranged in a big square.

The game designer moderating the session leaned forward, cocked his head, paused for dramatic effect, and unfurled his question with the seriousness of an explorer planting his flag on a new continent: "Who here has had a profound emotional experience playing a game?"

He waited expectantly for a raucous discussion to ignite. It didn't. Instead, his question hung in the empty air.

No one in the group had an answer for him. They were all as silent as monks. In effect, the moderator's simple question had instantaneously transformed everyone in the group into accidental Buddhists.

If the subject of emotion in games is a new continent, it is an almost completely uncharted one.

Obviously, things aren't black and white. Many designers are hard at work trying to inject emotion into their games, and no doubt all of us, if we think about it, can recall one or more times we were moved while playing a game (with emotions other than excitement, fear, or frustration, that is). The problem is that such game moments are far too rare, and no creative technology (no series of techniques) exists for producing rich emotional experiences in games over and over again.

The solution certainly isn't a set of handy formulas; no artist wants the word "cliché" emblazoned on his or her flag. The solution is an expansive palette of techniques that can be layered, adapted, mixed, and reworked in infinite combinations. Van Gogh, Rembrandt, and Picasso all dipped their

---

1. The Game Developers Conference is the world's largest convention of game designers and others intimately involved with the creation of games. (For details, see **www.gdconf.org**.) It's held annually, traditionally in San Jose every March. Besides the lectures, workshops, and exhibits, it provides opportunities for game designers to mainline Colombian coffee and expand their minds by hobnobbing with their peers late into the night.

brushes in the same three primary colors, but their artwork couldn't be more varied.[2]

In this book, I'm attempting to do for game design what I did for screen-writing. During years of not only writing myself, but also studying the best writers in film and television, I created and distilled over a thousand tech-niques for creating characters, dialogue, scenes, and plots that were refreshingly unique and layered with emotional depth. After finding a way to assemble them, I made them the essence of "Beyond Structure."[3]

As I began designing and writing games, I stumbled upon far too many accidental Buddhists. When my game design colleagues were faced with the need or desire to put a greater depth and breadth of rich emotion into their games, their creativity would come to an abrupt halt and they'd screech into a dark, dead-end, ideational cul-de-sac. They'd become silent as church mice.

In truth, who can blame them? Emotion is created in films as a series of scripted circumstances that occur to a character, in an exact order, with exact timing.

Games, on the other hand, may have some linear elements, but these are often combined with any number of nonlinear and what I call "multi-linear" (multi-path) elements and structures. In a game, it's not unusual to have some events that unfold in an exact sequence, while others might be encountered by the player in any number of possible sequences. Other environments or situations might be bypassed by a player all together. Still other events and tasks are often offered as optional, yet useful, diversions.

And even when it comes to linear elements, the timing between the differ-ent events (in other words, precisely when they're encountered) will differ from player to player.

So how do you create emotion in experiences that are this variable?

---

2. Perhaps it sounds a bit extreme to compare games, which right now are primarily entertainment, to masterful artworks. But most of the game designers, programmers, artists, animators, and game composers I know definitely consider what they are doing to be art, and they strive to raise their art to continually higher levels.

   Also, just as with films and television, as games mature, entertainment and art will increasingly merge. For art is entertaining. When you see the *Lord of the Rings* films, the artfulness of the writing, acting, direction, sets, and photography all contribute to the entertainment.

3. "Beyond Structure" (**www.beyondstructure.com**), the course that presents some of these techniques, has grown to become the most popular screenwriting workshop both in Los Angeles and New York.

One clue is life itself. Your life has linear elements—things you need to do in a certain order. There are other activities for which you pick the time, and others still that are optional.

Yet amidst these different structures, you still experience a wide breadth and depth of emotion. Well, if it can be done in life, it can be done in a game.

But the task is difficult, and we get a clue as to the scope of the challenge when we compare games to film and television. The primary means of evoking emotion in those media is:

1. Create one or more characters with whom the audience identifies.

2. Have that character, or those characters, undergo a series of moving experiences.

In games, because the player *is* the main character, or at least operates the character, what will be the primary way of creating emotion?

You can't just suggest an emotion and assume the player will feel it. Nor can you tell the player he is supposed to experience a state of being or play a role, and assume that the player will experience things the way you hope he will. For instance, just because you tell a player who he is supposed to be, doesn't mean that the player buys into the role. You might tell the player that he is playing a jet pilot with a shameful past. But more likely than not, the player will feel neither like a jet pilot nor ashamed. Instead, the player is likely to feel just like himself.

So, to create emotion in games, we can't rely on the film and television mechanisms of:

+ Always controlling the order of events.

+ Controlling the timing between events.

+ Creating characters with whom the audience identifies, who then undergo moving experiences.

Nor can we easily create a character with a role that the player will necessarily "inhabit."

Thus it's no wonder that game development studios across the world, one by one, have been converted into temples for accidental Buddhist.

I've seen many a cocky screenwriter sure that he or she, in a minute or two, without any study of games, can swoop in and zap these problems into oblivion. These screenwriters quickly find their brains deep-fried and served up as snack food to weary game designers and programmers who knew from the start that linear writers are the crash-test dummies of interactive entertainment.

Perhaps I had a bit of a head start, for many of the techniques from "Beyond Structure" could be applied to games. Still, these techniques didn't even begin to solve the entire problem.

There *is* a way to put a breadth and depth of emotion into games. Actually, there isn't one way—there are at least 1500 ways.[4] These techniques fall, as far as I can tell, into 32 distinct categories. These are the techniques of Emotioneering.

But we've gotten ahead of ourselves. The first question is, why would one *want* to put emotion into games?

---

4. As I was given a mandate by my publisher to keep the length of this book somewhat less than the *Encyclopedia Britannica*, this book will offer more than 300 of them.

Why Put Emotion into Games?

Entertainment becomes art.
Art becomes commerce.

Why put emotion into games?

The answers are: art and money. Sure, it's an unholy alliance, but so are pineapple and pizza, windmills and tiny golf courses, military intelligence, and fruit and Jello™ molds.

Don't get me wrong. I think of myself as an artist first, a businessman second. Game companies that don't make a profit, however, aren't game companies for very long.

There are at least nine reasons why putting emotion in games can lead to greater profits, and it's worth taking a few minutes to mention them.

Reason #1: Expanded Demographics

I asked Jason, a close friend of mine, if he ever played games.

"No," he said. "If I'm going to invest my time in entertainment, I want it to have meaning. There's no meaning to games."

Upon further questioning, I learned what he meant was that he wanted entertainment experiences that also contributed to or enriched his life in some way; experiences that weren't just fun diversions.

My friend speaks for a vast group. There are many more people who watch film and television than play games. Many of these will never be lured into playing games until games begin to offer the emotional range and depth of the entertainment they're used to enjoying.

Reason #2: Better Buzz

A more involving game experience means better word of mouth or "buzz." Just as much as the movie business, the game business depends on buzz.

Reason #3: Better Press

The press likes to write about games that find new ways to be immersive. More press means more sales. (If you were around back then, think of all the free press received by the first *Max Payne*.)

Reason #4: So Games Don't Seem Amateurish

The better game visuals get and the more games look like films, the more we'll instinctively compare them to films. Weak writing and shallow emotional experiences will increasingly stand out in games featuring stories and characters. Although publishers and developers will (and do) have games that look like films, most games don't have nearly the emotional sophistication of films.

Reason #5: An Inspired and Dedicated Creative Team

When a game has emotional complexity, combined with fun gameplay, the creative team becomes more inspired by the game they are producing.

For they know they're creating not just superficial entertainment, but something that has depth, meaning, and impact.[1]

Reason #6: Consumer Loyalty to the Brand, Which Is Worth a Fortune

People seek out branded experiences that touch them emotionally. The *Lord of the Rings* films and the *Spider-Man* film helped ignite game sales, because people wanted to continue to be involved in the brand.

Reason #7: So You Don't Burn Millions of Dollars of Potential Profit

Metal Gear Solid II was an eagerly awaited game. Did it satisfy people's hunger for great gameplay? Many gamers said yes. But gamers complained that the story was unengaging—even trite and silly. The game, despite its great look for the time, sold a million less units in the United States than its predecessor.

How many millions of dollars more could the game have made if it had been more emotionally involving? And how much damage was done to the brand? How much will the next sequel *not* make because of the lessened passion U.S. game players felt for *Metal Gear Solid II*?

Reason #8: Competitive Advantage

Once upon a time, the technological evolution between games was so dramatic that games could trump one another in sales just by having a better look or slightly more fun gameplay.

Today lots of games look great, and consumers have no shortage of choices for truly fun games.

Games that involve a player emotionally will gain a competitive advantage. Obviously, however, games still need to have fun gameplay besides looking great.

---

1. Please don't feel I'm knocking superficial entertainment. Uplifting people and giving them an arena for play by creating fun and exciting entertainment experiences—from games to roller coasters to river raft rides—is, to me, extremely worthwhile. But many creative teams find renewed inspiration when they're also creating experiences that enrich the interactive participant.

Reason #9: So You Don't Come in Last

Certain game developers are working hard to advance emotion in gaming. Game designers and publishers creating games with stories and characters but not emotion will find themselves further and further behind. Their games will be eclipsed.

A Little Baring of the Soul

My greatest personal motivation for putting emotion into the games I design and write isn't any of these nine reasons. I add emotion because, as an artist, it's what I do.

When we think of ancient Greece, we remember its temples, its statues, its plays, literature, and mythology. We think of its art.

So, though the primary reason for putting emotion in games might be to make money, that's not what fuels my greatest passion, nor the passion of many other game designers I know. The fuel is the desire to create entertainment and art.

If we can get used to tiny Dutch windmills taking up residence on small golf courses upholstered with green indoor-outdoor carpeting, then we should be able to survive money interwoven with art. When a breadth and depth of emotion is added to games, then profits are increased and art is enhanced.

Summary

When emotion is added to a game, then the game will appeal to wider demographics. The game gets better press, gets better buzz, and is more likely to generate allegiance to the brand. The development team will have increased passion for the project. All this translates to increased profits and a much richer game experience.

Regarding *Metal Gear Solid II*, a game designer friend of mine commented, "My feeling is that a game without a story is better than a game with a bad story, because anytime a player is taken out of their connection to the game it gives him the opportunity to walk away from the game entirely."

If my friend is right, and I think he is, then poor writing can pull the player out of the story—the exact opposite of what we're trying to accomplish.

The solution seems easy: Just hire a professional writer. The next chapter, however, shows why this might not be the simple solution it seems to be.

17 Things Screenwriters Don't Know About Games

Game experiences frequently have little to do with linear storytelling.

If traditionally trained

screenwriters are to be effective in writing artfully for games, they will need to learn the many types of writing skills games require. Likewise, developers and publishers may need to learn the finer points of dealing with Hollywood agents if they want to hire a screenwriter for their game. Some of the difficulties that might ensue for screenwriters and developers are discussed here.

This chapter, however, presents only half of the story. The next chapter, "Why Game Designers Often Find Writing to Be So Challenging" shows why *not* using a professional writer might potentially get a game developer in trouble.

Some specific tips for handling this conundrum are provided at the end of this chapter.

Having kicked around in the worlds of both films and games, I've come to appreciate the gap between them. Their surface similarities disguise their enormous differences.

Still, many game companies are reaching out to try to incorporate films' emotional spectrum into their games. At first glance, it seems like the answer is simple: Either train your existing staff (game designers, programmers, and so on) in the craft and art of writing (much tougher than it sounds), or, more likely, hire a trained screenwriter.

While my background as a screenwriter (especially armed with the "Beyond Structure" techniques) served me well for games, I've come across more than a few game developers who've had bad experiences with writers and now shun them.

Sometimes it's because they dealt with amateur writers—writers who simply weren't good enough to make it in film and television, and who turned to writing for games, thinking their weak writing wouldn't be as noticeable there. But, in the end, their lackluster writing skills did little to improve the games they worked on, and the developer realized that if the writer stopped receiving paychecks, sooner or later he or she would hopefully stop showing up.

Some developers incurred other problems with trained screenwriters. Obviously, as a screenwriter now working heavily in games, I must feel that my skill set is of value. But I understand the difficulties some developers have faced. Why isn't simply hiring a screenwriter—even a famous or a talented one—always the "magic pill" that games need?

It's because there are so many aspects of games that most screenwriters don't know.

What Screenwriters Need to Learn About Games

There are at least 17 points that screenwriters need to learn about games if they're to be effective as game writers, let alone designers.

The Shortest Distance May Be a Straight Line—But Who Wants a Straight Line?

Point 1: The screenwriter might feel that the player should follow a set route through the game to make sure that the player experiences the story in the way he or she (the writer) intends.

But the screenwriter needs to learn all the ways to give actual or apparent freedom to the player, so that the player doesn't feel trapped into merely being a pawn in a story. Gamers want to feel they're playing a game, not being played by it.

Point 2: Many screenwriters don't realize that, even in games with stories, there may be ways to play the game that completely avoid the story altogether (example: enjoying "vigilante mode" in *Grand Theft Auto III*).

Therefore, the screenwriter needs to learn dozens of other ways to make the game emotionally immersive so that it will be compelling, even if the player never experiences the story or puts the story on hold.

Point 3: Many games are designed so that a player might come upon elements of the story in a variety of orders. Most screenwriters create emotional experiences by making a story unfold in a particular sequence. They need to learn how to keep a story emotionally engaging when the different parts of it can be experienced in multiple orders.

Stan acquainted himself with nonlinear and multi-path story structures.

Game designers, take pity on the linear writer who drowns in a chaos of plot possibilities, gasping for air while going down for the count in a sea of infinitely expanding flow-charts.

Creating Playable Roles

Point 4: A screenwriter will often get quite excited about the idea of a player acting out a certain role in the story. But if the game, or the story in the game, casts the player in a role—say a space pilot—that doesn't automatically mean that the player *feels* like a space pilot.

The screenwriter needs to know techniques for getting the player to identify with a role.

Point 5: Screenwriters need to learn how to induce a player to identify with the personality of the character he or she has been cast as. Let's say that the character played by the gamer is someone who is cunning yet generous.

Bad news: Just because this is the personality the screenwriter wants the player to pretend to have, that doesn't mean that a player who picks up the game will suddenly feel cunning yet generous. Instead, the player will probably feel like himself or herself.

Screenwriters need to learn how to create an environment in which the player willingly adopts a different personality in the make-believe world of role playing. By *role playing*, I don't mean RPGs (role-playing games); I mean any game in which the character being played has a supposed personality.

Point 6: One solution some screenwriters might seize upon to the problems discussed in Point 5 is to cast the player in the role of a hero. After all, wouldn't any player readily want to identify with a hero?

Perhaps not. You see, what screenwriters often don't know is that for every angel that sits on a game player's right shoulder, there's usually a grinning psychopathic devil on the left, who, just to be mischievous or rebellious, might attack foe and friend alike.

A screenwriter needs to allow the player this freedom, yet still provide incentives for the player to follow the story in the role the player is supposed to be inhabiting. Granting freedom yet prompting behavior with incentives is tricky business.

Similarly, just because the character you play is supposed to grow or change in some way during the game (undergoing what screenwriters call a *Character Arc*), doesn't mean the player will feel any different at the end of the game than he or she did at the beginning.

I'm not saying that creating a First-Person Character Arc is impossible (see Chapter 2.20, "First-Person Character Arc Techniques," for more about this). I am saying the way to do this effectively doesn't have much to do with the process screenwriters use for writing linear scripts.

Dialogue in Films Versus Games

Point 7: Because dialogue is often minimal in a game, the writer needs to be a proven master at creating complex characters—and maybe complex *and* likeable characters—even if that character speaks few words.

Point 8: NPC[1] dialogue is often used to convey information. But having NPCs dialogue *only* convey information can actually end up squashing emotion instead of enhancing it.

A screenwriter needs to know how to work with short bursts of dialogue to convey simultaneously not just information, but also emotion—and have this emotion not be conveyed in a cliché or bluntly over-obvious way.

Well, at Least They Can Write the Cinematics[2]

Point 9: Most screenwriters feel comfortable writing cinematics, because they're the part of games most like film and TV. They may not understand that these "mini-movies" are the *least* game-like part of any game. Although cinematics won't completely disappear any time soon, many game designers consider reliance or over-reliance on cinematics to be a weakness in a game.

A Different Kind of Process

Point 10: In films, a writer comes up with an idea and then writes a script. Many writers don't understand that in games, the idea is often evolved by a group.

---

1. An NPC is a *non-player character*—any character in the game not controlled by the player.

2. A *cinematic* is a section of the game in which the player has no control and, instead, watches action unfold as if watching a short movie.

When in a meeting with the design team, a screenwriter might not realize that the other members of the team are likely to have ideas that may be just as imaginative, viable, and artful as the screenwriter's.

Here we find a real mixed bag. I have found most screenwriters to be warm and responsive people. But there are a few who can't or simply won't adapt to the kind of group process games demand. You don't have to forage far for anecdotes from designers who have had extremely distasteful experiences with professional screenwriters because of these issues.

Point 11: Screenwriters may not understand that they need, when working in games, to be flexible—to the point where yoga masters would pay them homage and pretzel makers would use them as prototypes. As games are made, quite often all sorts of aspects of the game are changed in process.

This can greatly impact the way story or character information is revealed. A writer has to be able to creatively "wing it" as the ground keeps shifting under his or her feet.

Point 12: A screenwriter might find himself brought on board a game after the characters and locations for the game have already been established. The screenwriter might then be asked to create both a story and personalities for characters that fit in with the existing locations and character designs.[3] In such cases, the screenwriter needs to be able to operate creatively and easily within this kind of process.

Point 13: Screenwriters usually don't realize that they might be needed at some points in the game, and then, after story and character descriptions are worked out, that they'll probably be sent away for three to seven months while the game continues to be built. Then the writer will be called back to write the NPC dialogue—and expected to be available.

Point 14: When it comes to knowing how to emotionally draw a player into the story, the screenwriter should be aware of what's been done in other games, so as to not retread the past. In other words, screenwriters who want to write games should do their homework. They need to sit down and deconstruct game after game.

---

3. Lest you think this isn't possible, it has happened to me several times. Stranger things have happened, too, but they were in Tijuana and a lot of alcohol was involved.

Point 15: This point was contributed by one of America's top game designers who is helping to push the envelope of story, character, and emotional immersion in games. He wrote to me:

> "Game writers have to be able to master the technical aspects of writing for games. There's a coding element to game writing that's the stiffest challenge new writers face."

He was referring to a kind of writing that creates emotion while presenting the player with a wide range of options. In game design and writing, there are often an enormous amount of game experiences structured to unfold as:

> If the player does A then X happens; if the player does B then Y happens—and Y is twice as intense if the player has done not only B but C as well.

In this scenario, X or Y might take place soon after A or B, or they might occur much later in the game.

The applications of and variations in this kind of design, programming, and writing are almost limitless in nature. The screenwriter has to not only be able to think easily in this manner, but, importantly, needs to also be able to create a wide range of emotional experiences with these tools.

Hello, Hollywood

Point 16: In life, it ain't over until the fat lady sings. In games, it ain't over until all the NPC dialogue is written.

I was speaking to a high-placed executive at a large game company. He was quite excited; he had just begun a relationship with one of the biggest and most prestigious Hollywood agencies. I could almost hear his heart pound as he told me some of the famous writers these agents had introduced him to.

I asked him what he had been told he'd have to pay these famous writers, and his voice lowered a bit as he mentioned that he was supposed to shell out hundreds of thousands of dollars, plus offer them all sorts of back-end revenue, in exchange for their story ideas.

I paused for a moment of sad contemplation, the way I always do when I watch the innocent get led to slaughter. Then I took a deep breath, and explained how he was about to get fleeced. I pointed out:

- **Agents have one goal in life: to make money for agents.** They aren't on the developer's side; they're on their own side.

- **The big-name writers he was talking about are always booked for several years out.** This means that they'd spend a few weeks (at best) to whip together a story for him, take the hundreds of thousands of dollars, and then run back to their much more prestigious and lucrative screenwriting deals.

- **Because of the way games are developed, who even knows how much of their story ideas would actually be present when the final game was done?** And yet the game company would be out tons of money.

- **Because of all these problems, the agency would probably end up trying to get the company to accept some of the agency's writers "from the bottom of the deck."** These are writers who haven't worked for a while, not infrequently because they're not very good. And the game company would still be overcharged.

- **Are the famous writers he was speaking about going to stick around and write 500 or 1,000 or 10,000 lines of NPC dialogue, one line at a time?** Or, are they going to keep the exorbitant money they've been paid, grin as they walk away from their NPC writing duties, and go back to making serious coin writing screenplays and soaking in the glamour of Hollywood?

I asked the executive, if he's hiring a famous writer, *exactly* what is he getting for his money?

There was a long pause on the other end of the line, as the executive realized he was on the verge of becoming 21st-century roadkill, blindsided by a ten-ton semi in a B-rated Hollywood shark-o-rama.

The game executive was by no means an unintelligent man. He had just never been a bit player in a real-life episode of *Jaws* before.

And It Doesn't End There

Point 17: A screenwriter might think that giving a game a story is the only way to make a game emotionally engaging. However, sports games and racing games have little story but can be very emotionally engaging. Screenwriters need to learn that there are many other ways to create

Many game developers find their first encounter with Hollywood quite memorable.

emotional immersion in a game besides story. The screenwriter should know how to:

- Integrate the story with the gameplay mechanics.[4]

- Make the player care about the world of the game.

- Create emotionally complex relationships between the player and the NPCs—and, for that matter, between the NPCs and other NPCs.

- Figure out to what degree and in what way the world of the game impacts the player, and to what degree, if any, the player impacts the world of the game.

- Make sure the player is motivated to play through to the end of the game.

- Know many other ways effective ways of creating emotional immersion in the game by the player.

---

4. *Mechanics* are actions that can be performed by the character or characters being played by the gamer.

Putting It in Focus

Lest you misunderstand, the warnings in this chapter aren't to convince game companies not to hire a professional writer and pay him or her very well. The goal here is to stop a game company from paying the *wrong* writer extremely well.

Just as extraordinary writers turn movies into gold at the box-office, extraordinary designer/writers can help increase a game's visibility and profits. (See Chapter 1.3, "Why Put Emotion into Games?") To cite some old chestnuts, *Grand Theft Auto III* and *Vice City* each use dozens of techniques to keep players emotionally engaged, and their success is legendary.

> Thanks a lot, Dave. We were set on hiring a screenwriter because our guys aren't professional writers and we need help. Now we're so depressed that we spend our days glumly reorganizing our sock drawers and searching for meaning, and it's all your fault.

If, indeed, that's how you feel, before you touch those socks, consider this: My only intention is to save game publishers and developers from throwing away tons of money and ending up feeling (and being) burnt and used.

And this is what will happen if they latch onto the idea of hiring famous or talented screenwriters as the magic pill that will instantly give their games some kind of emotional depth and competitive edge.

> Ah, I see. We should just hire comic-book writers.

I love reading certain comics, and make a yearly pilgrimage to that mind-warping orgy of popular aesthetics, Comic-Con.[5] I always come away from the event inspired and even awed by the talent I've met. I understand why some game companies might turn toward comic-book writers. After all, they have a proven ability to convey story and characters with minimal dialogue. You'll even find some images from comic books in this book.

My personal belief, however, is that if a game requires complex and rich characters and stories, the skills and talents needed could very well exceed that of many comic-book writers. (Of course, there are exceptions to this statement.)

---

5. Comic-Con is the Super Bowl, Rose Parade, and Fourth of July of the comic book and graphic novel world, all rolled into one and served piping fresh annually in the San Diego Convention Center. See **www.comic-con.org** and wear comfortable shoes, because you'll be on your feet for days.

If you read Chapter 2.31, "Pre-Rendered and In-Game Cinematics,"[6] you'll see exactly how 35 writing techniques can be layered on top of each other in one short scene. Only a very few comic-book writers have the skills necessary to go back and forth from comics to film or television, and I think that's because the majority of comic-book writers don't have an easy command of all these techniques, not to mention the additional couple hundred that a savvy writer should have at his or her beck and call.

This isn't to say that comic books aren't a remarkably rich medium. The expressive combinations of words and images, and even the imaginative and evocative ways pages are often laid out, make comics a unique and amazing art form.[7] But comic-book writers aren't the perfect "quick fix" for games any more than screenwriters are.

To truly be a strong asset to game design, a screenwriter or comic-book writer must be superb in his/her craft and meet the conditions described next.

Facing the Challenge: A Guide to Hiring a Screenwriter

Obviously, I think that games with stories and characters need great writers. I just think a game designer or developer is destined to search in vain if he or she thinks that there's a single answer out there somewhere.

The solutions I believe are:

1. **Don't get star-struck.** Choose a writer by his/her writing ability; read his/her writing and decide what you think. Don't drop your jaw just because they're represented by a big agency.

   Even if you're using a "name" writer, be aware that often films and TV episodes go through many rewrites by writers who aren't even credited.

2. **Absolutely insist on reading a film or TV script.** (It doesn't have to be a film or TV episode that was actually shot.) Is this a great writer? Can he or she make both major and minor characters unique,

---

6. A *pre-rendered cinematic* (short movie-like sequence) is one that is rendered as a self-contained animated recording and stuck in the game. An *in-game cinematic* is one created in real time by the game engine.

7. If you'd like to learn how some comics are truly an advanced art form, read *Understanding Comics* (©1994, Kitchen Sink Press) by Scott Mccloud for an enlightening experience.

interesting, dimensional, and emotionally rich? Is the story imaginative and gripping? Can this writer captivate you from beginning to end?

I should mention that in Hollywood, people often write in teams. If the writing sample is from a team but you're only dealing with one of the writers, forget the writer. You have no way of knowing who wrote the best material in the script, no matter what the agent or writer claims.

Similarly, many Hollywood scripts are rewritten many times, by many different writers. If you're shown a script and you're told that the writer wrote "this draft," the sample is useless, even if it's by a famous writer. The agent and writer will protest and say the writer did a "page one rewrite," but, in truth, you'll never have the faintest idea who created or wrote some of your favorite plot twists, characters, scenes, and dialogue.[8]

3. **Even if the writer has worked on other games, still read a writing sample.** I know one writer who has worked on one game after another—and has done a poor job on all of them. People hire him off his resume, without stopping to read and assess his talent and skills. The proof has got to be in the pudding: Any writer must be able to prove his or her ability.

4. **Confirm that the writer knows the medium.** Make sure the screenwriter understands the difference between writing for films or TV and writing for games.

5. **Make the screenwriter prove that he or she can execute Point 9.** Can the screenwriter create emotionally complex NPC characters—some of which are likable, some of which are not—with very few words of dialogue?

---

8. I don't even begin to consider bringing a writer to work for me as part of my game design and writing consultancy, The Freeman Group, unless that writer has at least one TV or film script that utterly floors me with the complexity of its artistry and the excellence of its craftsmanship. For what it's worth, while it's conceivable that I might receive such a script from someone who is not yet a member of the WGA (the Writers Guild of America, which you can join only by selling film or TV scripts to major Hollywood companies), it hasn't happened yet.

Once I find a writer who is talented, skilled, imaginative, passionate, and available, and who has an upbeat and warm personality, then comes the very long process of training him or her in Emotioneering™. (*Emotioneering* is the vast array of techniques for creating emotion in games, illustrated in the next section of this book.) Otherwise, he or she will be of little use to me.

If the writer doesn't play games and can't think in terms of gameplay, then that writer might be helpful in certain circumstances, but the kinds of ways this person can be utilized are limited.

6. **Educate the writer to the group nature of the creative process in games.** Make sure they're absolutely fine with it.

7. **Use your gut to assess the screenwriter's motives.** Does he or she actually care about games?

If you find someone who meets these criteria, they're probably going to contribute to the quality of your game, and to the buzz and profits your game generates.

I can tell you from personal experience that the task isn't easy. As I was asked to help design or write more and more games, I formed The Freeman Group, a band of professional writers who are trained in my techniques and who often work with me on game projects.

My first criterion in bringing a writer on board is that he or she has sold film or TV scripts to major Hollywood companies, and therefore is a member of the WGA (Writers Guild of America). Also, the writer needs to have writing samples that blow me away. This is a must. And he or she needs to be genuinely warm and upbeat, and comfortable working as part of a team. A strong familiarity with games is a big plus, but not nearly enough.

If a writer meets these criteria, I give him or her several writing tests to evaluate his or her skill and artistry in the kind of writing and thinking games require. Most writers, even though I only work with WGA members, fail these tests. But for those who excel, and who meet all my other criteria, I then start training them in Emotioneering and in writing for games. It's been a long haul, and I still haven't been able to fully clone myself. But I keep on trying.

My difficulty of finding writers who can assist me in doing superlative, artful, and ground-breaking game design and writing has given me great sympathy for any game publisher or developer who tries to do the same.

Final Thoughts

The process of recruiting for The Freeman Group has certainly given me an appreciation of the difficulty a developer or publisher might face in trying to find a writer for a game—a writer who isn't burdened by the 17 potential problem areas.

But these problems are only one side of the dilemma. The next chapter presents the flip side.

Why Game Designers Often Find Writing to Be So Challenging

It's hard to master
what you don't even perceive.

The last chapter

pointed out all the areas where a traditionally trained screenwriter might run into trouble when working in games. At first glance, the apparent solution is to have a programmer, artist, animator, or someone else on the development team do the writing in the game. But that approach has its problems as well.

When I step into my role as a screenwriting teacher, I repeatedly see one phenomenon that never ceases to astound me: My students rarely read the screenplays of famous films.

No one would doubt that, barring from being born Picasso, becoming a masterful painter takes a lot of study and practice. No one doubts that much study and practice is needed to become a great ballerina. Or a great pianist.

And yet, my students continuously come to me believing that, because they grew up on films and television, they can be great writers without study and practice. Even on the face of it, this is illogical. They grew up listening to rock songs on the radio; why don't they feel they can be great guitarists just by listening?

These students of mine certainly aren't stupid; they're just naïve. They "don't know what they don't know," as the expression goes. They simply haven't a clue to the amount of craft and artistry that goes into writing a great screenplay.

Please don't misunderstand: This isn't a way of covertly boasting about my own writing. I can give you a long, long list of writers whose work I revere. And even if you asked these writers, they'd have their own similar list.

The Same Problem Often Besets Game Designers

Many of the game designers I've met are, in some ways, as naïve as my writing students. Just like the students, because they grew up on film and television, they naturally assume that they can write well.

Like my students, they don't realize how much goes into writing. Sometimes in a film, a *single scene* will simultaneously:

- Advance the plot.

- Reveal new information about a character.

- Reveal new information about the relationship between two characters.

- Show multiple aspects of a relationship between two characters.

- Show a character struggling to grow emotionally or to resist growing.

- Use 5, 10, or 15 dialogue techniques to help the dialogue sound natural.

- Use a number of dialogue techniques to hint at what the character is feeling beneath the surface, even if the character is unaware of these hidden feelings.

- Use other dialogue techniques to show ambivalence between two characters.

- Employ specific writing techniques that give poignancy or emotional power to the scene.

- Reinforce the theme of the film or TV episode.

- Introduce small elements into the story that will be revisited in the plot later in either ironic or even momentous ways.

- Artfully employ one or more symbols.

And so much more.

Consequently, most professional writers I know rewrite every scene in their scripts five to ten times (and often more) before they even consider that they've arrived at a "first draft."

note

If you'd like too see most of the preceding done in a single scene, take a look at Chapter 2.31, "Pre-Rendered and In-Game Cinematics."

Game moments and experiences that operate emotionally on many levels end up being like gems, each facet of which serves a different purpose. To use a film example, did you know that the final script for *American Beauty* was only about 100 pages long? Yet, as a film, it was a rich experience. That's because almost every scene serves a multitude of purposes.

Yes, But Games Aren't Movies, so That Isn't Relevant

Games indeed aren't movies, and, in fact, games that overuse cinematics and try to replicate a film experience very often aren't very appealing, especially to an American market.

Thus, in games, even in those with characters and stories, we're not trying to make movies. We *are* trying to integrate the gameplay with the variety, the intensity, and, sometimes, the subtlety of a powerful film's constantly changing, rich emotional nature. Techniques for accomplishing this integration are described in Section II of this book. As you'll see, however, you can't divorce them from the need for solid craftsmanship in the art of writing.

Some game companies don't hire writers because they don't know how to find a good one. Some game designers feel that writing is the "fun part" and don't want to yield it to someone else. Some "don't know what they don't know:" One game designer told me that he had read a book on mythological story structure, so he now knew all there was to know about writing(!!). And, as mentioned in the last chapter, a few game companies have been burned by bad experiences with "Hollywood types."

Whatever the reason for its flaws, there's little disagreement that much game writing leaves a lot to be desired.

Final Thoughts

An audience, listening to a film score, rarely picks out every musical instrument, chord progression, or key shift. The listener simply feels moved.

Similarly, superb writing employs a vast array of techniques that operate outside the audience's or gamer's awareness. This is why writing techniques are almost impossible to assimilate without study. It's also why most untrained writers—whether they're in a game company or not—end up doing sub-par work. They can have control of only those techniques within their awareness. They can't, by definition, masterfully control techniques of which they are not aware.

As Chapter 1.4 pointed out, if screenwriters want to contribute heavily to the game experience, they need to learn a tremendous amount about games.

Conversely, if someone on a development team with no writing background wants to do all the writing for a game and to bring emotion into it as well, then that individual will need to buckle down to hone his or her writing skills and learn some of the available techniques.

Just as an alpaca is a sort of hybrid of a camel and a llama, the future of games with characters and stories will require a new kind of game designer/writer hybrid. Hopefully, this book will abet this process of "alpacafication." It's really just a codification of alpacafication information.[1]

---

1. This discussion of alpacas hardly scratches the surface of what kind of strange entities they are, and it stops woefully short of clarifying the full complexity of their troubling relationship to camels and llamas. Perhaps, most critically, it doesn't begin to address their relationship to Quinn the Eskimo, nor their role in the future hopes and dreams of mankind. However, these weighty issues will be examined in full detail in Chapter 5.3, "Gatherings."

Why "Writing" Is a Bad Word and "Emotioneering" Is a Better One

Dialogue is only a very small part of writing.

Dialogue is only

a very small part of writing. Take, for example, the film *Crouching Tiger Hidden Dragon*. (If you haven't seen the film and don't want to learn the ending here, you might want to skip this and the next five paragraphs. Begin reading with the paragraph that begins, "If writing for scripts....")

Li Mu Bai (played by Chow Yun-Fat) and Jen (Zhang Ziyi) "trade places." Li begins the film by abandoning the spiritual (monastic) life, reentering the world of swordsmanship and passion. Even as he dies, he says he'd rather be a ghost by Yu Shu Lien's (Michelle Yeoh's) side than enter nirvana. Jen begins the film totally enveloped by narcissism and passion. By the end, she abandons these attitudes—and her boyfriend—for an act of spiritual redemption (jumping off the mountain).

So these two trade places. When two major characters trade places, this is about one of 60 techniques that, when applied artfully, can give depth to a plot. Thus, it's a *Plot Deepening Technique*.

This "Plot Deepening Technique" has little to do with dialogue, but much to do with writing. But, in addition to this technique, there are hundreds of others that you can use to create emotional experiences, and only a small percentage of them apply to dialogue.

In fact, if you were the writer of *Crouching Tiger Hidden Dragon*, how would you even know what dialogue to write in the final scene between Chow Yun-Fat and Michelle Yeoh if you hadn't worked out this "changing places" thing first?

If you thought of "writing" to mean "dialogue," you would miss this and all the other Plot Deepening Techniques in *Crouching Tiger*.

If writing for scripts involves much more than dialogue, this is even truer for creating emotion in games. Some techniques involve dialogue, of course, but many do not.

This is why I created a new word: *Emotioneering*™. As discussed in Chapter 1.2, "An Introduction to Emotioneering," Emotioneering is the vast body of techniques that can create, for a player or participant, a breadth and depth of emotions in a game or other interactive experience, or that can immerse a game player or interactive participant in a world or a role. It also means the application of these techniques.

The goal of Emotioneering is to move the player through an interlocking sequence of emotional experiences.

Emotioneering entails much more than great dialogue. Dialogue does play a role, however. Bland, clichéd, unnatural, or wooden dialogue—dialogue lacking emotion beneath the surface (lacking "subtext")—or dialogue that makes several or all the characters sound the same can mitigate otherwise powerful and artful Emotioneering.

How to Hopefully Be Unappreciated

The better you are, the less they'll think you did.

No one expects

the game player to pick out every instrument in the game's score, nor every sound used in the game's sound design, nor notice every tiny shadow configured by the game's art team.

So too, an extraordinary amount of Emotioneering is designed to emotionally affect a game player, but *not* to be consciously noticed.

Almost all the techniques in this book, when used well, will operate either just on the edge of or, preferably, just outside of a game player's conscious awareness.

As discussed previously, one of the prime reasons that beginning screen-writers usually do such artless work is that they've only noticed the *obvious* aspects of films and television shows. They are unaware of the 75% of techniques that create powerful emotional effects but that are designed *not* to be noticed.

When examining *Crouching Tiger Hidden Dragon* in the previous chapter, we looked at an example of one of those "hidden" techniques: the Plot Deepening Technique that I call "Two Major Characters Change Places."[1]

To be artful as a writer is to have most of your work go unnoticed, for it operates outside the conscious awareness of the audience. Skillful Emotioneering will encounter the same fate—most gamers won't notice the techniques that you employ.

If you do your work well, the gamers will be drawn emotionally into the game, but they will have no idea why. They'll have no idea that you did tremendous work over countless hours to cause that effect.

So, oddly, their thinking you did almost nothing will be your greatest reward.

---

1. That film uses many more Plot Deepening Techniques as well, and all of them could be applied to games. Some of these techniques will be examined in Chapter 2.17, "Plot Deepening Techniques."

Where Screenwriting Leaves Off and Emotioneering Begins

Approaching emotion logically. Approaching playing seriously.

Make things interesting and make them deep.

Over the course of a decade, as I created and distilled screenwriting and story techniques for "Beyond Structure" and elsewhere, I found that they all fall on one of the two axes of this grid:

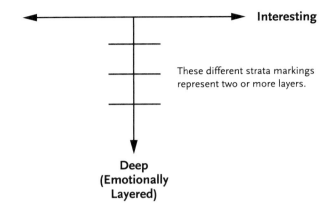

The arrow across the top represents techniques to make things *interesting*—unique, imaginative, original, etc.

The vertical arrow represents techniques to make things *"deep"*—to give them the feeling of emotional depth or to make them emotionally layered, poignant, soulful, emotionally complex, psychologically complex, etc.

These two categories—making things interesting and making them deep—apply to five areas of writing:

- Dialogue
- Characters
- Relationships between characters
- Scenes
- Plots

Any of these five can be interesting, deep, or both. Techniques that cause any of the five to be deep are what I call *Deepening Techniques*.

Deep Isn't Necessarily Interesting

Emotional pain is just one of many ways to give depth to a line of NPC dialogue. Depth, however, isn't necessarily interesting.

Let's say you're playing a WWII game. You're an American soldier in France, entering a destroyed town from which the Germans just fled. You walk up to a distraught young woman and have this interchange:

```
YOU: Where did the Germans keep their
munitions?

The woman doesn't even look at you. She's in
shock as she points to some burnt-out
rubble.

WOMAN: That used to be a church. I had a
two-year old son, Michael, who was baptized
there. The Germans killed him, and now I
feel very sad.

She breaks down and sobs.
```

Deep? Yes, for emotional pain gives a character depth. But is this woman interesting? No. Her dialogue is flat and over-obvious, or, as screenwriters say, it is "on the nose."

Take another look at the interchange; this time it has been made deep *and* interesting:

```
YOU: Where did the Germans keep their
munitions?

The woman doesn't even look at you. She's in
shock as she points to some burnt-out
rubble.

WOMAN: My son Michael -- he was baptized in
that church.

She breaks down and sobs.[1]
```

The fact that "depth" isn't in and of itself necessarily "interesting" applies to all the categories of "deepening" that have been discussed, not just dialogue.

By the way, you probably noticed that, in both examples, the woman didn't answer the question. That was intentional. To get the answer to your question, you may need to ask her again. Or you may have to ask another character, one who isn't as emotionally devastated.

---

1. Many specific techniques for making NPCs both "deep" and "interesting" will be discussed later in this book.

From Screenwriting to Emotioneering

There are at least 1,500 distinct techniques a writer can use to make these five areas of storytelling either (1) interesting or (2) deep, thus creating ten categories in all. All techniques for creating emotion in films and TV fall into one of the ten categories.

For instance, why even have a climax in your story? It's because it makes plots more interesting.

Why is it usually important to care about the lead character, and sometimes other characters as well? Same reason: It makes the plot more interesting if we do.

When it comes to games, as you'll see, there are not ten but rather 32 categories of techniques that you can use to emotionally engage a player.

The line had to be drawn somewhat arbitrarily. For instance, one could keep extending the list of categories to include such elements as lighting, sound design, animation, music, level design, and so on. After all, these can be used to enhance the breadth and depth of emotion in a game as well. However, these get into specialized areas or involve gameplay issues that exceed the scope of this book.

So, please understand that a line had to be drawn. Now, let's get into the techniques.

part II

The 32 Categories of Emotioneering Techniques

Emotioneering Techniques Category #1

NPC Interesting Techniques

Boring people never rock your world, and they always leave before the party gets good.

This chapter deals

with techniques to make major NPCs interesting. The term "NPC Interesting Techniques" at first seems awkward. It makes sense to call a technique that makes an NPC deep an "NPC Deepening Technique." If a technique makes an NPC interesting, however, it sounds awkward to call it an "NPC Interesting Technique." Still, this makes more sense than calling it an "Interesting NPC Technique," for then the technique itself sounds interesting, instead of the technique being about a way to make an NPC interesting.

Thus you'll find many places in this book where the word "interesting" is used after the noun it describes ("NPC Interesting Techniques," "Plot Interesting Techniques," and so on), just as "Deepening" is used after these same nouns.

If you wouldn't invite a bore to your dinner gathering or marry one off to your daughter, sister, or pet, then don't put one in your games.

Boredom comes in many forms. Sometimes the problem is that the NPCs have no interesting characteristics, so they radiate all the sizzle of a Hallmark get-well card.

Other times, though, the game designer or writer has gone trolling through the over-fished waters of Tolkien or Lucas, and has dredged up some poor character who's dying of overexposure. The game designer proceeds to stick this Gandolf or Han Solo knock-off in his game and smile as he watches us gag on his freshly-minted cliché.

If you want to sustain emotional immersion in your game, then don't let boring NPCs jar the player out of the flow.

This chapter discusses techniques that make major NPCs dimensional, fresh, and thus interesting.

Major NPCs (NPCs Who Recur Throughout the Game)

People are dimensional, and your NPCs should be too, especially the important ones.

For major NPCs, I create what I call a *Character Diamond*.

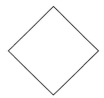

I try to give all major NPCs at least four different Traits—that is, one for each of the four corners of their Diamonds. For instance, say you have a Greek warrior. He's:

1. **Sly**: He steals some food off of a merchant's cart.

2. **Heroic**: He'll always jump into a fight for a just cause, no matter the odds against him.

3. **Absent-minded**: He forgets where he puts things.

4. **Aesthetic**: He likes to pause and enjoy a scenic vista or a striking sunrise.

I call the preceding attributes of the NPC his "Traits." A *Trait* is a major facet of the character's personality, and thus governs how the character sees the world, thinks, speaks, and acts.

All of the character's action and speech is guided by his or her Character Diamond, except for situationally appropriate emotions. For instance, if your Greek warrior was attacked, he might get angry, even though anger isn't one of his core Traits. But it would be situationally appropriate.

If the NPC trips a lot, that isn't a Trait. It's irrelevant as to how the NPC sees the world, thinks, and speaks.

On the other hand, a characteristic such as "Reckless" can be a Trait. If it's an important aspect of the character's core personality, then it affects how that character sees the world, thinks, speaks, and acts.

The Character Diamond is like an architectural blueprint. When building a house, you follow the blueprint. When creating a major NPC, the NPC's dialogue and actions conform to the Traits of the Diamond.

Let's say your character's Traits are:

1. Heroic
2. Loyal
3. Honest
4. Ethical

Would this NPC have a Diamond?

Yes, but a very boring one.

A *cliché character* is one who has a combination of Diamond Traits that we've frequently seen before in film, TV, or game characters. Even more commonly, cliché characters don't have three, four, or five familiar Traits, but rather just one or two—for example, a villain who is Cunning and Vicious.

Thus, we find that a cliché space pilot who's a knockoff of Han Solo has Diamond Traits that make him:

1. Swashbuckling
2. Brave
3. Have a dry wit
4. A bit arrogant

A cliché knockoff of Gandolf would be an NPC with a Diamond comprised of the Traits:

1. Magical
2. Mysterious
3. Good
4. Wise

A major NPC doesn't need to have four Traits to be interesting. Three would be enough.

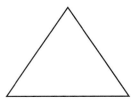

An NPC can also have five Traits. More than five for an NPC might easily turn the character to "mush." That is, it might be hard to get a strong feeling for who this character actually is.

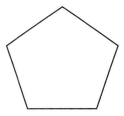

While major characters with five Traits aren't uncommon in film and television, even the most important NPCs are rarely around long enough so that you can easily squeeze in five Traits without their identities becoming confusing to a player. This isn't to say it can't be done, for it absolutely can. It just means proceed with caution.

If a character has three major Traits, or even five, I still call this combination the character's Diamond. (I use the word "Diamond" because four Traits is the most common number, and because it's easy to remember. You just need to wrap your mind around the idea of a three-sided Diamond or a five-sided one.)

While it isn't a hard and fast rule, your main characters will probably have more Traits than your minor characters.

More About Traits

Remember, a Trait can be manifested in action, dialogue, or both.

Here's an example. Let's say you're playing an action-adventure game with a swashbuckling, *Three Musketeers* type of feeling.

A character named Luther is your rival, but your relationship with him is complex. He might later become a friend.

His Diamond is that he's:

1. Cocky, ironic

2. Incredibly athletic and a superb swordsman, beautiful to watch in action

3. Touched by a deep sadness, which might be fueled by guilt

4. Keenly insightful into and empathetic with people

5. Sneaky and stealthy

The way Luther speaks, the choices he makes, even the way he fights—all these will be determined by his Diamond.

Notes on Game Scripts

There is no standard format for game scripts. The format for one game might be as different from the next as a porpoise is from a pickled ham.

In this chapter's example, I adapted the screenplay format. This format, however, doesn't allow for all of the "if X happens, then Y happens" type of events that are often written into games, although one such example is included.

The format must be further changed for the scenarios: "if X happens, then either Y or Z happens." In this case, Y or Z might be randomly chosen by the computer or, alternatively, selected based on whether events A, B, or C happened earlier in the game.

And, of course, if the script branched in any way, even for a short time, the format would have to change again.

So the following example is a simplified game script, but not a particularly representative one. It does, however, offer an easy way to study an NPC Character Diamond.

I've worked on scripts that were written with hot-linked documents, done using Microsoft Excel, and created using formats that you'd have to see to believe—all in an effort to assist programmers in programming all possible variations of "If X, then Y" scenarios.

The Hypothetical Game

(begin gameplay)

EXT. DIRT ROAD THROUGH THE FOREST - NIGHT

You're driving a stagecoach at night on a muddy dirt road lined by dense trees. You're moving at top speed because you heard Helena is in danger. You need to steer the stagecoach to avoid fallen logs, pits in the road, etc., that could overturn the coach.

(cinematic)

FOUR HIGHWAYMEN step out from the trees. They block your path. The horses stop and rear up. The Highwaymen pull out pistols.

> HIGHWAYMAN #1
> (to you; coolly threatening)
> Sweet night for a ride.

Suddenly, the end of a WHIP wraps around a high branch, and Luther SWINGS OUT onto the road, holding onto the handle of the whip. In his swing, he KNOCKS OVER Highwayman #1.

> HIGHWAY MAN #2
> (to LUTHER)
> You!

> LUTHER
> (to you)
> They all know me. But they never get the name right.
> (to Highwayman #2)
> It's not "you," it's Luther.

(resume gameplay)

You and Luther together fight the four Highwaymen. He's extremely fast and fluid in his movements.

(cinematic)

Your sword is knocked from your hand.

(scripted sequence)[1]

When your sword is knocked from your hand by one of the Highwaymen, Luther TOSSES you his and pulls out a dagger. You try to catch his sword. If you don't, you need to pick it up, but this exposes you to attack from the Highwaymen.

(resume gameplay)

The two of you eventually defeat the Highwaymen.

(cinematic)

You climb up on the carriage seat. Luther, like a cat, jumps up next to you, his dagger still drawn. Will he kill you?

(resume gameplay)

IF YOU DRAW YOUR SWORD [CHOICE 4a-1]:[2]

(NOTE: Choice 4a-1 mandates Cinematic 13c-2 in Mission 13.)

Then you two fight on the stagecoach for 45 seconds.

(cinematic)

He then jumps off the stagecoach.

>   LUTHER
>   (disappointed)
>   Betrayal -- it doesn't suit you.
>   And it's far too familiar to me.

He SLAPS the rump of the lead horse, and the carriage VAULTS FORWARD.

---

1. The definition of "scripted sequence" is too long and involved to insert here. Please see the definition in the Glossary

2. The numbers used in this example don't refer to anything specific here; they're inserted to merely to represent the kind of flow-chart system commonly found in game scripts.

<u>IF YOU DON'T DRAW YOUR SWORD [CHOICE4a-2]</u>:

(NOTE: Choice 4a-2 mandates Cinematic 13c-3 in Mission 13.)

Luther waits for a moment.

(cinematic)

>   LUTHER
>   (small smile)
>   My sword?

You hand him back the sword he had tossed you earlier.

>   LUTHER
>   (serious)
>   Helena is too pure. She'll
>   crack under his torture.
>   Godspeed.

He LEAPS off the carriage.

>   LUTHER
>   I have my burden. Helena
>   is yours.

He SLAPS the rump of the lead horse, and the carriage VAULTS FORWARD.

(resume gameplay)

<u>NO MATTER WHICH OF THE PRECEDING CHOICES IS MADE BY THE PLAYER</u>:

You must continue to steer the carriage around various obstacles without tipping it over. This time, your task is made more difficult, because other HIGHWAYMEN occasionally shoot at you from between the trees. If you're hit or if you don't kill at least one of them with your pistol, then you won't make it to Helena in time.

Normally, I don't go out of my way to put every corner of a character's Diamond in every sequence. I did it this time just as an illustration.

Let's look at the sequence again, picking out Luther's Diamond corners. Remember that he's:

1. Cocky, ironic

2. Incredibly athletic and a superb swordsman, beautiful to watch in action

3. Touched by a deep sadness, which might be fueled by guilt

4. Keenly insightful into and empathetic with people

5. Sneaky and stealthy

The Hypothetical Game

(begin gameplay)

EXT. DIRT ROAD THROUGH THE FOREST - NIGHT

```
You're driving a stagecoach at night, on a
muddy dirt road lined by dense trees. You're
moving at top speed, because you heard Helena
is in danger. You need to steer the stagecoach
to avoid fallen logs, pits in the road, etc.,
that could overturn the coach.
```

(cinematic)

```
FOUR HIGHWAYMEN step out from the trees. They
block your path. The horses stop and rear up.
The highway men pull out pistols.
```

HIGHWAYMAN #1
(to you; coolly threatening)
Sweet night for a ride.

```
Suddenly, the end of a WHIP wraps around a high
branch, and Luther SWINGS OUT onto the road,
holding onto the handle of the whip. In his
swing, he KNOCKS OVER Highwayman #1.
```

2. Athletic
5. Stealthy

```
                      HIGHWAY MAN #2
                        (to LUTHER)
                   You!


                          LUTHER
                        (to you)
                   They all know me. But they never
                   get the name right.
                        (to Highwayman #2)
                   It's not "you," it's Luther.
```

1. Cocky, Ironic

(resume gameplay)

You and Luther together fight the four Highwaymen. He's extremely fast and fluid in his movements.

2. Aesthetic athleticism

(scripted sequence)

When your sword is knocked from your hand by one of the Highwaymen, Luther TOSSES you his and pulls out a dagger.

(resume gameplay)

The two of you eventually defeat the Highwaymen.

2. Aesthetic athleticism

(cinematic)

You climb up on the carriage seat. Luther, like a cat, jumps up next to you, his dagger still drawn. Will he kill you?

(resume gameplay)

(NOTE: Choice 4a-1 mandates Cinematic 13c-2 in Mission 13.)

IF YOU DRAW YOUR SWORD [CHOICE 4a-1]:

Then you two fight on the stagecoach for 45 seconds.

(cinematic)

He then jumps off the stagecoach.

                        LUTHER
                (disappointed)   4. Insightful
    Betrayal -- it doesn't suit you.   3. Sad
    And it's far too familiar to me.

He SLAPS the rump of the lead horse, and the
carriage VAULTS FORWARD.

IF YOU DON'T DRAW YOUR SWORD [CHOICE4a-2]:

(NOTE: Choice 4a-2 mandates Cinematic 13c-3 in
Mission 13.)

Luther waits for a moment.

(cinematic)

                        LUTHER
                (small smile)   1. Cocky,
    My sword?   Ironic

You hand him back the sword he had tossed you
earlier.

                        LUTHER   4. Insightful,
                (serious)   Empathetic
    Helena is too pure. She'll
    crack under his torture.
    Godspeed.

He LEAPS off the carriage.   2. Athletic

                        LUTHER
    I have my burden. Helena   4. Insightful,
    is yours.   Empathetic
                                      3. Sad

He SLAPS the rump of the lead horse, and the
carriage VAULTS FORWARD.

NO MATTER WHICH OF THE PRECEDING CHOICES IS MADE
BY THE PLAYER:

(resume gameplay)

You must continue to steer the carriage around
various obstacles without tipping it over. This
time, your task is made more difficult, because
other HIGHWAYMEN occasionally shoot at you from
between the trees. If you're hit or if you don't
kill at least one of them with your pistol, then
you won't make it to Helena in time.

Clearing Up Some Possible Misunderstandings

The idea of creating Character Diamonds seems easy. Yet, in one of my most recent screenwriting classes, most of students struggled to create interesting Diamonds. Here are few guidelines:

- Remember that we're only talking about major NPCs here, not minor ones.

- In giving an NPC different Traits, we're not trying to make a character "well rounded" by somehow "balancing" the Traits. For instance, you don't give the character a "strong" Trait (Being a Leader) and then "balance" this with a "soft" Trait" (Having a Spiritual Take on Life).

- Nor is the idea to confuse the player as to who his friends are and who the bad guys are by making NPCs ambiguous, unless you desire this effect.

- Nor is the idea to balance out likable (or virtuous) and unlikable (or evil) Traits.

- What's important is that major NPCs are interesting, and this requires at least three Traits that form a colorful grouping.

- If a major NPC is designed with three or more Traits, but we go through long stretches without seeing a Trait manifested in the NPC's dialogue or behavior, then, to the player, that Trait might just as well not exist. The major NPC, without at least three Traits actively being used, will effectively have too few Traits and probably won't be very interesting.

- If you design a major NPC with three or more Traits, but the NPC starts saying or doing things not characterized by those Traits, then that NPC will seem like incomprehensible mush. You've strayed from the blueprint.

  There are two exceptions to this: One, as explained earlier, is *"situational emotions."* That is, an NPC might not have "Angry" as a Trait, but that NPC could still get angry if the situation called for it.

  The other exception is when an NPC grows emotionally and changes, and so one or more of his/her Traits change. This circumstance will be covered in Chapter 2.9, "NPC Character Arc Techniques."[3]

---

3. A *Character Arc* is the rocky path of growth a character undergoes in a story, usually unwillingly, during which the character wrestles with and eventually overcomes some or all of a serious emotional fear, limitation, block, or wound. Some examples are: a character overcoming a lack of courage, overcoming a lack of ethics, learning to love, learning to take responsibility for others, or overcoming guilt.

Artful or Arbitrary?

"If all you need is a colorful grouping of Traits to make an interesting major NPC," one game designer asked me, "then why not put a list of Traits up on the wall and throw darts? Whichever three, four, or five Traits the darts hit, you could use for a Diamond."

He might be right; this could potentially create an interesting character. I doubt, though, that random chance would create a useful character for your game.

Picking the Traits is where the art comes in. Many factors might weigh in on the selection, but ultimately it's up to the person who creates the character to make the difficult choices. I can teach craft; I can't teach art. This is exactly why I and so many other professional writers study the work of writers we admire: to examine what choices they made and to try to discern the thinking behind those choices.

Personally, I give very serious consideration to the Traits I pick when creating a major NPC's Diamond. Sometimes I use a list of several thousand Traits I've assembled to help spark ideas. I deliberate on the choices, because I, the other designers, and ultimately the players are going to have to live with these characters for a long time.

"Traits" Versus "Quirks"

Let's go back to that NPC who trips a lot. I've already mentioned that tripping over things wouldn't be a Trait.

Tripping frequently would be a "quirk." A *quirk* is something that gives individuality to an NPC without being as important as a Trait.

By using the word "quirk," I don't mean that the behavior needs to be extreme or odd. It's merely something less important than a Trait. If an NPC likes jazz, that's also a quirk. It doesn't measure up to the importance of a Trait.

Quirks are another way of making NPCs interesting.

Minor NPCs

Minor NPCs don't need three or more Traits. Two, or even one, can be sufficient.

At a minimum, these Traits need to be interesting and unexpected for such a character. If the NPC has two Traits, at least one needs to be interesting and unexpected.

For example: You lead a platoon, and one soldier is always depressed, but in a slightly funny way. He has just one Trait—Depressed in a Funny Way—but it's interesting.

You could argue that this is two Traits: Depressed and Funny. That would be true, if he was funny on a regular basis. If the funniness is just part of his depression and doesn't emerge anywhere else, then it's simply a modifier of Depressed.

Modifying Traits is fine. Just try to be clear to yourself whether you're modifying one Trait or adding a second one. Either case is fine; it's just helpful to know exactly what you're doing.

Or let's say you have an air traffic controller in your flight sim (simulation) game. He's a minor NPC. Give him two Traits, such as Sarcastic and Easily Excited, and have a sufficiently interesting character.

Let's go back to our soldier who was Depressed in a Funny Way. Could you give him just one Trait (Depressed)? Sure, and he could still be interesting. But the key there would be to make sure that his dialogue isn't a cliché. (See Chapter 2.3, "Dialogue Interesting Techniques.")

"But Game Players *Like* Cliché Characters."

I've been given this line more than once by game designers and publishers. The thinking goes like this: If the NPC is a cliché such as a "mafia type," then the player can instantly figure out "who the character is."

My argument is always the same: If people hate clichés in films and they hate clichés in television, then I refuse to believe that the minute they start playing a game, all their standards change and they're suddenly overcome by inexplicable longings for rehashed characters and formulaic dialogue.

Final Thoughts

The techniques presented here to create viable and artful Character Diamonds and make NPCs interesting just scratch the surface. Going into all their facets would add far too many pages and be too specialized, but here are a few last points to consider:

- You should give thought as to whether or not you want any of your NPCs to have Traits in common.

- There are matters of *false fronts*. Sometimes an NPC will have one Trait, such as arrogance, that covers up another Trait, such as insecurity. I call these false fronts *"Masks."*

- Sometimes an NPC might struggle against one or more of his Traits. For instance, a solider might be a coward but struggle to be brave. This takes fairly sophisticated writing to communicate artfully.

- Character Diamonds, or combining even a couple of interesting Traits, are useful techniques for creating interesting villains. Other methods besides Diamonds, however, can make villains more dimensional and lifelike, and therefore emotionally engaging. You can humanize them by seeing the fears or emotional wounds that drive them. You can reveal tiny pieces of their lives outside their acts of villainy. You can clue us in to their motivations, which, even though they're heinous sounding to us, make sense to them.

  But don't humanize a villain too much or the player will feel guilty for killing him or her, which in most cases is undesirable. On the other hand, if your villain is to change sides at some point and become good, then perhaps giving him or her more "humanity" in the beginning will make the player both be reluctant to kill the villain, and be glad when the villain changes sides.

- Traits and quirks can act in harmony or can fight a bit with each other. If they fight too much, the character will be unfocused. For example: A character who likes to have things "organized" (a Trait), always keeps his car messy (a quirk). These two seem to fight each other and will blur our sense of who the character is.

  If the character likes to keep things organized, but misplaces his keys on a regular basis, that doesn't fight his Trait of "being organized" too much and would probably work—although there's still the possibility that you'll confuse the player as to who the character is.

  Usually, quirks don't fight or harmonize with a Trait. They simply add more detail to the character, as in a character who is always organized (a Trait) and who enjoys watching baseball games (a quirk).

There's always something more to learn in this, or in any other art form, but if you keep these Character Diamond techniques in mind, you should have a solid basis from which to begin.

Emotioneering Techniques Category #2

NPC
Deepening Techniques

Giving your NPCs
heart and soul.

This chapter

focuses on techniques that give major NPCs emotional depth
and complexity.

They say children usually drown in the shallow end and I believe it. The word "shallow" itself has a cold breeze blowing through it, as in "shallow grave." Try diving into the shallow end of a pool, and there's nowhere to go. All that comes of it is an opportunity to get to know your local head-trauma specialist on a first-name basis.

No one comes to the defense of "shallow."

What about your NPCs? Are they shallow? If so, perhaps it's time to give them a shallow-ectomy.

In the last chapter, we looked at ways to make major NPCs interesting. There are also ways to give major NPCs emotional depth. I call these techniques *NPC Deepening Techniques*.

If you want your NPCs to have some depth, open an Emotioneering tool chest. Let's take a look at a few techniques you'll find.

> ## note
>
> For either major or minor NPCs, it's not a *requirement* that they have emotional depth. If your game is comedic in tone, you might not have a single NPC with depth. This would be completely fine.
>
> That having been said, you'll find that most comedic characters are enriched by a little depth. Think of *The Simpsons*, for example. Each one of them, at times, expresses deep, genuine emotions.

Emotional Pain

Pain, whether expressed or held in, gives an NPC depth.

Please take a look at the art. In this hypothetical game, you're a captain on a distant planet—a space outpost—accompanied by your Lieutenant. In this moment of the game, just before you arrived, an alien ship landed. The Lieutenant panicked and blasted the ship, killing the two innocent and peaceful aliens on board who were merely trying to escape. There's one survivor, a female alien.

You and your Lieutenant didn't expect to encounter an alien ship on this outpost. He's still freaked out and is about to kill the woman. So now find yourself in a potential firefight with your own partner.

The female alien is devastated. Those closest to her have just been murdered by your right-hand man.

Her pain gives her depth.

An Example of Technique Stacking[1]

Because a number of other Emotioneering techniques are used, this scene is also a good example of Technique Stacking.

For instance, here you find yourself siding with an alien you don't know and fighting someone you considered a friend. Defending a being you know nothing about, and turning on someone you know and care about, is an Emotionally Complex Situation (see Chapter 2.15).

It's also a big plot twist: A friend becomes an enemy, and a stranger becomes a friend. Plot twists can be valuable tools in eliciting a player's emotional involvement in a game (see Chapter 2.16).

If your lieutenant insists he's going to shoot the female alien, you've got to make tough a choice: Let him do it, or kill him. The two of you bonded due to earlier use of Player Toward NPC Chemistry Techniques (see Chapter 2.11). Because you care about him, the decision is even more difficult. Tough choices cause a player to reach inside himself or herself. This choice is a First-Person Deepening Technique (see Chapter 2.21).

Although there are many ways to create emotional immersion in games, if you want to begin to emulate the immersive qualities of life itself, one way is to carefully start layering Emotioneering techniques. In artful Emotioneering, techniques and layers of emotion are stacked like the crossing instrumental melodies and harmonies of a symphony.

Regret—and Hiding a Secret

In a hypothetical game, you're a commander of a platoon in WWII. War is a gritty business, and you've seen too much blood and lost too many men.

Of the men in your platoon, one, Riggs, is the most mysterious. His speech and behavior reveals an intriguing "Character Diamond." (Remember that we stressed in Chapter 2.1 that *major* NPCs without "Diamonds" are likely to be uninteresting.) Riggs' "Diamond" has five corners. He is:

1. **Emotionally Distant.** To the degree you can get a read on him, he's got a grim sadness about him.

---

1. *Technique Stacking* means layering several Emotioneering techniques on top of each other simultaneously, or utilizing them very close to each other in time, to create complex emotional impacts.

2. **Beyond Brave; Almost Suicidal**. He's the first to volunteer for any mission.

3. **A Superlative Warrior**—both in terms of tactical strategy and in terms of his fighting ability. Bullets seem never to find him. He's instinctually one step ahead of the enemy.

4. **Altruistic to a Fault**. He's always helping the other men.

5. **Obsessive Over Each Comrade's Death**. He reveals strong emotion only when one of the men in the platoon is lost. He obsesses almost more than any of the other men.

If the person writing Riggs' dialogue is a wordsmith with a hotline to the muses, and if the actor doing the voice over is gifted, and if the animation is expressive enough, then, as we play the game, we'll sense that something doesn't make sense about this character. His "Diamond" is too weird. Why is he so distant, so suicidally brave, and so preoccupied with each new death of a fellow warrior?

He's hiding a secret. No one has to say it; the player will deduce this because his "Diamond" is like a jigsaw puzzle that doesn't quite come together. It seems to contain inherent inconsistencies. Why would he be distant on one hand, yet be so distressed when one of the men in the squad is killed? How could he be so caring about others, yet be almost suicidal in his own behavior?

Finally, about three-quarters through the game, we learn the secret he's been hiding: He used to be a commander with a platoon of his own. In fact, he once even outranked you. But he caused a friendly fire accident and killed some of his own men. He was demoted to his current rank— a punishment that, obviously, he doesn't feel was harsh enough because he's full of guilt and self-loathing. This is why he has a taste for suicidal missions.

And so, all the corners of his "Diamond" now make sense. We see why he's such a good warrior: He has tons of battle experience. We see why he's emotionally distant. We see why he's suicidal. And we see why he obsesses over each man's death.

In this example of Riggs, we see two NPC Character Deepening techniques at work: Hiding a Secret and Shame or Regret.

Appreciation—and Wisdom

Appreciation for a friend, for nature, for a group...all these give an NPC depth as well.

Let's see an example of this in connection with another technique, Wisdom.

Here's the game scenario: You've been fighting slimy beasts on an alien outpost. The last one almost did you in. Your "health points" are just about down to zero.

You reenter the base. The Medic (male) looks you over, sizes up your beat-up condition, and digs a key out of a drawer. He hands it to you and says sincerely, "Want some privacy for a while? Here's the key to my quarters. Whatever you were doing out there, thanks."[2]

In a small way, the Medic has exhibited insight (he's noticed your condition and deduced you were doing something heroic for the benefit of the group, which includes him). Insight is one of many forms of wisdom. It gives him depth. His statement also includes appreciation, another NPC Deepening Technique.

In more than one game, I've seen wisdom is dispensed by a "wise old man," usually a Gandalf type.

But having a "wise old man" who gives advice to the player can be a cliché. Thus, hopefully, if you do have someone old and wise, and they're a major and recurring NPC, you'll construct an original Diamond for them.

A perfect example was done a number of years ago in the first installment of *The Matrix*. The wise Oracle was spellbinding, because she had a great Diamond. In the movie, she is:

1. **Secretive.** She likes to tease a bit with the knowledge she's holding back. And of course the biggest secret of all is, how'd she become the Oracle?

2. **Mystical.** She's endowed with prophetic powers, and we don't know how she got them.

---

2. In a game, this scenario makes sense only if there is something in that room that factors into game-play. For instance, there could be a weapon in there, or a secret underground passage out of the base that could be used later. Or this could be a hiding place if the base was later overrun. Perhaps, in that room, you'd learn a new piece of information that changes the entire direction of the plot.

3. **Calmly Powerful.** She seems untouchable by the agents of the Matrix, or they would have gotten her long ago.

4. **Maternal in a Mildly Cheerful, Amused Way.** She bakes cookies and, in some ways, treats Neo and the apprentices in her living room as if they are her own kids. Going to see her is a bit like visiting "Auntie Oracle."

5. **Profoundly Committed to a Noble Cause.** She's got a cause: overthrowing the Matrix.

We see that she actually has *four* NPC Deepening Techniques placed among her five Traits:

1. **Secretive** (hiding secrets)

2. **Mystical**

3. **Profoundly Committed to a Noble Cause**[3]

4. **She Takes Responsibility for Others.** That is, part of being maternal is the extension of her sense of responsibility to encompass the well being over those toward whom she feels maternal.

Had she just been "deep" without having an interesting Diamond, she would have been a cliché and a bore. As mentioned before, "deep" is an option; "interesting" rarely is.

Although this book doesn't nearly have room for all the ways to give depth to an NPC, let's look at a few more.

Cover a Real Emotion with a False Emotion

In the previous chapter, I alluded to the fact that there were many types of Masks—false fronts that can cover up an NPC's deep fear, shame, emotional wound, or problem.

Sometimes, however, a person puts up a false front for just a minute or two—a temporary false front. Consider an example: The hypothetical game is staged in a modern-day war located in a third-world country. You fight your way to the base, encountering one enemy after another. When you arrive, the Base Commander is there, waiting.

---

3. The Oracle from *The Matrix* has a strong Character Diamond, with three Deepening Techniques layered in. Her character construction is a great example of Technique Stacking.

He seems cheerful that reinforcements are coming, and says thank God the worst is over.

You go to check in with whomever is going to give you your next mission. But on the way out, using Eavesdrop Mode,[4] you overhear the Base Commander telling another officer how worried he is about the situation. Even with reinforcements, he thinks the group is doomed.

note

The emotion being covered up doesn't always have to be negative. For instance, an NPC could cover up love with feigned indifference.

The reason he hasn't told you or the other soldiers is that he didn't want to lessen morale. He presented you with a false emotion, covering a darker one. This gives him depth.

Combining NPC Deepening Techniques

In the last chapter, I mentioned that it's very hard to give a major NPC more than five Traits without that character becoming vague.

There is virtually no limit, however, as to how many Deepening Techniques can be used with a character, a plot, or in a "emotionally complex moment." (Deepening Techniques for each of these will be discussed a bit later in this book.)

Let's reconsider the female alien whose crew was killed by your partner (the one in the picture), and see how she could be given even greater depth than merely by using the "emotional pain" we've given her. We'll do this by combining NPC Deepening Techniques.

1. **She has a secret.** As you and she proceed through the game, you sense that she's hiding information. You're not sure what, but it's clear that she's holding something back. For instance, not all of her stories about her past add up. Time lines she describes don't quite match. She sometimes describes past events in different orders.

2. **A false emotion covers a darker, real emotion.** After her initial bout of grief, she gets herself together and admits that her two crewmen who perished didn't matter much to her. She claims that she was just recently assigned to their ship. This was their first mission as a team.

---

4. *Eavesdrop Mode* is my term for when you "overhear" two or more NPCs talking to each other. Some games use this as a way to get information to the player or to enhance the emotion of the moment. For instance, in *Star Trek Voyager: Elite Force*, you overhear a character talking to another express his fear about the upcoming mission. It has the effect of making that mission seem much more frightening.

Then, halfway through the game, you learn this is a big lie. In fact, she was engaged to one of those crewmen. She's emotionally devastated, and has been so since the time he died. Her indifference to their deaths has been total pretense.

3. **Emotional pain.** Of course, now we know the secret she's been hiding. We now see that she's got a tremendous amount of emotional pain.

4. **Fear.** The reason she hasn't told you all of this is because she's actually been afraid of you from the start. She saw what your partner did to her fiancé and fellow crewman, and she's come to the conclusion that humans are violent and erratic. She's been worried all along that you might flip out and kill her.

And so, this one NPC has four NPC Deepening Techniques. Trust me, she'll be an emotionally deep character.

This example shows why "Emotioneering" is a more useful word than "writing." We haven't even begun to write any of her dialogue, but we've already given her numerous NPC Deepening Techniques. How would you even know what dialogue to write for her if you haven't done this kind of Emotioneering first?

Having Emotion Relate to Player Actions and Decisions

I believe that simply creating emotional experiences in a game is its own reward, in the sense that it makes the game more engaging and rich.

It's even better, however, if the emotion can be used to influence the player's actions and decisions within a game.

Take the previous example. If you find that the female alien is actually terrified of you—and you need her help on an important quest but are afraid she might desert you out of fear—then you might need to take some kind of action in the game (go off on some mission) against an evil and dangerous enemy of hers to prove she need not fear you.

Perhaps, for instance, the technology in her ship is of great interest to your military superiors. They want to do a raid on her planet to capture some of this technology. Only by stopping them do you regain the woman's trust. She, in turn, is now willing to help you, which forwards the game.

The point is that the emotions you feel for her trigger action. They triggered your defending her from your partner, and they can trigger other actions as well. Emotion thus feeds into plot and gameplay.

Final Thoughts

This chapter has discussed ways of making NPCs seem more alive by giving them emotional depth—which the player only feels because his or her own emotions are triggered in turn.

Making any element of storytelling, including characters, interesting is different than adding emotional depth to that element. You can have deep characters who are still uninteresting, either because they lack enough corners in their Diamond or because the corners of their Diamond form a cliché combination.

There are a vast number of ways to give depth to characters. I encourage all of you to embark on the same Emotioneering training mission: When you see a scene in a movie or TV show where one of the character comes off as emotionally "deep," try to figure out what's going on to create that emotional effect. Then ask yourself, "Would it work in a game?"

Up until now we've been examining major NPCs. In the next two chapters, we'll see what can be done with *minor* NPCs, who may have only one or two lines of dialogue in the entire game. How do you make them interesting? How do you make them emotionally deep?

Emotioneering Techniques Category #3

Dialogue Interesting Techniques

Give players an Insta-Pass
to Your NPCs' personalities.

This chapter
focuses on making single lines of dialogue by minor NPCs interesting.

NPC dialogue often prompts action, sometimes gives crucial information, sometimes adds color,[1] and sometimes, of course, it performs two or three of these functions at once.

No matter what the function of the dialogue, giving the speaker one or two Traits can make that dialogue a lot more interesting.

Let's see this concept applied to different types NPC dialogue.

NPC Dialogue to Add Color

Say you're playing a game set in WWII. You and the troops have been battling your way across Europe. The going has been rough. To get health points, you've got to eat the slop that passes for food in your rag-tag regiment. (The war's been dragging on, and both the tent lodgings and the food look progressively less appealing.)

Let's look at some the dialogue of the Cook, a minor NPC. First we'll critique a weak example, and then consider how it could be made interesting.

An Example of Weak Dialogue

You approach the Cook, who's serving food. He says:

> **COOK: Here's your food.**

You might say that you'd never write a line like that. Maybe not. To my ears, however, far too much NPC dialogue hovers at that level of artistry.

How can you lure people who have become accustomed to hearing writing in films and television into your game, if they're going to have to suffer through lines like this?

I call this kind of writing *"robo-speak,"* because the dialogue might as well have been spoken by a robot. It *reveals no discernable personality* by the speaker. Have you ever met someone who has no detectable personality? Probably not. Thus, robo-speak breaks emotional immersion, because it's not realistic.

Believe it or not, I have actually encountered such a person. She's an elderly member of my extended family. In my entire life, I have never once

---

1. By dialogue that adds color, I mean dialogue that gives flavor to a scene or a person, and that possibly evokes emotion, but the dialogue doesn't prompt the player to take any specific action.

heard her offer an opinion on any subject or color a sentence with any kind of opinion or slant. If you told me that she was a Pod Person, I'd probably feel relieved to finally have an explanation.

The bottom line, though, is that she's hard to be around, because there's no "there" there.

So NPCs who only talk in "robo-speak":

- Won't appeal to people raised on the better writing often found in films and television.

- Seem unrealistic and, therefore, break the flow of emotional immersion.

- Aren't likeable. No one wants to hang around a lifeless person.

Let's see if the Cook's dialogue can be improved upon.

Better Dialogue

You walk up to the Cook to get your meal.

> **COOK (concerned): They said you were dead.**

At least he has some emotion; he expressed concern for you.

Or:

> **COOK (re: the food): Eat it -- before it eats you.**

He's sarcastic.

He has now shown at least one Trait. Let's see if we can give the Cook two Traits:

> **COOK (pleasant): It's probably chicken.**

Here he's both Pleasant and Ironic. Another example:

> **COOK (apologetic): It's bad, I know. But hey, at least you're alive to eat it.**

In this example, he has two different Traits. He's Caring with a sincere desire to feed the men well, and he's a bit Cynical.

You probably noticed that I needed to extend the length of the dialogue in the last example, possibly to an unacceptable degree, to get in the second Trait. The more Emotioneering you cram into a single line of dialogue, in general, the harder it is to keep that line brief.

Things get more complicated when the dialogue needs to not only add color, but to also *prompt the player to take action*. Most NPC dialogue prompts player action or gives the player important information.

NPC Dialogue to Prompt Action

Let's return to our Cook. First we'll feed him some weak dialogue, then add some technique to it.

An Example of Weak Dialogue

You walk up to the Cook.

> `COOK: I heard the Captain wants to see you.`

True, you know you need to seek out the Captain, perhaps to get your next mission, but the dialogue is amateur.

Better Dialogue

Approach that Cook again.

> `COOK: Captain says go see him so he can kill`
> `you.`

Or:

> `COOK: Captain's been by four times. Looking`
> `for `<u>`you`</u>`.`

Or, after you've done something heroic:

> `COOK (in an admiring tone): Captain's says`
> `go see him. Pick up a medal or two.`

Again, you notice that keeping better dialogue short is tough when it needs to provide the double function of prompting action and staying interesting.

These are the kinds of tradeoffs the game writer must weigh. In a game, short dialogue is almost always preferable to longer pieces of dialogue.

Splitting Up the Information

Often NPCs provide the function of supplying information. This dialogue can be quite dry and wooden. Of course, making the dialogue interesting is key.

One way is to "split up" the information so that, to understand what's needed to be known, the player must talk to more than one NPC.

This could be made even more natural if the player isn't just wandering around in a room or other environment, talking to one NPC after another. Instead, pieces of the needed information can be seeded into the game beginning earlier on, with the final NPC supplying the last piece.

Of course, this kind of detective work has several additional advantages:

- **It might allow the player to hear different points of view on the same subject.** These multiple points of view make the game's world richer and is a World Induction Technique (see Chapter 2.18).

- **It means that the dialogue from the NPCs doesn't have to simply convey all the information, thus leaving more room for color.** This adds to the atmospheric emotions in the game.

- **It can be used to create plot twists and missions.** For example, the player might learn that he or she needs to go to a different location where the rest of the required information can be found. Or the player might need to go on a mission to retrieve an item he or she must trade with a particular NPC to get critical information. Or the player might realize that another, more urgent task must be handled immediately, interrupting the task he or she thought needed attention.

- **And of course, ideally, information will also be given out in all sorts of nonverbal ways as well.** If the hospital is regularly being robbed of its medicines, you don't need to discover this from an NPC. You could turn the corner at night to see two men coming out a back door with boxes in their hands, and tail them.

> ## A Cautionary Note
> There's a danger to splitting information. Executing this technique poorly can drastically increase player frustration, if the players can't perform the detective work necessary to intuit what they are supposed to do next. This could happen because they can't find all the information, or they're just not clever enough to solve your "puzzles." Remember, a puzzle that might seem clear to the designer might not seem easy enough at all to the players. Sometimes only game testing reveals if you've gotten it right.

Combining these kinds of approaches with interesting NPC dialogue can contribute to a rich game experience and a feeling that the player is both discovering the plot and moving it forward amidst a world of life-like characters.

Some Common Fallacies and Problems

Some game designers and writers justify their poor NPC dialogue by claiming that most games have weak dialogue and, therefore, gamers won't object.

Sometimes, doing the writing is considered the "fun part," and those in the game studio don't want to turn it over to someone who might do a more professional job. This would be fine if they took the time to study and master the art of writing themselves—but the state of game writing lets us know this has rarely been the case.

Sometimes the justification is that weak doesn't matter, because the voice actors will add the emotion in the way they pronounce the lines. The truth is, there's only a limited amount a talented actor can do with poor dialogue.[2]

People who hold fast to these beliefs and behaviors are hurting the chances for good buzz and good press, and thus are restricting game sales and costing their publisher money.

Final Thoughts

It would be almost impossible to make every line of NPC dialogue interesting, especially when it needs to prompt player action. Sometimes it's okay, and even quite necessary, to have the NPC say colorless such lines as: "Over there!" or "Duck!" or "Drop the gun!" or "Back again?" In such situations, you just have to let the voice actor bring as much life as he or she can to the line. After all, in times of emergency or in urgent situations, people speak much less colorfully.

---

2. Even still, what a good actor can do with weak—or well-written—dialogue shouldn't be minimized. Poor voice acting can annihilate emotional immersion by the player. Most developers have finally conceded that it's worth spending the money to hire pros.

In other, less danger-packed situations, the ideal to strive for is to make NPC dialogue interesting, even when the NPC is giving crucial information to or prompting action by the player.

Now that this chapter has shown some of the challenges in writing NPC dialogue, and hopefully some of the solutions, let's complicate matters more (in a good way) in the next chapter, where we'll look at Dialogue Deepening Techniques.

Dialogue Deepening Techniques

Simple ways to create complexity.

In Chapter 2.2,

we looked at seven ways to add emotional depth to an NPC. For most of the examples, however, the sense of emotional complexity—the emotional or psychological layers—in an NPC couldn't be accomplished quickly. Those techniques required getting to know an NPC over time, as in the case with the female alien whom your partner almost killed (in Chapter 2.2, "NPC Deepening Techniques").

Can you give an NPC depth if he or she has only two lines or only one line of dialogue in the entire game?

Give Your NPC Some Depth

Yes, you can pull this off. To demonstrate a few of the ways, we'll return to Chapter 2.3's Cook who serves you after your return from battle in our hypothetical WWII game. He doesn't see his friend Tom in line for the grub.

Dialogue Deepening Techniques can add depth to the Cook, even though he speaks just one line of dialogue.

Worries

```
COOK (worried): You seen Tom? Just don't
tell me he took a bullet too.
```

Remember that just because a character—or even a line of dialogue—conveys a sense of emotional depth, that doesn't make the character or the dialogue interesting. Techniques to make characters, dialogue, relationships, moments, or stories *deep* are completely separate from those that make these same components of Emotioneering *interesting*.

If you made the Cook's worried line "deep" but not interesting, it would be weak dialogue. For example:

```
COOK (worried): I don't see Tom. Was he hit?
```

The two lines are very similar. They both convey the Cook's worry, but the first one is more interesting.

Sure, it's more interesting in that it picks up more of the flavor of spoken speech, but, as explained in Chapter 2.3, what truly makes it more interesting is that we sense a personality in the first example. The second offers no such glimpse of a definable personality. In the first example, we can at least gather that the Cook feels close to Tom, that he hates hearing bad news, and that he hears a lot of it. All three of these qualities are missing in the second example.

Thus, when it comes to any kind of Deepening Technique, including Dialogue Deepening, it's not a matter of making an element deep *or* making it interesting. Rather, when you choose to make an element deep, you almost always need to *also* make it interesting. The side effect of trying to do these two things (make the dialogue both interesting *and* deep) is that keeping the lines short is harder.

Remember, although making NPC dialogue *interesting* is worth striving for *in almost every case* where it's possible, making NPC dialogue "deep" is optional—a tool to be used *when appropriate*.

Let's try out a few other NPC Dialogue Deepening Techniques on our Cook.

Deep Doubts

```
COOK (looking over the battered and weary
men; cynical): How's "the cause"?
```

Regret

```
COOK (regretful): Tom was still limping. I
shoulda' stopped him from going.
```

Self-Sacrifice

```
COOK: Sorry about the slop. Up all night
with the wounded.
```

Wisdom or Insight

```
COOK (downcast): You know, our kids won't
even care about this war.
```

The Cook's wisdom is a Dialogue Deepening Technique. In the next example, I've given an NPC Wisdom, in addition to a second Trait, Bitterness, in order to make him more interesting.

The Hypothetical Game

You and your platoon just entered a German town. It's in ruins. You find an old man and, using Self Auto-Talk,[1] ask him which direction the Nazis retreated.

The Old Man points to some of the bodies of young German soldiers:

```
OLD MAN (cynical): They couldn't wait to
die. Your men have been of great assistance.
```

---

1. "Self Auto-Talk" is my term for when you're playing a character and you hear that character speak.

Once again, we see that the more Traits we stick in one NPC's speech (here, Wisdom and Bitterness), the more difficult it is to keep the dialogue short. Of course, the positive trade-off is that the NPC with two Traits is more interesting than the NPC with just one, assuming the two Traits make a colorful grouping.

You might have noticed that the Old Man *didn't answer the question*. That was intentional on my part. In life, people often don't answer questions. You might have to ask him again, or you might have to aim your rifle at him to get him to answer, or he may never answer the question and you might have to ask or threaten another NPC.

Combining Emotioneering Techniques

If he doesn't answer the question, even if you point your rifle at him, will you kill him? Well, maybe most gamers would. However, if the game designer:

- Dressed the old man in rags

- Placed his dead wife in the scene, behind him in his ruined house (we'd have to ensure the player knows it's his wife)

then you, the player, might both feel annoyed with him *and* feel sorry for him.

An Example of Technique Stacking

In one fell swoop, the previous example with the Old Man exhibits four separate Emotioneering techniques at the same time:

1. His dialogue is interesting; thus, it's a Dialogue Interesting Technique. It's even more interesting than usual, because he has two Traits instead of one: Bitterness and Wisdom.

2. He has depth, because he displays Wisdom or Insight. This is one of the Dialogue Deepening Techniques discussed in this chapter.

3. As mentioned earlier, you feel two separate emotions toward him. On one hand, you're annoyed or angry at him because he won't answer the question. On the other hand, you feel sorry for him. Having two different feelings simultaneously toward an NPC is a Player Toward NPC Relationship Deepening Technique (see Chapter 2.13).

4. You then will decide to kill him or not. Because of what he's been through, it's not an easy decision. Giving the player tough decisions is a First-Person Deepening Technique (see Chapter 2.21)—a technique that causes the player to reach inside to a deeper place within himself or herself.[2]

So far, we've focused on Dialogue Deepening, which is a tool to enrich dialogue, but we've left aside the idea of using NPC dialogue to prompt an action by the player—which is usually its key function.

So let's return to our Cook and up the Emotioneering challenge even more. Let's see if we can make the NPCs dialogue prompt player action *and* be interesting *and* be deep. Let's do *three things* with a single line of dialogue.

The Cook needs to direct the player to see the Captain. His example lines will use some Dialogue Deepening Techniques you've already seen, and introduce some new ones as well.[3]

Worries

```
COOK (worried for you): Captain wants you
for an assignment. The kind you don't come
back from.
```

---

2. You may read this and say, "No one would put that much thought into a single line of dialogue. Nor would anyone playing the game notice the subtle differences between a line like this and a less artful one." This kind of thinking, when it occurs, demonstrates a real naiveté about the art of writing and of Emotioneering. There's nothing wrong with being naïve, but this kind of naiveté is responsible for much of what amounts to little more than hack writing in games.

The professional writers I know—the good ones—often rewrite heavily to make their dialogue perform several functions at the same time. To them, writing has more in common with a composer creating a complex and layered musical score than it does with what most game designers consider "writing."

If you were to look at any one of many stunning television shows that have come and gone over the years—the better episodes of *Buffy the Vampire Slayer*, *Angel*, various episodes of the different *Star Trek* series, *Smallville*, *The Practice*, *The West Wing*, *The Sopranos*, *Six Feet Under*, and so very many others—you'd see techniques like these layered on top of each other in almost every single scene.

3. To see an example of writing with 35 Emotioneering Techniques stacked on top of each other in one three-minute scene, see Chapter 2.31, "Pre-Rendered and In-Game Cinematics."

An Example of Technique Stacking

This (long by game standards) piece of NPC dialogue by the Cook exhibits Technique Stacking by simultaneously accomplishing *four* things:

1. It's interesting. (He has two Traits: concern for you and a gallows sense of humor.)

2. It conveys depth via worry.

3. It prompts action.

4. It also creates suspense, because we're setting up the idea that something horrible is going to occur. Suspense helps make plots interesting, and it is a Plot Interesting Technique (see Chapter 2.16).

Let's take a look at a few more Dialogue Deepening Techniques.

The NPC Has Emotions Beneath the Surface

"Showing what a character feels beneath the surface" is a Dialogue Deepening Technique that perhaps deserves an entire book in its own right, but here's the short version.

Quite often, when someone feels a strong (and sometimes even a weak) emotion, they don't mention it. Rather, they hint at it through the words they speak, even if those words seem to be about something else. Or they hint at the emotion through their actions.

One example of this was given at the start of this chapter. Consider another from a hypothetical fantasy game:

You return, barely alive, from a fierce battle with an ancient, evil deity who has vowed to destroy a town that stopped worshipping him. He's a powerful boss.[4]

Your female companion (an NPC) has been waiting for you, not knowing if you were dead or alive. When you return to her, she *wants* to say that she loves you and missed you. But such direct statements of emotion are considered "on the nose"[5] and tend to be weak dialogue. Because such statements don't let the player "solve the mystery" of what the character feels, they don't draw the player in. Rather, they block player immersion. As a general guideline, avoid on-the-nose dialogue.

---

4. In games, a *boss* is a villainous or monstrous person or beast of some importance whom you fight, and who is difficult to defeat or kill.

5. "*On the nose*" dialogue is a film term that means a statement that is too direct or too obvious.

So, instead of stating her feelings directly, she expresses her love by saying:

> **WOMAN (angry): You go and fight that thing and don't even tell me?**

Or, she presents you with a cool gun, saying:

> **WOMAN: Took a couple hours to clean it but...thought it'd look good with that shirt.**

Or, she acts cold, and with Self Auto-Talk you say:

> **PLAYER'S CHARACTER: Why the freeze-out?**

> **WOMAN (icy): I never aspired to be a widow.**

In all of these variations, she means the same thing: "I love you."

Let's take a look at another example of the same technique.

The Hypothetical Game

Welcome to Russia, comrade. The game takes place in the present day, outside of Petrozavodsk, in Northwest Russia. The terrain is rugged. You and your Navy Seal squad, along with some Russian commandos, are trying to recapture a nuclear facility that has been taken over by terrorists.

```
INT. TENT - DAY

In a large, makeshift tent, a mile from the
nuclear facility, an ironic Russian NPC named
Nikolai is slow to heft his gear and get
moving. You just saved his butt in the last
mission. You play Carter. Calling him the
feminine name "Nikki" is how you good-naturedly
taunt him.

Outside, the rain pours down.
```

(gameplay)

```
You pick up various pieces of gear. You head
out of the tent. Nikolai isn't there beside
you. You turn to him. This triggers a...
```

(in-game cinematic)

```
    Carter (using Self Auto-Talk): Hey Nikki,
    aren't you coming?

    Nikolai (Russian accent; ironic): I was
    going to wait here. But if you're going,
    then I better protect you.
```

```
He picks up his gear and heads toward the tent
entrance. In the game, this triggers: A LOUD
EXPLOSION GOES OFF OUTSIDE, FOLLOWED BY GUN-
FIRE. SCREAMS of wounded Navy Seals and Russian
commandos are heard.
```

(resume gameplay)

```
You rush outside, followed by Nikolai...
```

Deconstructing the Dialogue

Let's take a look at Nikolai's lines:

```
    Nikolai (Russian accent; ironic): I was
    going to wait here. But if you're going,
    then I better protect you.
```

What he means is that:

- He says he was going to wait in the tent, but of course, as a commando on a mission, that's not an option. He's being ironic. So *beneath the surface* he's saying he has no choice but to go.

- He's saying that he better go because otherwise you'll probably get killed if he's not there to protect you. Thus, he's taunting you in return for you calling him "Nikki." *Beneath the surface*, this taunting shows that he considers you a friend.

- He may be saying he needs to protect you, but *beneath the surface*, he's trying to "save face" and deny that he needed to be rescued by you in the last mission.

So, in two sentences, *beneath the surface of the words*—underneath their literal meanings—Nikolai is saying three distinct things. Meanings and emotions beneath the surface of dialogue are one way to make even a single line or two of dialogue "deep."

Ambivalence

If I was to ask you how you feel about your father or mother, or your brother or sister, you might say, "That's complicated."

Most people feel ambivalent[6] about many of the people and situations in their lives. Ambivalence in dialogue is always a "Dialogue Deepening Technique." Let's look at one of the ways it can be done. This particular technique is called NPC's "Words are Neither Positive Nor Negative."

Here's the game set-up: You've been driving a tank, and are now getting out of your tank to attack the enemy on foot. With Self Auto-Talk, you ask the gunner in the tank if he'll join you.

> GUNNER (wry): Last driver asked me the same thing.

His answer is neither positive nor negative. It reveals ambivalence. Or he could say:

> GUNNER: No way. (Pause) On the other hand, I do owe you one.

That technique is called "The NPC is First Negative, and then Positive."

In both examples, because he's ambivalent, we can generate some suspense. You jump from the tank and launch into a fight with the enemy. Will that gunner later appear by your side? Maybe yes, maybe no. With his ambivalent answer, either one is possible.

Here's another Dialogue Deepening Technique:

Let's say that woman we discussed earlier truly is angry at you after you return from fighting the evil deity. She says:

> WOMAN (dryly): Weather turned cold while you were away.

note
The sentence has two meanings: both a literal meaning and an emotional one beneath the surface.

---

6. Ambivalence means feeling, simultaneously, both positive and negative about a person or situation.

Now, assuming the weather really *had* turned cold, she'd be talking both about the weather *and* her feelings about you.

Final Thoughts

It's been stated before but bears repeating: When I offer tools like the ones here, I'm not necessarily implying that each tool (such as Dialogue Deepening Techniques) always *should* be used. I'm simply supplying some of the tools of Emotioneering.

While adding *depth* to characters, dialogue, plots, relationships, and game moments might often be an attractive *option*, making all these facets *interesting*, including NPC dialogue (whenever possible), is not an option but instead is something to strive for, unless there's a good reason not to do so.[7]

Because so much NPC dialogue either conveys information or prompts player action, the challenge is to make this dialogue interesting and, if appropriate, deep. As we'll see later in this book, by doing Technique Stacking, it's sometimes possible to layer into NPC even more functions, such as having the dialogue tie into a theme in the game or serve symbolic value.

It's also worth nothing that the way a character speaks can, obviously, change as the game progresses. This could relate to a change in the character's Traits, a shift of allegiances, emotional growth, attainment of depth, or other kinds of change.

---

7. For instance, in a battle, a commander might yell out "Take cover!" It might be a line of dialogue without any discernable personality behind it (and thus not interesting), and it might be cliché, but it could still be the right line of dialogue for that character in that situation.

Emotioneering Techniques Category #5

Group
Interesting
Techniques

Get rid of boring aliens and
Boy Scouts forever!

This chapter discusses

ways of making groups[1]—groups as small as a squad or as large as a
tribe or even an entire culture—fascinating and intriguing to the player.

___

1. Here the term "group" refers not to a few friends who might know each other, but instead to any
   collection of people who have, to some degree, their own distinct, collective identity. "The Celts"
   are a group, for example, as are "the Marines."

When you create a major NPC, you can make that character interesting by giving him or her a colorful grouping of Traits. The same goes for a group. To make the group interesting, of course, the mixture of Traits has to deviate from expectations and clichés.

Whereas major NPCs usually can't support more than five Traits, a race or a culture or any other group that's been around for a long time can. Even still, to stay consistent, I call these groupings of Traits a "Diamond." I suppose the term "Trait grouping" would be much more accurate, though.

The Basic Idea of Klingons

The basic idea of Klingons is that they're not like us. Let's take a look at some of their Traits. Just as a refresher, a Trait determines how the character (or in this case, the race or culture) sees the world, thinks, speaks, and acts.

Klingons have a colorful grouping of Traits:

- They love war and battle. They have special weapons and rituals that accompany it.

- They consider honor important.

- Lying *isn't* necessarily dishonorable. You can exaggerate your deeds in battle and this is acceptable—even expected. This apparent contradiction (honor versus lying) doesn't bother them. In fact, to them it's not a contradiction.

- Passionate attraction for someone of the opposite sex is shown dramatically without hesitation.

- They have a number of traditional rites of passage for different stages of life, and they consider it important to maintain these traditions.

- They believe in an afterlife and that if they live and die honorably, they will end up there.

- They have a loyalty to their race, but an even stronger loyalty to their clan and lineage.

Relevance for Games

When you're creating a group that has its own culture (such as the Marines or a prep school's students), or an alien race or species, that group, to be interesting, needs to be composed of a colorful grouping of Traits.

If the group or race has too few Traits, it can be boring. The same problem occurs if the grouping of Traits isn't interesting enough. As with the creation of a character, the grouping can't be cliché (one we've seen before).

Two Important Considerations

Of course, if players are going to meet only three members of the group and hear only one line from each of them, you'd be wasting your time evolving a complex Diamond for the group or race. You'd never have any way to reveal the group's Diamond.

Indeed, the amount of dialogue in most games is sparse. Players are looking to engage that world and the characters or entities within it primarily through action, not through talk or reading.

So you might have some great ideas for your group or race, but is there even room to bring them into the game?

The second consideration involves the importance of the Traits you give the group or race. How do they figure into the plot? How do they figure into the gameplay? (There will be more about this in Chapter 2.30, "Tying Story to Gameplay and Mechanics.")

For instance, if you say that an alien race is "war-like," we can see how that can feed into gameplay.

But let's say they also love playing music. Well, that could certainly make them more interesting, and perhaps that's reason enough. If you want to make it factor into gameplay, however, the challenge is harder. Some ways this could be achieved are:

* Maybe their musical instruments are so fine that they're treasured throughout the land (or this sector of the galaxy) and you can trade one for items of great use to you.

- Perhaps you befriend one of the female musicians, and her music has healing powers you need at some point. Because previously you did something for her (like defending her from an enemy), now she will heal you when your life force is almost expended and you're on the edge of death.

- Maybe you can kidnap one of their top musicians, bring the musician to someone from whom you need a favor (if this character had said earlier that he'd do you the favor if he could just hear his favorite tune one more time).

Traits Versus Quirks— Carrying the Analogy into Groups

With a major NPC, a *Trait* determines how the character sees the world, thinks, speaks, and acts. For a group, a Trait would be a core aspect of that group's identity.

For a major NPC, a *Quirk* is something smaller that adds further individuality to the character. The same definition would apply to a group.

So, being "war-like" would be a Trait for a race. So would being musical. On the other hand, if the race had an interesting handshake, I'd call that a Quirk. It doesn't determine how they see the world or think. It isn't part of their core identity.

With groups, however, sometimes the line is a little blurred between what's a Trait and what's a Quirk. To me, this blurring is not a problem. The techniques are here to facilitate brainstorming. They're in the service of the final product.

Hypothetical Game Case Study

Three times in the last year I've been hired to work on games in which my responsibilities included creating human or alien groups, tribes, or species.

One project was for Microsoft. As often happens in the game world, the project was terminated after the prototype was complete. (It was decided that the gameplay wasn't quite unique enough.)

The game takes place on a post-Apocalyptic Earth, which has turned into a dumping ground for human and alien prisoners. These groups have divided into seven (what I called) "tribes."

Here is a small portion of what I created for Microsoft. However, unlike the document I gave them, here I'll point out the number of Traits in each tribe. Here is my description of three of the seven tribes.

Tribe 3: The Blades

"The Blades" is an ironic title for a group of humans that never uses swords or knives. They took their name from the Samurai of old, adopting the Samurai code of ethics and morals—if, that is, you filtered those ethics and morals through a heavy dose of unmitigated self-interest.

The truth is that, like many groups in Badlands, they're not easy to peg with a word or two. They do believe in honor, and they have a Code of Honor to which they strictly adhere. Part of the code is that violence is never used except when necessary. On the other hand, it's amazing how often they find violence necessary. (*Trait 1.*)

The Blades live by an exact hierarchy. Each man knows who's above him and who's below him, all the way up the their leader, whom they call "The Point." Members of the tribe advance only by challenging the man above them. If the man above them ducks out of the challenge or loses the fight, then the challenger ascends. (*Trait 2.*)

The Point is always at the front of any battle, for he's always the bravest and best fighter in the tribe. (*More about Trait 2.*)

The Blades have ritualistic katas, or fighting patterns that they practice as a slow series of almost lyrical movements. The katas stem back to karate—except in these moves, the warriors all hold guns. (*Trait 3 shows an aesthetic side.*)

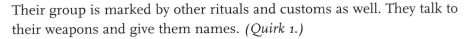

Their group is marked by other rituals and customs as well. They talk to their weapons and give them names. *(Quirk 1.)*

Anyone who's been shamed can get redeemed in the eyes of the community by going on a "siege." They can invade another tribe to steal a piece of machinery, a vehicle, and so on. *(Trait 4 shows concepts of shame and redemption.)*

Unlike the Sidewinders, the Blades are monogamous and marry for life. They believe in family integrity, and there are numerous customs surrounding family roles. *(Trait 5.)*

Upon meeting this tough, fierce, and disciplined group, you wouldn't suspect that this tribe was originally composed of the outcasts and runaways from the other human tribes. They banded together, adopted a rigid but effective way of life, and grew strong and even feared. *(Not a Trait, not a Quirk—just backstory.)*

Of course, being too rigid can also be a drag, and everyone needs to let off steam. It's not uncommon to hear loud, boisterous, drunken laughter echoing down the hills from a late-night Blades party. *(Trait 6.)*

Tribe 4: The Tabrene

The Tabrene are one of two alien groups on the planet. They're tough—and they have to be. They're outsiders, and no one wants them here.

The Tabrene are not composed of one species. All alien species (except for the Korimutay) on the planet banded together into this one group, forced into unity for mutual self-protection. Despite their various origins, though, they've established a quite unique identity.

Others will often remark on the Tabrene's cruelty. The Tabrene would probably counter that they had to become this way out of necessity. In any case, they paint vicious faces on their vehicles, and no one has ever seen a Tabrene run from a battle. Their sheer determination to win at all costs has rewarded them with the admiration, fear, and hatred of other tribes. *(Trait 1.)*

For many of the species in the Tabrene, this world doesn't provide the right climate. They need to drink a lot, or they'll dehydrate. *(Quirk 1.)*

They're a people of many customs. The strangest is, by using a process that no outsider has ever witnessed, they're able to "sync up" their minds so that, when in proximity to each other, they can act with such coordination that they almost fight as one being. In fact, Tabrene, when near each other, will often complete each other's sentences. Once further apart, they again become full individuals. *(Trait 2.)*

While no one has ever witnessed the method by which they create this cross-penetration of minds, outsiders have certainly *heard* it. That's because the practice involves forming a drum circle that goes late into the night.

The Tabrene feel that death is inevitable, so why not live as intensely as you can while you're alive. They're a people who take everything to extremes; they're beings of great passion. *(Trait 3.)*

Once in a while a Tabrene will get it in his head to just go off and single-handedly take on another tribe or tribe's village. These impulsive acts of insane courage are called "crazy strikes." *(Trait 4.)*

The Tabrene also have a tradition of literature, poetry, and music. They protect their artists, who will paint, make music, weave tales, or coin phrases. It's common for them to quote from "Teeoch," the "Book of Insights." The Teeoch is a group of sayings and proverbs, written by Tee-nalo, one of their great writers. *(Trait 5.)*

While most of the human tribes look down on the Tabrene as being inferiors—even a cancer to the planet—the Tabrene, in turn, look down on humans. *(Trait 6.)*

They revere the species called the Korimutay and would protect them from harm even at the cost of their own lives. *(Not a Trait, but sets up a mystery.)*

Tribe 5: The Korimutay

The Korimutay is a small, alien tribe, and all its members are of the same species. No one sees much of them. They tend to hide. Little is known about them. Always on the move, they're hard to locate. They leave no evidence behind as to where they've been.

Human tribes keep their distance from the Korimutay, claiming that the group has voodoo and will turn you into a tree or a rodent. The few people who've seen the Korimutay say that each member of the species carries himself or herself with fearless, calm dignity, like the Indians in old Edward Curtis photographs. *(Trait 1.)*

In fighting, they use two types of weapons. One is a simple, though high-powered, rifle. They fire just one bullet at a time. Though these rifles seem modest, other tribes are terrified of them. This is because, in the entire history of this world, no one has ever seen a Korimutay miss a single shot. *(Trait 2 shows their ability to focus and implies they can use this ability in other areas.)*

Their other weapon is a wide-barreled, high-tech gun (of sorts) that definitely looks quite alien. When they blast someone with the beam from this weapon, the target turns into a boulder, a tree, a pond, or some other natural element. You can see why no one wants to mess with the Korimutay, including Govan (the ruthless warlord who aspires to rule this land)—at least until he gets enough weaponry to overpower them. *(Trait 3. It's a Trait because it implies an ability to alter the material world.)*

The Korimutay are said to have strange rituals involving starlight. It's also said that they speak to the rocks and to the trees. All of these are rumors. *(More about Trait 3.)*

The Korimutay hide a secret of unimaginable proportions. Everyone assumes they're here as prisoners, like everyone else in Badlands. After all, no one would come to this wasted world voluntarily. And yet that's exactly what the Korimutay have done. *(Not a Trait, but it sets up a mystery.)*

So, All Groups Need a Diamond?

The answer to this is no, not at all. As with all the other techniques in this book, the techniques here are just options. If you create an alien species (for example), and they don't have a colorful Diamond, however, that group will most likely be pretty boring.

A friend once asked me, "So, if you have a group of friends, then that group too should have a Diamond, right?"

I replied that you only give a group a Diamond when you want that group to have its own distinct identity.

The Diamond of the Group and the Diamond of the Individual

Even within a group, individuals still need their own personal Diamonds. The art is to have these characters be unique, but not violate the Diamond of their group. For example, in *The Lord of the Rings*, Gimli has some of the Traits of a Dwarf, but he is also an individual. Arwen shares the Traits of the Elves, yet she's still unique.

Final Thoughts

Whether you're creating an individual or a group, clichés, boredom, and lack of imagination are always the enemy.

There's more to making a group interesting than just having a Diamond. Some ways of accomplishing this can be found in the next chapter, "Group Deepening Techniques," and in Chapter 2.14, "Group Bonding Techniques."

Group Deepening Techniques

If one person can have depth,
so can a bunch of 'em.

This chapter

focuses on techniques that make groups—groups as small as a
platoon or as large as a race or culture—embody a feeling of emotional
depth.

Just as there are ways to give depth or layers to an NPC, there are ways to do the same for a group or a culture.

We actually encountered a few in the last chapter among some of the tribes of post-Apocalyptic America, but I didn't point them out at the time. Let's look at those tribes again now, and focus on the Group Deepening Techniques.

Giving Depth to Groups

Among the Blades, the leader doesn't command his men from a distant outpost; he spearheads the attack. Thus, they have *Honor*. Also, their beautiful training routines, or katas, show *Aesthetics*. This was also true of the Tabrene, who had a tradition of music, literature, and poetry.

The Korimutay hide. They're *Mysterious*. Also making them mysterious is the secret they hide: Why are they here voluntarily?

Additionally, the Korimutay have some special rapport with nature and can even transform it to some degree. Therefore they are *Mystical* or *Spiritual* and have mystical or spiritual abilities. You might say that their incredible accuracy with their weapons has either a spiritual or aesthetic quality.

All these characteristics can give emotional depth to a group.

Let's examine techniques for adding depth to a group in the context of a hypothetical game.

The Hypothetical Game

In our example game, a time-travel mishap delivers you to the time of Cro-Magnons, who fight off Wooly Mammoths and other hominids who've got their own ideas about being progenitors to man.

Initially, the game sets up situations that would lead you to think that these Cro-Magnons are fairly dumb and shallow. But then, as you get to know them as a group and as individuals, you discover that certain aspects of their culture give them depth.

Wisdom

They have a mythological explanation of the world that, although not very scientific, has more emotional and spiritual truth than perhaps even our own world-view.

For instance, they claim that children are inhabited by river spirits, which is why they are free, playful, and always on the run. When children get older, the river spirits leave, replaced by tree spirits, which is why adults are more inclined to stay in one place.

The way a tree offers shelter with its green canopy, adults give shelter to their children. But, as water nourishes the tree, the river spirits in the children, in turn, bring life to the trees that are the adults. Thus their proverb, "The sound of children is life."[1]

Obviously, merely believing in spirits doesn't make an individual or group "deep." But being able to think in terms of metaphorical relationships based on observation of subtle energies would certainly show wisdom and thus give the group "depth."

Aesthetics

If there's a beautiful sunset, members of the clan gather to watch in complete and utter silence and awe. The children watch too.

Also, the clan creates beautiful cave paintings.

Nobility

There's something noble just in the way they carry themselves.

A Deeper Group

Suddenly, by applying a few Group Deepening Techniques, the group no longer seems possibly unintelligent or shallow.

---

1. It goes almost without saying that this spiritual background is a lot of information to relay in a game. Those who enjoy the extra level of detail and depth will truly appreciate your efforts here. But because some players couldn't care less (since their primary reason for playing will be the gameplay and not any story elements), ideally your game should accommodate both.

One way of dealing with this is to not force information like this down players' throats; don't make learning information about these tribes' beliefs and practices something that all players must experience in order to progress through the game. Instead, it can be made available in some way or another just to those who seek it out.

Some designers feel that every piece of information a player learns should influence how the game is played or how the story unfolds. But this is simply one ideal. If the information colors the player's emotions, then I would say that it does influence the game. If liking children makes these people more likable to the player, then that also influences the game.

This doesn't mean that it isn't worth striving to have all information that is learned by the player be useful in a more active way in the game.

Of course, as you get to know various NPCs among the group, if a number of them possess either NPC Deepening Techniques (Chapter 2.2) or Dialogue Deepening Techniques (Chapter 2.4), their depth will also rub off on your feelings about the culture as a whole.

Final Thoughts

This talk about Deepening Techniques may make it sound like a game is deficient if such techniques are lacking. That's not the intended conclusion. Most of the tools of Emotioneering are optional.

If a game is purposely designed to be fun and off-the-wall, the designers might choose not to use Deepening Techniques of any kind whatsoever. That having been said, you'll note that in even the silliest of Hollywood films (*Liar, Liar,* for instance), there are almost always moments of "depth" to give the story a periodic emotional anchor. These moments are usually designed to sneak up and grab us when we least expect them.

NPC Toward NPC Chemistry Techniques

Some NPCs belong together,
the way toothpaste belongs on a small
plastic stick with spiky, translucent fur.

This chapter discusses

techniques that, with very little reliance on dialogue, make it feel like two
NPCs have *Chemistry*—i.e., that they belong together as friends or lovers.

Although the bar was crowded, you caught each others' eyes instantly. It's as if time stood still and you were ripped out of this universe into another one, a swirling space held together by pure animal instinct. Magnetic forces within your bodies propelled you toward each other, like the raw energies of nature, like a fire about to burn this world to cinders.

Has this ever happened to you? Well, it might have been fun, but it wasn't very artistic.

If the only reason two characters come together as lovers or even friends is physical attraction, then your imagination well has run dry and you should pray to your favorite nature deity for a creative monsoon.

In real life, there are reasons you are friends with the people you're close to. Maybe you have a shared history, maybe you have similar interests, and maybe you're just a good fit. These are all Chemistry Techniques, and there are many other viable ones as well.

If you're going to have some NPCs in your game who know each other (an occurrence in some games), and they're supposedly friends, then it's important to make these friendships credible so that they mirror life itself.

Here are a few techniques for the taking.

The Characters Think in the Same Way

Consider a game scenario:

You're a 1930's San Francisco gumshoe in a film noir-styled game. You meet a sexy, dubious damsel in distress, who dresses in red and looks at you with bedroom eyes while relaying a sad story that may or may not be true.

She describes San Francisco as a "toy box masquerading as a city."

Later in the game you meet her sister, who mentions that she likes cable cars, because "they're like toys for grownups."

These two sisters think in similar ways. This helps convince us that they are at least friends, and it won't surprise us to learn they're sisters.

This technique can also be used if the two sisters are present together in the same room. Let's say you're in a cinematic.

```
SISTER #1: How do you like the city? You
picked a good time to --

SISTER #2 (interrupting): The cable cars are
a hoot --

SISTER #1: (interrupting) -- like riding
around inside a big toy box. I know.
```

Or, we could be a little more layered, by writing them so they have things in common, but also some disagreements.

```
SISTER #1: How do you like the city? Spring
here is so...springy --

SISTER #2 I'm not the one who gets depressed
in winter.

SISTER #1: It's a condition.

SISTER #2: The cable cars --

SISTER #1: I know. Like riding around inside
a big toy box.

SISTER #2: (realizing) That dress -- It's
mine.

SISTER #1: We both know it looks better
on me.
```

Is there anyone who, reading the preceding, wouldn't think these two people are sisters or at least friends?

That's because this example uses *five* NPC Toward NPC Character Chemistry Techniques:

1. **The two sisters have things in common.** They both see San Francisco in a playful way. If Sister #2 didn't, she'd say something to contradict her sister.

2. **They have Shared Bits.** We get the feeling that they have this kind of inconsequential disagreements on a somewhat regular basis—and that it actually might be an expression of affection.

3. **They have shared experiences or history.** They must have a past together if #2 knows that #1 gets depressed in winter or if #2 had had an opportunity to take her sister's dress.

4. **Sister #1 knows what the other is thinking.** When she says "I know—like riding around inside a big toy box," she's accurately guessing what her sister was about to say.

I had mentioned there were five Chemistry Techniques at work here. The fifth, **fighting**, deserves a more in-depth look.

Fighting

I sometimes point out to my screenwriting students that the opposite of love isn't hate—it's indifference. As long as two people are fighting, they're still emotionally engaged with each other. Therefore, we're not surprised when, in a romantic comedy, the man and the woman who've fought all along suddenly fall in love. In fact, we almost expect this.

In the game example given earlier, the fact that the sisters disagree sometimes makes us more likely to believe they're emotionally involved with one another. It's a sign of Chemistry.

Perhaps one of the best examples of this technique was in the first *Star Trek* series. Bones and Spock would continuously make jabs at one another, which heightened our feeling that they belonged together. And who can forget the back and forth jabs between Han Solo and Princess Leia?

In the cases of Spock and Bones, as well as Solo and Leia, they wouldn't just fight with each other, but they'd also risk their lives for each other in a heartbeat—lest anyone wonder if there wasn't real Chemistry there.

Thus, Chemistry can be more complex than just having two people fight or just having them be friendly. The conflicting feelings can derive because the characters feel different layers of emotion toward each other (described in Chapter 2.8, "NPC Toward NPC Relationship Deepening Techniques") or because one or both of the characters feel actual affection for the other but covers up this affection by pretending to be antagonistic. (Covering up emotions is an NPC Deepening Technique. See Chapter 2.2.)

These kind of approaches are more sophisticated, but that doesn't mean they're always the better choices. They're simply additional options for creating emotional engagement on behalf of the player.

Person #1 Talks Warmly About Person #2 in Person #2's Absence

In our noir detective game, we never got very far into the noir portion. Let's rectify that here.

You meet up with your client, Sister #1, in a smoky, dimly lit bar. A pianist in the corner threads the air with nostalgic standards that fit the night like a warm hand fits an old leather glove.

She's paying close attention to you and makes a flattering remark. You think her heart, or at least the steamy pulse of her sexuality, is turning in your direction—when she pauses, and then comments that this was the bar Kyle (her missing husband, who she has hired you find) liked the most.

Written out, the cinematic might look something like this. Remember, your character is a noir-style detective.

```
You walk into the bar. She sits there, a
drink in front of her. She observes you as
you approach.

SISTER #1: You're the best thing I've seen
all day.

PLAYER: I'm flattered -- but only if you've
had a great day.

SISTER #1: A great day? What's that? (Pause)
Kyle loved this place.
```

Because it's a game, my guess is that it's just about now that some mobster who wants either you or she dead will appear, and the next thing you know everyone's guns are pumping lead, the bar is reduced to shambles, and those patrons who don't get hit are screaming and fleeing in panic.[1]

The bottom line: Simply by talking about Kyle, the woman shows she has Chemistry with him.

---

1. There's really nothing so fun as shooting up a fancy bar, although the police, as they took me to the station, failed to see my point.

Another Example of Technique Stacking

As you know, I stress the use of Emotioneering Techniques in combination. In the film noir bar scene, four techniques are used:

1. She talks about Kyle, so she and Kyle have Chemistry.

2. The dialogue is interesting. He has one trait (Dry Humor), and she has one (Depressed). (See Chapter 2.3, "Dialogue Interesting Techniques.") And it stays within the noir style.

3. The scene itself is interesting in that it reverses itself. She starts by flirting with you and ends by talking about Kyle, whom we presume she has feelings for. (For more on these kinds of reversals and other ways to make cinematics interesting, see Chapter 2.31, "Pre-Rendered and In-Game Cinematics.")

4. Suspense is present: Will she end up, at the end of the game, with you or with Kyle? (See Chapter 2.25, "Motivation Techniques.")

That's a lot of Emotioneering, crammed into a very short cinematic!

Underkill Is Sometimes Better than Overkill

In the example cinematic, I kept the extent of the woman's feelings about Kyle a bit vague, although we can sense she's concerned about him or she wouldn't have brought him up. Her last line was:

```
WOMAN: A great day? What's that? (Pause)
Kyle loved this place.
```

Now I'll add an extra line at the end, so her dialogue becomes:

```
WOMAN: A great day? What's that? (Pause)
Kyle loved this place. (Worried) I hope they
haven't messed him up.
```

Let's look at the entire interchange, with this new ending:

```
You walk into the bar. She's sitting there,
a drink in front of her. She observes you as
you approach.

WOMAN: You're the best thing I've seen all
day.

SELF: I'm flattered -- but only if you've
had a great day.
```

> WOMAN: A great day? What's that? (Pause)
> Kyle loved this place. (Worried) I hope they
> haven't messed him up.

The interchange now has a fifth Emotioneering function: Worry. Worry is another NPC Dialogue Deepening Technique, so it gives her more depth.

This isn't to say her worry improves the cinematic; in fact, I think it definitely *lessens* it for two reasons:

- Her worry diminishes the suspense that comes from the earlier version, where her feelings were more indeterminate about both you and Kyle—and thus created suspense by making us wonder if she'd end up with you.

- Simply by talking about Kyle in the earlier version, we can deduce she's worried about him. To then restate that ("I hope they haven't messed him up") is telling us something we already know, and thus is boring.

Person #1 Can Read Person #2's Hidden Feelings

Here's another game scenario:

You play the captain of a starship. You've just learned that your spaceship has received orders from Admiral Jensen to cross the neutrality line for a secret mission into enemy space.

> CREWMAN #1: To hell with Jenson, and to hell
> with his orders.
>
> He storms out. Crewman #2 turns to you.
>
> CREWMAN #2: He just found out his wife's
> pregnant. Think he's a bit reluctant to die.

Crewman #2 can read what's beneath Crewman #1's feelings. Thus, we know he and #1 have Chemistry.

Now, to know for sure whether this Chemistry Technique is present, we'd need to know a little bit more about Crewman #2. That is, if he can read *everyone's* feelings, then this wouldn't have as much to do with Chemistry as it would the fact that he's very intuitive or insightful, which is an NPC Deepening Technique.

If he's insightful in this way *only* with Crewman #1, however, then it's definitely a Chemistry Technique.

(Even if Crewman #2 is insightful only into Crewman #1, as I'm setting it up in this example, that's *also* an NPC Deepening Technique for Crewman #2. Genuine insight always gives a character depth, even if it's just into one other person.)

They Have Shared Bits

This is one I mentioned earlier, as part of the Chemistry between the two sisters. A *Shared Bit*, as I define it, is a recurring routine. It can be something physical, like a special handshake. Or, it could be verbal, like two friends who always try to show they have a bigger problem than the other one. A bit can be comedic, but doesn't have to be.

Here's an example of a verbal Shared Bit: There are two friends, and one is always announcing the subtext (the buried feelings) of the other. This would be their Shared Bit.

Take a look at another case study: In this game, you play a paramedic. You walk into the employee lounge at the hospital. There you see Jim and Steven, who are frequently seen together.

> **PLAYER (to Jim): You're eating my sandwich.**
>
> **STEVEN: He's upset, he brought in a stiff. Baloney calms him down.**

And then later in the game, you find Jim and Steven in your ambulance, about to pull out of the parking lot. Jim's at the wheel; Steven's riding shotgun. You walk up to them.

> **PLAYER: (to Jim): Get out of my ambulance.**
>
> **STEVEN: Your ambulance is newer. It helps his self-esteem.**

This Shared Bit between Jim and Steven shows Chemistry between them.[2]

---

2. As a side benefit, if Jim never said a word in the entire game but Steven was his "spokesman," it could be quite funny.

Shared Bits don't prompt player action and they don't advance the plot. Their purpose is, like all the techniques in this chapter, to make us believe that two NPCs belong together.

Final Thoughts

If the goal is to create emotional immersion in a game, then we need to make the NPCs life-like. Drawing upon NPC Chemistry Techniques helps create that sense of realistic relationships between the NPCs, in cases where they're supposed to be friends, lovers, and so on.

Conversely, setting up a situation where two NPCs are supposedly friends or lovers, and not using such techniques, pulls us out of the game because it will feel unnatural and the poor writing (or lack of Emotioneering) will stand out and call attention to itself.

Emotioneering Techniques Category #8

NPC Toward NPC Relationship Deepening Techniques

Giving NPCs layers of feelings toward their fellow digital creations.

This chapter

illustrates ways, with very little reliance on dialogue, to make it feel like two NPCs have a rich and complex relationship.

Revisiting a thought from Chapter 2.4, if I were to ask you how you felt about your mother, father, brother, or sister, you might respond, "Well, that's kind of complicated...."

Which is exactly the point of this chapter. We often feel several emotions simultaneously toward a person. If we can capture this in the relationships between NPCs, we add to their life-likeness. If we don't, we've missed a great opportunity to create a more emotionally immersive environment.

Two NPCs can have *layers* of feelings toward each other.

Here's a hypothetical game example: You lead a SWAT team. On your team is a seasoned Veteran, as well as a Rookie. The truth is, the Rookie is braver and a better shot than the Veteran. The Veteran, however, is a smarter tactician and less likely to get the group killed.

In this kind of situation, I like to diagram the layers of feelings of each character toward the other. To simply this example, we'll focus on only the feelings of the Veteran toward the Rookie. The diagram could have one, two, three, or more layers.

For example:

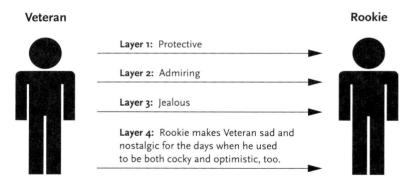

Veteran   **Rookie**

Layer 1: Protective

Layer 2: Admiring

Layer 3: Jealous

Layer 4: Rookie makes Veteran sad and nostalgic for the days when he used to be both cocky and optimistic, too.

In this relationship, the Veteran feels a variety of things toward the Rookie: (1) Protective, (2) Admiring, and (3) Jealous, and the Rookie makes him (4) Feel Nostalgic for His Youth.

I call this technique of a character feeling several layers of feelings toward another *Layer Cakes*. I use this expression because the image of a layer cake easily conjures the image of layers.

If you're designing a relationship like the one between the Veteran and the Rookie, you might decide that one or two of the layers the Veteran feels toward the Rookie are present more often than the others, or you may opt to give them all equal weight.

An Analogy to the Character Diamond

As will be discussed in greater detail in Chapter 2.22, "Revealing Complex Characters Through Their Actions," I don't differentiate between dialogue and action. A Trait such as Courageous could be revealed through an NPC's courageous actions or through his or her dialogue.

In a similar way, if the Veteran possesses different layers of feelings toward the Rookie, then they could emerge in the Veteran's words, in his deeds, or in both.

Different layers could emerge at different places in the game, or several layers could be revealed close together or simultaneously.

Let's say your SWAT team is storming a house where a terrorist is thought to be holed up.

> **The Rookie advances, but when gunshots emerge from the house, the Veteran shoves him down and takes point.**
>
> (The above shows protectiveness—Layer 1 in the drawing.)
>
> **The Rookie charges into the house anyway. The Veteran turns to you.**
>
> **Veteran: Let's not let the imbecile get all the glory.**
>
> (The above shows both his admiration—Layer 2—and jealousy—Layer 3.)
>
> **You and the Veteran charge in after him.**

So, in *less than 15 seconds*, we've presented three layers out of the four the Veteran feels toward the Rookie.

If, for some reason, we didn't want the scripted sequence of the Veteran pushing the Rookie down, we'd still have two of the Veteran's Feeling Layers toward the Rookie in the cinematic.

More Than One Layer Can Be Present in One Line

As we saw with the Veteran's speech, one line of dialogue ("Let's not let the imbecile get all the glory") can reveal more than one Feeling Layer, just as one line of dialogue can reveal more than one Trait of a Character Diamond.

There Doesn't Need to Be a Relationship Between the Two Characters' Layer Cakes Toward Each Other—But There Can Be

The layers of feeling that the Veteran has toward the Rookie need bear no relationship to the layers the Rookie feels toward the Veteran.

Their two characters' Layer Cakes toward each other are, in most cases, completely separate and unrelated.

The exception is when they fall into some kind of familiar and recognizable pattern, such as a father/son type of relationship, where both play out certain established roles. You could even tweak it to "critical father and rebellious son."

Some Dangers in the Familiar

Having the characters portray a familiar relationship as in the preceding is fine, but there are two possible pitfalls you must guard against.

Let's say the Veteran acts out the role of critical father, and the Rookie metaphorically takes on a role of delinquent son. If you make either character a cliché, the Great Emotioneer in the Sky who oversees us all will look down from on high and give you an F on your psycho/creative report card. For if you do fall into the cliché trap, you are not implementing the techniques in Chapters 2.1, "NPC Interesting Techniques," and 2.3, "Dialogue Interesting Techniques."

Another danger in using a familiar, metaphorical relationship such as this is that there's a tendency to do the *opposite* of Layer Cakes. That is, there's a tendency to have just one layer of feeling from each character toward the other. That's shallow. Layers are what cause Relationship Deepening.

And, of course, if the Veteran acts out the role of a critical father, there's absolutely no need whatsoever to have the Rookie act out the complementary role of rebellious son. As I mentioned earlier, in most cases there's not much of a relationship between the Layer Cakes the two characters feel toward each other.

Final Thoughts

NPC Toward NPC Relationship Deepening is particularly useful when you are part of a squad, platoon, team, strike force, or other continuing group. If this group is around you for a long period of time, then Layer Cakes can make the relationships between the characters richer.

Or, if you have two NPCs around you frequently, they can each have their own Layer Cakes toward each other.

As we saw with the Veteran and the Rookie, many layers can be conveyed quite quickly. Let's say you're working for a mob boss and a mob boss from another city enters the room. In just a quick exchange, using Layer Cakes, you can detect a quite complex relationship between the two.

Emotioneering Techniques Category #9

NPC Character Arc Techniques

NPCs can grow and change—
but hopefully not easily.

This chapter

discusses techniques that, when applied, give an NPC a Character Arc.

Quite often in a film, one or more characters have something wrong with them. More specifically, they start the film with what I call a *fear, limitation, block, or wound* (*FLBW*). For example, they:

- Are a coward.
- Are irresponsible.
- Lack ethics.
- Are self-destructive.
- Feel guilty over something they've done.
- Have low self-esteem.

There are a vast array of possible FLBWs.

Let's say the character's FLBW is that he has no idea who he really is as a person. He might have felt this way all his life, or maybe some devastating experience happened to him last week that left him in this condition. For our purposes, it doesn't matter. What matters is that, by the end of the story, he will have grown though this FLBW, and he'll have a good sense of his uniqueness.

This is exactly what happens to Luke Skywalker. In the beginning of *Star Wars—Episode IV*, Luke doesn't know who he is. By the end, he knows he's a Jedi Knight—or at least that he's meant to be one. A little later in this chapter, we'll look at how this character growth is brought about.

A Character Arc Doesn't Come Easily to a Character

A *Character Arc* is the rocky path of growth a character undergoes, usually unwillingly or with difficulty, during which the character wrestles with and eventually overcomes some or all of a serious emotional FLBW.

The character is unwilling to grow because it's tough to grow though a FLBW. Usually, the character has created a life in which his or her FLBW doesn't get in the way.

For instance, if the character lacks ethics, his life is fixed up at the beginning of the story, in a way so that he can get away with his unethical behavior without consequences. Perhaps he has an entire system of cover-ups and excuses to explain where he is and what he's doing when he's really off doing something unethical.

Another example would be a shy person who has gotten himself or herself employed in a job or even a field where interacting with others isn't required.

And then something happens to the character. He or she falls into a new circumstance or an adventure or simply a change in events, and now that FLBW gets in the way all the time. The character is forced to grow, like it or not.

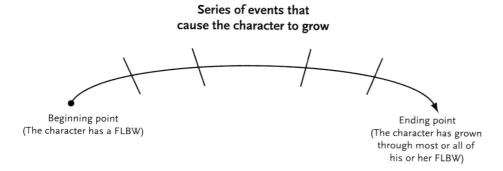

**Series of events that
cause the character to grow**

Beginning point
(The character has a FLBW)

Ending point
(The character has grown
through most or all of
his or her FLBW)

As I mentioned, going from "not knowing who you are" to "knowing who you are" is the Character Arc that Luke Skywalker undergoes in *Episode IV*.[1]

Luke is forced to grow due to the new experiences he undergoes, such as:

- Exposure to Obi-Wan's teachings and life examples
- Luke's needing new skills and powers to deal with the threats from the Empire
- Luke's desire to be a Jedi because his father was

One of the key factors that makes a film or other story emotionally gripping is watching one or more of the characters struggle through their fear, limitation, block, or wound.

It's not easy for Luke to become who he is. It's not easy for Princess Leia to learn how to love. It's not easy for Han Solo to learn how to go from being an outlaw loner with just a sole friend in the world (Chewbacca) to being an ethical team player. It's not easy for Obi-Wan to "get back in the game." (When we meet him, he's living by himself in a cave, doing nothing to fight the Empire.) It's not easy for C-3PO to learn courage.

---

1. It's also the Character Arc that Neo undergoes in *The Matrix* (he learns he's "The One"). Arnold Schwarzenegger undergoes the same Arc in *Total Recall*. In fact, because the memories of Schwarzenegger's character have been altered, he goes on a *literal* quest to find out who he is.

note

You might say that C-3PO never completely learns courage. It's true that he complains, but due to various external and internal pressures, he usually ends up doing the brave thing anyway. However, he seems to always be perpetually "mid-way" in his Character Arc: first complaining, then doing the brave thing, but never totally becoming the unflappable hero. Although I can't read George Lucas' mind, I suspect Lucas didn't want to lose the comedic benefits that came from C-3PO's continual anxiety. I think most people would agree that it was a good choice. Also, Luke, Leia, and Han were all heroes of different kinds; C-3PO's worry-wart style of heroism rounded out the mix.

Relevance for Games

Giving a character we care about an FLBW, and then watching him or her grow through a difficult and stressful Character Arc, is one of the key ways of making a story emotionally gripping.

If your game has major, recurring NPCs, then, ideally, at least one of them should have a Character Arc. It's fine if others do as well. If you don't do this, you might be bypassing a major opportunity to help create an emotionally gripping game.

Again, this is a general guideline, not a rule. There are always exceptions.

Ins and Outs

The ins and outs of Character Arcs could fill a book by themselves, but here are a few pointers.

One Arc

Try to give a character just one Character Arc. There are ways to give a character more than one, but they're tricky. They'd also require more dialogue than most games have room for.

Rocky Growth

A character's growth should be rocky. It's okay if the character resists growing—for instance, if the character is put in a situation where he or she *should* grow, but doesn't, instead clinging on to his or her old ways. Sometimes a character needs to be "hit over the head" a few times before they start growing.

In *Star Wars—Episode IV*, for example, Han has lots of exposure to the ethical group of Luke, Obi-Wan, and Leia before he finally starts changing and becoming concerned for purposes other than his own personal financial problems.

Happy Events Cause Growth Too

Although it's always difficult and uncomfortable for the character to grow, some of the events that force a character to grow can be happy ones.

In *Episode IV*, for example, when Luke first learns to use his light saber and hit a little flying target while wearing his blastshield, it's a happy moment, but still one that pushes him along the path of his growth.

Growth in Increments

Usually, like Luke in *Episode IV* or Neo in *The Matrix*, a character is forced to face his or her FLBW many times throughout a story. In some of these situations, the character may not grow at all and may even get defensive. (Luke is this way in the beginning, when he protests to Obi-Wan that he's too insignificant to do anything about the Empire.) When growth does occur, it's often in increments. Usually, by the end of the story, the character reaches the end point of his or her Character Arc.

For example, let's say you have a female character who lacks ethics. She's caught doing something unethical. She doesn't need to grow at that moment. Instead of repenting, she might justify her actions.

Darkness Before Growth

Characters can go through some very dark periods (emotionally) before they emerge on the other end of their Character Arc.

For example, in the film *Good Will Hunting*, Will (played by Matt Damon) is a young man who is afraid to let anyone become close to him. This fear stems back to terrible physical abuse as a child by his foster father that made him, on an unconscious level, equate intimacy with pain. So terrified is he of closeness that he even pushes away the woman who loves him and his therapist who only wants to help him. Rather than grow, he retreats into a very bleak situation. By the end, however, he makes his way through his FLBW and learns to allow people to be close to him.

The game *Max Payne* is another example. In it, Max feels responsible for his wife's murder. This guilt propels him into bleaker and bleaker situations and states of mind. One level is even played inside one of his haunting nightmares—twice. By the end, though, he does avenge his wife's death.

The designers and writer decided not to have him feel fully restored from his feeling of guilt, however, believing that a rosy ending of that nature would violate the noir feeling. There's some real bleakness to Max's circumstances at the end, and a certain amount of bleakness within Max himself.

To make the emotions at the end even more layered, this darkness is mixed in with a feeling of resolution from Max killing his wife's murderer. All these choices show a daring move by the designers and writer, and, I think, a sophistication by the players who embraced the game so widely.

A Mask to Hide Limitations

Some characters hide their FLBW behind a Mask (see Chapters 2.1, "NPC Interesting Techniques," and 2.2, "NPC Deepening Techniques"). If you've given a character a Mask, once they grow through their FLBW, they no longer need their Mask and it will disappear.

Let's reconsider our woman who lacks ethics. She puts up a Mask, or false front, that she's a respectable citizen. She goes out of her way to impress everyone of the civic contributions she's made. When she finally obtains ethics in the end, she can drop her constant promoting of what a wonderful civic contributor she is.

Imply Success, Don't State It

It's usually poor writing to have the character overtly state how he or she has grown at the end of the story. You wouldn't want Luke to say, "I didn't know who I was, but now I do." Instead, by the end, we should infer from a character's actions and dialogue that they've "made it" to the end of their Character Arc and overcome their FLBW.

Failed Character Arcs

Not every character we're "pulling for" necessarily needs to reach the end of their Character Arc. If they fail, they become a tragic character, doomed to live forever ruled by their fear, limitation, block, or wound. Characters who fail tragically in their Character Arc can bring a "down" feeling to the end of a story, so think carefully before doing this with one of the characters you want the player to like.

For example, the character begins as a coward and still chickens out in the big battle at the end, although we thought he was gradually becoming more courageous. That would be a tragic character.

The Consistency of Villains

Villains rarely have Character Arcs. If they change, it's usually for the worse.

Exceptions

Remember that the preceding points are guidelines, not rules. There are always exceptions.

In Hollywood, by the end of the film, if the lead character has a FLBW, he usually grows all the way or a major part of the way through it by the end. There are rare films, such as *Taxi Driver*, where the lead character gets worse.

Final Thoughts

Character Arcs undergone by characters we care about can add significant emotion to a film experience, and they can perform a similar function in a game.

In a game it is challenging to have an NPC go through a Character Arc when that NPC has relatively little "screen time," compared to the characters in a film or television show. Nonetheless it's absolutely possible in many games in which there are recurring NPCs. How would I know? I'm adding NPC Character Arcs in most of the games I'm currently helping design and write.

Emotioneering Techniques Category #10

NPC Rooting Interest Techniques

We know you care about your NPCs— but will anybody else?

This chapter offers
ways to give an NPC Rooting Interest.

Rooting Interest Techniques are techniques that make us "root for"—or, more precisely, identify and empathize with—a character. The term sounds like it means we cheer on the character who has Rooting Interest. We do, but that's just a byproduct our identifying with him or her. Thus a character with Rooting Interest is one with whom we empathize. This term, and "Character Arc" are the only two phrases in the book that come from the film industry.

The Sorcerer Among Us Is You

Luckily, the witch trials of Salem are behind us, because I suspect you're
a sorcerer.

note

Because this chapter focuses on ways to help
make the player identify with one or more of
the NPCs, you might well ask the question,
"How do we get the player to identify with the
character he or she is playing?" That topic is
tackled in Chapter 2.19, "Role Induction
Techniques."

In the *Lord of the Rings*, we're introduced to
Palantiri, or "Stones of Seeing." They're enchanted
rocks used to see what's happening in the vicinity
of other Palantiri, no matter where the stones are
placed in the land. Sauron ends up controlling one,
much to Gandolf's dismay, for it gives him visual
access to the vicinities of the other stones,
wherever they're scattered.

You don't need to be the evil overlord of a planet, however, to have access
to the same sorcery. You too can cast your eyes far out into the oceans of
human experience. In fact, I suspected that you daily adopt the viewpoints
of complete strangers and see the world through their eyes.

It's called *empathy*.

The two biggest reasons artfully written films or television shows move
us are:

+ We identify or empathize with one or more characters.

+ What happens to them then feels just like it's happening to us. If the
  character or characters undergo an emotional experience, so do we.

If you can get the player to identify with one or more of the NPCs, then he
or she isn't just experiencing his or her own emotions, but the emotions
of the NPCs as well.

Thus you can actually experience viewpoints of several characters simultaneously. It's certainly one way to create emotional immersion.

This happens in *Star Wars—Episode IV*. We simultaneously feel what's
going on inside the hearts of Luke, Obi-Wan, Han Solo, and Leia, among
others. Is it any wonder people became very attached to those characters?

Relationship to the Character Diamond

The Character Diamond enables you to create colorful and fresh characters. Season them with a few quirks and the characters develop even more
uniqueness. They may become *so* unique and so unlike us, however, that

we can't identify with them. If we don't identify with them, we've lost a major opportunity for creating emotional immersion in the game.[1]

It's worth reiterating that NPC Rooting Interest Techniques are just another Emotioneering tool and not necessarily one that benefits every game. For instance, if you were creating an urban game where you were alone in a hostile city, fighting and killing everyone you encounter, then you probably wouldn't want any of the NPCs to have Rooting Interest.

Even in this situation, however, it might be worth asking the question if it wouldn't be worth changing the design of the game and using Emotioneering to create greater emotional engagement by the player. In this example, I might ask the developer if the game wouldn't be improved by having a few NPCs in the game who are more than cannon fodder.[2]

But how do you create Rooting Interest for an NPC?

Put the NPC in Danger

Sword-and-sorcery games have gotten short shrift in this book, so let's rectify that by using one to illustrate several ways of adding Rooting Interest.

Picture a rolling green landscape. There's a forest in the distance. Stick a few medieval villages over here, a castle over there, inject some trouble into paradise, and suddenly there's a gaping need for a hero like you.

The enemy, Alrik the Dark, has unleashed a wild, powerful dragon that has been passing time by barbecuing a few of the neighboring towns.

You enter the village and find it crowded with refugees. One in particular is terrified. It's a young woman, Serilda, who is descended straight from a line of powerful wizards. To protect her, her parents gave her up at birth. Thus, she walks the earth unaware of her own latent powers.

Because of these powers, she could potentially pose a threat to Alrik. Dead, her blood can be infused into his and make him more powerful.

---

1. This assumes, of course, that it's a game in which at least one or more NPCs play an important role. If it isn't, there are still scores of techniques in this book that can be used to make the game more emotionally engaging.

2. The discussion is by no means academic. Just as this book was being completed, I was hired to help design and write a game in which there wasn't a single character with Rooting Interest. I persuaded the developer and lead designer to allow me to introduce one major and several minor NPCs with whom we'd identify, precisely to make the game more emotionally engaging.

The reason the dragon has been destroying town after town is Serilda. Alrik, through magic, knows she's somewhere in the land, but doesn't know how to find her nor identify her. She's the target that the dragon and the man who controls it (a henchman of Alrik) are seeking.

Though Serilda is normally strong, confident, and smart, these events would be harrowing for anyone. Having narrowly escaped death from the dragon once, and knowing that it's continuing its pursuit of her (although she doesn't know why), she's terrified.

Where will she turn? The villagers, learning that the dragon is after Serilda, have rightfully concluded that if Serilda dies, the dragon's path of destruction will cease. So, just as you enter the village, Serilda is being attacked by an unruly mob.

She's *in grave danger*, and we "feel for her." We identify with her.

Some might say that we would understand Serilda's plight but not feel for her. If the writing and animation are artful, you will. To use a film analogy, start the film off in a galaxy far, far away. Immediately introduce a small group of people in a spaceship being chased, fired upon, and boarded by shock troops from an Imperial Starfighter. The danger closing in on the small group causes you to instantly identify with them.

Self-Sacrifice

Serilda joins you on your quest to kill the dragon, as well as the unknown henchman of Alrik who controls it.

At some point in the game, Serlida comes to grips with the truth: If she allows herself to get killed, no more innocents will be harmed. She *decides to sacrifice herself.*

This too gives her Rooting Interest; it makes us identify with her.

In *The Lord of the Rings*, each member of the Fellowship is willing to sacrifice himself to prevent Sauron from returning to power.

This particular technique was also used extensively in the first *Star Trek* series, and in many of the succeeding *Star Trek* series as well. Kirk, Spock, and Bones never think twice about sacrificing themselves to save their comrades, and often risk their own lives to protect others.

Undeserved Misfortune

At a certain point, you learn that Alrik's henchman who created and now controls the dragon isn't who you thought it was. He was a wizard whose mind was taken over by Alrik. In fact, this wizard (the one whose mind is being manipulated) is, in fact, Serilda's father Valdemar. (She has never met him until this point.)

He struggles against the spell that controls him and begs for your help. He wants his mind and soul back. In short, he has experienced Undeserved Misfortune, and he'll thus have Rooting Interest, too.

In the first few minutes of the film *The Fugitive*, Harrison Ford's character fails to prevent the murder of his wife. Then he's arrested, charged with that murder, and found guilty. Because of his Undeserved Misfortune, we strongly identify with him.

Learn About a Painful Part of Their Past

In the village, you meet an NPC named Spengler, a cynical man. He doesn't care if his entire village is destroyed.

Initially Spengler is set up as someone you dislike. But later in the game, you learn that he wasn't always this way. His wife and young son were visiting friends in one of the first towns destroyed by the dragon. They all perished.

Spengler was devastated. All purpose and meaning evaporated from his life in an instant. His life effectively ended at that point.

The next time you meet Spengler, despite his cynicism, you'll understand *the pain underneath it*. And even he will have Rooting Interest.

In *Sling Blade*, Billy Bob Thornton plays Karl Childers, who is mentally retarded. At one point, he relays a painful part of his past to a boy for whom he feels protective. Karl tells of how he had a terribly physically abusive father. When Karl's mother gave birth to a very sickly child, his father forced Karl to bury the child, even though the child was still alive. Karl was horrified and distressed by the act. Karl, afraid of his father, did as he was told—but the experience emotionally devastated him. This painful part of Karl's past causes us to identify with him, despite his retardation.

Bravery

When the dragon comes to the village, one of the first NPCs to attack it is Spengler. Now this *brave* man, whom at first we disliked, acquires even more Rooting Interest.

Where do we begin? William Wallace in *Braveheart*. Luke Skywalker. Frodo Baggins. Indiana Jones. And hundreds of others.

Some Techniques Fall into Two Different Categories

As the book progresses, you might notice some overlapping techniques. Some Rooting Interest Techniques are also Character Deepening Techniques. For instance, Spengler, the man with the Mask of cynicism, may have Rooting Interest because we learn of his pain—but pain is also NPC Deepening Technique. So is self-sacrifice, which he does when he attacks the dragon.

Not every NPC Deepening Technique (an NPC exhibiting insight, for example) is a Rooting Interest Technique. And not every Rooting Interest Technique (an NPC being genuine, for instance) is a Character Deepening Technique. But some of these techniques do overlap.

Characters You Invest with Life

Characters you *invest with life* also have Rooting Interest.

It's easy to observe that childrens' stuffed animals have Rooting Interest, for kids love them immensely and easily identify with them. They'll often imbue the animals with characteristics, give them voices, use them to enact stories, and get caught up in the personalities they've created.

So, like the NPCs discussed in this chapter, the animals are used by kids to extend their imagination into new viewpoints, at least for a time. It's empathy—even though it's empathy for characters for whom they themselves create.

The Sims is a great example of characters that have Rooting Interest because players invest them with life, as well as their Sims' families and even neighborhoods.

Of course, many additional factors contribute to *The Sims* being emotionally engaging, but we're just talking about Rooting Interest for now. In that regard, *The Sims* exemplifies another Rooting Interest Technique as well: being responsible for characters.

Characters for Whom You're Responsible

In *The Sims*, players do something more than invest the characters with life. Compared to a stuffed animal, Sims already look fairly alive, so it doesn't take an extreme amount of "investing."

Players are also *responsible* for their Sims. Characters for whom we feel responsible have Rooting Interest (meaning that we empathize with them).[3]

You can see this even in real life, for instance, parents suffer when one of their children experiences a major setback or disappointment.

Going back to our game with the dragon: You come to know the villagers, and they depend on you to save them. Assuming they're made life-like enough and with techniques to give them Rooting Interest, you want to save them. You feel responsible for them. This increases your empathy for each of them.

Take a look at another example.

In the hypothetical game illustrated on the following page, you play Jen Cranston, a surveyor under contract with the government of Peru. Your life is pretty drab and uneventful, until you get lost one day (which happens to be where our game begins) and hear screams from inside a cave.

You explore and discover this ancient artifact, as well as Citlali, the woman who's been trapped by it and who's been writhing in pain for 1,000 years.

You smash the artifact and free the woman from her agony.

It's true that empathizing with someone leads us to wanting to have some responsibility for them. But the reverse is also true: taking responsibility

---

3. It's important to state that different players relate to their Sims characters in quite different ways. Some players strongly identify with them and try and get quite involved in creating their lives. Other players, however, are simply amused, and we all know that more than a few players have tried to get their Sims into all sorts of horrible situations, and even kill them off in loathsome ways. Thus, though Sims characters have Rooting Interest to some players, the game offers players many ways relate to the characters. This is a Self-Created Story Technique and, as we'll see in Chapter 2.24, it's a great way to foster player immersion in a game.

My guess is that if you could never control more than one or two Sims, you'd be more emotionally invested and there'd be a greater likelihood they'd have Rooting Interest.

for someone causes us to empathize with him or her. In this case, you'd empathize with the woman for whom you took responsibility, and whom you liberated from her torment.

We can see this in life not just with parents and children, but even with pets. If you take care of a dog or cat, soon you start empathizing with it. Thus, if the animal gets sick or wounded, it will affect you emotionally.

The parameter of our being expands to encompass those people, and even animals, trees, and things, for whom and which we feel responsible.[4] For them, we'll feel empathy. This is that almost mystical ability I noted at the start of the chapter—our ability to see through the eyes of others.

Citlali also has Rooting Interest due to two other techniques. First of all, she's in Danger—and an NPC in Danger is one we're likely to identify with. Additionally, she has Undeserved Misfortune, which also gives her Rooting Interest. (To be fair, we don't yet know if Citlali's misfortune is undeserved or not, although the way I envisage the game, she wouldn't have deserved this punishment. And even if, later in the game we learn that her misfortune is deserved, she'd still have Rooting Interest until then.)

A Note About Multi-Function Techniques

Some Emotioneering techniques, as you might have noticed, perform more than one function—for example, Taking Responsibility for Another. In our hypothetical game, when you (playing Jen) take responsibility for Citlali, four Emotioneering functions are performed simultaneously:

1. You (through Jen, the character you play) rescue Citlali, and you'll protect her from many dangers during the game, as the beings who trapped her there now try to find her and capture her again.

    As was discussed a bit earlier, responsibility for an NPC makes us identify with the NPC for whom we take responsibility. Thus, it's a Rooting Interest Technique.

2. Taking responsibility for another character emotionally bonds you to that character. It's one of many ways of creating Chemistry between you and that character, and is thus a Player Toward NPC Chemistry Technique (see Chapter 2.11).

---

4. If a person has restored a vintage car and labored tremendous time and love on it (taken responsibility for it) and that car gets injured, the person will feel pain. This is what I mean by being able to even empathize with objects for which we feel responsible.

3. When you are bonded to one or more characters in a game, as you'll be bonded to Citlali, you're more willing to participate in the world of that game. Thus, this Taking Responsibility is also a World Induction Technique (see Chapter 2.18).

4. When a player takes responsibility for another character, it actually gives the player himself or herself emotional depth—just as taking responsibility for a friend or a child in real life gives a person depth. That's because you need to expand your vision to see not just what you need, but what that other person needs. Thus, you taking responsibility for Citlali is also a First-Person Deepening Technique (see Chapter 2.21).

It's rare to see techniques function in so many ways. I certainly know no other technique such as "Taking Responsibility," which occupies a slot in four distinct Emotioneering categories.

Usually techniques don't perform multiple functions. For example, a Character Exhibiting Insight is an NPC Deepening Technique, but it isn't an NPC Rooting Interest Technique. A Character Being Genuine is an NPC Rooting Interest Technique, but not a Character Deepening Technique.

But some techniques do occasionally overlap into different categories. I therefore thought it worth pointing out so that it doesn't seem confusing or even a mistake when you periodically come upon other examples later in this book.

Using Rooting Interest Techniques and Their Opposites to "Dial Up" or "Dial Down" an NPC's Likability and the Degree to Which We Identify with Him or Her

Any Rooting Interest Technique, flipped upside down, can make a character unlikable and make us unwilling to identify with that character. For instance, it's a Rooting Interest Technique to have a character risk sacrificing himself for another person who's in danger. Flip this upside down, and it makes the person unlikable.

Thus, we have a sort of dial by which we can control exactly how much we like (or identify with) any particular character.

There are many uses for this "Rooting Interest Dial," such as:

- **Creating flawed heroes**, and preventing heroes from being "too perfect."

- **Creating villains whom we like some of the time or about whom we're ambivalent** (for example, "cool villains" of the films *Pulp Fiction, Get Shorty*, and *The Usual Suspects*).

- **Making a character who would normally be unlikable into a hero.** If you remember the movie *Rocky*, you'll find that he's a quite likable hero (because of all the Rooting Interest Techniques employed in the creation of his character). It makes us overlook his job—he's an enforcer for a loan shark.

- **Making a character go from being unlikable to likable over a stretch of time.**

Final Thoughts

When, as game designers, we give an NPC Rooting Interest, the player will, as if using Tolkien's "Stones of Seeing," we look at the world through that character's eyes and experience that NPCs emotions.

It becomes even more of an Emotioneering tool when you start having the player experiencing the emotions of numerous different characters simultaneously.

How many characters did you identify with in *Star Wars—Episode IV*? How many in *The Matrix*? How many in the *Lord of the Rings* films? It's no wonder these films take up permanent lodging in our hearts.

Giving NPCs some Rooting Interest becomes a valuable tool in creating emotional immersion.

Player Toward NPC chemistry Techniques

Getting emotionally entangled
with someone made
of polygons.

This chapter offers

ways to make the player feel chemistry with an NPC. That is, these
techniques make the player feel close to an NPC, either romantically
or non-romantically.

When you have *chemistry* with someone, you want to be friends with them.

In Chapter 2.7, we examined NPC to NPC Chemistry Techniques. This chapter is about creating NPCs with whom the *player* has Chemistry.

It would seem, at first, that techniques that make a player feel like he or she has Chemistry with an NPC would be the same as those that give an NPC Rooting Interest. After all, if we identify with a character (i.e., if they have Rooting Interest), wouldn't we therefore also have Chemistry with them?

The difference is subtle.

Because of an artful use of Rooting Interest Techniques, in a game you might end up identifying with an orphaned elf, or a brave and kind but hideous-looking alien, or a peasant who is genuine and self-sacrificing.

But, curiously, this doesn't mean you'd necessarily want to be friends with any of them. And Chemistry, by definition, means you'd like to be friends or lovers with a character.

To use some film analogies, you might emotionally identify with troubled and somewhat retarded Karl Childers (played by Billy Bob Thornton) in the film *Sling Blade*, or with Forrest Gump (Tom Hanks) in the film of the same name, or with Billy Elliot (Jamie Bell), the boy from a British coal-mining town who wants to study ballet in *Billy Elliot*, or with a number of the troubled young teens in *Stand By Me*—but this doesn't mean that you'd want to be friends with any of them.

It's a curious thing, but true—techniques that make us identify with a character (NPC Rooting Interest Techniques) are, in large part, different than the techniques needed to make us feel like we'd want that character as a friend (Player Toward NPC Chemistry Techniques).

Following are a few techniques to make a player feel he or she has Chemistry with an NPC. We'll examine them in the context of a hypothetical game.

The NPC Admires You

Here's our case study game scenario:

You're a police captain in an elite unit. You fight back the provoked and angry mob that is trying to kill Jason Falconer, a prisoner you're guarding.

He's been accused of treason, and they want him drawn and quartered. Not that you like Falconer—but guarding him is your job.

After the fight, one of your lieutenants tells you he's never seen anyone fight like that, and that he's glad to serve under you. My guess is you'll like that junior officer. We all love admiration, and thus this builds Chemistry.

The NPC Reads Your Mind

Can an NPC have insight into you? It certainly sounds impossible. But let's see....

You have to transport Falconer across town at night in an armed jeep.

But a lot of people want to get at Falconer, and the cross-city journey deteriorates into one hair-raising battle after another. Bullets fly, blood splatters. The route you took was supposed to be secret. There's no way the mob could have known your plans.

One of your would-be killers, now dying on the cold city pavement from your merciless onslaught of lead, spills the beans:

The reason that this hoodlum armada knew where to repeatedly ambush you is that one of your own men, a lieutenant named McCully, purposely leaked your route.

Now understand, McCully had been a friend of yours until now. You went out on missions together, and he even risked his life for you once. So, when you learn he's a turncoat, it comes as a total shock.

The harrowing cross-town mission continues. Barely alive, you make it to the jail where Falconer will be guarded (for his own protection). Your officers there have already heard how McCully sold out you and the unit.

One of them approaches, looks at your ragged condition, and comments, disgustedly, "McCully, can you believe it? After what you guys have been through...."

And that's exactly the way you feel. The fact that what you're feeling is acknowledged by this fellow officer creates chemistry between you two.

The NPC Has Things in Common with You

You just risked your life to get Falconer across town.

Falconer (who up until now you assumed was guilty) explains why his enemies in the government framed him for treason and want him killed: He knows their plans.

They're going to instigate riots in several cities simultaneously, and then use these riots as an excuse to declare martial law. Once martial law is declared, they'll use the "state of emergency" as a reason to round up all their opponents and have them imprisoned or killed.

You give yourself the mission to search out corroborating evidence, which you find. Falconer was telling the truth.

So now you're off on a mission to locate the compound where the secret plans to instigate a national state of emergency are hidden. This compound is the base from which the entire conspiracy is organized.

You need to find the compound and retrieve those written plans—the "smoking gun"—so you can bring them to the press and expose the conspiracy.

One minor setback: You don't know the location of the compound. You know someone who does, however, and that's your "friend," McCully, who earlier betrayed you. So you set off to capture him.

note

It's worth reiterating: Weak dialogue can undo the best Emotioneering, and most game dialogue is very weak. Weak dialogue from the rookie could make the preceding situation hokey and undo the effectiveness of this quite useful Self Toward NPC Chemistry Technique.

One of your men, a young rookie, volunteers to help you. He joined the force to "Serve and Protect," and he believes in those ideals. The notion of police being used as a tool for those who would abuse power is more than he can take.

So he joins you on this next mission. What you two have in common, of course, is your similar feelings about what's right and wrong.

The NPC Anticipates Your Needs and Desires

You locate McCully, the cop who betrayed you, in a complex outside of town. You and the rookie sneak in, but soon guards swarm you and an intense firefight erupts.

At a certain point in the battle, when you're outgunned, the rookie tosses you a powerful automatic weapon (one you've used before so you know the controls). You catch the gun—it comes just at the right time, and its firepower allows you to blast your way through this assault and complete the mission.

Trust me, you'll have chemistry with the rookie.

An NPC Makes You Grow to Become a Better Person

Game Case Study: *Ico*

One of the most interesting games to date that employs this Player Toward NPC Chemistry Technique is *Ico*. (Please note: I'll be discussing *Ico* in great detail here. If you haven't played the game and don't want to learn the ending, please skip this section.)

Ico is set in a strange land, in a large and foreboding castle. There you must protect a young woman from all sorts of dangers and a terrible fate that awaits her, while trying to lead her to freedom. The look of the game is luscious and the animation is wonderful, but it's a puzzle game with some redundant gameplay. Thus, players often decide not to pursue the game to its finale.

Those who do finish it, however, are treated to some of the most emotional experiences any game has delivered to date. The end's emotional power is due to the artful application of a number of Emotioneering techniques. Some of the techniques that contribute to the emotion are:

1. The girl's Rooting Interest, which stems from:
    * Her being in danger.
    * Her undeserved misfortune.
    * The fact that you constantly take responsibility for her safety and freedom.
    * There's an aesthetic quality about her as well.
2. Plot Deepening Techniques (see Chapter 2.17), including:
    * A story that doubles back on itself in an interesting way. In fact, the plot folds back on itself near the end in numerous ways that are both inventive and moving.
    * The ending is a little open-ended—but not so much that it frustrates us. Much is explained, but still some crucial pieces are left for us to fill in with our imaginations.
    * We're swept into a world where mystical forces are made palpable. (The *Lord of the Rings* films do this as well.)

continues

continued

3. Plot Interesting Techniques (see Chapter 2.16) in the form of some incredible plot twists near the end that are completely unpredicted on one hand, yet also resolve many mysteries.

4. Player Toward NPC Chemistry Techniques, which are the most important factors in creating the emotion we experience and which are the subject of this chapter. Some examples are:

   - The girl admires you—and in fact slowly falls in love with you.
   - As you constantly take responsibility for her, you experience yourself growing and becoming a bigger and better person.

     Normally, taking responsibility for another NPC, especially one who can't hold her own weight in a battle, might annoy the player, because it forces the player to slow down. But because of the girl's strong Rooting Interest, that isn't the case here.

The last 45 minutes of gameplay uses Technique Stacking to the max.

Let's return to our story about Falconer and the conspiracy to instigate riots in order to justify the declaration of martial law. You had just fought with McCully, and retrieved the information as to the location of the compound in which the conspirators are using as a base of operations and in which their plans are kept.

Now there's a further twist: Falconer's 10-year-old daughter is being held prisoner in the compound. It's his former bosses' way of making sure Falconer doesn't betray them. If he does, she'll be killed. He's terrified this will happen. He shows you her picture. She looks beautiful, innocent, and playful.

You have to get into that compound, rescue Falconer's daughter, and find the plans to trigger that state of emergency. Armed with this evidence, you can then provide concrete proof to your superiors and stave off this disaster—or so you think, until you discover that they too are part of the conspiracy. And the clock is ticking....

If you choose to save Falconer's daughter and not just go for the plans, you'll be facing a much greater risk.

And there are other consequences if you go on this mission. You might get tried for treason, just like Falconer. You will, at the least:

- Be stripped of your rank.

- Be fired from the police force.

- Be portrayed as anti-American in the eyes of the public and broadly reviled.

- End the game with nothing—no weapons, no title, and no prestige.

All this is made quite clear to you. And it's not just that all these losses will come in a closing cinematic—you'll have to finish out the game in that state of privation and disrepute.

To effectively pull this off in the game, we might want to set up two alternative endings. If you're the player and you don't want to infiltrate the compound, there would be some big boss fight to serve as the game's finale.

But if you decide to risk it all, the question is, will this just be another mission, or will the experience have any emotional impact on you?

If you've really come to like, respect, and care about Falconer, and thus care about his daughter...

And if you really like the rank, weapons, and respect you get in your current job but which will all be sacrificed if you take this mission...

Then this won't be a mere mission. The decision should be difficult to make. But if you make it, you'll feel noble and heroic.

Emotion could be further heightened in the following way: Once you fight your way into the compound, you break into the heavily guarded room where the girl is being held. You're entering the room triggers a scripted sequence that makes it seem as if you arrived just as if she was about to be killed by a guard with a long knife.

However, you get creamed. First of all, in that room is a sub-boss who beat you earlier in the game and left you barely alive. Because of his rain of bullets, and because of extremely heavy gunfire from another man in the room, you're forced to retreat or get killed. The game leaves you no other option.

Your retreating triggers another scripted sequence: A few seconds after you back out of the room, you hear the girl's terrified scream, as if she had just been cut (which indeed she has).

You'll definitely be weary, and maybe even a bit afraid of going into the room a second time, for fear of dying. After all, earlier in the game you learned that your nemesis in that room is actually a better fighter than you are. Additionally, you almost got killed a minute ago.

These factors, coupled with the fact that saving the girl is optional, would make the choice to go back into that room truly a heroic one, because you know the mission to save the girl is not necessary—only collecting the data is. You can walk away from this dangerous situation, and if you choose to fight (and save the girl who's screaming in pain), you're likely to be very emotionally rooted in the situation.

Quick-Saving

The game element that can break this whole situation, though, is *quick-save*. In most PC games, the player can hit F5 (or some other designated key) any time he wants to save his game. This means that the player can hit F5, run in, and if he dies, reload instantly and try again, and during the face-off with the nemesis character, every time he successfully gets another shot off at him, he can hit F5 again. This is called a *quick-save crawl*, where the player never has any immediate threat to his person because he always has the get-out-of-jail-free card at his disposal. It's something that has the potential to sap a lot of the emotional intensity out of any situation.

Most console games, on the other hand, let you save only at check points or at specific points in the level (such as the couches in *Ico*). Because of this saving strategy, these games have the potential to offer a much more exciting experience to the player. If our example game is a console game, your decision to save the girl is significant, because if you die, you'll go back to the last check point and have to fight your way through again. This means there are real consequences to your actions. In a quick-save game, though, there are no consequences.

Most PC developers, however, feel that replaying an entire section of a game, just to finally make it back to the point when you died, is too frustrating. And the player's frustration increases the further back the player is thrown into the game after dying. (I think we've all had that experience.) Therefore, the argument goes that quick-saving gives you the freedom to experience the game in the way you want to and ultimately makes a stronger experience.

It's a hotly debated topic, and a worthy one to discuss, as it can impact the emotional experiences a player does or doesn't have in the game.

I believe the answer might depend on the situation. When designing, ask yourself if a quick-save option will eliminate the emotion of the experience. If so, perhaps it's best not to make that option available. On the other hand, if the scene has no emotion at all, there might be a much better argument made for a quick-save option.

To me, the compromise for this case study game lies in tuning the game so that the player can't quick-save, but also doesn't get thrown an aggravating distance back into the game when he dies.

What are you going to do? You need to charge back in, but this time the game allows you to be victorious, if you're very skilled with your weapons—although you wouldn't know that victory is possible when you blast your way in, because the previous time you were in the room you would have been killed if you tried to rescue the girl.

In this hypothetical game, I've introduced the idea of self-sacrifice for a higher causes (or causes) to force the player to become a better person. The causes were:

- Stopping the conspiracy
- Protecting and ultimately freeing Falconer from false charges
- Rescuing his daughter

It should be noted that stopping the conspiracy is the *least* emotional of these causes. This can be fixed, however, if earlier in the game, you have gotten to know and really like a person or people who will be hurt or killed if the conspiracy goes forward. Liking this person or these people would come from their having Rooting Interest, as well as the use of NPC Toward Player Chemistry Techniques.

If you're the player, let's look at the sacrifices you'll make if you decide to rescue Falconer's daughter. You will:

- Go into this final mission knowing that, even if you survive, you will have to give up your job, reputation, and weapons, *and* be hated by the public.

- Possibly get arrested and charged with treason if you succeed.

- Be making a choice much more likely to get you killed, if you rescue the girl instead of just going for the evidence.

In life, almost any taking of responsibility for anything or anyone requires some kind of sacrifice. Here, the sacrifices have been multiplied and heightened. If you, the player, care about Falconer, and you risk or accept these sacrifices, you'll feel like a better person at the end, just as players who finished *Ico* did.

The game shouldn't end after this mission. The player should be forced to live with the consequences of his or her choice.

So, let's say you save the girl. You're not tried for treason, but all the other horrible consequences you were warned of do unfold. You're fired, your weapons are taken from you, and the public scorns you as being anti-American.

Now comes the final boss fight—against the man in charge of the entire conspiracy. And you have to go into it with just one lousy gun.

So the consequences you suffer aren't just revealed in a final cinematic, but are woven into the gameplay itself.

The fight begins inside a security installation and you're vastly outgunned. It's all you can do to hide and dodge bullets to stay alive, because your opponent is like an enraged, walking weapons depot on steroids. At best, perhaps you get off an occasional shot that forces him to retreat a little.

But if he retreats just enough, this allows you to finally make it to a weapons cache, where you can grab all the firepower you want. Now that you're loaded for bear, the real fight begins.

Why give you so many weapons at this point? First, you've already made the sacrifice and experienced the consequences, so that plot twist has been milked. Most importantly, we don't want to deprive you of a great boss fight at the end.

By the way, if you were designing this game, there are two ways you could end it. The first is that the evidence you retrieve about the conspiracy hits the press. Belatedly, after first being accused of treason, you're redeemed in the eyes of the public, all the conspirators are brought down, and you get your old job back.

Or, you could end it in a much darker way. You've foiled the conspiracy and killed the man at its head. All the others who were involved retreat into the woodwork. But the public never knows what occurred and of all the good you did. Instead, although you're not tried for treason, you are nonetheless painted as a traitor in the eyes of the citizenry.

There are a few people, though, who know what a hero you are. And that's Falconer, his daughter, and a handful of others who are overwhelmed by your bravery and integrity.

Which ending is preferable? Arguments could be made for either one. It's a matter of taste and artistic judgment. Which ending would you choose?

Summary of This Example

By getting the player to care about Falconer and the mission of rescuing his daughter, the player has to put himself or herself at risk to ever greater degrees. And there are extreme negative consequences, even for success. However, the player will be admired by those he or she has come to care about.

The player will, as in *Ico*, feel like he or she has become a better person.

Final Thoughts

In these last two chapters, we've focused on ways to cause players to bond with NPCs. Chapter 2.10 detailed a few methods to make a player identify with an NPC. This chapter dealt with techniques to make a player feel close to (i.e., have Chemistry with) an NPC:

- The NPC admires you
- The NPC reads your mind
- The NPC has things in common with you
- The NPC anticipates your needs and desires
- The NPC makes you grow to become a better person

Certainly our emotional immersion in life is enhanced by the existence of people with whom we feel close. Emotional immersion in a game can be significantly enhanced from a player feeling close to one or more of the game's NPCs.

Emotioneering Techniques Category #12

NPC Toward Player

Relationship Deepening Techniques

NPCs may not be alive,
but that doesn't mean they can't have
complex feelings toward you.

This chapter discusses

ways to make it feel as if major NPCs have emotionally complex relationships with the player.

In this chapter, we're not talking about how you, the player, feel toward the NPC characters in the game, but how they feel toward you.

Layers of Feeling

Remember how Princess Leia had mixed emotions toward Han Solo?

- She thought he was selfish and arrogant.

- She was attracted to his headstrong manner and his resourcefulness.

- She begrudgingly admired his heroic deeds.

- She was repulsed by his desire to help himself, instead of those who were oppressed by the Empire.

This is an example of a technique called Layer Cakes, which I described in Chapter 2.8. It means giving one character layers of feelings toward another. It's a Deepening Technique because layers equal depth.

What if you're playing a game and have taken on a role like Han Solo's, and there is an NPC like Princess Leia?

Hypothetical Game Case Study

Post-Apocalyptic America Game

For example, you're a swaggering gunslinger in a post-Apocalyptic America. It's survival of the fittest, but there are people in need and in danger: a group of innocents who are hiding in mountain caves, terrorized by the thugs who roam the landscape. They could use your help—but will you choose to give it?

There are incentives to help them. Initially, the incentives are mostly internal, moral ones (if you're leaning that way while playing the game, which you might not be). Down the line there are more tangible rewards, although you don't know that yet.

But there are also incentives to *not* help them, such as dangers to you. Perhaps if you help, you'll miss out on riches, weapons, excitement, and so on. (Chapter 2.20, "First-Person Character Arc Techniques," offers more detail on balancing incentives.)

Let's say you're thrown together with, or periodically run into, a sexy, headstrong woman named Kira (an NPC). She's all heart, with her courage directed toward helping those who need protection.

Periodically you join forces, but at other times you pursue your own agenda.

She could exhibit all those layers of feelings toward you that Princess Leia felt toward Han Solo in *Star Wars—Episode IV*.

NPC Toward Player Relationship Deepening is part of Emotioneering because when a character has mixed feelings toward you, it resembles life itself, and thus is emotionally engaging. I'm sure there are people who have various layers of feelings toward you, just as there are people toward whom you have different feelings simultaneously.

In the example, the types of feelings Kira exhibits toward you might depend on your actions and other choices—which means the game would have to keep track of (or "flag") the choices you make, so these can govern Kira's actions and dialogue around you.

Hypothetical Game Case Study

The Detectives

The two illustrations depict two moments in another example game.

You play the guy. You and the woman, Carey, are both detectives. The first illustration shows her regular feelings toward you. She's generally annoyed with your cocky, swashbuckling attitude. (But you've a right to be cocky because you're so good at your job, right?)

The moment depicted in the second drawing comes later in the game; you stumble upon a loving drawing she's done of you.

Carey obviously feels both annoyance and love toward you. This is classic Layer Cakes, and it results in NPC Toward Player Relationship Deepening. Layers, remember, create depth.

In summary, why not take one of the major NPCs in your game and see if it's appropriate to have that character feel different layers of emotion toward the player?

Hypothetical Game Case Study

Another Hypothetical Game Example

Take a look at the color painting on page 1.

In this hypothetical game, there's a boy who turns into a dragon. It's due to no fault of his own, but is rather the result of a curse put on his parents by an angry wizard. The people of the land want to kill the boy, for when he takes the form of a dragon, he wreaks destruction.

Yet you know that the only chance of destroying the big boss you must fight at the end of the game is with the help of this boy/dragon, so it's critical that you ensure his safety. During the game, you must lead him across the land. When he's a boy, you need to protect him from those who try to kill him. Yet when he turns into a dragon, *he* tries to kill *you*—he can't help himself. In those situations, you need to injure or weaken him without killing him. So sometimes you're protecting him, and sometimes you're fighting him.

Other factors make your relationship with him even more complex. In one situation, when he's a dragon, he kills some innocents who don't deserve to die (they weren't even attacking him). Further complexity is added in that, to help you fight the big boss at the end, he is willing to sacrifice himself as penance for the innocents he hurt earlier.

You're likely to have many layers of feelings toward the boy:

1. A desire to protect him.

2. Fear of him when he's a dragon.

3. Pity toward him for being the victim of a curse.

4. Admiration for his willingness to sacrifice himself to help you kill the big boss.

This would truly be an example of Player Toward NPC Relationship Deepening.

An Example of Technique Stacking

Because the breadth and depth of emotion in a game is heightened when Emotioneering techniques are used in combination, I feel it's always worth pointing out such examples when they occur in some of the hypothetical games described in the book. The game with the boy/dragon employs a few other Emotioneering techniques in addition to Player Toward NPC Relationship Deepening:

1. Because the boy is the subject of undeserved misfortune, he has NPC Rooting Interest (see Chapter 2.10).

2. Protecting an NPC and taking responsibility for him causes a player to bond with him, which I call having Chemistry with the NPC. It's a Player Toward NPC Chemistry Technique (see Chapter 2.11).

3. When the player finds himself protecting the boy, even though the boy, in dragon form, has tried to kill him, and even though, while a dragon, he killed some innocents, this is an Emotionally Complex Situation (see Chapter 2.15).

4. When the boy is willing to sacrifice himself in penance for the deaths he has caused (even though these were the result of a curse put on his parents), this not only gives him additional Rooting Interest (see Chapter 2.10), but Self-Sacrifice and Wisdom are each techniques that give him depth. They're NPC Deepening Techniques (see Chapter 2.2).

5. By the end of the game, the player will have truly experienced some emotional and moral complexity. For example, the player will have seen that the boy is right in wanting to live; the villagers are right in wanting to kill him. The boy's willingness to sacrifice himself in the end, to restore his feeling of self-worth and to punish himself for his crimes while in dragon form, could be equally argued to be reasonable and unreasonable. The player's character will be loved by many people in the land for daring to take on the big boss—but the player's character will also be despised by others who were victims of the boy when in his dragon form.

   Experiencing the emotional and/or moral complexity of a situation, especially when these complexities develop over the course of a game, can leave the player wiser and thus deeper. They're First-Person Deepening Techniques (see Chapter 2.21).

Final Thoughts

Games traditionally have NPCs feel one way or another toward the player (or the player's character). They react to the player as a friend or foe. In your own life, however, there are, no doubt, people whose feelings toward you are complex.

NPCs with complex emotions are more life-like. So, why not have one of the major NPCs in your game feel different layers of emotion toward the player?

Why All This Matters: A Brief Philosophical Diversion

It might seem odd to treat NPCs with this much attention. I discuss them as if they're alive—or at least, as if they should act that way.

But shouldn't they?

Granting life is exactly what artists do. A song is just modulations of sound waves, and yet it can move us, inspire us, and maybe trigger in us a desire to dance. It can depress us or wrap us in feelings of exhilaration. The singer, the songwriter, and the musicians have joined together to actually *put life* into something inanimate: sound waves.

Screenwriters have long treated their characters with the idea that they have life, and all of us have, at one time or another, participated in discussions about various film and television characters and talked about them as if they were alive.

NPCs only await deft Emotioneering to also assume life.

Emotioneering Techniques Category #13

Player Toward NPC

Relationship

Deepening

Techniques

If you truly feel something
toward an NPC,
why not feel several things?

This chapter explores
ways to give the player emotionally complex relationships with major NPCs.

At the end of the last chapter, I speculated that some people in your life probably have mixed feelings toward you. Are there people toward whom *you* have different layers of feelings?

Many people have a variety of feelings toward one or both of their parents, their siblings, or even their spouse.

If it happens in life, it's appropriate to put one or more NPCs in your game toward whom the player will feel a variety of mixed feelings simultaneously.

Hypothetical Game Case Study

Our Post-Apocalyptic Gunslinger

Going back to the example from the last chapter, again take the role of a gunslinger in the post-Apocalyptic world.

In the game, a guy named Kovar sells you weapons. Your feelings about him are complex because:

1. Sometimes he cheats you.

2. He almost steals the heart of the woman you like.

3. While he doesn't get her, he does land the heart of a well-known hottie who never falls for anyone.

4. He risks his life to save you, and even takes a bullet for you.

5. You find out that he has suffered incredible tragedies in his life; his own wife and son were murdered by the same enemy you're going after.

It's likely that you'll have Layer Cakes toward him—a variety of layers of feeling. If you're a guy, you might simultaneously:

1. Feel annoyed at him for swindling you.

2. Be angry that he's making a play for the woman you like.

3. Grudgingly admire him for winning the heart of a woman everyone thinks is untouchable—or perhaps be a bit jealous.

4. Appreciate him and like him for the risks he takes in saving your life.

5. Feel sorry for him for the tragedies of his past.

Remember, you may feel these different emotions sequentially (feeling different emotions at different points in the game), or, at any given moment when you're with him, you might feel several of them at the same time.

The reason to do this in a game is to emulate life itself. This book is about creating complex states of emotional immersion in a game, and Player Toward NPC Relationship Deepening is a useful type of Emotioneering.

A Hypothetical Game:
Mixed Emotions in WWII

The illustrations depict a game in which you play a WWII soldier. In the first scene, you, the player, would probably feel annoyed at your fellow soldier, an NPC named Conrad, because the sexy and spunky girl he's flirting with turned you down in favor of him.

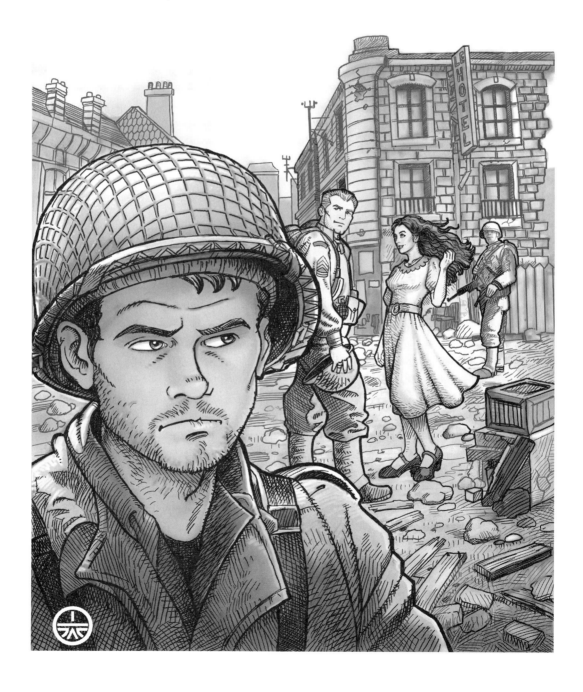

Then, in a battle, Conrad bravely defends you when you get injured.

How are you going to feel toward this NPC? You'd most likely feel a variety of things. This is another example of Player Toward NPC Relationship Deepening, and it is just one of many Emotioneering techniques yet to find its way into many games.

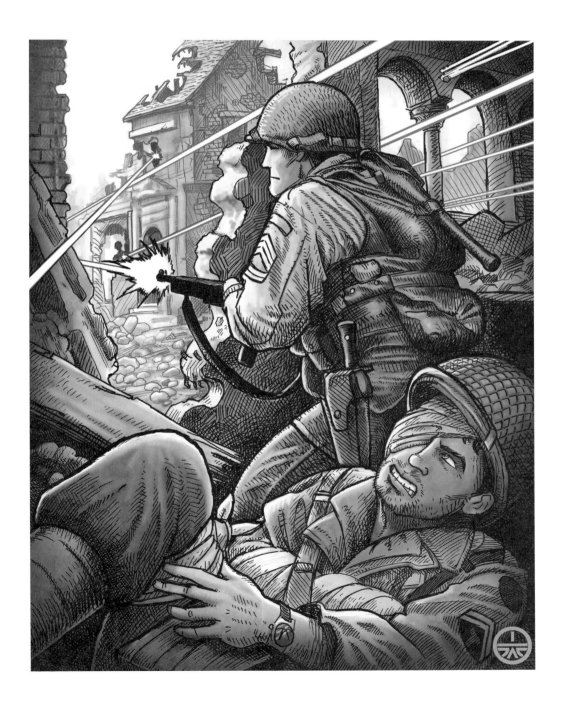

Final Thoughts

Depth is possible in a relationship, whether it's the way an NPC feels toward the player or how the player feels toward an NPC. If you're trying to get a player to feel a variety of emotions toward an NPC, then that NPC will have to do and say things that prompt a variety of internal reactions to the NPC.

You can also have a progression of feelings. For instance, you could be a member of a Navy Seal team and have a variety of feelings toward one of your fellow Seals who, on one hand, is an irritating hot-head, but on the other hand is a skilled asset to your squad. As the game progresses, your annoyance with him could gradually give way to admiration.

Emotioneering Techniques Category #14

Group Bonding Techniques

Why go it alone?

This chapter discusses
techniques for making a group (such as a squad) feel bonded. If the player
is part of that group, the player will feel bonded to the group as well.

A group may begin as just a number of people with a series of agreements and shared purposes, but we all know that groups evolve their own "culture."

Perhaps you've once been forced to be a member of a group you didn't like. For me that group was my junior high school. Inside some generic, mustard-colored buildings swirled a toxic whirlwind of runaway hormones, social paranoia, bullies, and teachers heroically trying to keep chaos at bay. Thank God I figured out how to turn 15 so I could escape that place. I'm proud to say that at least half of the emotional scars have healed.

But most of us have had the opposite experience too: being a member of a highly motivated, tight-knit team, infused with an inspired purpose and sky-high morale. Maybe it was a Boy Scout troop, a marching band, a choir, a sports team, a church organization, or the group of people with whom you currently work.

Some games involve the player working as part of a team, often a military group, such as a squad. You may want to create "Group Bonding," the feeling of a close-knit, high-morale group.

Here are a few techniques.

Elements of Shared Appearance

A shared appearance fosters bonding. By this I mean that you can create or enhance a sense of Group Bonding by matching uniforms or clothing, tattoos, or other visual symbols of group identity.

Shared Goals

Having shared goals can make friends out of very disparate people—take Luke, Leia, Han Solo, Chewbacca, and C-3PO. Their goal, of course, was to destroy the Death Star and bring down the Empire.

Shared Rituals

Consider a game scenario: You're a member of a squad, and all the guys do the same "high five/low five" hand slap after a victory. This shared ritual brings group bonding.

This kind of thing is hard to animate, and harder still to animate for the player's character. But if used artfully, similar group rituals in which the player can participate, increase the bonding the player feels with the group.

Obviously, to do it right, if the player didn't participate, he would be ostracized by the NPCs. If he did participate, he would be rewarded by them. They could open up to him, act more loyal to him, or tease him in a good-natured way. In short, rewarding the player for participating in a group ritual reinforces the bonding.

There are many types of group rituals. For instance, in your squad, soldiers could scratch markings on their guns to represent each successful kill or each kill of an officer from the enemy's side.

Going Through Shared Ordeals and Adventures

You probably have a few friends whom you knew when you were younger. If you met them today, would you still befriend them?

We draw close to those with whom we share ordeals and adventures. If the NPCs seem lifelike, then the shared ordeals will bond the player to the group.

Taking Heroic Actions to Protect Each Other

When members of a group take heroic actions to protect each other, group bonding increases. These are physical actions taken by the NPCs in your group. For instance, in a battle, they station themselves over a wounded comrade and fight to save him. If you're their leader, they may try and protect you at all costs.

This becomes a bit richer experience if the characters are a bit more dimensional. For instance, the NPCs could sometimes complain about each other, but then, in battle, their true loyalties could comes out. This was done wonderfully in the original

> ### A Possible Difficulty with This Technique
> There are other factors that must be taken into account when having NPCs taking heroic actions to protect each other and perhaps the player. The teammates in the game *Star Trek: Elite Force* were at first programmed to fight with full zest, but then developers realized that this stole away the action from the player. The solution was that they were toned down to fire single shots at a slower rate, to allow the player to kill the enemies while the group still seemed as if they were fighting too.

Star Trek series, where Spock and Bones complained about each other and bickered, but didn't think twice about putting their lives at risk to protect each other. (It's also a classic example of NPC to NPC Relationship Deepening, which is discussed in Chapter 2.8.) Similarly, Captain Kirk wouldn't hesitate to put his life on the line if he thought it could save his crewmates.

Complementary Skills

If each member of the group has a slightly different skill, when they work as a group, they're capable of doing things as a group that would be impossible if they worked as individuals. After awhile, you'll come to think of the group as a single organism.

This technique can be taken to a higher level if the NPCs are programmed to act as a group in a choreographed way. For instance, one guy in your team runs out of ammo, and without missing a beat, one of the others in the group throws him a clip.

This could be done by way of a scripted sequence, triggered by some event in the battle.

Say Good Things Behind Each Others' Back— Even if They Don't to Their Faces

If NPCs tend to say good things about the others behind their backs (nothing too schmaltzy, of course), even if they say teasing or mean things to their faces, then this too increases the group bonding. Why would they not show their admiration openly? Because:

- Antagonism or teasing isn't always what it seems, and, in fact, can be chemistry. (See Chapter 2.7, "NPC Toward NPC Chemistry Techniques.") Just as it can show chemistry between two people, it can do the same when performed by a group.

- They have Layer Cakes in their feelings for each other. (See Chapter 2.8, "NPC Toward NPC Relationship Deepening Techniques.")

- One or both is wearing a Mask that prevents them from expressing admiration. (See Chapter 2.1, "NPC Interesting Techniques.")

Whatever the reason behind it, this technique can create bonding when used appropriately.

Bam-Bam Dialogue in Cinematics

Bam-Bam Dialogue is my term for dialogue that moves quickly between NPCs, often with them interrupting each other. It's a sign that the characters know each other well. An example of Bam-Bam Dialogue will be provided a little later in this chapter.

Shared References

After you have been through an experience with the NPCs, especially an intense one, you'll feel part of the group when one of the NPCs references that experience. Shared references are allusions made to current or past events or to information that the entire group understands.

An Example from a Hypothetical Game

As always, you can layer techniques for a fuller effect. In this cinematic example, Good-Natured Teasing, Bam-Bam Dialogue, and Shared References are all used to show Group Bonding.

```
In a modern-day war in a country like
Afghanistan, you're in a fox hole with your
guys: Granger, Lee, and Steadman. Steadman's
searching for the enemy with his binoculars:

    GRANGER (to Steadman, who's looking through
    binoculars): Hey dogface...

    LEE (to Granger): You insulting dogs again?

    GRANGER: You're holdin' 'em backwards.

    LEE: I think he's still in shock from...

    STEADMAN (looking though the binocs): Found
    'em!

    GRANGER: Where?!

    STEADMAN (grabs his gun, moves out): Love to
    tell you, but I'd probably explain it
    backwards.

    Granger and Lee exchange looks. They
    scramble out of the foxhole to catch up with
    Steadman, and you follow.
```

Lee's mention of Steadman being in shock from something is the technique of referring to past shared experiences.

Also, if teasing is a form of bonding and showing affection employed by the group, they should also tease you, the player, especially when you screw up.

Of course this means more lines of NPC dialogue, triggered by a number of possible circumstances you might find yourself in.

Group Bonding Challenges in Squad-Based First-Person Shooters

Some squad-based first-person shooters move so fast that there may be no moments to hear a line from or give a line to an NPC, outside of urgent battle chatter. In games like these, it's hard, if not impossible, to get a sense of the NPCs who fight alongside you.

Therefore, in such games, creating Group Bonding is a much greater challenge. Of course, you can use techniques like Elements of Shared Appearance and Shared Ordeals. Otherwise, though, you may need to slow down the game here and there in order to increase Group Bonding. This might be considered a tradeoff, and no formula will work for every game.

I've seen designers take three different approaches to bringing emotion into squad-based first-person shooters:

1. Some feel that all that matters are fast-paced, non-stop, running battles. Variety in such games derives from changing the locations and the objectives of different levels and missions.

2. Some designers feel that emotion belongs in the game, but nothing should be added that will slow down the action. These designers feel that the way to bring emotional variety into the levels is (besides changing locations and mission objectives) to have each mission have a distinct beginning, middle, and end (which aren't predictable or cliché), and also include highs and lows, as well as unforeseen twists.

3. The third group of designers believes that the pacing should be slowed down here and there to allow for various additional Emotioneering techniques to be utilized, above and beyond plot twists, highs and lows, and possibly Emotionally Complex Moments and Situations (see Chapter 2.15).

It would be foolhardy to try and say that one of these approaches would work for all squad-based first person shooters. However, I'd guess that, if your intuitional radar is on line or your psychic powers have had a recent power-up, you can probably deduce that I favor approaches (2) or (3), depending on the game, or perhaps some mixture of the two.

Final Thoughts

By reversing various Group Bonding Techniques, you can adjust how fast the group's ties coalesce.

For instance, the group could undergo shared ordeals, but one of your NPCs could have different purposes than you (the lead character) possess. Thus, in some ways, you'd feel like that NPC is part of the group, but in other ways not.

This was done in *Star Wars—Episode IV*. Han Solo slowly becomes part of the group by going through ordeals with them, and because he has chemistry with Princess Leia (mostly using the Chemistry Technique of Fighting).

His purpose—to make money—is very different, however, than that of the group. Therefore, in some ways he's part of the group, but in other ways not bonded to them at all. This very gradually changes, but his bonding isn't complete until the very end, when his purposes and the groups become identical.

You could start a game with a number of people who work together toward a goal, but they'd have no feeling of Group Bonding. That is, there's no feeling of the group having its own collective identity. And then the "group feeling" could grow, as techniques like those in this chapter are slowly introduced. Anyone who has worked on a political campaign, or who has gone on a rafting trip with strangers, or who ever joined a Boy Scout troop or a fraternity, has experienced this kind of Group Bonding.

The point, though, is that you can get a little fancy with the techniques by regulating the speed at which a group comes together or falls apart, or by slowly bringing in a new member or pushing him or her out. My guess, however, is that, in most games that involve the player being part of a squad or other group, establishing Group Bonding early on will probably be the chosen route.

Whether you're trying to quickly establish Group Bonding or whether you're getting a little fancy with the techniques, making a game player feel that he or she really *is* in a group can heighten that player's emotional engagement in the game.

Emotionally Complex Moments and Situations Techniques

Get your player into an emotional mess.

This chapter discusses

ways to put the player in the middle of emotionally complex moments and situations.

You just got a promotion. You call your best friend to share the news flash on your upwardly mobile ecstasy—but before you can even squeak out one gleeful, artificially modest yet subtly self-congratulatory news flash, he hits you with a bombshell: His wife is leaving him.

You can't share your good news. It would be insensitive, and maybe even cruel.

This is an emotionally complex moment. Life is full of such moments. Movies are full of them. Television shows are full of them. Even the best comic books are full of them.

They are far too scarce in games.

When it comes to emotionally complex moments and situations, if these other art and entertainment forms are giant redwoods, games are still bonsai trees. Isn't it time for these interactive, emotional shrubs to gain a little altitude so they can go one-on-one with the giant Sequoias of film and television?

While there are a vast number of potentially emotionally complex moments and situations, let's focus in on a few choice techniques.

You Are Forced to Do Potential Evil

For this example, first take a look at the color illustration on page 2.

In this game example, you're the leader of a rebel force, fighting against a tyrannical, planetary government. Your forces have been decimated. Your only hope for survival is to resurrect an ancient and banned practice— using a disturbing mixture of sorcery and mechanics to build and bring to life a monster that can save you and your band of rebels.

However, there's no predicting the monster's actions. You know the creature will also be capable of great harm, yet you have no choice. The creature is your only chance for survival, and the only chance for the survival of your fellow rebels.

Yes, as the game progresses, the monster will save you. But later it will establish its own agenda—just as such monsters did in a previous era, which is why they were banned. When the monster turns on some innocents, to protect them you'll be forced to fight it. This new foe, which you have created, is much worse than the enemies you built it to destroy.

Even as you were building the mechanical beast, you knew this was likely to happen. That's why creating it was an Emotionally Complex Situation.

You Are Forced to See Through the Eyes of Someone You Don't Like or Are Ambivalent About

Consider the hypothetical game illustrated on the preceding page.

The game is set in a strange, undefined land. There is a woman (an NPC) who was the spiritual leader of her people. You (the man in this picture) and she have mutual enemies, but there are many personality conflicts between the two of you. Because you don't share her mystical religion, she treats you as unimportant, and even with pity.

What I'm doing here is flipping upside down some of the Rooting Interest Techniques to make her somewhat unlikable. In this case, we'd make her extremely arrogant and dismissive toward you. Also, she cares about her own people, but no one else (such as humans like you). Additionally, there's an instance where you could use her help and she doesn't come to your aid—not because she hates you, but because she could care less.

I wouldn't flip so many Rooting Interest Techniques, however, that I'd make her loathsome. The idea is to make the player highly ambivalent about her.

She is killed by your mutual enemy, but her spirit can survive for a short time—inside of you. If you can take her spirit through enemy terrain, you can reach the Shaman of the Mountain Pass, who can then conjure up a new body for her. But if you don't make it in time, her spirit will die, and she'll never be able to take corporeal form again.

Even though you might not like her, her own people completely depend on her. They're in grave danger if you fail. In fact, without her leadership, they'll all be slaughtered by your mutual enemy.

Furthermore, some of these people have helped save you in the past, so you feel you owe them your support.

Thus, you bear her essence inside you as you travel across a hostile land. However, things get even stranger—for her spirit is strong, and at any given time, with no predictability, you *change into her*.

When you become her, your weapons change. Your way of moving changes. Your abilities and skills change.

This is emotionally complex for several reasons:

- You have to rescue her (for the good of her people), even though you don't like her or are ambivalent about her.

- Even though you are ambivalent about her, you *become* her.

Now, becoming this woman would be simply an interesting way to swap one set of skills for another, but the emotion of the situation can be beefed up in a number of ways:

- **Even though she's without a body, she can still talk to you.** You learn that she has great insight and kindness. Past trials of her people, and her own past hardships, forced her to become calloused. But that outer shell isn't reflective of who she truly is. Your opinion gradually changes until you see her not as strange and snobby, but as strong and wise.

- **She occasionally manifests in a sort of beautiful, translucent form, to plead for your continued help.** (These manifestations happen during times when you're in your own body, not hers.) This makes her easier to relate to because you can see her.

- **The longer she's "out of body," the more her spirit fades.** She's dying, and thus there's a ticking clock (a limited time). After a certain point, she'll no longer be able to be given human form again. The increased jeopardy will make you care for her even more.

- **She begins to go through an NPC Character Arc in that she starts to appreciate you.** However, this wouldn't be overdone—she'd just *begin* to change.

Because of all these techniques, you'll increasingly feel close to her.

You'll also increasingly be willing to "be" her (feel like her) when you take her form. That's because, when you're in her form, her people defer to you, admire you, and fight to protect you. They tell you of all the great things she did for them at great risk to herself, and you realize that she's been quite a hero.

Of course, the skills you possess when she takes over will ultimately prove important in your accomplishing tasks that are necessary to fighting your way to the Shaman—the man who will make her whole.

Here's another game example, set in a contemporary, realistic setting:

A villain has gotten hold of a terrible biological weapon. He's the one you're after.

Along the way, however, you come across the scientist who created the weapon. He's not sane. Sometimes he's rational, but sometimes he's delusional. Sometimes he doesn't remember what he's done, but at other times he remembers and is filled with regret. These emotions flit through him at a rapid rate.

He begs you not to kill him. You know that he's nuts, but not evil. Yet you also realize that if you don't kill him, he could create the biological weapon all over again, during one of his crazy fits, and once again give it to someone with evil intentions.

You'll kill him; you really have no choice. But the act won't sit well with your sympathy for him. It will be an emotionally complex situation.

Ambivalence Toward a "Friend"

Imagine a game in which you are given telepathy. Suddenly you can hear the thoughts of the people around you. You learn that your best "friend" is jealous of your success.

You still like him and respect him—you two have been through a lot together and he's come to your assistance many a time—but now things are more emotionally complex between you.

Ambivalence Toward an "Enemy"

Many writers I know seem to have minds that blossom late at night. The mysterious realm of darkest night is a unique time for many reasons, but where I live, there's an especially enticing aspect to the depths of night: It's when a local TV channel shows reruns of *Buffy the Vampire Slayer*.

According to the show's mythology, at any given time in the world, there's usually only one woman, with superhuman strength and skill, destined to be the vampire slayer. At this time in history, Buffy's the one.

In an episode I recently re-watched, Spike, an often-evil vampire who's nonetheless capable of doing some very loving things, tries to instruct Buffy on ways of killing vampires. He tells Buffy how he has killed other vampire slayers over the last several hundred years. These were vampire slayers who came before her. Spike wants her to learn from the mistakes made by her predecessors.

Spike's teaching Buffy how to avoid getting killed takes a strange turn, and ends by his confessing that he's in love with her. She rejects him coldly and treats him like dirt.

He goes back to his lair (lairs are apparently de rigeur if you're a vampire). He grabs a shotgun and marches to her house, intent on killing her. But when he arrives, she's crying on her porch. It takes the wind out of the big confrontation he had envisaged. Spike puts down the gun and comforts her.

What if we transported this general idea of a villain with some good qualities (like Spike) into a game? What if your enemy is evil, but is also occasionally capable of great good? What if he is dying a terrible death, and only you can save him. Will you?

Or what if you go to kill him and find that his wife has just been brutally murdered, and he is beside himself with grief—and he even begs you to kill him so his misery will end. How will you feel? What will you do?

Whatever action you take in the above scenarios, one thing is likely: You'll find yourself in an emotionally complex moment.

Let's take a look at a similar instance, from the Top Cow comic, *Witchblade*, illustrated on the following page.

Sara, through destiny—a destiny she doesn't want—is the bearer of the Witchblade. It's a magical, organic bracelet with a long history. It can metamorphose into different forms of armor and weapons that turn her into an awesome warrior.

Nottingham is both her foe and friend. Their relationship is difficult to characterize, much like Spike's and Buffy's.

Here he's gotten possession of the Witchblade. Owning it has been his life-long ambition, but it's not his destiny to wield it. It begins growing across his body and face, strangling him and killing him. Only Sara can save him.

If this was a game and you were playing Sara, it would be an emotionally complex moment due to your ambivalence toward Nottingham.

But it would also be emotionally complex if you were playing Nottingham. You'd need to give away the powerful weapon you'd fought so long to get, and you'd need to rely for help on someone toward whom you felt ambivalent.

Game players don't particularly desire to lose power and forfeit their favorite weapon. And, to be honest, some men might not want to rely on a woman they don't like to save them. If you designed the game for players to play the role of Nottingham, and if you wanted to hedge your commercial bets, then you could flip the plot at some point. That is, you could later give the player an even cooler weapon than the Witchblade (which the player wanted, worked for, and finally got, but was forced to abandon), and you could even have a plot turn-around where the player gets to rescue Sara at some point.

Consider another hypothetical game example, pictured on the following page.

Every time your health points get low, you actually see Death. She's a beautiful, melancholy, but cruel woman. (We'd use NPC Interesting Techniques and NPC Deepening Techniques to make sure she's dimensional and intriguing.)

As you come to know her, however, she starts having mixed feelings toward you. As Death, she wants to claim you. However, she also begins to admire and like you. After all, you've heroically faced and overcome death many times. You're not like the others whom she has so easily snatched. (Because she feels conflicting feelings toward you, this would be NPC Toward Player Relationship Deepening, which is described in Chapter 2.12.)

And, because we'll use some Player Toward NPC Chemistry Techniques (see Chapter 2.11), we'll arrange it so that you also come to like her. For example, after you are victorious in a battle in which your fighting was spectacular, and during which you saved some innocents, Death makes you aware of her admiration for you—despite the fact that, by saving so many people, you've robbed her of some of her prey.

Though you might, on some level, like her, you also fear her and loath her. After all, she didn't just admire you; she also eagerly whisked away the souls of your friends who fell in battle.

The result would be that you'd have several different feelings toward her— and thus it would be a classic case of Player Toward NPC Relationship Deepening (see Chapter 2.13).

At some point in the game, you will die—but instead of taking you to the next realm (in a cinematic), she revives you.

God gave Death her role in the universe, and he doesn't like her disobeying him by reviving men who are dead. After all, the world's balance is delicate, and those who are supposed to die all play a role in the grandiose plan.

And so God has imprisoned her and is torturing her. He would have killed her, but as Death, she can't die.

At this point in the game, your feelings toward her would be ambivalent. You'd like her—she saved your life—but she's also taken the lives of some of those closest to you.

Yet you're compelled to free her because of what she did for you. Risking your life for someone for whom you feel both love and hate is a very emotionally complex situation.

Another Way You Could Employ This Technique

You could have a boss whom you encounter several times during your missions. Each time you set out to fight, you learn aspects that not only "fill in" his Character Diamond (making him more dimensional), but you see qualities in him that gradually begin to give him Rooting Interest (see Chapter 2.10). Then, during the final encounter, he could approach you for help, creating an emotionally complex situation.

The question would then be, who would the player fight in the final battle? Perhaps the boss you thought was the big enemy—the one who asks for your help—was really doing the bidding of an even worse boss who now you'll meet.

You could make the situation even more complex if, in the fight with this new boss, the boss who has changed sides sacrifices himself to save you. So the character you've spent so much of the game hating now gains instant Rooting Interest by sacrificing himself for you.

Ambivalence Toward a Situation

Consider a different hypothetical game case study.

You're training to be the pilot of a space fighter. After the game's training level, you take a test—and pass, but don't score quite high enough to make the grade. So as the game begins (the first level after the training level), you're stuck at the helm of a cargo ship.

At this point, your character—and probably you, the player—aren't too happy—especially when you learn your first job is to ferry two children to a distant planet. You wanted to command a space fighter but now you're just a babysitter!

Very soon into the journey, when you look over your shoulder, you spot the children levitating objects! These kids have a secret power that makes them targets for every nasty human and creature in the universe—including the one who's currently breaking into your ship from another dimension.

You want action? You've got it, for in about two seconds you and that creature will be in a heated battle over those kids.

The scene is emotionally complex, because the job you thought was awful is beginning to look a lot more intriguing.

Later in the game, simply as a Role Induction Technique (a technique that makes you more willing to adopt your role, described in Chapter 2.19), we'll throw in a plot twist. That twist is that you'll learn that you were picked for this assignment not because you failed your test, but because of your outstanding abilities and potential. You weren't told at the time because everything about these two children is classified and revealed only on a need-to-know basis. So it turns out that being picked for this "baby-sitting" mission was really a very high honor.

note

This is actually is harder to pull off than it might first seem. The player will suspect that this job isn't awful, anticipating that although he's merely ferrying kids, this will soon turn into some kind of adventure. To make the emotional experience work, it might be worth taking a risk and really have the player perform some drudgery. It would only need to go on for a few minutes, in order to build up some frustration in the player. (Testing the game would reveal the right duration of this drudgery.)

You Discover You've Been Tricked

One of the first jobs I ever had was working in a phone bank, raising money for a very worthwhile charity. It wasn't the world's greatest job, but I didn't have a lot of job skills. The money was okay, and I took pride in doing a job that had tangible benefits to people in dire need.

One day, however, I skipped the morning injection of caffeine, slowed down, and did some serious math. I realized that only 5% of the money being raised in this office was actually going toward the charity. A very large percent went to the guys who ran the phone bank.

It was a very weird feeling to realize my good intentions had been preyed upon and used. I quit that day.

What if the situation was even more emotionally complex? In *The Road Warrior*, "Mad" Max Rockatansky (Mel Gibson) is "played," or used, by a peaceful group surrounded by enemies in a post-apocalyptic world.

I won't reprise the entire plot here, but suffice to say that, as a skilled driver, he ends up at the helm of a tanker truck filled with water, vital for the peaceful group's survival. Enemies continuously besiege the truck.

As Max later learns, he was just a decoy; he was really driving a truck filled with sand. He was duped, set up to draw off the enemy, while the tribe made their secretive escape with the real water.

Unlike my experience with the phone bank, the group that misled Max were good guys, and misleading him was, perhaps, the "right" thing to do. He realizes all this in the end—but he has still been used. He has been used by good people for a good cause. This is a very complex moment.

If you were playing the role of Max in a game, and this happened to you, you'd feel a complex range of feelings.

Here's a similar complex moment from another Top Cow comic, Michael Turner's *Fathom*.

Aspen is a woman who has seemingly magical abilities and strange links to the sea. Her own nature and history are a mystery to her.

In this illustration, Killian, whom she thought was a friend but who is actually evil, has manipulated her into using her powers. Not realizing the magnitude of the force she wields, she accidentally kills a man and is consumed with regret.

What if this scenario was transposed into the world of games? In fact, it has been. In the game *Thief II*, you play Garrett and run a number of missions for Victoria before you realize she's evil.

What if we made the situation even more emotionally complex? Let's say you were playing the role of Fathom, and you were tricked by someone like Killian into killing a man, just because Killian didn't like him.

Of course you'd be angry at Killian, and angry at yourself for being fooled.

But what if you then learn that the man you killed was evil and had slaughtered many helpless people? So you'd been used—tricked—into killing someone who was even more evil.

That would be a truly emotionally complex moment.

Further Thoughts

In most games, you expect to kill bad guys. So, if someone *tricks* you into killing the bad guys—imagine the shock of the player. It would be an emotionally complex moment.

Of course, you could be tricked not just into doing the right thing (like Max in *The Road Warrior*), but tricked instead into doing the wrong thing.

Or the trickery could be woven right into the gameplay itself. For example, the beginning of the game finds you carrying out a hazardous mission with great fighting and action involved (and you feel quite cocky about your abilities and power). Your motive is that a group of people in grave danger had begged and pleaded with you to carry out your mission in order to save them.

The game is designed so that the more you use a skill, the faster and more effective you become at it, thus encouraging you to specialize in certain modes of combat.

Then later in the game, you realize that there is more to the game than just shooting. For instance, there is hacking, stealing, sneaking, and using disguises. The people who asked you to carry out this mission are actually more powerful than you, and they tricked you into building up the "wrong" skills (skills that they can defend themselves against), so that later you'll pose no threat to them when they initiate their nefarious plan.

So you've been tricked not just into doing the wrong thing, but even into building up the wrong abilities. The people who tricked you are evidently quite clever.

In short, you'll realize that a lot of your first assumptions were wrong—not just about these people, but about the game itself. It would truly be an emotionally complex situation.

To now stop this group, you need other skills such as stealth, disguises, and so on. However, you've built up your shooting skills (such as accuracy), but you've done nothing to increase your stealth capabilities.

And then I'd consider adding even another layer of emotional complexity. Perhaps, after you've become certain that those who tricked you are evil, I'd put in a twist and you'd then learn they're actually good. They only tricked you because they felt they had no choice. Someone like you (someone of your order or guild, or someone wearing a uniform like yours, etc.) did great harm to them just a few days ago. So they had a legitimate reason to fear you and trick you.

This example starts pointing the way as to how Emotioneering techniques, when combined, can be used to create games that begin to have the same emotional richness we expect from some films and television shows.

Helpless to Aid Someone You Love

The hypothetical game depicted on the left is set in ancient days. You play the warrior. Your true love has been captured—by aliens! She's a thousand miles away—you don't know where—but you can see her image in the magical waters. And you're unable to help her, at least for now. To be able to see someone you care about who's in grave danger, but not be able to help, is emotionally complex.

Consider a related example, illustrated on the following two pages.

This is an emotionally complex scene because the trees watch on, unable to help the forest nymphs, whom they love.

But another technique is used here that also makes the moment emotionally complex:

What's Good and What's Evil Is Not Black and White

The beast used to live here first, long before the nymphs moved in. They invaded his land, and ate the same food he depends on. (They were forced out of their own lands by the encroachment of humans.) By diminishing his food supply, the nymphs had endangered the beast's survival, although unintentionally. Thus, who is good here and who is evil is a bit muddied.

Other Techniques at Work in This Scenario (An Example of Technique Stacking)

Beside the two Emotionally Complex Moment Techniques noted previously in this scenario, there are added Emotioneering techniques at work as well:

- **The nymph in the cage is distraught because of what happened to her friend.** Her pain makes us identify with her; it creates NPC Rooting Interest (see Chapter 2.10).

- **She's also in grave danger herself.** This creates further NPC Rooting Interest.

- **It's because of these and other Rooting Interest techniques that you care about the nymphs.** Taking responsibility for them also makes you care more about the *world* of the game. Thus, it's a World Induction Technique (see Chapter 2.18).

- **Taking responsibility for others in a game, just as in real life, gives us depth.** Thus it's also is a First-Person Deepening Technique (see Chapter 2.21).

Forced to Violate Your Own Integrity

In the hypothetical game illustrated on **pages 196–197**, you play Brianna. You and your brother were fighters together on this distant world.

But the enemy built a war machine—this mechanical centaur—and it just killed your brother. You, the player, really liked him, because of NPC Rooting Interest Techniques (see Chapter 2.10) and Player Toward NPC Chemistry Techniques (see Chapter 2.11).

But now he's dead. And the enemy is almost here, about to swarm in over-whelming numbers.

You escape the only way possible—by riding on the very creature who killed your brother. It's emotionally complex because, given your choice, you would have rather destroyed the thing. But now you have to use your brother's killer to escape. On some level, it's a violation of integrity.

Creating Emotionally Complex Moments and Situations Through Incongruence[1]

When incongruence occurs, the way our minds or spirits function is to try and assemble the pieces into a story or a mood in which the disparate elements make sense. Incongruence snaps us out of a lulled state of complacency.

There are many forms of incongruence, and many uses of it. I want to talk about one form of visual incongruence, which can help create a rich world. (Other uses of incongruence will be discussed in Chapter 2.18 ("World Induction Techniques"), Chapter 5.2 ("Techniques for Creating Fun"), and Chapter 5.3 ("Gatherings").

Sights, sounds, language, and just about any other media can also be incongruent. When the incongruent items themselves have a richness or emotional resonance to them, the incongruence can help create a rich world.[2]

Example 1: In a game, your Guide, who has been leading you, takes you out of the dark forest and to the edge of a huge meadow, surrounded by towering peaks. You're caught up on their beauty. He looks at you and says:

> `"This is where the our great leader, Kalnar,`
> `was slain. Thousands died. It's where our`
> `slavery began."`

---

1. I define *incongruence* as putting things together that normally you wouldn't think of as belonging together.

2. This discussion leads to the question: "What constitutes an emotionally resonant image?" Well, it's safe to say that images of profoundly happy or sad or momentous events are emotionally resonant to many cultures—images such as those of birth, marriage, death, war, or physical triumph. (Case in point: the Olympics.) So are images of the elements or aspects of nature, such as mountains or forests.

   But many other images that are emotionally resonant are culturally relative. For instance, an angel might be emotionally resonant in Christian Western cultures, but not necessarily to the Eskimos. An eagle's feather might be emotionally resonant to the Sioux Indians, but not necessarily to Russians.

His sad words are incongruent with the scenic meadow. The emotional resonance in the image and in the words mean that, when combined, their incongruence create an emotional depth and complexity to the moment.

Example 2: In a game set in the American Revolution, the Americans have taken a pounding. Many lay dying in the mud. Your captain is injured and can barely drag himself along the ground.

Suddenly, a runner enters the scene and whispers something to him. He cracks a small smile, and says in a loud, hoarse whisper, "We've won."

Here we see a reverse of the incongruence with the meadow. In this situation, the battlefield is a place of ruination and very emotionally resonant. But his words are happy. The incongruence creates a moment of emotional depth and complexity.

Final Thoughts

Creating Emotionally Complex Moments and Situations is one of the best ways to mirror the complexity of life itself.

If you want to open the door to emotionally engaging games, this is a great place to start.

Emotioneering Techniques Category #16

Plot
Interesting
Techniques

Is a plot still a plot
when it's different for each player?

This chapter focuses

on ways of making game plots interesting, while taking into account the
many different kinds of story structures—linear, nonlinear, and multi-path—
unique to games.

I squirm a little just to think about combining the words "plot" and "game" in the same sentence.

Plot suggests events moving in a straight line, it suggests external control, and it suggests order.[1]

Game suggests something open-ended and chaotic. It suggests fun and play.[2]

Putting "plot" and "game" together is like trying to combine order and chaos. It's like trying to tidy up the Big Bang.

You Call This a Story?

As linear writers make the transition into games or become demented, frothing beasts in the attempt, one of the things they'll need to adjust to is that games aren't very much like films. Even if the game has a plot, the story is likely to unfold through some very unorthodox structures.

Forget film structure; a game's story is just as likely to unfold in a structure that resembles any or several of these:

- The game, "Capture the Flag"

- Solving a crime, with clues you can seek out in any number of orders

- Exploring a landscape and figuring out how to get past the seemingly impassable parts

- Playing poker

- Accumulating weapons and spells, and calculating which ones serve your needs—often on the fly, during battle

- Waging a war, including all the strategic elements and the resource-management aspects

- Building a city and making sure all its inhabitants have everything they need

- A shooting contest

- At least a dozen other such interactive structures

---

1. And thus, by extension, it connotes people who can't leave the beaten track, who can't dance, and who won't try exotic foods.

2. And thus, by extension, it connotes irreverence, rebellion, and teens who seek attention by having their underwear or bra-straps showing.

Within these structures, can we say something even has a plot?

And so, when working on a game, my colleagues and I frequently stretch our synapses to the breaking point as we riddle ourselves with questions such as:

> Which *plot information, character insight, character information, or emotional experience* is it critical for the player to eventually learn or undergo during the course of the game?

The following examples shed light on what I mean:

- **Plot information**: This city was built on the ruins of another. That one was destroyed so quickly and cataclysmically that the ghosts still yearn for life.

- **Character insight**: Your best friend had been here once before, but never told you. He has met those ghosts.

- **Emotional experience**: You try to defend your friend in a battle, but he gets severely wounded.

Almost any game with even a modicum of a story has many of these "critical bits." And in some games, for instance some RPGs (role-playing games), the number of these critical bits can balloon astronomically.

Once you've created and decided upon your critical information and experience bits, you've got to determine:

- Which of these bits need to be revealed by certain points in the game?

- Which of these bits need to be revealed sequentially, and which can be revealed non-sequentially?

- Which bits have (for instance) just three different places and ways they can be revealed? Is there flexibility in the order? (Meaning, that some bits can be revealed in more than one place, but not in an infinite number of places.)

- What different methods can be used to reveal them?

- Which of these bits must be experienced by every player, so that they'll even be encountered by players who just want the quickest route through the game?

- Which bits are optional, and thus won't be "forced" on players, but instead will be saved for players who want to explore every nook and cranny of the game?

- Which bits will be experienced by the person who wants to break every rule and play the game in a very different way than it was designed to be played?

- Which bits will be learned, discovered, encountered, or experienced only the second time the player goes through the game, or the third? Which are saved for bonus levels or bonus experiences?

Designers in game company after game company wrestle with these issues. And when the variables really seem overwhelming, especially when it's crunch time and the clock is pushing midnight after a 14-hour day, game designers across the country invariably arrive at the same solution:

"Let's take a break and order pizza."

Breaking These Different Structures into Elements

I'm going to hone in on some of these unwieldy story structures and identify some of the structural building blocks used in games. And I'm going to do it the best way I how: by talking about a 7-11.[3]

Here's the game scenario:

I want to get to the 7-11, which is a mile away. I can only walk only along one path. Along the way, I'll encounter obstacles and enemies.

This first version is a straightforward *linear* structure.

Consider some other example structures:

I walk out of my front door, but can go any direction. There are many things for me to do that are fun and adventurous. At some point, I'll learn that there is such a thing as a 7-11, which I may elect to visit, or may never visit.

This is a *nonlinear* structure.

Halfway between home and the 7-11 is a bridge I need to cross. I go there but it's blocked. I need to find a number of objects, pieces of a code, clues, etc. to be able to get across the bridge.

---

3. 7-11 is a convenience store chain across the U.S. The stores never close, much like the eyes of fish.

So I go back and explore my neighborhood, enjoying various adventures, collecting clues, fighting enemies, and polishing my skills. These activities can be done in any order. Eventually I learn, retrieve, or attain whatever I need to get over the bridge.

This is a combination of *linear* and *nonlinear* structures.

I have a choice: I can start walking toward the 7-11, but, along the way, there are many side-quests—fun adventures—I can go on. I can enjoy them in almost any order.

On these side-quests I might get money, weapons, and the like, but if I never did a single side-quest, I could still make it over the bridge. So the side-quests aren't technically necessary.

This is a combination of a *linear* structure and a different form of *nonlinear* structures.

I can make it to the 7-11, but laying in wait are a spectrum of enemies and obstacles. I have a wide range of weapons and spells I can use for offensive or defensive purposes, and I must select among them.

Furthermore, I have different styles of making it to the 7-11. For instance, I can sneak there and try to not alert attention. Or I can unleash my firepower and act like the Grim Reaper's bastard stepchild.

This is a *multi-mode* structure. *Almost all* games are multi-mode to one degree or another. Sometimes the player can take on different roles, and each role has its own mode (sets of weapons, skills, defenses, etc.).

I can go to the 7-11, but when I come to the bridge, I find that there are actually two bridges, going off in different directions. I have a choice, but they'll both end up at the same place in the end.

This is a combination of *linear* and *multi-path* structures. Diverging paths aren't done very often, because this approach requires the creation of up to twice the assets—money that could be used for other aspects of the game. Still, some games do have paths that split for a period of time.

As I get toward the 7-11 along a linear path, near the end, I have a choice of which direction to take. One takes me toward the 7-11, and the other takes me to its arch-rival, the notorious Circle-K store.

This is a combination of *linear* and *multi-endgame* structures.

I can play the hero or the villain. As the hero, I try to get to the 7-11 and kill the villain. As the villain, I try to kill the hero, and get everyone in a five-square-mile radius to be my slave. As the villain, I can accomplish my goals in a variety of orders.

> **note**
>
> Examples of emergent gameplay can be found in such highly popular games as *Sim City* and *The Sims*. Instead of the game supplying a narrative or a contest (such as with driving games or sports games), emergent games give the player advanced or somewhat "intelligent" building blocks that you can use to create your own story. Did you ever play with Lego™ as a child? It's the same basic concept.
>
> Unlike Lego, in emergent games, there's often some kind of instability built into the system, however. Either you constantly need elements you don't have but are required to get, or the system needs to constantly be attended to so that entropy doesn't destroy it, and so on. Thus, in many games that use emergent gameplay, you're continually prompted to take action to maintain or expand whatever world or system that you've created using the building blocks.

This is a *multi-role* game; the hero role is *linear*; the villain mode is *nonlinear*.

I can make it to the 7-11, fighting all sorts of baddies along the way. There are other missions to run as well. They can be run in any order. Each is a complete adventure unto itself. The missions are only loosely related to each other.

This is a *modular* structure.

My goal is to build a city, with a happy population and a complex, functioning infrastructure. And, of course, the city will include lots of 7-11s. If you built a city, yours would only vaguely resemble mine.

This is *emergent* gameplay. And because "The Sims" could have infinite "endings," or no ending at all, games based on emergent gameplay are often called *open ended*.

Creative Toolbox or Wellspring of Psychosis?

Most games have combinations of some of these basic structures—linear, nonlinear, multi-mode, multi-path, multi-role, multi-endgame, modular, and emergent. Add to this all the ways of creating fun (see Chapter 5.2, "Techniques for Creating Fun"), and then factor in the innovative genius of today's and tomorrow's game designers, and it's easy to see that there is an infinite number of ways to create a game.

This is one of the reasons why writers coming from traditional, linear storytelling occasionally are plunged into psychotic breaks when they begin working in the field of games. However, evolving effective psychotherapies to help linear writers who've crashed and burned against some of these game structures isn't our focus here.

We're here to talk about making game plots interesting—while we redefine "plot" to mean all the structures mentioned earlier. How can you make a game plot interesting?

One way, of course, is to assess all these different structures, and then do a mix-and-match to arrive at the combination that best serves your game. It's very possible that parts of the game will use a few of these structures, while other parts of the game use wholly different structures.

Here are few plot twists that could work in some of the preceding structures.

Structure Twists

Structure Twists means surprising the player with the way some of the basic structures are used. For instance, it could be interesting for the player to discover that a game has non-linear elements, just when he or she thought that it was a linear shooter.

Let's look at a few more plot twists in the context of a hypothetical, contemporary war game.

Hypothetical Game Case Study

A Revelation Changes Everything

You and your squad have been making it across hostile terrain toward the enemy's stronghold. You've been getting orders from your higher-ups over a radio carried by one of your men.

And then comes the revelation: You learn that your radio is bugged. Your enemy knows where you are and everything you've been planning.

You can make it even more interactive if you didn't *have* to bring that radio with you, but you elected to do so as one of the five accessories you could carry on the mission. Because you chose to bring the radio, this plot twist won't seem as if it's "rammed down your throat."

Innocent People Are in the Way

The enemy has put his compound in the middle of a densely populated area. If you shell it, you'll kill many innocent people.

A Key Piece of Equipment Breaks Down

You're making a final assault on the enemy's fortified compound. The rocket-grenade launcher, your main and only sure way of destroying the ramparts, breaks.

A Character Changes Sides

Continuing the preceding story...You turn around, and there's the enemy's right-hand man. You panic! Assuming he's here to kill you, you shoot first. *Blam!*

As he dies, he confesses he had deserted the enemy and was changing sides. He tells you there's a lightly guarded, secret back entrance to the compound. He's about to tell you exactly where it is, but he dies.

You Fall into a Trap

You find that entrance and storm it—but your enemy's men are inside, waiting. It was all a trap.

A Hostage Is Taken

No sooner are you inside the walls of the enemy fortress when your best buddy is captured. Do you go to rescue him, or do you go after your enemy?

Forced to Carry Out Another's Agenda

The enemy's henchman has got you in his sniper scope, and you're in an open area with no place to duck for cover. The way you discover you're doomed is that he's tapped into an ear microphone you've been using as part of a communications system, and he taunts you.

The henchman says he'll kill both you and your buddy (the one taken hostage earlier, who's still their prisoner) unless you tell your men to leave—that you'll take it alone from here.

So, to save your and your buddy's life, you dismiss your very confused men. You've been forced to carry out another's agenda.

Mini-Goals

A *Mini-Goal* is a goal you need to accomplish first before proceeding to the main goal.

Let's say that there's an enemy soldier up in a guard tower, picking off your men. Before you charge the enemy's HQ, you've got to take out that soldier one way or another. This becomes a mini-goal.

Out of the Frying Pan, into the Fire

The solution to one problem gets you into an even worse problem. For example:

- The enemy has a futuristic catapult that it was using to bombard you when you were outside the walls. You break inside, but can't get to the center of the compound because it's too heavily guarded. You get an idea: Have your men catapult you. You'll use your parachute as a break to slow down your descent. It seems like a great solution—but when you do this—

- You land in the wrong place—right in the middle of a munitions storage area. Enemy troops are swarming you. The solution is to use your flame thrower to start a cascade of explosions—

- You start the explosions, which destroy the troops, but they ignite a fire that rapidly spreads your way. You run out of the munitions area—into some worse problem.

I think you get the idea.

A Problem with No Obvious Solution

In the hypothetical game depicted on the left, a destructive spirit has taken refuge in your space ship. You can't dislodge it or even harm it without damaging your ship.

Finally, you're forced to blow up your own ship. You don't kill the spirit, but you do succeed in injuring it. Unfortunately, you've also eliminated your only way off this planet.

Getting your player into problems with no obvious solutions can be quite dramatic and emotionally engaging.

Pancaking Scripted Sequences

Pancaking Scripted Sequences means that, at certain points in a mission (I'll call these points *nodes*), scripted sequences are stacked on top of each other like a stack of pancakes. When you reach that node of the game, any one of a number of scripted sequences could be triggered.

Here's an example.

In a "Desert Storm" type of first-person shooter, you go to take out an enemy radar antenna. One of your men follows you. Once the two of you shoot your way through a ring of enemy troops, one of two scripted sequences are triggered. Either:

1. Your comrade gets injured by an enemy who ambushes you, or

2. You blow up the antenna, but it falls in such a way that it blocks your and your comrade's best exit route.

So these two scripted sequences are pancaked on top of each other, and you don't know which one will occur. Either the computer picks one randomly, or selects one of the other factors that occurred earlier in the game.

Each one of these two scripted sequences demands separate courses of actions. Let's say option (1) occurs, and you drag your wounded comrade to a medic. This will be the next node. At this node, one of two pancaked scripted sequences could occur:

1. The medic could save your friend. Just as it seems that everything worked out well and you're relieved that your comrade didn't die, the medic himself is unexpectedly shot and killed by an enemy. Now you've got to find and take out that sniper. Or:

2. Your comrade, who has been treated, is now okay. He stands up, and notices that some other members of your squad are pinned down 50 yards away. The two of you rush off to help them.

No matter which of the two options occurs, once you go off and do what you need to do, you'll hit another node and another series of pancaked scripted sequences.

What pancaking scripted sequences means is that two people playing the game will experience very different stories. And if at each node where the scripted sequences occur, you could end up experiencing one out of three possible scripted sequences instead of one out of two, then the variance between the stories experienced by different players will increase manyfold.

The big disadvantage of pancaking scripted sequences is that is costs a lot of money and time to program—time and money that could be otherwise used to enhance different aspects of the game. This disadvantage is large enough that it would dissuade most developers from utilizing this technique. The advantage of this approach is that makes repeat gameplay a lot more fun.

However, because many gamers only play through their games once, before taking this approach you've got to decide if your game is one intended to be played many times.

Electronic Arts has discovered that many gamers play their *Medal of Honor* games more than once, so EA is introducing some pancaking of scripted sequences into their game *Medal of Honor—Rising Sun*. In fact, I first heard the term "Pancaking Scripted Sequences" from one of their executives who was discussing *Rising Sun* in particular. Because the game wasn't out when this book was completed, it will be interesting to see if they pull off pancaking in a way that also keeps the varying story-lines within each mission both exciting and emotionally gripping.

Meaningful Nonlinear Re-Sequencing (MNR)

Meaningful Nonlinear Re-Sequencing means that the player in a game can undergo a variety of experiences, or pursue a variety of tasks, in any order he or she pleases (thus, they can be "re-sequenced" in any number of ways, and so are "nonlinear"). These experiences and tasks, which can be re-sequenced nonlinearly, have *meaning*. By meaning, it's implied that the experiences and/or tasks have *emotional content*, and they feel like *they hang together coherently as an emotionally engaging story or as part of a story.*

But is MNR truly possible?

The Problem with Past Efforts

Pancaking Scripted Sequences is just one possible way to allow a game to be played in any number of orders. But one doesn't need to get nearly so fancy.

Almost all games allow players to, at one point or another, undergo a variety of experiences or pursue a variety of tasks that can be re-sequenced nonlinearly. For instance, as a player, you might, at some point in a game, have a choice of:

- Retrieving an amulet that will open the door to the next level of the game

- Killing a few enemies, and by doing so gaining some kind of benefit to your offensive or defensive capabilities

- Locating certain precious stones that can be later traded for weapons, goods, or services

- Going off and creating mayhem just for the heck of it

- Seeking out and speaking with NPCs who give you information about the history of this place, or about current events

- And so on

There are a thousand variations of the preceding. Games set in present time have their own versions.

While events and activities such as these can be re-sequenced nonlinearly, they aren't meaningful—i.e., they don't evoke emotion (except perhaps fear when fighting a difficult enemy). Nor do they lead you through a sequence of experiences or insights that by any means constitute an emotionally gripping story, or even a piece of one.

A Fatalistic Argument

There's a fatalistic argument in favor of keeping events like the preceding meaningless—i.e., without emotional content and not constituting a gripping story or part of a story. The argument goes something like this:

In a (non-game) story, if Ethan secretly yearns to kiss Britt, who barely notices him—but eventually he does and she falls for him—then this is *meaningful* (i.e., it has emotional content and it constitutes a coherent story or part of a story). However, if you were to reverse the order of events, so that first he kisses her and she falls for him, and then he later secretly yearns that someday she'll kiss him, it doesn't make sense.

Therefore, the only events that can be re-sequenced nonlinearly are those that have no emotion, such as something like the list of potential game experiences and tasks I enumerated a bit earlier. Otherwise, certain combinations of experiences or activities won't make sense.

I call such a viewpoint "fatalistic" because it assumes there's no solution. The result of stringing together activities and tasks that are meaningless is that huge nonlinear portions of a game might end up being meaningless. Don't get me wrong—this isn't a condemnation. Chess, skiing, laying on a beach and getting a tan, or playing basketball might not contribute to an emotionally gripping story, but they all can be quite satisfying at different times.

However, this brings us right back to Chapter 1.3, "Why Put Emotion into Games?." If we're trying to increase games' demographic appeal and reach out to people who desire meaningful entertainment experiences (i.e., who watch films and TV but who won't play games because they're too "meaningless"), then this hurdle needs to be crossed.

Applying Meaningful Nonlinear Re-Sequencing to Games

Let's take a look at a hypothetical game example. In this game, you could undergo the following three experiences in any order, and they'd still be meaningful:

1.

After many (gameplay) struggles, you retrieve the pendant that allows you to hear the voices of the dead Elders. The Elders give you a new name that means, "Wing of Time." This name refers to the fact that, someday, you may be able to change the very fabric of time itself.

The Elders tell you not to tell the people of the village that you can hear them (the Elders). This secret is for you alone. If you tell anyone, you will die.

2.

In gameplay, you battle enemies and make your way to the quite ill Shaman, who declares that you are the awaited one—the one of uncanny ability.

Before dying and joining the Elders, he advises you to keep your own counsel, and ignore the people of the village. Sadly he confesses that they've always treated him quite strangely—he doesn't know why...

Having said all this, he dies, his mission in life fulfilled at last. His time is at an end.

3.

In gameplay, you perform a unique fighting move and save the village from enemies. People are aghast, for no one has been able to do that move since olden times. To them, your place in the ancient lineage seems likely. You may be the fulfillment of their dreams. They wish the Elders were still around to guide them and tell them for certain...

And they tell you, if you see the Shaman, or have already seen him, ignore him, for they expelled him from the village long ago. He always made them uneasy.

4.

You discover that the Shamans have no independent existence. They are created by the unconscious dreams of the people, during times of great stress. Distrusting their own counsel, they unconsciously weave together a life form called a Shaman out of their own psychic energy, without even realizing they're doing so. Then, supposedly, they would turn to the Shaman for advice.

You can undergo these four experiences in any order. The story and emotions change, depending on the order, but in each case the story remains emotional and coherent.

Each order has its own unique flavor. If you experience (3) after experiencing (1) and (2) (these last two in any order), you live with the secret that you can talk to the Elders, something the villagers think is impossible. And you know the secret that you're the "awaited one," even though they're not totally certain about this.

If you experience (2) after experiencing (3) and (4) first (these last two in any order), then the Shaman's statement—that the people always treated him strangely—has a sort of tragic quality, for you know the reason. It's because he is made out of their own unconscious dreams. Obviously, there's something about their dreams they're uncomfortable with, and thus they view the Shaman with that same unease.

If you experience (2) after experiencing (1), then you find yourself holding a secret from the Shaman. He says his time is at an end, but you've already learned that may not be true, since the Elders have told you that you may be able to alter time.

If you experience (3) after experiencing (2) and (4) first (these last two in any order), then the villagers' statement that the Shaman made them uneasy is ironic, for you know that he was created out of their own unconscious.

Also, if you experience (3) after (4), there's a further irony. When you get to (3), you've got to wonder if, on some level, you're like the Shaman. You were both "created" out of the villagers' dreams. He was created literally, and you were "created" metaphorically—i.e., created as a hero out of their need for one.

Let's change the order again. If you experience (3) before (4), the sequence will still be meaningful, but the preceding irony disappears. However, the irony that the people were made uneasy due to their own unconscious creation (the Shaman) still remains.

Each order of these four experiences is meaningful (emotional and coherent). The emotions you'll experience in all the different orders will vary, but all will be emotional. Even the story will shift a bit, but not so much that it mandates any new, alternative paths through the game.

Coherence is created in the MNR in various ways. One is some of the previously mentioned ironies. Another is your Character Arc (learning that you're special and have an important role to play).

A third method is by exploring themes, of which there are at least four in this brief example.

1. One is secrecy. The Elders have secrets from the villagers. You hold secrets from both the villagers and the Shaman.

2. Another theme is time, although this theme has just begun to emerge. The Shaman says "his time has come," and you're told that you may be able to alter time.

3. Yet another theme is people not knowing who they are. For instance, you're just learning who you are (the "awaited one"). The Shaman doesn't know who he is (that he was created out of the villager's psychic desires). And the villagers don't even really know who they are—i.e., that the Shaman is part of them.

4. The final theme, discussed a bit earlier, is how the people require saviors of different kinds, such as the Shaman or yourself.

Summary

In short, Meaningful Nonlinear Re-Sequencing is indeed quite possible in a game. It can be done with both emotion and with coherence.

To me, MNR represents a sort of ideal. However, it's not always practical, or even the best solution in all cases.

MNR offers players experiences unknown to audiences of the linear media of film and television. It's a way of unfolding story (advanced and revealed through gameplay whenever possible, of course) that many people think is impossible, due to their assumption that storytelling can't be emotional or coherent if it isn't linear.

The difficulty *linear writers* might face in trying to create MNR is their linear training. The difficulty *game designers* are likely to have in trying to create MNR is a lack of understanding of all the different kinds of continuities that usually operate outside a player's awareness, but which MNR depends on to work effectively.

Unfortunately, these continuities often operate outside the awareness of game designers and inexperienced writers as well, unless they've been explicitly studied. These "hidden" continuities, critical to making MNR work, include elements such as:

- Character Arcs

- Ironies

- Symbols that gradually accumulate emotional power or increased emotional associations

- Set-Ups and Payoffs

- Emotional continuities and emotional contrasts between game experiences

- Revelation of details

- Revelation of plot twists that can work at different places in a story and in different orders

- Themes[4]

—to name but a few.

Game designers and developers still often pursue interactive storytelling in a sort of topsy-turvy, non-emotionally engaging, afterthought kind of way. Add the challenges of time, budget, and the need to create stories often in coordination with a large team, and I don't anticipate the widespread use of MNR in the near future. It remains a powerful technique, yet barely touched upon in today's games.

But the future won't wait. Games with a breadth and depth of emotion are needed and wanted. Meaningful Nonlinear Re-Sequencing can be a valuable tool in their creation.

---

4. If "Character Arc," "Set-Ups and Payoffs," or "Theme" are not completely understood terms, you'll find them exactly defined in the book's Glossary.

Final Thoughts

Man Cannot Live by Twists Alone

Some amateurs think that plot twists are themselves enough to make a story interesting.

But a story that has no emotional content is rarely interesting, no matter how many twists are involved. *Indiana Jones and the Temple of Doom* was filled with action and twists, but at times seemed strangely empty and slow, even when the pacing was at its peak. The lack of emotional content meant that, even amidst the heavy action and jeopardy, it was sometimes hard to care about the twists or the danger.

Games have an advantage in that the action and twists are happening to *you*, the player—so there's a good bet you'll care.

I've played games with plenty of twists and no emotional content, however, and it's hard to get excited about them. I'm sure you've had the same experience.

Why then include mention of twists as an important facet of Emotioneering? Although twists might not be enough, a game without them could be simply tedious. When designing a game, I usually spend a lot of time trying to think of twists that will surprise the player and alter the context of the gameplay, as well as each level's, and indeed the entire game's, big and memorable moments.

Emotioneering Techniques Category #17

Plot Deepening Techniques

Why some stories touch us.

This chapter presents

techniques to give game stories the emotional depth and resonance found in such films as the *Lord of the Rings*, *Crouching Tiger Hidden Dragon*, *The Matrix*, *American Beauty*, *Blade Runner*, and *Casablanca*.

Plot Deepening Techniques are woven right into the flow and fabric of a story, whether the story is for a film or a game. The best way to understand these techniques is to deconstruct a story that uses them effectively. The film *Crouching Tiger Hidden Dragon,* which we touched upon in Chapter 1.6, "Why 'Writing' Is a Bad Word and 'Emotioneering' Is a Better One," is a wonderful example. It has a lyrical plot full of nuances.

While Chapter 1.6 discussed that film briefly, here we're going to examine it in great detail. Unfortunately, there's room for only a brief summary here. (Please note: Most of this chapter focuses on Plot Deepening Techniques used in this film. If you haven't seen the film and don't want the story ending given away, please skip this chapter. If you haven't yet viewed the film, I strongly recommend it.)

An extraordinary swordsman, Li Mu Bai (played by Chow Yun Fat) has left his monastic training to re-enter the world. He loves Yu Shu Lien (played by Michelle Yeoh), who loves him in turn. Various complications prevent them from acting on their love.

Young and "innocent" Jiao Long Yu (also called "Jen" and played by Zhang Ziyi) has a secret life: She's also an incredible swordswoman, a fighter of tremendous skill. She, Li, and Yu have all been trained in a special martial art that allows them to run up walls and over the roofs of buildings.

Jen steals a special sword that belonged to Li's deceased master, and much of the film involves Li and Yu on Jen's trail, both to retrieve the sword and to stop her from doing any damage with it. Their concern is well-founded; Jen's narcissism and stubbornness cause her to injure many people along her way, although she does have a passionate affair with a young, nomadic leader whom she comes to love.

Li doesn't want to punish her for stealing the sword; his goal is to teach her ethics so that she doesn't use her power to harm others. Both he and Yu end up fighting Jen at different points, but with the intent to stop her, not kill her.

Near the end, Li protects Jen from an evil and powerful woman, the "Jade Fox," who trained Jen to be a warrior but who envies Jen's superior martial accomplishments. This woman is the same person who stealthily killed Li's master long ago.

Although Li saves Jen and kills the Jade Fox, the Jade Fox fatally wounds him with a poisoned dart. After confessing the depth of his love to Yu, who's also present, he dies. Jen is overcome with guilt. She finally attains the ethical awareness that Li had tried so hard to impart to her—but her wisdom comes too late.

Up on a mountain is a monastery with a magical history. Legend has it that if you leap off that mountain, you don't die—although it's not clear what happens to you, for you don't return either. But whatever you wish for comes true.

Jen turns down the chance to return to her nomadic boyfriend, and in fact turns down life itself, for she jumps off a bridge in the monastery. We see her sailing down the mountain, but we never find out what becomes of her—nor even what she wished for.

Let's examine some of the Plot Deepening Techniques employed so artfully in this film.

Two Key Characters Trade Places

Li begins the film by abandoning the spiritual (monastic) life, reentering the world of swordsmanship, and letting himself be led by his deep passion for Yu. Even as he dies, he says he'd rather be a ghost by Yu's side than enter nirvana.

Jen begins the film totally enveloped by narcissism and passion. By the end, she abandons these attitudes—and her boyfriend—for an act of spiritual redemption (jumping off the mountain).

So Li and Jen trade places. Having two major characters trade places can give depth to a plot.

The Story Makes a Spiritual Power Palpable

When you posit in a film or a game that there are spiritual forces in the world, you can make that spiritual force seem quite real by giving a key character who possesses the spiritual force power or influence over others, even over those who might be much better armed.

Gandalf, in *Lord of the Rings*, is not afraid of those who wield mighty weapons. Obi-Wan's, Luke's, and Darth Vader's use of The Force to overcome others who have more firepower makes The Force palpable. Similarly, at one point in *Crouching Tiger*, Li holds a stick and fends off Jen, who wields a sword.

The spiritual power a character manifests doesn't need to emerge in fighting, however; it can also emerge just through the character's inspirational nature. For instance, at one point in *Crouching Tiger*, Li touches Jen's forehead, and we can see that, at least for a moment, some kind of wave of understanding sweeps through her.

At another point in the film, because of Li's perfect "spiritual balance," Jen can't dislodge him from a thin tree limb on which he stands with serenity, no matter how much she shakes the branch. There are many other such moments in the film. Like Obi-Wan, Li makes the spiritual world palpable.

A Symbol Takes on More and More Emotional Associations

Symbols can add emotional depth to your story. Chapter 2.23 discusses some game examples in depth; here, we'll look at an example from *Crouching Tiger*: The sword, in the beginning, has the significance that it once belonged to a master swordsman. Thus, we can assume it is a superior fighting instrument and perhaps is even endowed with a bit of the master's spiritual energy.

By the end of the film, it comes to signify spiritual and ethical purity. Li has been chasing Jen the entire film to get the sword. At one point, he finally gets it from her. When this occurs, she claims she's finally ready to be taught from him—only to belie this with another selfish outburst.

Li tells her she doesn't deserve the sword and throws it in the river. The sword at this point means the ethics and spiritual perfection that are the essence of his teachings. It's these teachings that she doesn't deserve.

So, just as the American flag has picked up many emotional associations over time, so does the sword that once belonged to Li's master and that is the focus of much of the plot.

A Character We Like Dies

In this case, it's Li who dies—and maybe Jen as well, although her final fate is a bit uncertain. Some might hate Jen because of the destruction she leaves in her wake. I believe, however, that we are intended to see her as a sympathetic figure, just as Li does. She certainly becomes more likeable when she decides to sacrifice her life, or at least her current form of existence, for the greater good.

A Bittersweet Ending

While there is no "formula" for creating a bittersweet ending, I have noticed that many films with such endings use this technique: A major character accomplishes his or her Character Arc (his or her journey of character growth), but not his or her goal.

Li's goal is to forge a life with Yu, which can never happens due to his untimely death. Before he dies, however, he finally confesses his love and passion for Yu. This completes his Character Arc, for he has traveled from monastic detachment to acknowledging his love and passion.

Yu's goal is to build a future with Li, which doesn't come to pass. Before she loses him, however, she finds it within her to communicate her love.

Jen's intentions throughout the film are to keep the sword, called the "Green Destiny," to stay with her nomadic boyfriend Lo, and to continue to get whatever she wants. Her goal certainly isn't to jump off a mountain. But before she does, she bravely undergoes a spiritual and ethical transformation that requires her to sacrifice her life as an act of redemption.

Thus, all three of the major characters undergo a similar fate: They attain the difficult character growth they need, but they fail in their outward goals. Bittersweet endings give plots depth.

An Ending That's a Little Uncertain

I rate "open endings" on a scale of 1 to 10, with 10 being the most open. *The Empire Strikes Back* would be a 10, for it left us with a cliffhanger that demanded a sequel.

Of course, George Lucas knew he could get away with it for that particular film. Usually you don't want to make an ending that open, because it leaves a story feeling unfinished. Your player, who has worked so hard to reach the finale and who finds there's no "end" there, will usually feel cheated and manipulated.

On the other hand, the ending of *Crouching Tiger Hidden Dragon*, is about a 3 on that 1 to 10 scale. We know that when Jen jumps off the mountain, she's going to get a wish fulfilled, but what did she wish for?

This question emotionally engages us because each viewer will complete the story in his or her own mind, in his or her own way.

My belief is that, if Jen turns down her boyfriend's invitation to return with him to his home, which she does, it must be for a pretty important wish. I believe that she wished for Li to come back to life, and that all her other misdeeds will be undone as well.

Given that she has completed her Character Arc (she has learned ethics and responsibility), this would seem to be a logical motivation for her decision to make such a great sacrifice. (Because I think Li will come back to life, I don't even see his death as final. To me, the film had an uplifting ending, not a sorrowful one.)

Of course, I can't *prove* that that's what Jen wished for, and you might have a quite different and equally valid opinion. And that's exactly the point: The ending is a little open, but not so open that it frustrates us by providing us too little to base any speculations on.

Greetings from a Land Outside Your Awareness

Most people who see *Crouching Tiger Hidden Dragon* and who are affected by it emotionally still aren't aware of all these Plot Deepening Techniques at work. The film provides a good demonstration of how, if you've got someone emotionally engaged, they won't notice the specific techniques you're using.

As discussed previously, though Emotioneering dramatically can increase a player's emotional involvement in a game (or, in this case, an audience's emotional involvement in a film), the techniques that are used to accomplish this usually operate outside the player's or audience's conscious awareness. And, after all, if all Emotioneering techniques were self-evident, then there'd obviously be no need for this book.

Relevance of *Crouching Tiger* for Games

It might seem odd to spend so much time discussing a film in a book about games, even if it is a great film.

However, there's not one Plot Deepening Technique pointed out in the film that couldn't also work in a game.

A number of powerful lessons can be taken from the film. One is how many ways a story can create deep emotion, even when dialogue plays a small role.

Another is that giving depth to a plot isn't a matter of some kind of magical process. Emotioneering always *involves the artful application of exact techniques.*

The film also demonstrates how many Plot Deepening Techniques can be combined in one story.

A Downside to Victory

The drawing on the preceding page depicts a moment from a hypothetical game. In this game, you play a character who has mastered some psycho-kinetic abilities. You've killed a sub-boss, and now you call your blade back to you.

But at this point in the game, your power is so great that some people are afraid of you. It doesn't matter that you've never harmed them; it doesn't matter that you've established a friendship with them by working together to overcome mutual foes. They're simply afraid of the power you wield, and there's nothing you can do about it.

Your victories have had a downside: You've frightened off some of those you hold close to you.

I call this "A Downside to Victory," but it could also be labeled "A Downside to Great Attainment." It's another Plot Deepening Technique.

Emotion Mapping

When I'm brought in early enough in the game design process, I like to see if I can include *Emotion Mapping*. This means taking the player through an emotional journey, or even a roller coaster. I like to know what emotion the player is likely to experience where, and to ensure that a spectrum of emotions come into play.

Part of Emotion Mapping involves creating powerful emotional moments.

There's a macro component—arranging these powerful emotional moments in key places throughout the course of the story—as well as a micro component—creating these moments within a particular mission or segment of the game.

Powerful emotional moments include such things as:

- The time when you see you have little option but to do something unbelievably brave, and you launch into it
- A moment when all seems lost
- The feeling that you've finally won—only to suddenly learn that the real hell is just beginning
- Moments of parting, or moments of reunion, with characters you care about
- Times when you and possibly your squad are running like hell from a better armed enemy

- Painful moments when you lose one or more characters you're close to

- "A-ha" moments when a big mystery is suddenly resolved

- Huge action sequences that aren't cliché

- Unbelievable plot twists that leave you amazed or stunned

- Other such powerful emotional moments

Also involved in Emotion Mapping is building into the game Emotionally Complex Moments and Situations, as discussed in Chapter 2.15.

Unfortunately, when I'm brought in too late in the game design process, often there isn't much I can do in the way of Emotion Mapping.

Idea Mapping

Idea Mapping means taking the player through a variety of viewpoints, usually inconsistent ones, during the game.

I was brought in as a designer/writer on a game about a man who hunts monsters. Unfortunately, the basic game design was fairly complete by the time I came on board.

It didn't allow me to do any Idea Mapping. If I had been part of the original design team, I probably would suggested that:

- At one point in the game, the player would feel that humans are good and monsters are bad.

- At another point, the player would feel that monsters are good and some humans are actually monsters.

- At another point, the player would feel that he or she was a monster.

The first two points are done in *Blade Runner*, where at first we feel that the replicants are inhuman monsters. By the end, however, our opinion has changed and it seems clear that some of the replicants are much more "human" than those who are trying to destroy them.

That's Idea Mapping.

The third idea I would have suggested is harder to make work in a game. I'd probably put the player in a position where the player (i.e., the player's character) was near two people or monsters the player liked, but who were both in mortal jeopardy—and the player can only save one of them.

Later in the game, a friend of the person (or the creature) the player allowed to perish, would call the player a monster. Perhaps several NPCs the player cared about and respected would feel this way about him or her, and the player's character would be shunned.

It would take artful writing to make all the intended emotions carry weight, but if those emotions were brought to life, it would certainly be an interesting exploration of the theme of "monsters."

Idea Mapping Is Often Synonymous with "Theme," But Doesn't Have to Be

In the preceding example, there's really no difference between Idea Mapping and "theme," because the ideas the player would hold at different points all revolved around a particular subject ("monsters"). "Monsters" would be the theme of the game. Here, the term "theme" means "a subject central to the story and explored from different points of view, but with no final conclusion drawn."[1]

However, Idea Mapping could be performed on subjects other than the theme.

For instance, in this game, at one point you could make viable the idea that a person should do his or her noble work (hunting monsters) alone. At another point, it would be clear that it's better to hunt monsters as part of a group.

These diverging ideas would be "Idea Mapping," but they wouldn't be central enough to the story so as to constitute its theme.

If this all seems a bit irrelevant to emotion, because it deals with ideas, I'd like to point out that in *Lord of the Rings—Fellowship of the Rings*, the idea of "power" is explored from many points of view:

- The power of innocence (Frodo)
- The power of friendship (Sam)
- The power of a group (the Fellowship)
- The seductive power of evil (Saruman)

---

1. Another type of theme is "a subject explored from different angles, with a conclusion drawn at the end."

- The corruptive power of evil (the ghoulish, haunted, wasted faces of the Ring Wraiths)

- The power of guilt (Aragorn)

- The power of love (Aragorn and Arwen)

- The power of self-restraint (Gandalf resists taking the ring)

- The power of magic (Gandalf, the ring, the elves, and the objects they make)

This highly artful Idea Mapping helped deepen the plot and contributed significantly to the emotional scope and impact of *Fellowship of the Rings*.[2]

An Important Note: Ideas Are Not Enough

It's important to point out that ideas in themselves are dry and don't deepen emotion in a game. Ideas only contribute to a game's emotional power and resonance when they affect or manifest themselves through the acts or decisions made by characters we identify with, care about, fear, or hate.

Therefore, Idea Mapping can't deepen emotion in the absence of the artful use of techniques that cause players to become emotionally involved with NPCs (Chapters 2.10, 2.11, 2.13, 2.14, and 2.15) and techniques that cause players to become emotionally involved with the role they're playing and the world they play in (Chapters 2.18, 2.19, 2.20, and 2.21).

Better Late Than Never, But Better Early Than Late

Emotion Mapping and Idea Mapping, like just about all the Plot Deepening Techniques, can only be effectively put into a game when they're part of the initial design. This is true for many Emotioneering techniques. How much Emotioneering can be done, both in terms of quantity, variety, and power, depends on how early they're woven into the game design and gameplay.

When I'm asked to involve myself on a game in its last stages, I can polish the dialogue and often enrich the characters, but there's a tremendous amount that I can't do. For instance, I certainly can't do any Emotion Mapping or Idea Mapping. In fact, I can't use any of the techniques described in this chapter.

---

2. Here, the idea that was "Mapped" was the theme ("Power").

Final Thoughts

Plot Deepening, like many other aspects of Emotioneering, can't be injected into a game near the end. It has to be woven into the story right from the beginning.

Here and there, you come across games with genuine depth to their stories, such as *Ico* or *Final Fantasy X*.

I'm not focusing on how "good" these games are; 20 people will probably have 20 different opinions. All I'm saying is that their plots had depth. There was even some Plot Deepening in the generally comic *No One Lives Forever 2*.

Whenever you feel depth in a story, be it a story in a game, film, or novel, that's because one or more Plot Deepening Techniques are used.

There exists a wide array of Plot Deepening Techniques. In fact, *Ico, Final Fantasy X,* and *NOLF2* all use Plot Deepening Techniques not discussed in this chapter, as do many films, such as the *Lord of the Rings* trilogy and *The Matrix*. Perhaps you can do a little detective work and ferret out what techniques contributed to the depth of those plots.

Plot Deepening Techniques are an excellent way to enrich a game's story.

World Induction Techniques

If you create a world for the player,
don't forget the welcome mat.

World Induction Techniques

are techniques other than realism that cause a player to become emotionally immersed in the world of the game. It doesn't mean the teaching of skills and weapons. It refers instead to techniques for making a player want to spend time in the world of the game.

Birth.

From our moms' point of view, it's all contractions and screaming. But for us, it's being squeezed like toothpaste. Then there's a welcoming committee comprised of a stranger with a surgical mask who dangles us upside down beneath a five million watt lamp before walloping us on the butt. Paradise.

Before long we're drenched in an exploding cacophony of sounds and images, places, situations, and people. And the initiation rituals of childhood begin.

We gradually get the hang of it—what's an adult, what's a kid, what's a boy, what's a girl, what's a family. Soon we're off to elementary school and the initiation continues. We learn about teachers and students, and find that the day is no longer an unbroken string of uncertain possibilities, but now has a rigid structure demarcated by golden moments of ecstasy— lunch and recess.

And just when you think you've got it licked, there you are in junior high school, and it's like starting all over, but with a giant boot on top of you in the form of social pressures, "in crowds," and "out crowds."

It never ends. Once you're initiated into one sector of life, there's always another with entrance rules, rituals, status emblems, and lingo.

Each game takes place in the context of the world. Does your player care about this world? Just because the game takes place in post-apocalyptic Toledo doesn't mean that players want to spend the next 20 or 40 hours of their lives frenetically twitching their thumbs to become the lord and master of a nuked outpost in doomed Ohio.

The player needs to be made to care about the game's world. The way to do this is with World Induction Techniques.

Let's take a look at a few.

Creating a Rich World

A subset of World Induction Techniques are Rich World Techniques. These have much to do with offering players a variety of things they can be, do, and have, as well as adding a history to all of these. Let's examine some ways to create a rich world.

What Can You Be?

Think of the choices of what you can be in America:

- Flippant athletic insurance salesman
- Over-caffeinated novel-writing retro-beatnik
- Cat-hating, guilt-ridden veterinarian
- Code-breaking paranoid intelligence expert
- Belly-ringed bored nubile tenth-grade goddess

Did I leave anything out?

The menu of possible roles you can be exceeds even the sandwich list in a New York deli.

Does your game offer a variety of roles to choose from? Can you be good or bad, man or woman, human or alien, warrior or shaman?

Can you work solo or as part of a group? Can you be friendly, or can you be ruthless? Can you change sides, or are you stuck in one viewpoint?

Giving choices helps the player make the game his own, and thus encourages emotional engagement.

Obviously not all games can or should allow you to make these kinds of choices, and many of my favorite ones don't. But we're just exploring ways here to induct a person into the game's world.

Choice of Actions

If the game has a story, do you have to play in story mode (following the game's plot) or can you find other ways to enjoy the game? What kinds of activities does the game make available?[1] Can you:

- Solve a puzzle?
- Explore a section of the game's world?
- Cause trouble?
- Kill bad guys?
- Kill good guys?
- Accumulate wealth?
- Accumulate status?
- Sneak around?
- Blast your way through?
- Race a competitor?

---

1. *Grand Theft Auto III* and *Vice City* are examples of games that offer players a tremendous amount to do other than follow the plots.

Choice of Possessions

Another way for the player to make the game his or her own is a choice of possessions. In the game, can you:

- Have different weapons? Spells? Charms?
- Drive a variety of vehicles?
- Change clothing or armor or bodies?

One size does not fit all. Give the player a choice.

Adding History

What makes a rich world isn't just a matter of what you can be, or do, or have, but the sense of tradition and history behind these things.

Ideally, the information you learn about the history should figure into gameplay. Although this is an ideal, it isn't an absolute rule.

For example, let's say you're a soldier in a high-tech uniform. Let's explore how we could add history to the soldier's being, actions, and possessions.

> **Being:** You are being soldier on a planet like Earth, but not like Earth.

> **Add History:** You wear a badge. When you touch it, you can bring up a hologram of your grandfather, your father, or your uncle, all of whom were soldiers.

> Because of technological developments in psycho-photonics, though they are dead, echoes of their life forces can be funneled from the ether (to whence their spirits were dispersed when they died) and enter those holograms. Thus your dead family members can guide you on the code of honor of a warrior and even give you tactical advice. *(Note how history contributes to gameplay.)*

> When a soldier has done a feat of extraordinary bravery at great possible cost, he is rewarded with the Boots of Hermes—special shoes that allow him to run about three feet above the ground, at incredible speed. They were developed by an ancient race that once inhabited this world.

> Solving the puzzle of what happened to your family is the plot of this game. But as you go on, you learn that you might be descended from the ancient, vanished race. And when you learn these secrets, it will

unlock other abilities you have within you but of which you were unaware. *(Note how history contributes to gameplay.)*

Summary: We've made your being a soldier richer by adding in very specific histories to different aspects of what you can be.

Actions: You can kill, protect, sneak, and so on.

Add History: The soldiers here perform certain traditional ritualistic actions: They stand outside at sunrise so that the first rays of light can add new power to their guns and their other weapons.

That's because Telan Ku, the founder of their order five centuries ago, discovered Sentia, a form of metal that, like plants, is nurtured by sunlight. He forged the first bio-guns that have been a staple of soldiers ever since. No non-soldier is allowed to own anything made of Sentia. Some of your missions therefore involve protecting the Sentia mines. *(Note how history contributes to gameplay.)*

Your platoon sings an ancient yet vigorous marching song as they walk home from victory.

It's the tradition here for small children to offer soldiers chocolate and bullets. When you shoot a bullet given to you by a child, you can faintly hear children's innocent laughter after it slams into an enemy. *(Note how history contributes to gameplay.)*

Summary: We've added history to some of the things soldiers do, and made these actions richer.

Possessions and Other Objects: You can have different uniforms, guns, other weapons, a house to live in, and so on.

Add History: You possess a curved sword that was given to you by a general after you fought heroically in a recent battle. This sword, when you whip it over your head, lets loose the death screams of every person it has ever killed. This terrifies your enemy and temporarily immobilizes them.

Telan Ku, the founder of the soldier order, was originally a farmer. He developed the art of war, which you now follow, in order to throw off an oppressive government, which has long since disappeared.

There's a well outside of town. In his first major defeat, Ku lost his son and his two closest friends. It is said that he went to that well and cried. When you dip you special sword in that well, it becomes super-charged for awhile. You can move it so fast that you can even use it to stop bullets. *(Note how history contributes to gameplay.)*

Summary. We've made an item—the sword—richer by giving it a history.

Level of Detail

Detail also contributes to making a world rich. Ideally, as with history, it should contribute to gameplay whenever possible.

Consider an example: There's a tree—the Great Tree—in the center of the village. When you stand under the mottled shade of its branches, your health is restored. Now let's add some details, both in terms of the tree's present and its past.

The great Singers of the village all compose their songs under the Great Tree. At the full moon, the villagers gather under the Great Tree for their monthly energy renewal. At that time, under the silvery moonlight, for one minute, they all turn into small trees themselves. It's a very weird sight.

The tree was planted by The Stranger, a man of peace who wandered this land 1000 years ago. Wherever he rested, there grew trees with healing abilities. You'll use these trees whenever your health points are low.

Furthermore, the path of his wanderings is marked with guide stones. When you stay on that path, you're much more impervious to weapons wielded by your enemy. *(Note how details and history contribute to gameplay.)*

Unique Cultural Art Forms

Unique cultural art forms also contribute toward creating a rich world. Let's continue with our fantasy culture that worships the Great Tree. *Ideally, as with history and details, unique cultural art forms should contribute to gameplay.*

Sometimes, when you're away from the village on a mission and you get injured, one of The Singers from the village can feel your danger. If you've earlier been kind to them, one might sing a healing song or melody that you can hear even miles away.

The song can restore your health and even repair your armor and weapons. *(Note how this unique cultural art form contributes to gameplay.)*

The point here is that unique cultural art forms can help make a culture, race, or world rich.

Creating a Rich World Through Visual Incongruence Using Emotionally Resonant Items

Although this book has stayed away from visual design, I would like to discuss art direction a bit, and show how some forms of visual incongruence can help create a rich world.

In Chapter 2.15, "Emotionally Complex Moments and Situations Techniques," I discussed how some forms of incongruence can help make an emotionally complex moment—if the different elements were each, in their own right, emotionally resonant.

Similarly, incongruence can contribute to creating a rich world if the different visual elements are all emotionally resonant.

Take a look at the color painting on page 3. An empty canoe sits in the middle of a lake, with ripples going out from it in 360 degrees. The canoe is on fire, yet not burning. Birds fly in and out of the flames, but aren't scorched.

These images are incongruent. When incongruence like this occurs, our minds or spirits try to assemble a congruence that makes the disparate elements make sense. Yet the incongruence doesn't fit into any normal framework, so it snaps us free from those mental mechanisms that make us take reality for granted.

In trying to mentally or spiritually assemble it into an image that holds together as a unity, we're drawn into a rich world.

However, this is not *only* because of visual incongruence. If there had been a refrigerator in the middle of the burning canoe, and Mickey Mouse was sitting on top of it, it would be incongruent, but it wouldn't have a feeling of richness about it.

Because the incongruent items—flying birds, water, fire—all are quite emotionally resonant images in their own right, combining them creates a feeling of richness to the world.

Take a look at the color painting of the man assembling a towering monster on page 2. What if, hovering in the heart of the monster, we saw the image of a sad angel—either trapped there or perhaps even powering the beast.

The beautiful angel would be totally incongruent with the monster, and would completely change the picture. In fact, it would add emotional depth to the image and make it rich. But this would occur only because the monster and the angel are both emotionally resonant in their own rights. Putting a big martini glass where his heart should be wouldn't create any richness, because the martini glass isn't emotionally resonant the way an angel is.

Having the Visual Incongruence Relate to Gameplay

How could we make the visual incongruence of the mechanical monster with the sad angel in its heart factor into gameplay? That trapped, sad angel is the "power source" that fuels the monster.

Let's say that the monster goes on to ravage the land. The only way to stop it is to right some great injustice (which of course involves you going into battle)—an injustice that had caused the angel to be sad in the first place. Once the angel is released from its sorrow, it can finally leave the monster, and the mechanical monster will be immobilized. The angel's sorrow emotionally weakened it (the angel) and kept it trapped.

This would be an interesting way of "defeating" the monster. More importantly, however, it means that *the element that created the richness—the sad angel in its heart—would then also factor into gameplay.*

There are many other World Induction Techniques besides Rich World Techniques. Let's look at a few.

A World That Takes A While to Figure Out

In the fantasy world with the Great Tree described earlier, the most important people are The Singers. Yet even they defer to a class called The Dreamers, who can actually change the landscape with their dreams. The Dreamers defer to The Warriors, and The Warriors defer to The Singers. So it's all a weird circle.

How all these pieces fit together takes a while to figure out—as do the pieces of most complex cultures such as our own.

In America, how many ways does the President have power over Congress? How many ways does Congress have power over the President? Well, these powers are spelled out in The Constitution—but things aren't so simple. If the President is popular, then those in Congress are loathe to oppose him. So there are situations in which either the President or Congress have powers not described in American law.

Some cultures take awhile to descramble. That's part of their richness.

Friendship or Responsibility Toward NPCs You Care About

Would you like the city or town where you live if you hated everyone in it, and didn't have a single friend? Conversely, if you had a wide circle of close friends, do you think you'd hate living there?

Caring about others is a World Induction Technique.

We looked at ways of making the player care about NPCs in Chapters 2.10, "NPC Rooting Interest Techniques," and 2.11, "Player Toward NPC Chemistry Techniques."

Once you employ these techniques toward an NPC or a group of NPCs, if the game prompts you to take responsibility for one or more of these NPCs—for instance, because they're likable or because they've helped you in the past—you'll feel more willing to involve yourself in the world of the game.

The same thing goes if you're part of a group of NPCs (such as a squad) and Group Bonding Techniques (see Chapter 2.14) are artfully used. If you feel part of a group, you'll also like the world of the game.

Revenge

It may not be the most noble of motives, but if you can stir the player to hate an enemy enough, in its own way this also causes the player to be emotionally involved with the world of the game.

Don't Hold Back on Cool Weapons or Cool Things to Do

In some games, you fight and fight and finally get hold of some cool weapons. Suddenly you're fighting the boss—and then the game is over. In such games, the player never gets to really enjoy some of the best weapons. Why not give the player some extremely cool weapons right from the start?

And even if you hold back on giving the player cool weapons, you can at least give him or her cool things to do. Returning to *Grand Theft Auto III*, even before you've collected an awesome arsenal, there's no end of very cool and fun things you can do in the game. Just a few of these are: You can run people off roads, create a chain reaction of exploding cars, mow people down with your vehicle, toss people out of their cars, steal their cars, drive off the road, or chase criminals in a stolen police car.

Don't Change All the Rules at the End

In some games, the player makes his or her way through the game, getting progressively better at it. He's finally having fun beating the baddies—when he hits the end portion and suddenly is confronted with having to learn a new set of rules. *Half-Life*, for all its ground-breaking innovations and great gameplay, did this: You fight alien creatures and soldiers on earthly soil. But near the end, you find yourself jumping around in a floaty alien space with portals in it. In *Undying*, you end the game by fighting on an island with newly acquired weapons against a hydra-headed monster that spits fire.

Max Payne, on the other hand, avoids this problem. The final level is grand, breathtaking, with new enemies and set-pieces for action. But the final level still has its feet planted on the ground. There are no new alien creatures, no new weapons, and no new skills to learn. Nor is there any new puzzle-solving or platform jumping. You just do what you've been doing all along, but do it real good.

Obviously, what's both critical to achieve, and difficult to achieve, is balance. You want enough twists and surprises at the end so that it's not simply "more of the same," and rewards the player for having made it through that far. On the other hand, you don't want to give the player the feeling that he or she is starting all over again, with new weapons and new rules.

I always enjoy filmmakers who break established rules and get away with it. *Pulp Fiction* is a case in point, breaking just about every established rule on plot structure. The same thing applies to these last two points, about the importance giving players cool weapons or cool things to do early on in a game, and about not switching the rules at the end. Some game surely will come along that does both of these, and that is utterly amazing, enjoyable, and fulfilling to play.

In my screenwriting classes, therefore, I tell my students I'm offering tools, not rules, and the same goes for the techniques in this book.

World Induction Techniques Commonly Used in Massively Multiplayer Online Games (MMOGs—Sometimes Called MMOs)

MMOGs (sometimes called *MMOs* or *persistent world games*, among other names) often use a number of the techniques mentioned in this chapter to create World Induction. However, they also use a number of distinct techniques of their own. A few of these are (depending on the game):

- **Becoming an insider.** Some MMOGs take a while to get the hang of. Once you've learned the ropes, you're no longer a newbie—you're an insider. The enjoyment of being a knowledgeable member of the group is an incentive to spend time in the game's world.

- **Participation in social networks.** Some of these networks are long-lasting (existing over time); other social networks are formed with each new game experience, involving people you just met and with whom you go on adventures and quests. Players often have friends with whom they play online.

- **Building up a character over time.** Once you've invested a lot of time earning and enhancing your character's abilities, you want to enjoy the fruits of your efforts.

- **Being part of a social meta-group revolving around the game.** A meta-group is a group that discusses the group game experience. This means, when you're not playing the game, there are websites through which you can communicate about the game with other people who often play it.

- **Admiration from and status in the eyes of other game players.** This can occur during gameplay, generated by the power commanded by your character. It can also occur through meta-group communications, where the status or admiration comes as a result of your rank or your reputation in the game, or your providing a service to the group. Examples of such services can be disseminating inside information about the game to which you might have access, or creating assets that other players can use.

- **The unpredictability of playing with or against other people in real time.** Some people enjoy playing first-person shooters or real-time strategy games online for just this reason.

Final Thoughts

Right now, in your own life, you're part of a world and many sub-worlds, if you count your family and your workplace as groups you belong to as "worlds."

One problem faced by game designers is balancing World Induction with exciting gameplay. Designers are reluctant to slow down the speed of the game just to make the game's world richer and worthy of study or exploration.

Yet look how people get mesmerized by and emotionally attached to the world created by Tolkien. Those books use countless World Induction Techniques, and the payoff is widespread devotion. Much of that richness was left out of the films, however, to keep the pacing moving quickly—although it's truly impressive how much was retained.

So, in the end, it's a balancing act between how fast you want the game to move and how rich you want the game's world to be. Certainly having the elements that contribute to the world's richness be used in gameplay, as was stressed repeatedly in this chapter, is one solution.

Emotioneering Techniques Category #19

Role Induction Techniques

There's an art to pretending.

Role Induction Techniques
are techniques that make you willing to identify with the character you're playing.

What roles do you play willingly? Friend? Husband? Wife? Father? Son? Daughter?

Are there any roles you play unwillingly? At home? At work? In your family?

Children slide and in and out of roles at dizzying speeds. But by ten years old, psychological sediment has set in and they're expected to lock down into predictable personalities—although I'm proud that many gamers seem to have escaped some of this cultural curse.

It seems to me that some "role-playing" games are misnamed. The game might allow you to choose a variety of characters to play, and yes, these characters might have different bodies and faces. You might learn a bit about their pasts. And each has a different set of skills, weapons, specialties, spells, and so on.

Yet, in such games, taking on a role is really like being dealt a hand of cards, if each card was a skill or ability. One chooses a role depending on what that character can do.

It's not expected that you'll *feel* like one of these characters.

The opposite problem also besets some games. They actively cast the player in a role that he or she is *supposed* to emotionally embrace. But just because, for instance, the game says you are the last surviving pilot of your squadron, that doesn't mean you *feel* like you're a pilot, nor that you are willing to be one.

Yet we know from our own lives that people are quite willing to emotionally involve themselves in a role if it's one that appeals to them. After I graduated college, I spend my weekends in spring singing at a massive Renaissance Faire, where, every Saturday and Sunday, 10,000 visitors would be entertained by 2,000 people quite willingly delving into the roles of sixteenth-century British nobility, peasant, minstrel, or craftsman.

How do we create this kind of emotional connection between a player and a role in a game?

Skill Sets

Let's say that the game involves you taking on the role of an FBI agent.

A major part of identifying with a role involves learning the skill set of that role. If you can do a heart transplant, there's a good chance you'll feel like a heart surgeon. Of course, this education works particularly well if it takes place during early missions or training programs that offer genuine suspense and lots of fun.[1]

What are the skill sets of the agent? Surveillance? Hand-to-hand combat? Mastery of a variety of weapons?

As we master the skills and tools of a trade, we begin to assume the identity that goes with them.

There are a number of other ways to encourage a player to become emotionally caught up in a role. The following sections describe a few. I'm certainly not saying you should use every one of these. But, while some of these can be used in combination, you'll note that many of them can't.

Rewards for Playing the Role

In real life, there are all sorts of obvious and subtle rewards for doing a good job in certain roles, such as the roles of friend, father, mother, citizen, and so on. Rewards can encourage players to adopt a role as well.

These rewards can come in a variety of forms, such as:

- ◆ Admiration by strangers.

- ◆ Admiration by NPCs who are your colleagues.

- ◆ Having a reputation that spreads to NPCs you haven't met, but who, by your reputation alone, place you on a pedestal (or fear you) when they meet you.

- ◆ Admiration or fondness by an NPC who's an attractive member of the opposite sex.

- ◆ Admiration by the NPC who is your boss or superior in the game.

- ◆ Immediate rewards for a job well done. For instance, if you do a good job on a mission in your FBI role, you're given a better car to drive or a new group of great weapons.

- ◆ Access to places that others in the game are denied. Maybe it's a penthouse office.

---

1. This last point is important: A training mission, if the game includes one, needs to have suspense or fun. It should also relate to the main story of the game. It can be like a mini-story in itself, but if this is the case, it should be tied to the main plot. The fact that the player is being trained should be disguised, as much as possible, by Emotioneering.

- ◆ Being let off the hook from debts, obligations, and the like.

- ◆ Negative attention. In *Grand Theft Auto III*, it's tremendous fun to cause so much mayhem that every cop in the city is after you.

The illustration on the left is of an example game scenario. You play the bad-ass gunslinger who just rid the city of its worst villain—the leader of a heavily armed crime ring.

And now you're being rewarded with the red-carpet treatment and a choice of great, high-tech weapons.

The scene shows several rewards:

- Admiration
- Acknowledgment
- Access to special places (the penthouse)
- Tangible rewards (the weapons)

All of these work as Role Induction Techniques.

Against All Odds

A *badass* is a character who's able to stand on his or her own, without the need of a social network, and who is willing to take on incredible odds. It's a role players are often glad to assume. The character might be out for the social good, as Batman is, or just out for himself, as is Mel Gibson's character in *The Road Warrior is.*

Even people who, in real life, are politically correct goodasses, will secretly confess over their fourth beer that there's nothing like playing a badass.

Accomplishment

Make the character the best at something, or at least a master at it. For instance, in *Thief,* you play a character who is a master of stealth. If the player doesn't start the game as the best, make it known that he or she can rise to that level.

Leadership Attitudes and Abilities

We have a natural propensity to identify with someone who exhibits leadership abilities and attitudes. These include being:

- Ambitious
- Daring
- Original

- Confident

- Respectful; treating others as if they're important

- Responsible

- Ethical

- Not shaken easily from a path

- Able to handle tough situations instead of being overwhelmed by them; not shirking from situations that would intimidate others

Remember, some of the techniques in this chapter are incompatible with each other. For instance, a number of qualities on the preceding list wouldn't jive with the badass personality described in the section "Against All Odds."

A Valuable and Appreciated Role

In massively multiplayer online games (MMOGs), you often see people congealing into guilds and getting very involved in roles like my experience at the Renaissance Faire.

Even if you're not the leader, occupying a valuable and appreciated role can be a powerful Role Induction Technique.

A Story About Bread

I was speaking to a designer of MMOGs who was talking about the roles played in his games by NPCs. He said, "No one would want to play the baker who makes bread." Thus that role, he reasoned, would best be played by an NPC.

I took up the challenge, and suggested he imagine a society in which:

- Bread offers not just sustenance and health, but, if you eat certain breads, they give you superhuman abilities, at least for a time. For instance, you could gain the ability to see through walls.

- The Lead Baker controls the flow of bread and decides who gets how much.

- The Lead Baker is the most respected person in town. He gets more attention even than the Mayor. People offer him free goods and services wherever he goes.

- Bakers from this and other towns gather for secret ceremonies in which they renew their abilities to make magical breads. No one else knows what goes on in these ceremonies, but everyone is dying to know.

- The tradition of being a Baker is a long and rich one, and pieces of that story are engraved on the front of City Hall.

- Bakers, because they can eat their own breads and gain special powers at will, can, when required or when they feel like it, exhibit extraordinary abilities—speed, strength, or even wilder abilities like the ability to walk through hills.

The game designer looked at me and nodded. Who *wouldn't* want to be a baker in that game?

License to Break the Rules

In some ways, curiously, this technique is the opposite of the leadership traits mentioned earlier in this chapter. In this technique, your character can enjoy taboo thrills that would normally be frowned upon.

We're all indoctrinated into a cultural straightjacket. Break the rules at your own risk. If you don't believe me, wear a bright orange jumpsuit and walk along a downtown sidewalk, playing with a yo-yo. Strangers will shun you like the plague.

The straightjacket begins from the moment you wake up in the morning, and many people are only freed from it when they're dreaming.

Now, perhaps the word "straightjacket" might be a bit harsh. Certainly reigning in some impulses is critical for the greater good, or real life would resemble the chaos of the Internet.

But a game that allows us to take on a role in which we can ignore or break many of those social conventions and strictures can be quite involving. *Grand Theft Auto III* and *Vice City* bear testimony to the power of this Role Induction Technique.

Beguiling New Identities

Part of the previously mentioned cultural shackles involves submitting to a personality lock-down.

At the Renaissance Faire, there was one young woman who played the Queen of England, year after year, at Faire after Faire. As she was carried aloft in her traveling palanquin² by a dozen young men, all others at the Faire would fall silent and bow when she passed by.

I remember observing this one day, as I stood alongside a cynical news reporter. He leaned over to me and said, "How sad that this woman feels she has to pretend to be a queen."

I can still remember my response. "How sad that she lives in a society that doesn't see she has the nobility of a queen."

A role that allows a person to take on a beguiling new identity is a role the player will assume quite willingly, of course modified by individual taste. Even at the Renaissance Faire, those who enjoyed playing nobility wouldn't dream of playing a peasant, and visa versa.

In a game, we can escape our cultural shackles and become:

- A dark and mysterious hero
- The most feared man or woman in the county
- A benevolent god or the ruthless dictator of an entire community
- Mario
- An alien
- A superhero
- The leader of a fearless band of space militia
- The world's best thief
- A dancer in Britney Spears' stage troupe
- A noir detective
- A funny but slightly insane animal

Or we can choose hundreds of other roles that normally aren't available to us.

Abilities Beyond the Norm

Abilities Beyond the Norm can certainly make playing a character more enticing. Who didn't enjoy being undetectable in *Thief*? Or juggling an enemy in the air with blasts from your duel pistols in *Devil May Cry*?

---

2. A *palanquin* is seat or throne set on two poles. The throne and the poles are conveyed aloft, parallel to the ground, on the shoulders of a group of carriers.

Character Diamonds

In Chapter 2.1, "NPC Interesting Techniques," I introduced the idea of giving a major NPC a Character Diamond of three, four, or five different traits to make their personalities more dimensional.

There are a couple ways to use Character Diamonds in Role Induction—if it's a Diamond a player wouldn't mind occupying, at least in fantasy.

To be effective and entice the player to identify with the Diamond you create, take one of the preceding roles—from leader to badass to playing a valuable and appreciated role in a group to playing a beguiling identity— veer a bit away from the cliché Diamond, and include a few interesting traits.

For example, playing a detective who is always cynical probably isn't as compelling as the character who is:

1. Often cynical
2. Occasionally brilliantly insightful
3. Cool and unflappable under pressure
4. Slyly generous

That is, we've created a non-cliché detective with an interesting Diamond.

The key, though, is to, along with the Diamond, use at least one of the other techniques discussed in this chapter, such as being a master at something; being a badass; having leadership qualities, and so on.

The Character Has Emotional Responses We Recognize and Can Identify With

If something great happens that makes the player exalt, the in-game character should do the same as well. For instance, if the player gets an awesome power-up that gives him exciting new abilities, the in-game character should be excited by that as well.

However, if the character has a large exuberant response to every little reward you get in the game, but the player doesn't feel the same way about receiving those rewards, the player will start to break his or her emotional connection with that central character.

The opposite also holds true. If you feel excited about a big accomplishment but your in-game character has no reaction, that can also diminish or break the bond.

The exception is if part of your character's Diamond is to show no reaction to triumphs or setbacks.

Self Auto-Talk and Self Auto-Thought

Earlier we looked at ways to use a single line of dialogue to reveal insight into a character. Self Auto-Talk and Self Auto-Thought[3] can be used to reveal some of the character's Character Diamond or unique traits.

These techniques can enhance identification with a role.[4] For example, Self Auto-Talk is used effectively as a Role Induction Technique in *Thief*.

Fewer Words Usually Invites the Player to Identify with the Character

As we saw in Chapter 2.4, "Dialogue Deepening Techniques," a lot of meaning and emotion can take place beneath the surface of few words. Using fewer words can also create a sense of mystery.

If we hear the character we're playing talking, it's helpful if the character isn't overly talkative. A less talkative character allows us to project ourselves into the character.

A character who hints at what he or she is feeling, instead of spelling it out, also allows us to project ourselves into the character. It forces us to fill in the pieces, and thus draws us in.

Also, if we hear the words of the character we're playing and the words are slightly mysterious, we are similarly pulled in as we fill in the pieces.

In the game *Final Fantasy X*, we're supposed identify with Titus, the teenage hero, who leads a group of comrades on a fantastic journey. Most players identify most strongly, however, with his elder protector, Auron, because he's the one who speaks few words and has an air of mystery.

---

3. *Self Auto-Talk* is when you hear the character you're playing talking. *Self Auto-Thought* is when you hear his or her thoughts.

4. It's important to note that weak writing will annihilate the effectiveness Self Auto-Talk or Self Auto-Thought.

Character Silence (No Self Auto-Talk and No Self-Auto Talk)

Many game designers prefer to have the character you're playing be silent. This technique has also been shown to be effective in creating Role Induction.

Grand Theft Auto III is just one of many, many examples. By *not* giving the character a diamond or even any speech at all, each player can take the badass role and make it his or her own. Still, most players I've spoken to preferred playing Tommy Vercetti, the character in *Vice City* who does have a voice.

Generalizing a Problem

In *Final Fantasy X*, you play the role of Titus, a young man who is angry because (as far he knows) his father deserted him. But unless your own father deserted you, it might be hard to identify with his anger.

However, if Titus complained about the unfairness in life—the fact that one person is born rich and another poor, that one person lives long while a child might die of some dread disease, and, in his case, his father deserted him—then his anger would have been *generalized* and thus be easier to identify with.

Tradeoffs When Using Role Induction Techniques

Opening one door means not opening another. There is a tradeoff with every choice of Role Induction Techniques, and the tradeoff with keeping the character silent is that you can't create and define a complex and fresh new character, like Garrett in *Thief*, for the player to identify with.

A Case Study in Role Induction: *Thief*

Thief, in fact, uses a number of techniques discussed in this chapter:

- **License to break the rules.** You get to steal things, and you get to act as narcissistically as you want.

- **Accomplishment.** You're great at being a thief.

- **Abilities beyond the norm.** You can make yourself unable to be detected.

- **He has a sense of mystery about him.** He has mysterious abilities.

- **Garrett says few words.**

Because of the preceding five techniques, when you play the game, you're willing to identify with Garrett, the character you play. And because you're willing, that identification is then enhanced in the game with:

- Use of Self Auto-Talk
- Garrett's Character Diamond; he (you) have the following traits:
  1. You're a master thief
  2. You're out for yourself
  3. You're dryly ironic

By the end of the sequel, you begin to develop some empathy.

Final Thoughts

How emotionally involved will you be in a game where you don't identify at all with the character you're playing?

Well, perhaps a lot, if many other Emotioneering techniques are used.

However, to cast the player into a role and then not try to make the player identify with that role, is to actually diminish the player's emotional engagement in the game to a greater or lesser degree. It also means passing up a superb opportunity for increasing the player's emotional immersion in the game.

Role Induction and First-Person Character Arcs (see the next chapter) are two of the biggest hurdles in game design. Games that conquer these challenges and that also offer intoxicating gameplay will become signature fixtures in the next generation of games.

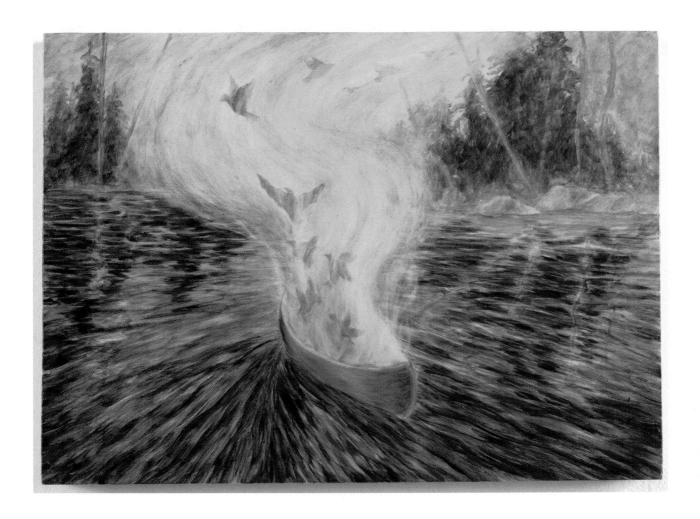

Emotioneering Techniques Category #20

First-Person

Character Arc
Techniques

Leave the player changed by your game.

This chapter focuses

on ways to induce a player to personally experience emotional growth and change during the course of a game.

In Chapter 2.9, "NPC Character Arc Techniques," we looked at ways to create emotional growth in an NPC. A *Character Arc*, as we discussed on Chapter 2.9, is the character's difficult path of growth through an emotional fear, limitation, block, or wound.

note

Refresher example: If a character grows from being and feeling like a nobody (his fear, limitation, block, or wound) into feeling like and being a leader, that's his Character Arc.

To create the experience of the player himself or herself undergoing personal change, however, requires quite different techniques—techniques that have no parallel in film or television.

If you succeed in creating a game that leads the player through personal growth, the game can be quite emotionally gripping. But how can you honestly lead a player through emotional change?

Defining the Problem

I think it's safe to say that if therapists struggle for years to transform people, we're not going to succeed in helping players expunge deep-seated emotional dysfunctions during the course of a game.

However, if we narrow the scope of our goals, there's a lot we can do. After all, on some level, don't we vicariously experience the emotional growth of those characters in films with whom we identify? And haven't all of us been affected, if not changed, by one of those experiences?

After experiencing films with characters who go through change and identifying with those characters, are we ourselves actually changed? For instance:

- Are we inspired to be more honest by watching Fletcher Reede (Jim Carrey) in *Liar Liar*?

- Are we galvanized to leave the safe and familiar and instead strike out to find our own path by watching Neo (Keanu Reeves) in *The Matrix*?

- Do we learn to be appreciative of the people around us by watching Phil Connors (Bill Murray) in *Groundhog Day*?

- Are we inspired to make decisions based on the greater good instead of our own selfish desires because of Rick Blaine's (Humphrey Bogart's) changes in *Casablanca*?

- Are we made more willing to courageously do the right thing by watching Frodo Baggins (Elijah Wood) take on the impossible in *Lord of the Rings*?

Well, hopefully, we're changed at least a bit. If these films don't encourage us or even motivate us to change, even a little, then a lot of screenwriters, directors, actors, and other talent have spent great amounts of effort in vain.

If our goal in games is no more or less ambitious than those of filmmakers, I think we can succeed.

Of course, we already have available to us the tools filmmakers use. We can create empathy for one or more characters (see Chapter 2.10, "NPC Rooting Interest Techniques"), and we can then have these characters undergo a Character Arc (see Chapter 2.9, "NPC Character Arc Techniques").

But we want to do more. We want the player himself or herself to undergo change directly—not just by empathizing with an NPC who changes.

Past Attempts to Create a First-Person Character Arc

Some games have taken on the challenge of having the player experience emotional growth of some sort (a Character Arc) by trying to give the player the most obvious Arc: to become courageous.

Assuming you're the player, this is done (or emulated) by your acquiring enhanced military skills or weapons as the game goes on. By the end, you can accomplish acts of daring-do that you couldn't accomplish at the start of the game. You're thus supposed to feel more powerful and courageous.

Does this work? Probably a little bit—and that's not bad. After all, as we've seen from this book, to create emotional experiences in games we should grab every tool and technique we've got, and use them whenever they're appropriate.

The game *Ico* tried another method to encourage the feeling that you've become powerful: by having the smoky demons who are such a threat in the beginning becoming afraid of you by the end, as if you've become quite intimidating to them.

Whereas early in the game these smoky demons are very aggressive, by the end, after you've gone through and triumphed over countless ordeals, these same demons practically flee every time you thrust out your weapon to kill them.

Does this method work? Sure, a bit. When I played the game, watching those smoke phantoms cower, I did feel somewhat smug and tough.

The player spends much of that game protecting a young and innocent girl. Did this leave me more willing to take responsibility for innocent people in real life? Yes, a bit—although perhaps someone else would have a different response.

To reprise the earlier idea, I think a game can change us about as much as a good film can change us. But films have traditionally been much more successful in this arena than have games.

I applaud every game that tries to take on the difficult challenge of creating a First-Person Character Arc. Hopefully, we'll see many interesting experiments in the future.

Still, there's a lot more that can be done...

Problems with Past Efforts

The problems with past efforts are several-fold:

- **To always have the player's First-Person Character Arc be "going from cowardly to courageous" is boring.** What about other kinds of Character Arcs?

- **The male character in *Ico* became powerful at the expense of making the girl weak.** In doing so, *Ico* alienated a potential demographic. Many of the women I know didn't like the game because the female character was so helpless. Even some guys I know found this to be an objectionably retro view of women.

- **When you have the player go on a journey from being cowardly or weak to being courageous, what if the player feels pretty courageous and powerful right from the start?** Then the player won't identify with the character he or she is playing, and this actually diminishes the player's emotional engagement in the game.

Some Exceptions

Silent Hill, *Resident Evil*, and *The Thing* all attempt to create fear in more complex ways (some much more successfully than others). In the context of games like these, having a player learn to be more courageous might make real sense and be a viable and emotionally charged First-Person Character Arc. That's because such games succeed to the degree that they create genuine fear. And if they create genuine fear, then that fear can be overcome. If they fail to create genuine fear, then it's impossible to have the player overcome that (nonexistent) fear.

There have to be other techniques to create a First-Person Character Arc than the limited ones used in the past. What are they?

Perhaps we designers should take the Character Arc of a person becoming more courageous and put it on a back shelf. That's because not only is it the obvious Arc, but, as in most games, if the player can die infinite times, it's hard to make a player afraid (cowardly), at least by the threat of death.

Emulating Life Itself

To see how to create change in a player, it's helpful to see what forces cause a person to change in real life.

In the course of your life, have you changed? I'll bet you're not the same person you were ten years ago. Sometimes what changes us is simply our ongoing observation of ourselves, of others, and of life. We study life and we grow.

More often then not, however, we're changed by a system of rewards and punishments. And this is just how you might do it in a game. What kinds of rewards and punishments are viable?

Applying This to a Hypothetical Game Case Study

Let's say that we want the player's Arc to be to learn to take responsibility for others. In the film *Schindler's List*, Liam Neeson's character, Oskar Schindler, went through such an Arc. He started off selfishly, but eventually grew. By the end, the most important value he held was to try and use his power to protect Jews who otherwise would be killed in a German concentration camp.

But would something like this work in a game? No. Schindler began the film from a point of being selfish, but we can't cause a gamer to begin a game as anything but how he or she actually is in life.

So let's start with that as a given: The player begins the game with the personality he or she has at that moment. We won't try to convince him or her to have some kind of personality flaw or limitation that he or she doesn't really have.

In the beginning of our hypothetical game, there'd be no benefits and no punishments for the player acting selfishly.

As the game progresses, however, there would be steadily increasing rewards if the player starts taking responsibility for others—and steadily increasing punishments if he or she doesn't.

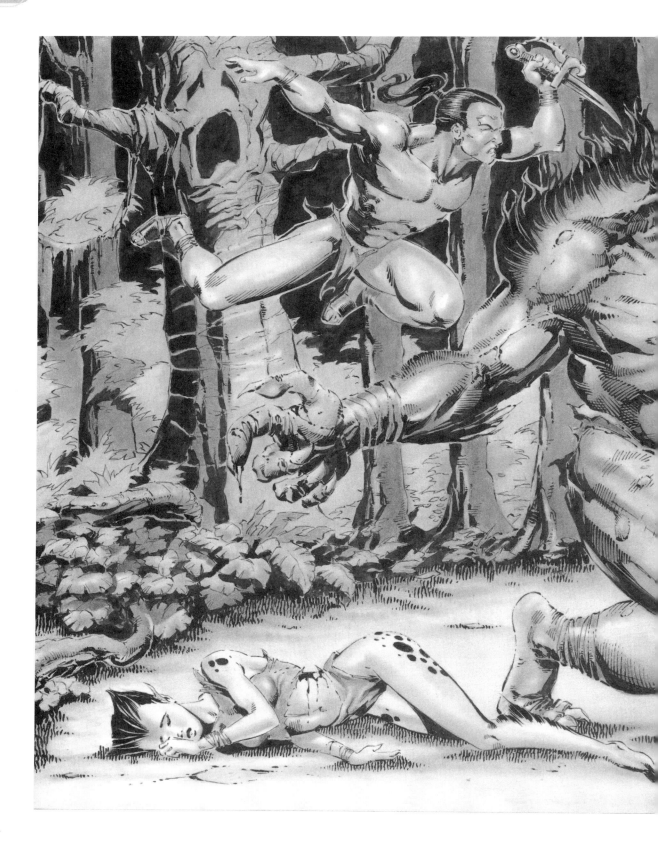

Another Hypothetical Game Case Study

We've seen the drawing on the preceding two pages before, in Chapter 2.15, "Emotionally Complex Moments and Situations Techniques."

There we discussed the powerlessness of the sentient trees to help the forest creatures that are being killed by the beast.

Let's expand upon the story. Let's say that, in the beginning of the game, the forest nymphs played impish tricks on you. They stole your weapons, mocked you, and, in general, annoyed the hell out of you, at least some of the time.

You probably wanted to kill a few yourself, and perhaps you did.

As the game progresses, however, you start to empathize with these characters. They are helpless before the beast (the one you're attacking in the preceding drawing) who kills them regularly.

During the game, you get to know them and see the emotional devastation they feel when one of their own is killed. You also come to learn they have a beautiful, though simple, culture—one that is quite endearing.

So, bonding with them would be one incentive to start to take responsibility for them. (The bonding would be caused by the use of the NPC Rooting Interest Techniques, discussed in Chapter 2.10.)

As mentioned earlier, however, there could also be some very concrete rewards for taking responsibility for them:

+ Perhaps, once they begin to trust you, they start showing you shortcuts through the dense forest.

+ Maybe they give you a magical implement or power that can help you traverse through the dense undergrowth at incredible speed.

+ Perhaps they teach you how to extend your "sentient net" through the forest, so you can feel and locate any living creature walking though the forest—including your enemies. In short, you can feel and know everything that, collectively, the creatures and trees of the forest feel and know.

+ Maybe they come to your aid and fight to protect you when you're faced with enemies.

In other words, the more responsibility you take for them, the more rewards you gradually receive.

The Role of Punishments

Punishments are also an option, if you don't go through your Arc. For instance, if you don't start helping the forest nymphs or if you start killing them, they could punish you:

- They steal your weapons.

- They whistle and alert your enemies when you're trying to sneak through the forest.

- They could even attack you in great numbers and injure you. Or, if you've been particularly vicious to some of them, they might kill you.

You would be induced to take responsibility for the nymphs by:

- Having empathy for the forest nymphs due to NPC Rooting Interest Techniques (see Chapter 2.10).

- Increasingly being offered rewards and punishments that guide your behavior.

Of course, had the beings for which you were taking responsibility been human and not forest nymphs, or if we made them more human-like, we could employ yet another Emotioneering tool: You could have chemistry with one or two of the people, using techniques explored in Chapter 2.11, "Player Toward NPC Chemistry Techniques."

Would This Character Arc Be Real?

Would you exit the game really having come to feel more responsible?

I think the answer is yes—you'd be changed at least as much as a film could create a change in you. After all, what we've done in the game is exactly emulate life and induce change the way life does.

Should Going Through a First-Person Character Arc Be Essential to Winning a Game?

You could debate this question back and forth, and undoubtedly score valid points for each point of view.

There's no right answer, just preferences. My preference would be that you should still be able to have a lot of fun and win the game even if you don't go through the intended First-Person Character Arc.

That is, even if you don't help the forest nymphs, you could still win the game. It would just be lot tougher and not as fun.

Perhaps we'd draw the line at murder. If you killed more than three of them, you couldn't win the game.

Again, these are just preferences. The game could be designed in many other ways.

Various Types of Rewards and Punishments

Life doles out all sorts of rewards and punishments, and games can too.

Consider a small list of some of the types of rewards a player could receive for moving through a First-Person Character Arc. To create a punishment, just deny the player these things, or make the player lose them (or diminish them) if he or she already has them.

Rewards Type 1

The first type of rewards are those that help you win the game. For example, you could be rewarded with *allies*, people who join your side or who work harder to help you. With enough allies behind you, you may even become their leader.

Another common reward is *increased abilities*. These could be more speed, accuracy, power, or other forms of effectiveness at skills that you already possess, such as:

+ Fighting (by hand or by weapon)
+ Stealth
+ Thieving
+ Manipulating objects
+ Ways you can traverse the landscape or buildings
+ Summoning spirits
+ Various magical abilities
+ Defensive abilities, such as protective spells

You could also gain:

+ Extra lives
+ Extra time on your mission
+ The ability to unlock new content
+ The ability to read people's minds

- The ability to change your face, body, or clothes
- The ability to slow, speed up, or change time

This list could go on forever, but you get the idea.

Items vital to your mission make good rewards. For example, you could receive:

- New weapons, armor, or spells, offensive or defensive
- Money (to buy weapons, etc.)
- Other items you can trade for weapons, spells, etc.
- A better vehicle

Finally, *various types of power-ups* are rewards that can also help you win the game.

Rewards Type 2

There are other rewards that are great to receive but that don't directly assist you in winning the game. For example, you could receive:

- Furnishings for your house/cave/castle/lodging, if you have one

- Access to special events or rituals

- Admiration from those around you or those who you meet who've heard of your reputation

This list is far from comprehensive. It's simply to suggest the range of possible ways to reward a player.

Where a First-Person Character Arc Begins

Rewards can direct a player along a Character Arc, but how do we start off that player's First-Person Character Arc?

In a film, a character who undergoes an Arc usually begins from the opposite end of the spectrum. Thus, someone who will end up being responsible will usually start off by being selfish. As I mentioned earlier, Liam Neeson's character, Schindler, undergoes such a Character Arc in Steven Spielberg's *Schindler's List*. But, you can't do this in games. You can't make the person playing the game any more or less selfish than they actually are at the start of the game.

I've seen games where the player is supposed to identify with a character who has a fear, limitation, block, or wound that he or she doesn't have in real life (such as being a coward, for instance), and it doesn't work. In fact, instead of encouraging emotional immersion, it distances the player from the game, for the player won't identify with the role. It would be the opposite of a Role Induction Technique. (For more on Role Induction Techniques, see Chapter 2.19.)

But there are some workarounds. For example, although you don't possess a particular flaw (let's say you're not particularly selfish), others could still see you with this flaw because of a misconception. By the end of the game, other characters would no longer see you as selfish. Of course, this isn't a genuine First-Person Character Arc, because it's more about changing the view of other characters about you, rather than about you yourself changing.

Still, this kind of solution has uses in certain scenarios.

Alternative Character Arcs

The subject of exactly which Character Arcs are possible in a game is one of those vast topics that goes beyond the scope of this book. There are many viable and interesting ones. We've already discussed two:

- ◆ To become courageous
- ◆ To become responsible for another or others

Here are few more.

To Become a Leader

For instance, your character could start out as a grunt, a no-account, and get rewarded for each act of decisiveness. A leader needs followers, and so you'd acquire followers as you move through your Character Arc.

To Learn You Are Worthy of Love

You start out hated. Your father had been ruthless, but your acts of heroism and goodness are rewarded to the point where you become the most beloved person in the land.

To Achieve a Spiritual Connection to the World

You probably can't try for a more challenging First-Person Character Arc than this. After all, do we dare suppose that you can give a spiritual experience to a player?

Yet it must be possible, for it occurs in films like *Crouching Tiger Hidden Dragon* and *The Karate Kid*. Some people might even put the films of the *Lord of the Rings* trilogy in that camp or the film *Phenomenon*.

Here are few potential approaches. In all of them, you start out just as you are. You are rewarded, however, for:

- Noticing minute variations in nature
- Mastering your sword in an increasingly aesthetic way
- Making tough choices wisely
- Gaining increasingly rigorous ethics
- Doing anything else we consider spiritual

The rewards themselves would have to have a spiritual quality to them, such as:

- The ability to see the life force pulsing inside of people and trees
- The ability to hear the voice of your loved one on the wind, from a hundred miles away

Of course, some might argue that these abilities and rewards might seem interesting (or magical) but not have a spiritual quality at all. It's all in the execution. For example, *Crouching Tiger Hidden Dragon* could have been completely lacking in spiritual overtones in the hands of a lesser writer and director.

Also, the spiritual overtones in the game wouldn't just come from the experiences that lead to spirituality or in the particular rewards, but in the linking of these two.

To Learn Ethics

You start out as a pirate, out for only yourself, but you receive increasing incentives (rewards and punishments) that guide you to make ethical choices—including eventually, perhaps, turning on the pirates you used to travel with and who've hurt or killed many innocents.

Final Thoughts

Is it critical that every game with a story try and create a First-Person Character Arc? Of course not.

It does, however, represent one of the forward edges of Emotioneering. The rewards for succeeding in making a First-Person Character Arc work are great, but the risks for failing can be serious. You could create a Character Arc that the player doesn't go along with in his or her heart. If that's the case, the player will feel emotionally distanced from the game instead of feeling more involved.

But, if you want to be part of the cutting edge of game design, step right up and take your best shot.

Emotioneering Techniques Category #21

First-Person Deepening Techniques

Making the player reach inside.

This chapter focuses
on ways to make a game player explore and perhaps even enhance his or her own emotional depth.

In this book, we've looked at ways to give emotional depth to an NPC (Chapter 2.1), even if the NPC has just one line of dialogue in the entire game (Chapter 2.4).

Although the ambitions of this chapter seem outrageous—to give greater depth to the player—it can be done. As with the Chapter 2.20, "First-Person Character Arc Techniques," here we will take our cues from life itself.

What causes people to gain emotional depth in life? As you will see in the sections that follow, the answers lead us to the techniques that will work in games.

Emotionally and/or Morally Difficult Decisions

Many games offer the player a wealth of strategic choices, often on a moment-by-moment basis. These can be a fun form of gameplay, but they don't cause the player to become a deeper person.

Here we're talking about Emotionally and/or Morally Difficult Decisions. The choices should not be easy.

You could find yourself with an infinite number of tough decisions when playing a game.

For instance, do you save your best friend—or the villagers who have come to need you for protection?

Another example: The villain has captured your sister. To free her, you'll have to run a mission for the villain, a mission that may result in hurting an old man—the very man who trained you in the martial arts you now possess. What choice will you make?

Hypothetical Game Case Study

Woman from the Future

Take a look at the color picture on page 4.

In this game, you play a character who is merely a guard—a guard, however, in a top-secret facility researching time travel.

Everyone there treats you like dirt, except one guy named Byron. He works for the Secret Service. Byron treats you well, because, as he says, he knows the only difference between you and him is the agency who issued you the gun and the badge. To him, you're both in law enforcement and, therefore, colleagues.

He's more than just respectful; he's actually a friend. When he sees you treated dismissively by one of the top scientists, he verbally defends you and berates the man.

And then, one day, there's a knock on your door. It's this desperate young woman, Dani (the one in the picture).

She tells you that she came from the future—three years in the future—and that she works on the same time-travel project that you currently help protect. By that point in the future, she tells you, the time travel project has succeeded. She knows, for she's the very first time-traveler.

Dani says she was just a secretary in the facility. On the day of the first time travel experiment with a human being, the time flyer—the man who had trained for months for the first time jump—shoved her into the device just as it was activated. The next thing she knows, she was sent back three years to your time period.

She has no idea why the time flyer shoved her into the device. Had he flipped out? Was it intentional? Is she a victim in some conspiracy?

Worse still, there's a man, right now, in this day and age, trying to kill her. She just escaped with her life from a close call.

Things get more complicated. The two of you look up Dani's younger self, in this time period—and she doesn't seem to exist. She doesn't live at the apartment that Dani claims she lived in during this time, and there are no records of Dani at any of the jobs or schools she claims to have attended.

Dani gets progressively more distraught and freaked out by these unfolding events. Someone has erased her from history.

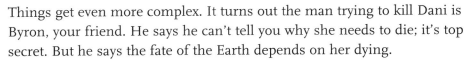

Things get even more complex. It turns out the man trying to kill Dani is Byron, your friend. He says he can't tell you why she needs to die; it's top secret. But he says the fate of the Earth depends on her dying.

Who will you believe? Dani, who you don't know but who seems sincere, or Byron, your friend, who seems equally sincere and anxious that Dani be killed for the sake of mankind?

It's a tough choice. No matter which choice you make, it will be a First-Person Deepening experience.[1]

---

1. This kind of choice brings up the problem of the potentially high cost of building assets to support a branching story-line. Some solutions are offered in just a few pages.

Another Example of Technique Stacking

By the way, the preceding scenario also uses a few other Emotioneering Techniques discussed earlier in the book, providing a good example of Technique Stacking.

- Because Dani is in danger, we empathize with her. That's an NPC Rooting Interest Technique (Chapter 2.10).

- She's confused and afraid, and these emotions give her depth. They're NPC Deepening Techniques (Chapter 2.2).

- Because you'll end up helping her (taking responsibility), you'll feel chemistry with her. That's a Player Toward NPC Chemistry Technique (Chapter 2.11).

- Because you take responsibility for her, you, the player, become a deeper person. That's another First-Person Deepening Technique, and we'll get to that a little later in this chapter.

In an ideal world, everything would flow exactly as written in the game with you and Dani. However, there are four challenges that make it difficult to pull off.

Problem #1: One Choice Seems Better than the Other

It's not much of an emotional choice or even a difficult choice if saving Dani is the clearly appealing selection.

The solution is to make the choice a bit more complicated. Therefore, we've got to make Byron a very good and believable guy, and make Dani's story questionable and perhaps make her not overly likable, at least at this point of the game. In short, we'll adjust both of their Rooting Interest Dials (see Chapter 2.10) until the choice is difficult to make.

Also, Byron can tell you that if he doesn't catch Dani, he'll be killed by his own superiors. He wasn't supposed to know anything about this time travel project with Dani, and now he's considered to know too much. His superiors see him as a liability—unless he proves himself by bringing Dani in. You get evidence that supports his story, so you know it's true.

Thus, making the choice as to whom to help is complicated by the harm that will befall Byron.

Problem #2: Save Points Mitigate the Emotion of Making a Tough Choice

If you can just save the game at the point where you need to decide whether to help Byron or Dani, then the choice doesn't matter. Your player can explore one option, and then return to the save point and explore the other.

Thus, there's nothing emotional about making the decision—and certainly nothing that would cause you to become deeper the way tough decisions cause us to become deeper in real life.

- **Solution #1.** Give the player a save point a few minutes earlier, before the decision point. That way, there are some consequences to the decision and the player will think more seriously about it.

   Of course, this requires a balancing act and some serious game testing before shipping. If the save point isn't back far enough, then it hardly makes a difference. If it's too far back, then the player will get frustrated and angry at the game.

- **Solution #2.** This is the more interesting solution: Make neither choice completely wrong or right. For instance, if you choose to save Dani, Byron will end up getting killed. There can be other bad consequences as well.

   If you don't save Dani, she'll get captured and incarcerated in a cell in a special location. But maybe, to handle this new threat, a man named Richard Hutton, who you suspect is evil, is put in charge of the time travel project, with some kind dire consequences resulting (explained a little later in this section).

But, there's still another problem.

Problem #3: This Scenario Means You Need to Build Assets for Two Different Paths

This problem is one of the key considerations that scare game designers away from forking paths in a game (multi-path structure). "Why build assets that many players won't see?" designers rightly ask. And they readily point out that the money you spend on these potentially unseen assets could have been better used if spent on other areas of the game that all the players will encounter.

When designers use a multi-path structure, the most common approach is for the game's path to fork for just a short period, and then for the paths to rejoin into a single route through the game.

This can be a satisfactory compromise, except (as frequently occurs) when there is *little or no plot consequences nor emotional consequences* as to what choice you make. And the truth is that, in many games that have offered sections of multi-path structure, no matter which path you take, it doesn't really make much of a difference.

How could we build not just plot consequences, but emotional consequences into our game about Dani, even if the path branches for just a short time?

Let's say you believe Byron and don't help Dani. Dani tries to escape into the time travel chamber. She's caught, but before she's apprehended, she accidentally does something that slightly alters the time stream.

Suddenly, a second security guard at the installation, who was a friend of yours, disappears into thin air. Whatever Dani accidentally did, in this new time-line, your friend has never been born. If *you sincerely liked him*, this would be an emotional consequence. As a result of this mishap, the head of the time travel project is dismissed and Richard Hutton, the evil man mentioned earlier, is put in charge.

Let's say you took the other path and decided to help Dani, and not help Byron. Then, as mentioned earlier, Dani's escape will lead to Richard Hutton being put in charge of the time travel project, and he'll blame Byron, who knows too much and who, in his opinion, has screwed up big time. Byron, therefore, will be killed by Hutton. Because he's someone you liked, you'll feel his loss.

Then the two paths come together again.

No matter which path you choose, we need to arrange it so that (1) your friend, the guard, is out of the game, and (2) so is Byron. Furthermore, (3) you need to end up with Dani, and (4) Richard Hutton needs to end up in charge of the time travel project.

We've already shown how Hutton could come to power in both scenarios. But how do we make sure the other three points are accomplished in both paths?

Let's say you help Byron, and as a result, Dani gets captured. We know the guard will disappear in the time-travel mishap Dani causes in her escape attempt. But how can we get rid of Byron now and make sure you end up with Dani? In this path, you'll discover Byron is part of an evil conspiracy, secretly in league with Hutton, and that Dani is innocent. You'll need to rescue Dani, and you'll kill Byron in the process.

note

The fact that the two paths come back together in a fairly short period of time means that giving the player the decision as to whom he or she will side with doesn't add significantly to the cost of the game.

Even still, giving the player choices like this does add some cost, so it's likely that, if you're keeping an eye on the game's bottom line, it's probably not a technique you'll want to employ frequently.

That having been said, Ion Storm, headed by Warren Spector with project direction by Harvey Smith, is perhaps the company most dedicated to having all sorts of short- and long-term consequences linked to a multitude of decisions made by the player. At the time that this book is being completed, *Deus Ex: Invisible War* hasn't yet been released. But rumor has it that the designers and programmers there are trying to take the entire issue of consequences for player decisions to levels of sophisticated repercussions never before attempted in a game. I've peaked at the software they created to track player decisions, and it's daunting.

Making decisions with meaningful emotional and moral consequences is probably one of the things the game will be known for, and this factor will likely serve as one of the key reasons players will buy it. My guess is that the folks at Ion Storm are trying to create a game that will entice players to go through it multiple times, experimenting with different modes of playing and making different choices at the numerous decision points.

So, all three of our remaining conditions are met.

Let's say that you side with Dani from the start. We already know that Byron will get killed by Hutton. The guard can get a promotion and say goodbye. So, once again, all the conditions are met.

So, no matter which fork you take, you're soon back onto a single path, with both Byron gone and the guard gone too. Furthermore, Hutton is in charge of the time travel project, and you're on the run with Dani.

Problem #4: There Are No Long-Term Consequences in the Game

Of all the problems, this last one is by far the least important. If the other three problems are addressed, then the player will undergo the First-Person Deepening experience we're intending.

However, if we want to be even more artful, it would be good to have some long-term consequences to the choice, even if they're not particularly emotional ones, for it makes the player feel like his or her decisions matter in the game.

The key is to make any long-term consequences not cost too much time (and therefore money) in terms of programming or building assets.

Here are some samples of possible long-term consequences for our example:

1. If you chose to help Byron, then Dani's failed attempt to travel in time could change the time-line and suddenly half the trees in the city could disappear—and never come back.

2. If you choose to help Byron, and your fellow guard gets a promotion, then someone could refer to having seen that guard in his new job later in the game.

3. If you choose to help Byron and then end up killing him, you could later run into a friend of his who has some pretty hostile things to say to you.

None of these would cost a lot of money or time to integrate into the game.

Case Study Summary

Let's recap the key points of this example:

- In a branching path, the decision as to which path to follow should be strategically and emotionally difficult, if it is to cause a First-Person Deepening Experience.

- There should be both plot and emotional consequences to the decision, at least in the short run.

- Ideally, the decisions should have some long-term consequences, even if they're not particularly emotional (although that would be preferable). It's important for the player to feel his or her choices matter.

Linking actions to consequences also helps connect one part of the game to another. It's a Cohesiveness Technique, as you'll see in Chapter 2.26.

To further illustrate the technique we've been exploring, let's take a look at another example game that involves the First-Person Deepening Technique of thrusting the player into an Emotionally and/or Morally Difficult Decision.

note

The bottom line in our example with Dani is that it's a First-Person Deepening type of choice because it involves an Emotionally and/or Morally Difficult Decision. By contrast, most choices in games don't promote First-Person Deepening because they're simply strategic; they're not difficult to make due to emotional or moral reasons. A strategic choice would be, for example, whether to use firepower or stealth to accomplish a mission, or deciding which weapon to use.

Hypothetical Game Case Study

Choice of Player Character

In this game, the plot is unimportant to our purposes.

What is important is that you have a choice in the character you play. You can select either the brother or the sister in the illustration. Furthermore, you can play either of them in their human form, or in their demonic form. Pre-game, you choose to be either the brother or the sister. Once that choice is made, during the game itself you can switch between human and demonic forms at will.

But there are tradeoffs. Obviously, each character will have different abilities when they're in their human form than when in their demonic form. But, in games, characters who look different having different abilities is nothing new; this is standard in just about every game in which you can choose to play a variety of characters.

The real tradeoff is this: If you play either character in their human form, people (NPCs) find you charismatic. They help you in numerous ways.

In your demonic form, even your friends are afraid of you. People either flee from you or try and impede you. No one helps you. In that form, however, you're much more powerful.

Which form will you assume, or will you alternate? These are tough decisions. It's a First-Person Deepening Technique.

A Problem with This Idea—and a Solution

You could argue that this is no different than a standard RPG (role-playing game) in that each character has different skills and abilities, and the decision whether to be human or demonic is simply a tactical one. Therefore, there's no emotion involved—and making the decision about which character to play wouldn't generate any kind of depth on the part of the player.

This argument could be 100% correct. The solution would involve how emotionally painful it is to have ones closest friends fear you and shun you when you take a demonic form. *Only* if you like these other NPCs and hate it when they turn away from you would the decision as to which form to choose be emotionally difficult and thus be a First-Person Deepening Technique.

Therefore, the game will have to have been Emotioneered in such a way that you really like your friends and feel bonded to them. This means that NPC Rooting Interest Techniques (see Chapter 2.10) and Player Toward NPC Chemistry Techniques (see Chapter 2.11) must be artfully employed.

Hypothetical Game Case Study

The Kidnapped Teenager

Take a look at the color picture on page 5.

In this game, you play Terrence Sloan, a special-forces operative. As your best friend, James, dies in battle, he asks that you look after his 16-year-old daughter Corrina.

When you meet her, she's distraught over her father's death, but also alienated and unhappy in life. She's a withdrawn misfit.

She's kidnapped by the creatures of Shadowland, a world that can only be entered between twilight and night. The inhabitants there are fairies and other mythical creatures. They didn't always live in Shadowland; they fled there as the ranks of mankind swelled and forced them out of our realm.

When you come upon Corrina, she doesn't remember you, her father, or her prior existence. Though she was a gloomy misfit in her former life, here she fits right in. In fact, her mind and soul are now threaded into this world and have brought it new life. She's a sort of empress here.

Of course, because she doesn't remember anyone or anything from her past, she doesn't want to come with you back to your world.

You have a tough choice:

- Will you leave her from this world where she's happy and has a purpose, but where her memory has been erased?

- Or, will you bring her back to a world where grief and alienation await her...but also the chance to grow through those problems and become who she's meant to be (by normal standards, anyway)?

There may not be a right or wrong choice, but wrestling with it will make the player face some potentially deep issues.

Technique Summary

Although giving a player Emotionally and/or Morally Difficult Decisions is just one of many First-Person Deepening Techniques, it's among the most difficult to achieve. That's because it implies a splitting of the path the player is taking, and that, in turn, means building assets that at least some of the players won't see (unless they play the game again and take the alternative path).

So while it might be easy to theoretically design and build tough decisions for the player to make, it's very difficult to build in meaningful choices like this that result in First-Person Deepening and still do it cost-effectively.

As pointed out earlier in this chapter, one solution is to have the player's choice result in meaningful short-term consequences, combined with some long-term consequences that don't cost much to implement.

The obvious question is: Is it worth it? Of course it depends on the game, but if this technique is employed in a cost-effective way, then I feel it certainly enhances the emotional depth of the game.[2]

Responsibility

Think of your own life. Do you now take responsibility for any things or people who weren't in your circle of responsibility when you were younger? Hasn't assuming those responsibilities—especially the ones for which you willingly volunteered for—made you a deeper person?

This isn't just an accidental phenomenon. Responsibility can promote depth because, to truly take responsibility for another, you must, to a lesser or greater degree, understand that person—who they are, their needs, their dreams. You need to expand beyond your own viewpoint and see the world they way they do. This causes depth.

Things can get even more complex. Take a parenting dilemma, for instance: You might see things from your children's point of view, but

---

2. The painting on the cover of this book depicts a hypothetical game in which the player also faces a First-Person Deepening type of choice, because it is emotionally and/or morally difficult to make. That choice is for the player to either (1) try to rescue the young woman while simultaneously fighting off the alien creatures, or (2) drop her so as to have both hands free to fire weapons and better save himself. How to offer the player this choice in a way that doesn't require the building of many new assets, and which is therefore cost-effective—while still having consequences within the game—is examined in Chapter 5.3, "Gatherings."

also see things from your own point of view. That means there might be aspects to the situations they face, or aspects of themselves, that you see clearly but that they don't see at all.

What can turn this broadened insight into a dilemma is when you know that the best thing to do is *not* intervene in a painful or tough situation they're facing and let them learn for themselves, even when your wisdom could save them misery.

So responsibility doesn't always mean solving someone else's problems. It might mean seeing that what they need is to solve their own problems, even if you love them and it kills you inside to see them suffer, when you could so easily whisk away their pain.

Responsibility makes us expand. We have to be ourselves, but on some level, be another or others as well. Thus, it makes us deeper.

When a game causes us to take responsibility for another, that also gives us depth. By "causes us," I don't mean that a game should *force* us to take responsibility. In games where it's relevant, I believe it's better to provide incentives for the player to take responsibility for NPCs, for a culture, for a planet, or for something else.

The player can be incentivized to take responsibility for NPCs by using techniques covered in various chapters in this book, such as:

- Empathizing with them (Chapter 2.10, "NPC Rooting Interest Techniques")

- Having chemistry with them (Chapter 2.11, "Player Toward NPC Chemistry Techniques")

- Bonding with them as a group (Chapter 2.14, "Group Bonding Techniques")

When you play chess, you have responsibility to protect your king. But playing chess doesn't make you a deeper person. First-Person Deepening results from taking responsibility for people, organizations, species, and things that we care about. This is why, for taking responsibility to cause a player to become deeper, the technique requires some of the other Emotioneering techniques to also be used, to bring about caring.

Hypothetical Game Case Study

The Terrellens

Parts of the planet Jaan are inhabited by the peaceful Terrellen, the planet's natives, while other parts of the planet have been leased by the Terrellen to human mining colonies. You're an anthropologist, here on a cultural exchange. You report, however, to the USIDF—the United States Interplanetary Defense Force. That's because you might be an anthropologist, but you're also a colonel in the USIDF. Before becoming an anthropologist, you were an experienced tactician and commander (trained in these skills earlier in the game).

Here's a bit about the Terrellens:

- **They love athletic competitions, and have a refined code of sportsmanship.** It is so developed that it's almost a code of life to live by.

- **Families are very important, and are run democratically.** At nine years old, each child undergoes a ceremony that changes their status within the family. From that point on, the child is a full member of the household with an equal vote.

- **Their religion is attributed to Tylaan, a figure who appeared 4000 years ago, bringing wise religious precepts.** They say he wasn't from this planet, but is immortal and was incarnated in a Terrellen body to bring truth. The Terrellen, upon learning about Jesus from humans, assume that Tylaan had been Jesus on Earth, and no amount of argument can convince them that the two men aren't the same.

- **Because they thought of Tylaan as a stranger visiting their world, they've always honored strangers.** This is why they've been so kind and generous to you. They've provided you food and lodging, and have even started teaching you some minor mystical abilities that they've mastered. This generosity toward strangers is also why they've allowed humans to mine their planet.

The planet gets attention when small amounts of Mitro3 are found in the mining camp. When super-cooled, this metal emits anti-gravity waves. Thus, it's the most coveted metal in the universe, for it can power space ships.

Suddenly, the mining camps are swarmed with American military, who want to seize all the Mitro3. Then much vaster quantities of Mitro3 are discovered in the sections of the planet inhabited by the Terrellens.

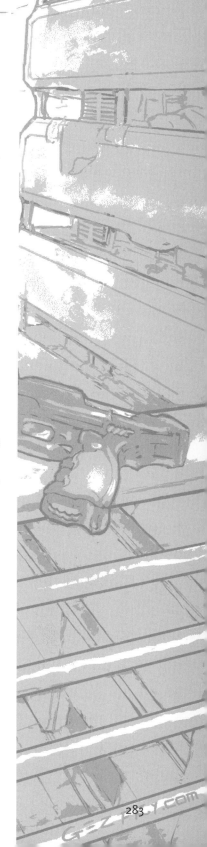

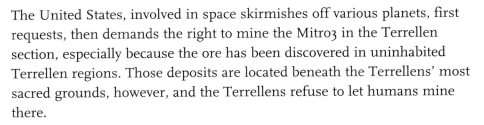

The United States, involved in space skirmishes off various planets, first requests, then demands the right to mine the Mitro3 in the Terrellen section, especially because the ore has been discovered in uninhabited Terrellen regions. Those deposits are located beneath the Terrellens' most sacred grounds, however, and the Terrellens refuse to let humans mine there.

The Terrellens haven't fought a war in 4000 years. Only one person can lead them to defend themselves—and that's you, because you have military and tactical knowledge they lack. Will you take the job?

Giving a Face to a Group

Everything's fine with the preceding scenario, except one thing:

It's hard to identify with or care about a group, unless we specifically care about *one or a few individuals in that group.*

So we'd need to come to know and love or admire a few specific, individual Terrellens. Then you'll care about the group and be willing to help them (take responsibility for them). If you freely elected to do so because you know them and care about them, this would be a deepening experience.

Of course, if the Americans *really* need that Mitro3 because they are losing a space war and Earth itself is endangered, then we add another First-Person Deepening technique into the equation: giving the player a tough choice.

Multiple and Sometimes Even Conflicting Viewpoints (Learning from Mr. Bill)

First-Person Deepening also comes when a game player experiences multiple and sometimes even conflicting viewpoints of a subject, event, situation, person, group, plan, object, or aspect of life that the player cares about—or that matters to at least one NPC whom the player cares about or identifies with because of the character's Rooting Interest.

"Multiple Viewpoints" vs. "Idea Mapping"

Earlier I mentioned that some techniques fall into more than one category. Taking responsibility is a prime example, and Multiple Viewpoints is another. The technique results in not only depth in the player, but also in the plot. That's why it's also a Plot Deepening Technique (see Chapter 2.17). It was discussed in that chapter, but from the point of view of the plot, not the player. There I referred to it as *Idea Mapping*.

There can be some slight differences, though. For instance, you could see a revolution as good at one point in a game, and see the same revolution as bad at another point in the game. Used that way, Idea Mapping would be the same as Multiple Viewpoints and would be not just a Plot Deepening Technique but a First-Person Deepening Technique as well. You're moved through different viewpoints on a subject.

However, Idea Mapping can also mean that we simply look at a subject's facets like facets of a diamond. If the subject is heroes, we can see an unlikely hero, a stupid hero, a fallen hero, a person who becomes heroic to seek redemption for a past sin, and so on.

In such a case, the player doesn't change viewpoints and become a deeper person, but the plot certainly is deepened through the exploration of a topic. Thus, this form of Idea Mapping would be a Plot Deepening Technique but not a First-Person Deepening Technique.

In a nutshell, different viewpoints generate First-Person Deepening when they force us to wrestle with the complexities of life or of a subject that matters to us—or that matters to at least one NPC whom we care about and with whom we identify because of that character's Rooting Interest.

If you simply look at different aspects of a subject (such as "friendship") but don't wrestle with any moral or emotional complexities regarding the subject, then it's Idea Mapping, which is a Plot Deepening Technique (but not a First-Person Deepening Technique).

In Shakespeare's *A Midsummer's Night Dream*, we witness many forms of love by watching the adventures and misadventures of many matched and mismatched couples. We see:

- The formal and stately love between two people from noble roots, Theseus and Hippolyta.

- Love used as a weapon, as Titania, the queen of the fairies, feigns love for a young boy to make Oberan, the king of the fairies, jealous.

- The arranged marriage (which never comes to be) between Hermia and Demetrius.

- The passionate eloping young couple, Hermia and Lysander.

- The unrequited love of Hermia for Demetrius.

- The foolish crush of Titania, queen of the fairies, on Bottom, a workman who's been transformed into possessing the head of an ass.

- At the end of the play, we experience the seasoned love between Oberan and Titania. What it lacks in newness and raw passion, it makes up for in familiarity and comfort.

That's love seen from a lot of angles. It takes a very wise (deep) person to write such a play, and we become deeper from experiencing his own rich vision.

Seeing a subject such as love from different points of view makes us deeper. This technique can work in a game just as well.

note

This note picks up where the previous note left off. Is Shakespeare's showing us different ways people can love a form of Idea Mapping that actually moves us through multiple viewpoints and, thus, is also a First-Person Deepening Technique? Or is it merely looking at love's different facets, but it doesn't leave us deeper (and thus would be a form of Idea Mapping that creates Plot Deepening but not First-Person Deepening)?

This Shakespeare example shows it might take some reflection to distinguish these two related techniques. However, remember that First-Person Deepening results when we're forced to wrestle with the complexities of life or of a subject that matters to us—or that matters to at least one NPC whom we care about and with whom we identify because of that character's Rooting Interest. Based on this, I think it's clear that the Idea Mapping in *A Midsummer's Night Dream* also generates First-Person Deepening.

By contrast, let's say that, in the play, we looked only at:

- The love of a mother for her child
- Love between two teenagers
- The love of a shepherd for his flock

Then we'd be looking at different facets of love without looking at multiple and sometimes even conflicting viewpoints of love. This example of Idea Mapping would result in Plot Deepening but *not* in First-Person Deepening, for we'd see different facets of love, but we wouldn't be forced to wrestle with love's complexities.

Hypothetical Game Case Study

Return to the Terrellens

Let's go back to our game where you're defending the Terrellens against the American military.

Earlier I had asked, what if the American military wants the Mitro3 for a very good reason: to stop an entirely different alien enemy who is heading for Earth?

So let's say you join forces first with the Terrellens, and later with the Americans, for now you're seeing more of the big picture. That is, at first you want to stop the U.S. military from destroying their sacred sites for Mitro3. And then, seeing more of the big picture and the threat to Earth, you side with the Americans to get that Mitro3. You can now see the issue equally from both sides. This is Multiple Viewpoints and it's a First-Person Deepening Technique.

Getting Even Fancier with This Technique

Could we explore, in the game, the subjects of loyalty and betrayal the way Shakespeare explored love in *A Midsummer's Night Dream*?

Sure we can. We start with the dilemma mentioned earlier: Should your loyalty be to the Americans, or to the Terrellens?

Also, we could, within the game, echo those same complex issues on a smaller scale. For instance, what if Shane, one of your military friends in the game, asked you to keep a secret—that he's addicted to senn, a serious drug. He's afraid if you tell his superiors, he'll be expelled from his military unit.

But, to save Shane, you're forced to betray him and rat him out. As a result, he is expelled from the military, but his life is saved. Depending on how we want the game to play out, he might or might not mature to the point where he sees that you were helping him.

In exposing Shane's addiction, were you being a loyal friend, or were you betraying him?

If, during the game, we see still more facets of loyalty and betrayal in a way that makes us wrestle with these issues then, by the end, we will have become deeper in the process.

note

By the way, when you have a subplot (like the question of what way you can best be loyal to Shane) that echoes the main plot (choosing your loyalties among the Terrellens and the U.S. military), this is a Plot Deepening Technique.

Another Way of Using Different Ways of Using Multiple Viewpoints to Create First-Person Deepening

This little section has just scratched the surface of what can be done by using Multiple Viewpoints. Another way to move a player through multiple and sometimes even conflicting viewpoints can be done by empathizing with several NPCs, all who have their own differing viewpoint of a subject, event, person, or plan.

Certain First-Person Character Arcs

Every First-Person Character Arc is also a First-Person Deepening Technique. The ability to grow emotionally and/or morally both gives a person depth and is evidence of their depth. At the very least, someone must have the depth to reflect upon his or her behavior and change it, sometimes bucking other impulses to refuse change and to stay the way they were.

A few Character Arcs, such as Learning to Take Responsibility for Others and Attaining Wisdom, have a bit more First-Person Deepening to them than the rest. How to accomplish a First-Person Character Arc of taking responsibility for others is detailed in the previous chapter. We'll look at Attaining Wisdom here.

One part of attaining wisdom is *coming to grips with emotionally complex consequences of your actions*. Consider an example.

Hypothetical Game Case Study

Returning to the City

In the game pictured on the previous page, you play the hero, the man re-entering the city. You find they've built a huge statue to you, and it, like the city itself, is in flames.

The city built a statue to you because the people there loved you. Previously in the game, they hid you and sheltered you when they found you heroically tried to liberate them from the dictator of the neighboring country, who had conquered them and oppressed them for the last 20 years.

And after you assassinated that dictator, you became their hero, and they built the statue (which you never knew about until just now).

After you killed the dictator, you didn't return to this city. Instead, the game had you do missions elsewhere in the country. What you didn't know, and what at this point in the game you're learning for the first time, is that the dictator's son took over where his father had left off. To punish this city for the aid they had earlier extended to you (at your request), the son destroyed the city and killed many of the people you knew and cared about.

Jarvis is the man who stands here waiting for you. You met him—and fought him—earlier in the game. He was the previous dictator's body-guard. However, the ruthlessness of the dictator's son disgusts him. Inspired by your own integrity, he has switched sides and now will help you in your effort to kill the son.

Jarvis has a spotted past because, before changing sides, he had killed some innocent people at the dictator's request. But you're in an emotion-ally complex situation (see Chapter 2.15) in that you'll need his help if you're to be victorious.

In summary, there have been some very emotionally complex conse-quences to your actions. A city you liked was destroyed; people you cared about were killed; and an evil man has been motivated by you to switch sides and now will help you accomplish great good. You will be left wiser and deeper. This is how the Character Arc of Attaining Wisdom can be a First-Person Deepening Technique.

Seeing Situations That Aren't Black and White

This next hypothetical game contains another example of coming to grips with emotionally complex consequences of your actions, as well as another component of the First-Person Character Arc of Attaining Wisdom.

However, we'll also look at another technique: *Seeing Situations That Aren't Black and White, and therefore require deep thought if you're to help those you care about.* You'll see that the technique of Seeing Situations That Aren't Black or White is closely related to the previous discussion of Multiple Viewpoints.

When you move a player, one way or another, through Multiple Viewpoints on an emotionally charged subject, this can be done in a way so that the player gradually comes to see that things are more complex than they first appeared—they aren't black or white. This is one of the fundamentals of wisdom: seeing the big picture.

Let's take a look how this could be used.

The game starts out with the player (you) in a situation that immediately looks clear cut. With no doubts that you are doing the right thing, you charge into the missions with a gung-ho Rambo-type of attitude about your rightness. To be a bit cliché, let's say you save a princess who has been kidnapped.

But then, as the game continues, it slowly becomes clear to you that you actually made the wrong assumptions to begin with. You discover that the princess is not all sweetness and light, and that the kidnappers were actually trying to put an end to her tyrannical reign.

And then, as the game goes on, further revelations change your view once again. You discover that the princess was forced into the position of ruling harshly because the kingdom she commanded needed to be delivered through a state of turmoil and unrest, which would have resulted in a full-out civil war if she hadn't ruled with an iron fist.

In fact, once you free the princess, civil war does erupt as parties that didn't want her ruling now rebel.

You would think, then, that by your returning the princess to her throne, all would be set right. But it isn't. The civil unrest is out of control—and the princess over-reacts with violence, further fanning the flames.

It is now up to you to fix this mess. You need to take down several war-lords who ignited the turmoil and are perpetuating it—even though they have some legitimate issues and aren't merely evil. Finally, you need to dethrone the princess herself and defeat her elite guard unit.

In short, after a series of what I call *Reveals*, you will see that:

1. The simplistic view of the situation that you used as a basis of your early decisions actually created a much worse situation than what was there to begin with.

2. All sides of the conflict have legitimate issues, and there's no one easy answer to the problems the kingdom faces.

3. In an effort to do the right thing, you brought about more harm than good, and thus created a situation that now you must fix.[3]

You, the player, will have grown wiser about the world as a result of the game. You will have learned that many issues in this game aren't black or white.

Final Thoughts

In this chapter, we looked at a number of ways to create First-Person Deepening:

+ Emotionally and/or Morally Difficult Decisions.

+ Responsibility. Responsibility could be something the player grows into, as part of a First-Person Character Arc, or something the player has from the start of the game (such as your responsibility for the young girl in *Ico*).

+ Multiple and sometimes even conflicting viewpoints of a subject, event, situation, person, group, plan, object, or aspect of life that you (the player) care about or that matters to at least one NPC whom you care about or identify with because of that character's Rooting Interest.

---

3. It should be mentioned that none of this story will have any emotional impact unless there is one or more people in the game who the player comes to really care about, and who are adversely affected by the degenerating condition in the kingdom brought about by the player's initial action in freeing the princess.

◆ Certain First-Person Character Arcs—specifically, Learning to Take Responsibility for others (mentioned earlier) and Attaining Wisdom. One common component of Attaining Wisdom is coming to grips with emotionally complex consequences of your actions.

◆ Learning that some situations aren't black and white, and therefore require deep thought if you're to help those you care about.

So, are games entertainment, or are they art? Obviously, like film, they're both. First-Person Deepening Techniques can help move games from being simply entertainment to also being art.

Let's define art as communication that operates on many levels and that brings us insight, complex emotional experiences, and potentially introduces us to new ways of seeing.

The *Lord of the Rings* films are entertaining because they're artful—they do all of the above. This, along with the thrills the films offer, is why audiences go to see them in droves.

When games become artful, they'll be more emotionally compelling and thus more entertaining. When applied artfully, First-Person Character Deepening Techniques can move a person emotionally with a power equivalent to a great film, but through experiences totally unique to games.

Emotioneering Techniques Category #22

Revealing Complex Characters Through Their Actions

Talk is cheap—and sometimes unnecessary.

This chapter focuses
on giving different facets to your characters, even if they have little or no dialogue in the entire game.

Sometimes you need to be able to portray a character—either a character you play or an NPC—as being multi-dimensional, even without dialogue. We've already seen how to do this when dialogue is used.

In previous chapters, we've talked at length about giving major NPCs a Character Diamond, which is a colorful combination of three to five Traits. (See Chapter 2.1, "NPC Interesting Techniques.")

We also looked at ways to get a player to identify with a role that has, as part of it, different Traits. (See Chapter 2.19, "Role Induction Techniques.")

One thing to keep in mind, whether the character is an NPC or one controlled by the player, is that the character's different facets or traits can sometimes be conveyed even without words.

This chapter doesn't contain techniques the way the other chapters do, but rather it focuses on applying principals learned elsewhere in the book to characters who don't speak or who rarely speak.

A Real Game Case Study

One of the games I worked on was Midway's *Gladiator—The Crimson Reign*. As sometimes happens in the game world, this game was cancelled before it was completed.

The game presented an interesting set of challenges. Consider just a few of them:

- I had to create ten different characters from the height of the Roman empire—seven men and three women. These characters would all be gladiators. Most would be forced against their will to fight, although a few would elect to do so for their own reasons.

- Each of these characters had to have unique personalities, quite distinct from one another. And each personality needed to be complex enough to intrigue a game player.

- Each character needed to be someone the gamer would want to play.

While the game afforded opportunities for some very interesting use of voice-over, there were very few opportunities for the characters to talk.

If I wanted to create Diamonds for each character, the challenges continued:

- If each character had three to five Traits, at least three of these Traits needed to be able to be expressed nonverbally.

- I had to repeat this for ten characters, and make each one of their clusters of personality Traits different from the other characters'.

- The characters came from all over the Roman Empire. Their Traits could not violate what might be possible within their culture. Hopefully, their Trait cluster could perhaps even shed light on their culture.

- If their Trait cluster was culturally based, it still couldn't be cliché. Their combinations of Traits needed to be colorful and fresh.

These seven requirements were a lot to pack in for ten different cultures, especially because most of the characters' personalities needed to be expressed nonverbally.

The challenge of creating these characters, and their Character Arcs, fell on my shoulders. However, the team, which was quite creatively adroit, quickly adopted my Emotioneering strategies and was able to make substantial contributions.

Khensa

I'd like to suggest we take a look at one of the *Gladiator* characters in detail, but there's not a lot I can say about the character of Khensa. It's not that there isn't much to talk about. Rather, if I discussed her in detail, I'd inadvertently summon a harrowing midnight attack by vampiric game lawyers who'd swarm my bedroom and mummify me, wrapping me tightly in thousands of strips of paper made from copies of the non-disclosure agreement I signed with Midway.

This fate wouldn't be so bad if they'd then follow through and stick me in a colossal pyramid that people would visit with slack-jawed awe for thousands of years. The last time I checked, however, creating monuments so huge that they're visible from the moon falls outside of Midway's current business plan. So I'll be a bit conservative about sharing information on Khensa.

In the game, Khensa comes from Egypt. She's 18 years old, the youngest of the characters. Khensa was an apprentice in the temple to Isis and hoped to be a priestess some day. However, she was forced into a terrible choice:

- She could marry the mayor of Alexandria, who lusts after her—but if she did, she'd betray her oath to the goddess Isis to never marry and to stay celibate. If she didn't marry the mayor, however, he vowed to burn down her beloved temple.

- Or, she could avoid both of these fates and become a gladiator. In doing so, however, she would be forced to kill, which would violate her religious vows, not to mention her spiritual nature.

You might notice that Khensa has Rooting Interest (meaning we empathize with her), because her Undeserved Misfortune is a Rooting Interest Technique (see Chapter 2.10, "NPC Rooting Interest Techniques").

Khensa's Character Diamond

I wanted to find five Traits to comprise Khensa's personality, and I wanted (as I did for all the characters) to have at least three that could be expressed without words.

The game offered a number of places a character could express himself or herself nonverbally:

- The way the character greeted the crowd when entering an arena to fight. (The gladiator fights took place in many small and large arenas spread across the Roman Empire.)

- The way a character taunted another warrior.

- The way a character killed an opponent if that character was in a good mood.

- The way a character killed an opponent if that character was in a bad mood.

- The way a character exited an arena.

The possibilities for nonverbal expression multiplied when we decided that we'd give the characters more than one way to do most of the preceding.

The first two traits I picked were ones that required words to show. She was:

1. **Innocent** and **Guileless.** This could be shown nonverbally, of course, if we had the option of close-ups on her face. But that wasn't part of the plan except for some very brief cinematics. Primarily we saw her was when she was fighting in one or another arena.

2. **Academically Astute.** The most famous library of the ancient world was the renowned library at Alexandria. Khensa studied there in secret.

Her next three traits could be revealed nonverbally, but don't take my word for it. Take a look at three drawings of Khensa done by Cheryl Austin, the artist on the team who was responsible for the look of the main characters.

In these pictures, you see Khensa's remaining three of her five Traits. She was:

3. Sensual and Graceful.
4. Lonely.
5. Mystical, with some minor magical abilities.

If I and the artists and animators and programmers all did our work correctly, anyone who plays Khensa would feel she's a very dimensional character, even in the way she moves and fights.

Depth Communicated Nonverbally

And she's not just mystical, she also has some depth, for two of her five traits—lonely and mystical—are also Character *Deepening* Techniques.

Final Thoughts

Whether the characters you're designing are made to be played by the gamer or whether they're NPCs, take a look at:

- The way they walk and run
- Their fighting moves
- Other ways they move
- Their idles[1]
- Other animations they might have
- Their taunts
- Their face
- Their clothing
- Their weapons
- Their tattoos or other body markings
- Their dwelling, if they have one

How many of these forms of non-verbal communication can you use to express traits on the character's Diamond?

---

1. An *idle* is the movement or movements performed by a character you play when you've stopped moving the character about. Idles are used so that the character doesn't seem stiff and lacking life. In some games, funny idles are occasionally used to provide humor.

Enhancing Emotional Depth Through Symbols

When an object or phrase is a window
through which the winds of emotion blow.

Film and television writers

have learned methods of using symbols to give characters, scenes, and
stories emotional depth and resonance. In games, the ideal is to go one
step further and create *Usable Symbols*—symbols that have emotional
power, but that are also useful in gameplay. This chapter shows a few ways
of creating such symbols.

Films and television shows use symbols. In *The Matrix*, the city of Zion is a symbol of rebellion and hope, even though we never see it.

Advertising uses symbols. The McDonald's arches? They're symbols.

The American flag is a symbol. And that photo on your desk of your loved ones? That's a symbol too.

Symbols resonate with emotion. They can be quite powerful.

When you create a symbol, you're not trying to create an intellectual puzzle, where the player tries to figure out what the symbol means. Such an intellectual exercise would work directly counter to the goal of increasing emotional immersion.

Instead, symbols should evoke emotions—even though, when you do your work well, most of the players won't consciously notice the symbols you use. It's not necessary for a player to notice a symbol to be emotionally affected by it.

It's certainly all right if a relatively small percentage of players who consciously notice your symbol might stop and think about the symbol's meaning or meanings.[1] This is only acceptable if, at the same time, the symbol generates in them an emotional experience too. This chapter will give you guidelines as to how to accomplish this.

Usable Symbols

Games often offer an opportunity that films do not. Symbols in film can enhance emotional depth. As you'll see, they cannot only do this in games, but they often can be used or given a function in gameplay as well.

Let's look at a few types of symbols that can add depth to a game.

---

1. A loose rule I often apply is that I want about 25% of the players to consciously notice a symbol I use in a game, with about 75% of the players not consciously aware of it. Of course, although they may not be explicitly aware of the symbol, they're still emotionally affected by it. If many more players than this are aware of your symbol and it's supposed meaning, then there's a good chance you're being heavy-handed. The emotional power latent in your symbol will be diminished or destroyed. I suggest that you avoid having a symbol in your game be obvious unless you have a specific reason for having it be that apparent.

Symbol of a Character's Condition or Change in Condition—Visual or Verbal

This is a kind of symbol that you use in a specific game moment or situation, but that you might never use again in the game.

To use this type of symbol, show an image on screen or have one of the characters say something in the game that reflects what one of the characters on screen is going through emotionally.

To understand how you might use this type of symbol, consider some examples from television and film.

Visual Example from TV

In one episode of *Star Trek—Voyager,* Captain Janeway finds herself in extended battle with the captain of a rogue Federation ship. The captain and crew of that ship are killing harmless aliens in order to use the chemicals in the aliens' bodies to propel their ship. Janeway is horrified that a trained Starfleet officer could so deeply violate the most basic Federation ethical principals. She takes the captain's murder of the aliens quite personally.

Janeway becomes so obsessed with stopping the other captain at whatever cost that she crosses the bounds of ethics and good judgment. In doing so, she imperils her crew by exposing them to extreme dangers. This generates a series of arguments between her and her first officer, Chakotay. In short, Janeway's obsession to stop the rogue captain, who has become a terrible leader, turns Janeway into a poor leader herself.

A metal plaque that reads "U.S.S. Voyager" falls off a Voyager bulkhead during a battle with the rogue ship. This plaque is a symbol that the spiritual core of Voyager—the moral codes of the Federation, the Starfleet tradition of honor and humanity, and the moral compass of people who uphold these codes and traditions—has been damaged. It's a Symbol of a Condition or Change in Condition of Janeway and Chakotay.

The plaque falling off the bulkhead affects us *emotionally*. If people make only an *intellectual connection* between the plaque and the abandoned Federation values, then the writer hasn't been artful enough in creating the symbol.

Visual Example from Film

In the 1957 Academy Award-winning masterpiece *Bridge on the River Kwai,* Alec Guinness plays Colonel Nicholson, who commands a group of British soldiers captured by the Japanese and forced to work like slaves in a POW camp in Burma.

I won't reiterate the convoluted plot, but suffice to say that, due to his ego, Nicholson has his men help the Japanese build a large, strong, and beautiful bridge. He tells his men it's to help keep their discipline intact and their morale high. In reality, it's because he thinks that this masterpiece of engineering and aesthetics will be a tribute to his own greatness.

The result is, in building the bridge, Colonel Nicholson has helped the enemy. But, near the very end of the film, during a battle at the bridge, he has a powerful realization, and says, "What have I done?"

At that exact moment, he reaches up and touches his commander's cap. This is the Symbol of a Character's Condition or Change of Condition. His touching the cap is a symbol of his changing back to becoming what he once was—an honorable British soldier.

An explosion goes off nearby and he is knocked to the ground, wounded from the shrapnel. When he stands up, his cap lies on the ground, but he's too dazed to immediately see this. He reaches for the top of his head and realizes that the cap is gone. Nicholson then bends down and picks it up off the ground. His reaching toward his head for the cap, and then his picking it up off the ground, again is the same Symbol of a Character's Condition or Change of Condition, signifying that he has become the honorable man he once was.

He puts his conversion immediately into action, for, as he dies from the shrapnel hit, he directs his fall onto the dynamite detonator, which in turn blows up the bridge he had so painstakingly guided his men to build.

As was the case with the *Voyager* example, most people in the audience wouldn't *consciously* notice this use of a symbol. And yet it would still contribute to the *depth* of their emotional experience. It's a strange moment when, as a writer, you realize that a great deal of your art involves trying to create emotional effects that *won't* be consciously perceived, perhaps ever, by anyone.[2]

---

2. But, on the other hand, it's not as strange as the expression on your parents' faces when you first tell them you're going to devote your life to video games.

Verbal Example from Film

In the provocative film *American Beauty,* the character Ricky Fitts (played by Wes Bentley) is a teen without fear of teen social pressures, and with a deep appreciation of the beauty all around him. He seems, in some ways, to be enlightened.

Contradicting his supposed enlightenment is the fact that he sells drugs, is completely emotionally detached, and is fascinated by death. In fact, his veneer of serenity is what I call a Mask, or false front (see Chapter 2.1, "NPC Interesting Techniques").

At a certain point in the film, Lester Burnham (Kevin Spacey's character) drops by Ricky's house to buy some dope from him. Lester is especially interested in some of the really potent marijuana he smoked with Ricky a few nights earlier. Ricky pulls out a bag of the dope and explains that it's:

```
RICKY: ...top of the line. It's called
G-13. Genetically engineered by the U.S.
Government. Extremely potent. But a
completely mellow high, no paranoia.

LESTER: Is this what we smoked last night?

RICKY: This is all I ever smoke.
```

Why is this a verbal Symbol of a Character's Condition or Change of Condition? Because Ricky, *unknowingly,* has just described himself. Ricky used to be a passionate young man, until his control-freak military father, as punishment for Ricky's perceived disobedience, had Ricky committed to a mental institution for two years, where he was heavily drugged.

This experience broke his spirit. So Ricky himself, his spirit crushed both by his Marine father and the mental institution, has been *government engineered.* His fake serenity (his Mask) is that of a *completely mellow high.* This Mask of serenity allows him to, in his core, remain numb. Thus, he's got *no paranoia.* But like all chemical highs, Ricky's is not real.

Verbal Example from TV

Sometimes, in the television business, you need to write a sample script just to show you can adapt your writing style to different shows. I wrote a sample *X-Files* script that has gotten me no end of work in the game industry.[3] In the story, Mulder no longer fits in professionally with Scully and Doggett. He was always driven in his paranormal quests by the search for the truth about his missing sister. But, with that case solved in the series prior to the point when I wrote my screenplay, Mulder no longer has a dream or ambition to push him forward.

In the middle of an awkward conversation with Scully, Doggett, and Skinner, in which Mulder is being forced out of the X-Files, Mulder notices Skinner's office clock. Checking it against his own watch, he says, "Is that clock right?"

No one responds to the question—the conversation merely proceeds. (Quite frequently, in dialogue, not every statement or question gets a response.) Why the throw-away line about the clock? It's a Symbol of Mulder's Condition or Change in Condition. In this case, it symbolizes that he's out of sync, or out of step with all the others. In effect, his time has passed.

Will anyone reading the script (or seeing Mulder say the line) consciously understand what I was going for with the line, or even notice it at all? It's unlikely, any more than they would note the line by Ricky Fitts in *American Beauty* about the government-engineered marijuana. As with the other examples, the symbol operates outside the audience's conscious awareness.

---

3. As you might recall from Chapter 1.4, "17 Things Screenwriters Don't Know About Games," I think game companies make a huge mistake if they hire a writer for their games solely based on previous work the writer did on other games. He or she might have simply done a lot of poor writing on a lot of games, but in doing so built up a game resumé. That's why I think it's critical that the game company reads not just some of their game work, if it's available, but also a piece of the writer's linear writing—a film or TV script—as well. This is to see if the writer really has what it takes, and if the writer can create complex, interwoven emotional effects that unfold through time in a story. These abilities are absolutely needed in game writing, just as much as is the skill of being able to create compelling characters who speak just one or two lines of dialogue.

Personally, I've never yet found a writer who has the "right stuff" who isn't a member of the WGA (the Writers Guild of America). That doesn't mean that such writers aren't out there; it means that you'll be looking for a needle in a lot of very large haystacks. And even many WGA writers who I've "auditioned" have been less than stellar. Most of the truly great ones are making so much money in film or television that they can't be lured into games. Thus the dilemma.

Game Case Study

Ico

In Chapter 2.11, "Player Toward NPC Chemistry Techniques," we looked in depth at the game *Ico*.[4] (Please note: If you don't want to know the ending, please skip the next few paragraphs.)

Near the very end of the game, the boy you play obtains a magical sword that crackles with a kind of spiritual electricity. This is a Symbol of the Boy's Condition or Change in Condition. It symbolizes that he's attained a level of power: The demonic creatures that used to attack him now flee him and the sword. And it also symbolizes that he now belongs with the girl, for the spiritual electricity the sword exudes looks exactly like the mystical energy that the girl can wield when she needs to, and that has the same magical abilities. So the sword symbolizes two conditions: the boy's attainment of power and his attunement to the girl's soul.

Because the boy uses the sword to accomplish his final tasks, this is a *Usable Symbol*, serving double duty: working to deepen the emotional experience, but also playing a role in gameplay.

---

4. To briefly recap: A boy in a different land or perhaps on a different planet (the character you play) helps lead a beautiful girl with mystical powers out of a towering castle where both of them are trapped. He bravely overcomes many terrifying obstacles in his journey, which is more focused on freeing the girl than on helping himself.

Hypothetical Game Case Study

Symbols of Sadness and Achievement

Let's say, in a sword-and-sorcery game, during a fight to save some villagers, the wisest and most beloved village elder is killed. The villagers are stunned. A cloud could pass in front of the sun at that point, throwing a shadow over the village. It would symbolize the villagers' sadness—and perhaps yours as well, if you had found the old man endearing (which you would have, if the character was rich enough and the dialogue excelled due to the application to the NPC Rooting Interest Techniques discussed in Chapter 2.10).

After great effort and many struggles and battles in other portions of the game, you attain the highest rank a warrior can achieve. At that moment an eagle flies diagonally overhead in the sky. It's a symbol of your lofty attainment.

To reiterate: It doesn't matter if no one consciously notices these symbols. They deepen the experience nonetheless. They have emotional impact.

Symbolic Subplot

In many stories, some of the most compelling emotional moments are wrapped around a character wrestling with, and eventually growing through, his or her emotional FLBW.

Some writers insert a symbol into the story that represents the character's Arc. That is, as the character changes and grows, the symbol changes right along with them.

note

In Chapter 2.9, "NPC Character Arc Techniques," and Chapter 2.20, "First-Person Character Arc Techniques," I spoke at length about giving NPCs and even the player a Character Arc, in which a fear, limitation, block, or wound (FLBW) is overcome with difficulty. The discussion on Symbolic Subplots is founded on information and techniques in those chapters.

A Symbolic Subplot is a *Plot Deepening* Technique, because it continues throughout all or most of the plot (unlike the Symbol of the Character's Condition or Change in Condition, which occurs in one moment or situation within the game).

In the *Star Trek* series, *Enterprise*, one of the crew, Ensign Hoshi Sato, is a woman with extraordinary linguistic abilities. In one of the early episodes, she's having a hard time adapting to life on a starship. She wants to go home, back to Earth.

She has brought a pet along with her—a yellow slug. And the slug isn't doing well aboard the ship. Environmental conditions threaten its health.

By the end of the episode, after discovering how much the crew needs her, she has made her peace with working in space. She drops the slug off on an Earth-like planet, where it will survive just fine.

Thus, the slug is a Symbolic Subplot. The slug not doing well in space equates with her not doing well in space. The slug being put on a new planet and doing well there equates with her surviving and thriving away from Earth.

With a Symbolic Subplot, you can know how the character is doing in their Character Arc, just by checking up on what's happening with the symbol.

Operating Outside of Conscious Awareness

Just as was the case with a Symbol of a Character's Condition or Change in Condition, a Symbolic Subplot may or may not be noticed by the audience or player.

Let's go back to the example from the *Enterprise* episode. In this case, unlike most, we are quite aware that the slug is a Symbolic Subplot, for the doctor on board the ship even points this out to Hoshi. That is, while speaking to her, he compares her difficulties to that of the slug.

This violates the guideline of having the Symbolic Subplot operate just outside most people's conscious awareness. In my opinion, this was a mistake. I think Hoshi's slithering slimy sick slug symbol would have generated more emotion if it hadn't been pointed out to the audience. "Look, here's a symbol" is usually not the best way to go. However, as every writer knows, to every guideline there are always successful exceptions.

The film *Wonder Boys* effectively uses an interesting Symbolic Subplot. In that film, Michael Douglas plays Grady Tripp, a character who wrote a great novel decades ago, and who is now a washed-up creative writing teacher at a prestigious liberal arts college. His life is a mess. He's depressed, and has been working seemingly forever on a sprawling, unfinished novel that he hasn't shown anyone.

The Symbolic Subplot is the novel he's working on. The novel equates to his life. We learn that he's been working on the book for decades. Then we learn it's a sprawling jumble, with plot-lines going off in all direction but without a focus (just like his life). It's comprised of tons of details without a unifying thread (just like his life).

Further along in the film, the pages of his manuscript—the only copy he has—are blown to the wind (symbolic of his life falling apart). Later still, when someone asks him what the novel was about, he can't answer— meaning he has no idea what his life is about. By the end, once he feels his life assumes meaning and direction again, he starts a new novel. This one has power and focus.

Using This Technique in Games

As we saw in Chapter 2.20, "First-Person Character Arc Techniques," trying to build in a Character Arc for a player opens up a can of worms. This upcoming section presupposes that you are completely familiar with that chapter.

A Symbolic Subplot can reflect the emotional growth not only of an NPC, but can also be applied to a First-Person Character Arc. In such cases, the changes in the symbol reflect the changes your character undergoes as he or she progresses through the rocky path of his or her Character Arc.

Remember that a First-Person Character Arc isn't just about the character you're playing growing; you, the player, should actually experience some change as well.

Let's say that in a game, the player's character is a samurai swordsman. He's a master of many weapons. Armed with a full range of finely honed steel instruments of death and sushi cutlery, he leaves his samurai Master's training to rescue his Master's niece from an evil warlord. This mission will start a much bigger plot in motion.

The obvious Character Arc is to have the character (the player) go from being a novice swordsman to being a master himself or herself. Because this is the obvious one, let's toss it out.[5]

So let's change your character's Arc to: attaining a spiritual connection to the universe. This was the Arc undergone by the boy in *The Karate Kid*. He wins his final fight in the first movie not because he's stronger, not because he's better at karate, and not because he's more courageous. By the end of the film, he achieves an understated spiritual connection to the universe. This is symbolized and demonstrated by his ability to easily maintain the "crane pose," standing on one foot with his other foot tucked under him and his arms extended.

In your game, as your character attains spiritual wisdom or abilities, perhaps the world will start looking different in some way. Perhaps he'll be able to do extraordinary moves similar to those by the fighters in *Crouching Tiger Hidden Dragon*.

Can we give this Character Arc a Symbolic Subplot?

Here's one possibility: Your Master has given you a sword. It makes a harsh, ringing noise when you swing it. But, as you progress along your Character Arc, the noise becomes more and more beautiful and harmonic.

Or, you recharge your life force by returning to a little, beautiful bamboo meditation hut suspended over a small stream. In the beginning of the game, the stream is muddy. But, as you progress along your Character Arc, the stream becomes increasingly clear.

---

5. As I often tell my writing students, when it comes to characters, lines of dialogue, scenes, or plots, a good general guideline is: "Find the cliché—then throw it away." This also means that the Master had best not be a cliché "wise Asian" character either.

In either of these two examples, the player might or might not notice the change in the symbol. This is just what we generally want: for your Symbolic Subplot to work just at the edge of the player's conscious awareness, or just outside of it.

Turning These into Usable Symbols in Gameplay

With the first example, perhaps it's when your sword makes its most beautiful, harmonic sound that something extraordinary happens. There's an old, frail man in the village who, in fact, is much more than the peasant he seems to be. When he hears that beautiful sound, he knows you're spiritually ready—and gives you some special weapon, amulet, potion, or secret that aids you as you struggle to accomplish your final and most dangerous task.

Or, taking a cue from *Ico*, perhaps it's only when the sword makes this beautiful sound that it's fully charged and able to be useful against your final and most formidable enemy.

You could also find a way to turn the river beneath the meditation hut into a Usable Symbol. Maybe it was your Master who built the meditation hut over the river, and he imbued it with magic of which you're unaware. Let's say your Master dies along the course of the game. But, when you attain your Character Arc and the stream becomes clear, your Master's face can be seen in the river and he gives you advice crucial to accomplishing your final task.

I don't think a symbol *needs* to be used in gameplay to justify its being there, for it's main purpose is to enhance the depth of the emotional experience. It's obviously an ideal situation, however, when it can also function as an element of gameplay.

note

In the previous examples, the suggested Symbolic Subplots would help the game's artfulness and aesthetics but not particularly deepen the game's emotion unless the First-Person Character Arc they symbolized truly had emotional power in it's own right. Means to achieve an emotionally powerful First-Person Character Arc can be found in the Chapter 2.20.

The same goes if the Symbolic Subplot echoes the Character Arc of an NPC. That is, the subplot might add some artistry to the story, but won't deepen the emotion unless we're emotionally caught up in that NPC's growth through his or her FLBW. How to achieve this can be found by combining techniques from Chapter 2.10 (to give an NPC Rooting Interest) and Chapter 2.9, "NPC Character Arc Techniques."

Game Case Study

Aidyn Chronicles

In the game *Aidyn Chronicles: The First Mage,* one of the close friends to the character you play is an NPC who's a reluctant knight. Though the knight has sworn off the violence of battle, he's continuously forced to fight for his king, both for his own honor, and to support a noble cause. He carries a pole bearing a flag or banner of the kingdom he serves. As a tool of gameplay, the banner has certain protective functions.

But it often gets ripped in battle—symbolizing how the knight's heart is torn every time he violates his decision to abstain from fighting. Furthermore, the banner, when torn, prompts discussions by the knight and those around him as to the ethics of his fighting in battle versus being a man of peace. The banner is a Symbolic Subplot, indicating, at any given moment, where the knight stands as he wrestles with the difficult decision to be, or not to be, a warrior.

This is one of those examples where a symbol serves double duty. Not only does it deepen the emotional experience, but it also is a Usable Symbol with a function in gameplay.

Does this Symbolic Subplot deepen the emotion of the game? That all depends on whether you feel that, as your character grows and changes, you, the player, are also experiencing growth and change, at least to some degree.

Symbols Used in Foreshadowing

Here's another Plot Deepening Technique. Though it only appears in one specific game moment or situation, it prepares us for something coming later in the plot. In foreshadowing, once again you're creating a symbol that usually operates outside the conscious awareness of the gamer or audience. The symbol, or what occurs to the symbol, suggests something that will occur later in the story to one of your main characters—usually something bad.

In the film *Shawshank Redemption*, Andy Dufresne (played by Tim Robbins) is a man who has been unjustly sent to prison. There he runs afoul of the warden, and the two become enemies. Later in the film, a another man is sent to the prison who has information that could clear Dufresne. The warden finds out about this and asks the man to step out with him into the prison yard at night. The warden grills the new prisoner, who confirms his knowledge of information that could help Dufresne.

The warden, finished, tosses his cigarette on the ground, and steps on it to put it out. He walks away—and the prisoner is shot from an unseen source in a guard tower.

The extinguishing of the cigarette was the foreshadowing that the prisoner—or at least the information he held—was going to be snuffed out. It's emotional: It gives us an ominous feeling when we see it happen.

Hypothetical Game Case Study

The Samurai

Let's go back to our samurai swordsman. Your Master has a bonsai tree that is 150 years old—cultivated, and handed down to him by his own Master who is long since deceased. Your Master has used the careful cultivation of the small tree to perfect his patience.

Then, during either a cinematic or during gameplay, the villain destroys the tree. This would foreshadow the fact that your Master is going to be killed.

The bonsai tree could be turned into a Usable Symbol, with a function in gameplay—its magic could heal you when you're injured or restore your life force when depleted. Thus, its destruction would not just foreshadow your Master's death; it would also affect gameplay by depriving you of a source of healing and thus increasing your jeopardy.

A Symbol That Takes on Increasing Emotional Associations—Visual or Verbal

This is another Plot Deepening Technique, as it too tends to extend throughout an entire plot. It can either be an object or a verbal phrase.

The American flag is an example of this type of symbol. What does the flag mean? It means a lot of things—democracy; courage; the right to live the life you choose; freedom of speech, thought, and religion; a nation ruled by law; Yankee ingenuity, and more.

Remember, when we look at the flag, we don't intellectually think of all these meanings. They're more like emotional experiences we *associate* with the flag. When we see the flag, we feel these emotional associations.

Symbols shouldn't make you think—they should evoke feelings. Or, if they *do* make you think, they should *also* evoke emotions.

When a symbol reappears over and over again during emotionally charged moments, some of the emotion rubs off on the symbol and the symbol literally takes on more and more emotional associations.

Visual Example from Film

An interesting symbol recurs throughout the film *Braveheart*—a thistle, and then a handkerchief with a picture of a thistle sewn into it. This symbol (the thistle and the handkerchief with a thistle) takes on more and more emotional associations as the film goes along.

Braveheart centers on William Wallace (Mel Gibson), an historic revolutionary leader in Scotland. When Wallace is a young boy, a little girl, Murron, gives him a thistle at the funeral of his father and brother, who were killed by the British. So the thistles are associated with *love*. When they're older, the two begin dating, and he gives her back this same, dried thistle. Once again, it is associated with *love*. When Murron marries him, she gives him a handkerchief with a picture of a thistle sewn on it. It still is associated with *love*.

Later Murron is murdered. Had symbolizing love been the only way the handkerchief had been used, whenever Wallace looks at it with sadness, we would understand and feel his personal anguish. It would evoke in him (and in us) emotional memories and feelings about Murron's specialness, the beauty of their love, and the sadness of her passing.

The handkerchief, however, continues to take on additional emotional associations throughout the plot:

- When Murron is killed by a British magistrate, Wallace kills the magistrate, then later stares at the handkerchief. By now it has begun to be associated with *revenge*.

- The handkerchief is with him as he becomes a leader of the Scots in their fight for independence, so it eventually comes to be associated with *freedom*.

- After Wallace is killed, wishy-washy land owner Robert the Bruce (Angus MacFadyen) takes up the fight. He overcomes his indecisiveness, his cowardice ends, and he leads his men into battle, holding the handkerchief, which now is associated with *courage*.

Throughout the film, the handkerchief with the thistle keeps reappearing, always during emotionally charged moments, and always associated with love, revenge, freedom, or courage. By the end, the handkerchief seems saturated with emotional associations, just like the American flag.

As when we see the American flag, or when we see the handkerchief in *Braveheart*, we don't think about all these meanings or associations. Instead, *the handkerchief evokes feelings in us drawn from all those emotional experiences* (the loss of his wife—the anger of revenge—the passionate struggle for freedom, and so on).

Hypothetical Game Case Study

The Pendant

How, in a game, could we create a Symbol that Takes on Increasing Emotional Associations and at the same time make it a Usable Symbol (something that has a function in gameplay)?

Let's say you're designing a game with a Tolkien-like story. (Yes, it's over-done, but we're just using it for instructional sake.) You play a relatively powerless Hobbit-type, going up against a fearsome enemy with supernatural powers.

Your motivation for undertaking this heroic quest is that the villain wiped out your family. It's your responsibility to both seek revenge and stop the villain from killing other innocents.

Before he died, your father gave you a pendant with your family crest, which had been handed down through the generations. The first time we see the pendant is in a cinematic, when your father gives it to you as he lies dying. So it is associated with *love*.

As you go on your quest to bring down the villain, you can recharge your life force (if you don't do it too much) by bringing out the pendant and clenching it. So the pendant comes to also be associated with *life*.

At some point, you need to permanently (or so it seems at the time) give the pendant to a fallen, dying friend—to save him by recharging his life force. So now the pendant is associated with *self-sacrifice for a friend*.

And if the pendant eventually comes back to you and gives you a decisive super-boost of life force for the final battle, it would then be associated with *victory*.

Although it would operate outside the gamer's conscious awareness, this would be a Symbol that Takes on Increasing Emotional Associations and it would add emotional depth to your story.

Because the pendant plays a role in gameplay, however, it's also a Usable Symbol, serving double-duty (enhancing the depth of emotion but also serving a function).

Game Case Study

Max Payne

In *Max Payne*, above the rough-and-tumble squalor of the city float billboards for the mysterious Aesir Corporation, with its logo (the R in AESIR has a little wing on it) and its slogan, "A bit closer to Heaven."

At first, the billboards have the emotional quality of taunting residents of the city by reminding them of *class distinctions*. After Max (played by you) discovers that the Aesir Corporation is responsible both for the city's decrepit condition and the murder of Max's wife and child, the logo and slogan are now associated with the *enemy*. And, when Max triumphs in the end and finally attains some inner peace, he adopts the slogan "A bit closer to Heaven" as his own. The phrase now is associated with *transcendence*.

If you played the game and this symbol only made you *think* about these associations, it was, to a great degree, unsuccessful (although still a wonderfully bold and inventive attempt at creating Plot Deepening). But, whether or not it made you think about the associations, if it evoked in you a variety of *emotions* that accompanied these different associations, then it was successful.

Hypothetical Game Case Study

The Hood Ornament

In the example game depicted here, set in a rough-and-tumble futuristic world, you play Kenneth Lassiter. America has dissolved into warring anarchy, with each man out for himself.

What brought the country to its knees? It was the creation, in a secret government lab, of RK-36, a metal that acts like a mighty fuel—a fuel that is never expended.

It could have been used to help mankind, but instead it was funneled into a covert weapons project. When the man in charge of that weapons program went insane and tried to blackmail the government with the threat of using the weapon on a series of domestic targets, perhaps the country's leaders should have met his outrageous financial demands. They didn't believe he'd carry out his threats.

In the conflagration, the country was all but destroyed, and so was all the RK-36...except one piece of the metal, which an artist fashioned into a hood ornament shaped like the head of Hermes.[6]

This ornament, when placed on the hood of a car and connected to the engine, powers that car to travel five times the speed of any other vehicle. In a land dominated by armed cars, this hood ornament has become the most sought after item in the land. Its energy can also be channeled into the guns on the owner's vehicle, making them significantly more powerful.

Because of RK-36's both incredibly constructive and destructive properties, the hood ornament would provoke a feeling of both *fear* and *cautious respect*, much like nuclear power is viewed in our own world today. Fear and cautious respect are its first emotional associations.

As everyone is scrambling for the hood ornament, it only falls into the hands of those tough enough to kill to get it. Over time it passes from one violent warlord to another. Thus, the ornament becomes a symbol of (becomes emotionally associated with) *power*.

Later in the game, when a young man takes possession of it, his own family steals the ornament and hides it to protect him from the ruthless

---

6. In Greek mythology, Hermes was the messenger between men and the gods. He wore a winged helmet and sandals.

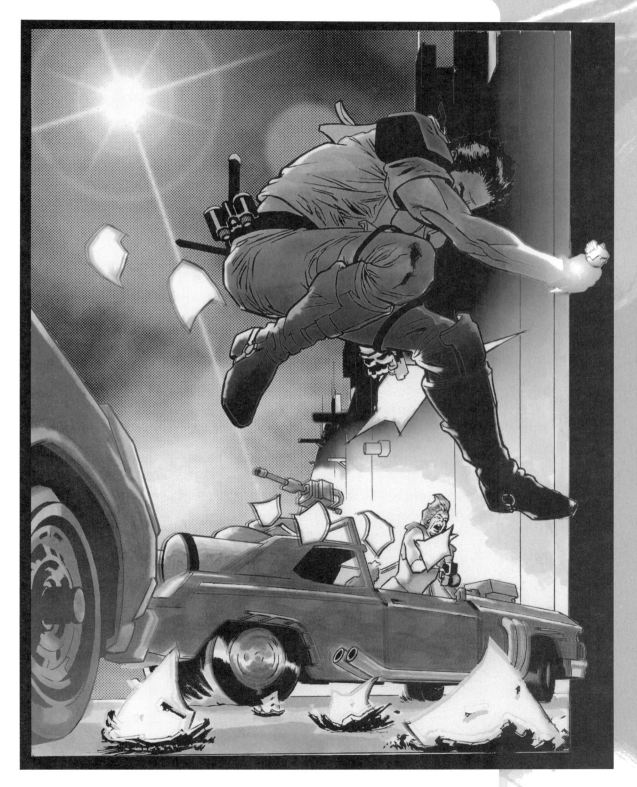

warlords who will surely come gunning for him. The family's plan back-fires: The local warlord wipes them out and reclaims the ornament.

This family has helped you in the past, and you've come to care about them. When they're killed because of the ornament, it takes on another emotional association: *tragedy*.

The young man was a member of the Book People. These people have a huge 18-wheel truck loaded with books—the only books still remaining in the world. They need to escape to a safer part of the country, where they can open up a school and begin to teach. They're the repository of all civilization.

Imagine if, earlier in the game, you were one of those selfishly jostling for power in this world. That is, let's say that the game encouraged you to do this.

But one of your missions accidentally results in the death of two of the land's most knowledgeable teachers—some of the only people capable of passing on knowledge.

Consequently, many Book People are emotionally devastated. Some are friends who have helped you in the past by sharing with you critical pieces of information that help you survive—information they know from books.

Now you've got to undo the damage you did in accidentally getting two of their teachers/leaders killed. So, as seen in the illustration, you steal the ornament (taken by the warlord from that family he slaughtered) to put on the Book People's truck, so can speed the truck to safety. At this point, you've helped make up for the damage you did earlier.

If the emotions evoked are real and the game's Emotioneering is done well, the ornament will take on the emotional association of *redemption*.[7]

When the Book People, in their truck with the ornament on the front, rocket through enemy lines to freedom, the ornament takes on the emotional association of *hope*.

---

7. I'd like to thank Terry Hayes, George Miller, and Brian Annant (screenwriters of *The Road Warrior*) and Ray Bradbury (author of *Farenheit 451*) for loaning me pieces of their plots for this example.

So, along the way, the hood ornament has picked up the emotional associations of:

1. Fear
2. Cautious respect
3. Power
4. Tragedy
5. Redemption
6. Hope

Just like the handkerchief in *Braveheart*, the hood ornament becomes a Symbol that Takes on Increasing Emotional Associations.

But, as befits a game, and as mentioned earlier, this would also be a Usable Symbol.

Final Thoughts

This chapter has covered four of the many distinct techniques for evoking emotional depth by using symbols. Each use of symbols is quite different from the other. They can, by the way, be used in combination. When you integrate symbols such as these into your games, if no one notices your skillfully imaginative work, that's just fine—in general, they're not supposed to notice.

It's always good to avoid cliché symbols—that is, ones we've seen many times before. Clichés don't involve us emotionally because they stand out like a sore thumb. For example, I don't recommend that a scary, mysterious man in a black robe, his face hidden by a black hood, have a seemingly chance meeting with one of your characters in order to foreshadow the fact that the character is about to die. The man in the black robe and hood is a cliché symbol of death.

When using symbols, you're not creating intellectual puzzles (having people try to figure out what a symbol means). Using a symbol for that kind of mind-game would detract from the emotion. Instead, when you use one or more of the techniques presented here, you're trying to *deepen* the player's emotional experience in the game, by letting the symbol evoke emotions in the player.

In short, when you create a symbol artfully, players will be emotionally affected by it, even though they probably won't consciously notice the symbol.

As we saw, quite often these different types of symbols can serve double-duty, also having a function in gameplay by being Usable Symbols.

Self-Created Story Techniques

(a.k.a. Agency Techniques)

Who's in charge—the game designer or the gamer?

Making the player feel

like he or she is impacting, or even (ideally) shaping the story is sometimes called "giving the player a sense of agency," or simply "giving the player agency." This chapter focuses on ways to accomplish this—ways to help the player feel that he or she is playing the game, rather than simply being taken along on a ride.

A game, to a greater or lesser degree, helps guide the player's choices and determines the possible consequences of his or her actions. However, it's important to make the player feel like he or she isn't just a pawn in the story.

In Chapter 2.21, "First-Person Deepening Techniques," we looked at ways a player could feel like he or she is impacting a game by creating (at least the feeling of) emotionally complex consequences to the actions the player takes in a game.

By feeling your actions have consequences, you feel you have an impact on the game. To the degree that impact is either real or feels real, it creates the sense that you're playing, to some degree, a *self-created story*.

However, there are many other ways of creating this feeling in a game.

At first it seems obvious that the player should be in charge of what occurs in a game, or at least the agent of much of what takes place. But in games that involve stories, or sequential missions, creating the feeling that the player is in change can become a challenge. For isn't the player following a path laid down by the game designers?

How much does the story happen to the player, and how much does the player create the story? Different games handle this question quite differently.

Every game, to some extent, is a self-created story. Even a game of chess is like a story with a beginning, middle, and end. And very, very rarely are two chess games identical.

When, in a game, you choose your weapons or your armor, you're playing the game differently than anyone else—so it's a self-created story.

There are some games, such as *The Sims*, where your impact on the game is extreme.[1]

On the other end of the spectrum might be *Final Fantasy X*. Many players were enthralled by both the rich fantasy story and the stunning visuals, but couldn't shake the feeling that they were simply being swept along by the narrative rather than really impacting the game. Sometimes it felt as if the gameplay's main function was to move you from one cinematic to another.[2]

---

1. All games might be, to one degree or another, stories, but not all stories have beginnings, middles, and ends. Some, such as *The Sims*, could go on forever.

2. This was problematic to U.S. players much more than to Japanese players. Why this was—the way the different cultures affect preferences in styles of gameplay—exceeds the scope of this book. But it is worth noting that the limited agency the game afforded wasn't, in general, considered detrimental in Japan.

A Spectrum of Impact

Thus, there is a spectrum of impact a player can have on a game.

Games without narrative stories are the ones in which you can have the most impact: sports games, *The Sims*, and chess are examples. Playing with a big box of Lego™, with all the accessories, would be an extreme example. Your impact on the way the Lego is used and the possible outcomes is huge.[3]

On the other extreme, you could have a game with two different endings. A decision you make near the end would determine the outcome. Here you'd have an impact, but on the impact scale, it would be much less than in *The Sims*. You could also have other forms of impact as to how you accomplish your missions in terms of stealth versus combat, the weapons you choose, the abilities you use, and even perhaps the geographic route you select.

One form of game isn't innately better or worse than the other; many players enjoy multiple forms of gameplay. And so one form of impact the player can have on the game isn't innately superior. The more of a "real" impact you have in the game, the less there can be anything that resembles narrative story. The more the game contains a narrative story, the more your impact in the game resides in the smaller details, but not the overall direction and shape of the outcome.

Mixing Impact Modes

One of the successful aspects of *Grand Theft Auto III* is the mixture of types of impacts the player can have on the game.

You can have significant impact when you jump into a cop car, chase down perps, and run them off the road. When you simply steal cars and run people over, that's also impact (literally and figuratively).

---

3. A Lego set is usually considered to be a toy, not a game. In fact, there are some game designers who call *The Sims* a toy for this same reason: Its gameplay involves the manipulation of (albeit very intelligent) building blocks. To these designers, it's a more advanced form of Lego. I won't try and define the difference between a toy and a game; different people draw the line at different places.

To make matters more complicated, people often create games using their toys, such as when a Frisbee™ (a toy) is used in a game of American football (substituting the Frisbee for the ball). Thinking about all of this could probably drive me mad, which isn't in itself a problem. However, I've already got enough of my own pet issues, quandaries, and conundrums that drive me mad, and I honestly don't have room for another one. This is why I'll choose to ignore this particular controversy of "game" versus "toy" and go into complete denial that it even exists.

I would note, though, that most people call *The Sims* a game, and we do live in a democracy.

But of course, there's no story involved with these sections of the game.

There are also elements of gameplay that have more limited impact. For instance, if you run missions for one gang, rival gang members will start shooting at you as a result of your reputation spreading. But it's a much lesser degree of impact, for no matter if it was you or if it was I who played the game, if we ran the same missions, the same rival gangs would fire upon us.

Different Ways of Fulfilling the Mission

GTA III skirts the feeling that you're being manipulated by offering many modes (see Chapter 2.16, "Plot Interesting Techniques") by which you can accomplish the missions, or at least some of them. Are you traveling by vehicle or on foot? What weapons are you using? What routes through the city are you taking?

The extreme impact you can have in choosing modes balances out the more limited impact you have on the narrative. As the sales figures proved, many people found it an extremely appealing balance. Adding to the balance was the fact that at any time you could leave story mode (following the game narrative) and go back into the more free-form types of gameplay discussed earlier.

Other Ways to Create Self-Created Stories

We've looked at a number of ways of giving the player the feeling that he or she can create his or her own story. Let's review that list and expand upon it a bit:

- Multi-path structure, so that the plot actually splits
- Different ways of accomplishing your missions
  - Choosing different weapons, armor, spells, and so on
  - Choosing different characters to play, with each role offering it's own abilities and choices of weapons, armor, spells, etc.
  - Different styles of accomplishing the mission, such as stealth or force

- Giving a game with a story some additional non-story ways of playing, such as:

  - Optional side-missions

  - The ability to explore environments (and usually find something of potential use or acquiring skills or ranking that allows you to pursue either story mode or non-story mode activities more effectively)

  - Mini-games (games within the game), which can be quite creative in nature. *GTA III* and *Vice City* allow you to steal police cars and get assignments to track down and kill criminals; you can grab an ambulance and rescue people; you can cause mayhem on foot or in cars in numerous different ways.

- Changing the game environment

  - Changing the sound-track

  - Changing the physical environment you play in

Final Thoughts

Game design requires a series of tradeoffs. Mini-games are fun, but if you put money and time into building them, you need to take away money from some other part of the game. Is the tradeoff worthwhile?

Making a game fun depends a lot on balancing such factors as:

- The *degree* to which a player can affect the game, or at least seem to affect it

- The *ways* in which a player can affect a game, or at least seem to affect it

- The ways and the degree to which the game guides or otherwise affects the player

- The ways the game delivers both expected and unexpected events and consequences to the player as a result of the player's decisions

- The types and amount of choices or actions available to the player at any given moment

- The type and amount of weapons, spells, defenses, and so on available to the player at any given moment

- When the player is performing a mission or even a small step within a mission, the amount and types of choices available to the player as to how to accomplish that small step or the entire mission

- The degree to which gameplay is repetitive, thus allowing a player to either continue practicing a skill or enjoy using a skill he or she has mastered versus the degree to which gameplay is new. (Of course, repetitive gameplay can be used in a new type of mission or in combination with other forms of gameplay, to balance out the familiar and the new.)

Getting these balances right is one big task; injecting emotion and meaning into the mix to enrich the experience is another.

The two aren't unrelated. For instance, the player will care much more about how he impacts the story if he cares about the NPCs and about what happens to them, about his own role and what happens to himself, and about the world of the game.

Emotioneering Techniques Category #25

Motivation Techniques

Baiting the player to
finish the game.

Motivation Techniques

are techniques to make the player want to keep on going and make it
through the game.

Trends come and go. And it's a good thing, or we'd all look like we stepped out of *The Brady Bunch*.

One current trend in games, at least in some genres, is to make games shorter. The game that takes 50 hours to complete is, in some circles, giving way to games that take 25 hours to complete—and sometimes games that are even shorter.

This trend is occurring to combat the fact that more than a few game players never make it to the end of a game. This occurs for several reasons:

- They get bored with the game, feeling that if they progress with the game, they won't get much more out of it than they already have.

- The average age of the typical game player is steadily rising. Adult gamers have other responsibilities in their lives and can't devote as much time to playing as they could when they were younger.

- They also have more disposable income, so they can afford to buy more games.

Shorter games might be one way to ensure that players make it through to the end of a game. But I know a publisher who swears that's the wrong answer, and that the right answer is to design games so that player can sit down for an hour—and perhaps even 15 minutes—and still have a fulfilling game experience. The player can then leave and later come back, and so digest the game in enjoyable installments.

I wanted to mention these two approaches, because I think we'll see game designers experimenting quite a bit with both of them.

Besides issues of length or segmented gameplay, however, there are definite mistakes to avoid if you want to keep your player motivated to continue on through to the end of your game. Here are a few.

Don't Interrupt Gameplay

Television writers live in fear of the commercial break. That's when a viewer is most likely to flip channels and see what's playing on a competitive network.

Many games have breaks in them. It's almost inevitable in games with sequential missions. Often it's because new assets need to load.

If at all possible, create the illusion of the game being ongoing, with no interruption. For instance, in *Grand Theft Auto III*, an area of blue light indicates where you need to go to receive your next mission. This device accomplishes many things simultaneously. When you play the game:

- You stay within the urban world of the game.

- You need to actively go and "get" a mission; it doesn't come to you. Thus, you don't become passive to get your mission briefing. Sure, you're passive as it's being explained to you, but the fact that you had to seek out the briefing gives the feeling that you've never left the game.[1]

Empire, Morrowind, and *The Sims* are examples of other types of games that keep the flow going. Online games like *Everquest* fall into this category as well.

Game designers will continue to pioneer ways to create the feeling of continuous game-flow.

Another way to say, "Don't interrupt the game" is to say, "Always give the player something to do."

---

1. Unfortunately, if you fail in the mission, you can't skip those cinematics. You must see them again in order to redo the mission.

If Possible, Try Not to Let the Way the Player Receives Information Interrupt the Game

Whenever you give information to the player, this can also have the negative effect of causing the gameplay to pause. Quite often game designers supply information or mission briefings in spoken or written forms to the player between levels or missions.

It's worth looking at some successful alternatives. For instance, in *GTA III*, not only do you get information and mission briefings from the men you seek out to send you on missions, but also over police radios while you drive. Getting information doesn't take you out of the game.

In *Deus Ex*, you get various people communicating to you through a screen in your helmet as you play the game. In the *Command and Conquer* games, there's a small square in the upper-right corner of your screen where various people on your side can communicate to you during the game. In *No One Lives Forever II: A Spy in H-A-R-M's Way*, your commander communicates to you through the mouth of a animatronic bird that seeks you at different points. It's effective—and hysterical. In all of these examples, gameplay isn't interrupted as these particular pieces of information are delivered.

We've all heard of a "babbling brook." In one fantasy game I worked on, I put in a brook that actually babbled. It was like the town gossip. You could lean down next to it and hear reports of other things going on elsewhere in the land.

Because the game took place in the land of fantasy, this fit right in with the genre, yet also provided information without taking the player out of the game.

A few other things to remember about information:

- If a person gives you information, make sure that person has a Diamond so they speak with a discernable personality.

- Try to convey information during tense moments. This is the exact opposite of what many game designers do, when they convey information between missions. (In these designers defense, they sometimes do this so that the missions themselves can proceed with an uninterrupted flow.)

- Don't give the player more information than he needs to know. If you've got other great stuff that might enhance the game world or characters but is optional, find a clever way that the player can seek it out and find it—but only if he or she wants to.

Don't Hold Back Too Long on the Carrots

Besides information, you need to give the player incentives. There is a wide variety of rewards that past games have offered players, and that future game designers will dream up.

These rewards include an expansion of abilities, weapons, and defenses. They can also include treating the player to intriguing pre-rendered cinematics.

There's a piece of street wisdom often repeated that a game should, early on, provide the player with lots of quick successes to get him or her excited about the game. After that, as the common wisdom goes, rewards should come less frequently, and be much harder to earn.

It's true that in games and in life, you want to take on progressively harder challenges. A player usually expects to and wants to get clobbered or killed by the game's biggest boss numerous times before finally being victorious.

But there's a danger if the game designer takes the player's willingness to continue through a game for granted.

Many game companies rely on extensive testing of their games to see where "good frustration" ends and "bad frustration" begins.

But in some games, the problem persists. Don't be overly stingy on giving the player those carrots.

A related issue is that not every enemy needs to be difficult to conquer near the end. You can throw in some fodder. The player has worked hard to build up skills, weapons, and defenses. Let him or her enjoy clobbering some baddies with his or her hard-won fighting skills.

Avoid the Feeling of Repetitive Gameplay...Sometimes

As mentioned in the last chapter, repetitive gameplay isn't necessarily a bad thing. It can allow a player to either continue practicing a skill or enjoy using a skill he or she has mastered. And, of course, some games rely on repetitive gameplay, such as race-track games—not to mention *Tetris* or chess.

And even in games where it's desired to minimize repetitive gameplay, quite often the gameplay *needs* to be repetitive. After all, the publisher doesn't have endless money to fund a hundred kinds of gameplay, nor an endless amount of assets. Also, there are only so many mechanics[2] a player wants to master during the game.

In games with stories, I've seen boredom set in when the gameplay gets too repetitive. In an earlier chapter I mentioned that many players never made it to the end of *Ico*, despite its many breakthroughs in terms of bringing emotion into a game. The principal reason some players quit was that they felt the gameplay was too repetitive.

---

2. *Mechanics* are actions that can be performed by the character or characters being played by the gamer.

There's no unexpected revelation in saying that boredom needs to be eliminated from gameplay. Boredom can be skirted by:

- Changing the setting of the gameplay in inventive ways

- Offering a variety of styles of gameplay, such as stealth or combat

- Modifying the weapons or adding the weapons

These are obvious and just about all games do them. There are other ways, though, to stave off boredom. Here are a few of them.

Keep Those Plot Twists Coming

I was watching a demo of a first-person shooter set in the Middle East. The mission demo took about 30 minutes to play through, and involved the rescue of a wounded soldier who was trapped behind enemy lines.

I was bored ten minutes into the level. I'd played other shooters and didn't see the compelling reasons that would make this one stand out. Why not put in a plot twist?

For example, let's say you're trying to kill an enemy soldier, and then headquarters radios you that that soldier is a high-level defector possessing key intelligence information. He's only shooting at you out of self-defense.

You stop shooting, so he stops shooting. But now others from his side come after the both of you. So, now you've got to defend the guy you were trying to kill as you try to make it back to safety.

Sometimes Provide Unexpected Consequences to the Player's Actions

Closely related to plot twists are unexpected consequences to your actions.

For instance, you shoot your enemy, but when he falls, the thud he makes alerts other enemies who otherwise wouldn't have known you were around. Suddenly you better get out of there fast.

Of course, if this happened every time, it would no longer be unexpected and thus would lose its effectiveness at combating boredom.

Action Puzzles

Action puzzles is my term for puzzles that take place in the middle of action. Furthermore, they're puzzles that take *doing something active* to solve the puzzle (i.e., achieve the desired result). They're not puzzles that merely require *thinking*. They aren't appropriate for every game, but for the right game, they can be quite involving.

For instance, maybe you're fighting in the American Civil War and it takes a long time to reload your rifle. A better way to fight might be shoot an enemy, pick up his gun and use it to shoot another enemy, pick up his gun and use it....

One of my favorite action puzzles was in *Star Trek Voyager: Elite Force*. You're on an alien ship and some very frightening aliens come through the portals. If you destroy the portals, beautiful little creatures that look like fireflies swarm around the portals and repair them. It's annoying as hell, because you can never keep the portals damaged for long.

Down a long corridor is a transporter you need in order to get out of there. But it's broken. Suddenly it occurs to you how to fix it: You go back to the main area and start shooting objects along the corridor. This lures the "fireflies" to follow you, for they're drawn to broken machinery or devices.

They repair each object you damage in turn, until they finally "see" the broken transporter. They swarm around it and repair it, allowing you to escape.

> **note**
>
> There are many types of action puzzles. I'd love to hear a description of your favorites. If you have some you'd like to share, go to **www.freemangames.com** and click on "Participate."

Not only was this a wonderful action puzzle, but it was also a great plot twist in that these "fireflies," which previously you hated, turn out to be the only solution to your problem of transporting out of this dangerous environment. Brilliant.

One big danger in action puzzles is making them so difficult that the player can't figure them out. The result can be a tremendous amount of frustration.

A Mysterious or Interesting World That Takes A While to Sort Out

Mystery works in films, it works on TV, and it works in games. When you play *Thief* or *Thief II*, you're thrown into a strange world, full of mysteries. Figuring out how they all fit together motivates you to continue. The same goes for a quite a number of games—*Myst*, *Morrowind*, the *Panzer Dragoon* series, and *Grim Fandango,* to name just a few.

There is a possible danger of swamping the player with too many mysteries. The result can be one big confusion. A solution is, once the player learns the answers to some of the game story's mysteries, you can then introduce some new ones.

An Example

In the game illustrated on the next page, you're a detective, spying on a mob boss. You had a hunch he was paying off someone in the police department to minimize police harassment and investigations. But here you find your own police chief paying off the mobster. What's going on?

You, the player, are suddenly saddled with a mystery. The desire to solve it will help motivate you to move forward in the game.

By the way, your motivation will be stronger to unravel if the corruption in the police department that you first suspected, and that caused you to spy on this mob boss, has a negative impact on you or someone you care about.[3]

---

3. We're going to revisit this game story and enrich it with all sorts of emotional variation, complexity, and depth in Chapter 2.29, "Injecting Emotion into a Game's Story Elements."

An Interesting Plot That Unfolds in an Interesting Way

It sounds obvious that a plot should be interesting, right? However, *Metal Gear Solid 2* sold about a million less units in America than its predecessor, despite greatly enhanced visuals. Many people felt this was in no small part due to problems with the plot. Quite a few American players regarded it as silly.[4]

There's no shortage of boring, cliché plots out there, and plots with no emotional engagement. I and The Freeman Group have been called upon to handle these problems on more than one occasion.

The truth is that coming up with a great plot, whether it be in a film or in a game, usually takes a tremendous amount of time, thought, creativity, and work.

Furthermore, the plot should unfold in interesting ways, with plot twists, unexpected revelations, causing the player to reassess what's going on or adapt to changing circumstances. You want the player to always be dying to see what happens next.[5]

A Higher Score

It's worth noting that a traditional way of keeping motivation going is to allow a player to compete against a previous high score—either a personal best or one set by another player.

This technique is a double-edged sword, however. On one hand, the player will want to continually get a higher score. At a certain point, however, the player's rate of improvement flattens out and previous scores are beaten only slightly, if at all.

When this occurs, the very thing that drove the player to try again—getting a high score—might now be a turn-off, because getting a higher score becomes difficult or impossible.

---

4. To be fair, there were probably other contributing factors, such as the fact that the game came out near the beginning of PlayStation 2's lifecycle, so that the console hadn't reached a high saturation point yet. But problems with the plot, as well as the character you play, were big contributing factors.

5. In fact, one of the ways I test writers who wish to join The Freeman Group is to give them a boring game plot, and see how they'd change it to make it both more riveting as well as more emotionally gripping.

Final Thoughts

It's a mistake to think a player will automatically want to continue forward in a game. We designers need to always be asking ourselves the questions, "What will make the player want to continue on to the next mission or level or game experience?" "What could turn off the player or cause boredom?"

Remember the problem zones, such as anything that can stop gameplay, like a break between levels or missions or the delivery of information. Try, if possible, to find inventive ways to handle these areas without ripping the player out of the game.

Or, if you need to rip the player out of the game to deliver this kind of information, have the information be presented in a way so that it's so entertaining or so intriguing that the player looks forward to it.

To some, it might seem strange to include, in a book on bringing emotion into games, a chapter that focuses so much on gameplay. However, an audience can get bored watching a film, a magic show, or a juggling act. A person can get bored on a theme-park ride. And a player can get bored in a game. It's the responsibility of the creators behind all these entertainment and art forms to know what it takes to ensure that boredom never sets in. For nothing will counteract an audience's or a player's emotional immersion faster than boredom.

The Big Picture

In a game with characters and/or a story, every trick in the book to motivate a player, in terms of gameplay and visuals, can all be mitigated when the player isn't emotionally invested in the game.

Here are some isolated segments from a *New York Times* review by Charles Harold of the game, *Zone of the Enders: The 2nd Runner*. The game is a sequel to the Konami game *Zone of the Enders*, which was released two years earlier.

> Because [the game] refers to characters and organizations I barely remembered from the first game, *Runner* became fairly confusing.

> While the sequel has little emotional depth and the character animations are inferior to those of the first game, the play has been much improved.

> *Zone* was notable more for its engaging story and intriguing characters than its somewhat pedestrian game play. Here the situation is reversed, with better action and a muddled story.

> [Regarding the final battle:] ...there is little strategy in that final tedious confrontation, and after getting killed a few times I gave up. I felt so uninvolved that I didn't even care enough to beat the final bad guy.

Mr. Harold, in just a few statements, about *The 2nd Runner*, sums up the entire point of this book. He found the plot confusing, the characters uninteresting, and the story lacking in emotional depth. So, even though the gameplay was *improved*, he didn't even care about winning the final battle.

The solution to motivating the player to passionately follow a game to its conclusion isn't just methods like those listed in this chapter. The solution lies in keeping the player emotionally engaged in the game from beginning to end. That won't occur with just a few tweaks in a game's design. It requires the entire gamut of Emotioneering techniques.

Emotioneering Techniques Category #26

Cohesiveness Techniques

Making it all hang together.

This chapter

deals with ways to make one part of a game feel connected to other parts that otherwise might feel separate in time or space.

It might seem strange to talk about connecting one part of a game to another. Is it really a problem?

I've experienced more than one game where the various missions seemed very disjointed, and the world they took place within felt fragmented.

In such games, the action may move from place to place, with new characters to encounter and new locations to explore. Newness is usually a good thing—it keeps the experience fresh. But continual newness of location and characters can, if mishandled, have one drawback: Sometimes it's hard to care much about a game's story if the characters and settings keep changing and there's little by way of a connecting thread.

The problem is not dissimilar to that in some road trip films that feel like little more than a string of disjointed incidents. Those road trip films that are the most engaging usually derive their emotional power from the rich relationships between the people taking the trip and their gripping Character Arcs.

But what if the game you're designing doesn't have a rich relationship between the player's character and an NPC? What will provide the Cohesiveness?

Here are some solutions.

Your Character Gets a Reputation

An example: NPCs in one part of the game have heard about your exploits in another part of the game and act toward you in a friendly or hostile way, based on your reputation. Or, they may simply remark upon it.

Karma

A kissing cousin to acquiring a reputation, the Hindu notion of *karma* is the idea that your positive and negative acts have long-range repercussions for your own well-being. Personally I tend to believe this, even though it takes a bit of time to prove.

For our purposes, *Karma* in a game is a Cohesiveness Technique. For example, if you help an NPC in one part of the game, and his or her friends or relatives help you later in the game, that's karma.

The flip side of this also applies. For example, if you kill the T-Rex early in the game, the other T-Rexes intuitively know this and come after you later on.

You can use this technique to create some interesting emotionally complex situations (see Chapter 2.15, "Emotionally Complex Moments and Situations Techniques"). For instance, imagine this sequence:

1. Early in the game, you kill Zack, a guy who was once good but who turned bad due to his financially desperate circumstances.

   This itself is emotionally complicated to you, the player, if you know that he didn't want to be evil. And it's even more complicated if his desperate circumstances were the result of being robbed by someone else and weren't a result of his own mistakes, bad judgement, or him having taken stupid risks.

2. Later in the game, you meet Conrad and Megan, two friends of Zack. They don't know he's dead, nor (obviously) that you killed him. If you like Conrad and Megan—especially if they aid you in some important way or if they help you get through a dangerous situation—then you'll have mixed feelings about the fact that they don't know you killed their friend. Once again, you'll be in an emotionally complex situation.

3. If they then learn you killed Zack, they could get furious and try to kill you. Now you have the choice of either having to kill your friends, or run from them—in order to save them from your killing them, which is what would most likely happen if you fight them. Either of these choices—to kill them or to flee—is emotionally complex.

In the preceding sequence, I took a simple notion—Karma—and then added emotional complexity to it. I call this process *Complexification*. Later in the book, Chapter 2.29, "Injecting Emotion into a Game's Story Elements," covers this in depth.

NPCs in One Part of the Game Refer to NPCs in Other Parts of the Game

Having NPCs within the game's world know each other or know of each other, and talk about each other, is a simple way to create Cohesiveness.

For example, you come into a village. One of the NPCs worriedly asks if you saw her cousin at the village you just came from (and which was the scene of a large battle).

Give Your Game a Theme[1]

What's your story about? Let's say we are were doing a *Buffy the Vampire Slayer* game.[2] The game could offer many rich themes.

For example, Buffy's a human who can do superhuman feats. She possesses powers that most people don't. What if power is our theme? If so, then we'd explore that through the various missions and side missions.

- Does one of her friends attain power that consumes her (the friend) and causes her to do evil? (This was done in the series.)

- Does Buffy find that she can have the power to overcome demons... but lack the power to fix the relationship of two friends of hers whose love is on the rocks? (The idea here is that one can be powerful in one realm but not another.)

- What if Buffy confronts Tanya, another slayer gone bad? What if Tanya offers strong incentives for Buffy to become evil as well (at least for a time). For instance, maybe by becoming evil for a period, Buffy can get some temporary abilities that would allow her to hopefully defeat the big boss at the end of the game?

In short, the game could be used to delve into the theme of various kinds of power, as well as the positive and negative sides of power.

The theme would need to be explored in the plot, the subplots, the characters, and maybe even the gameplay itself. We could explore it in gameplay by, on one hand, giving Buffy some special abilities that would be magnified when she's doing evil, while, on the other hand, giving her rewards for not doing evil. Let me explain:

---

1. The word *theme* can mean many things. Two ways it has been used in this book are:
   - A subject central to the story, explored from many points of view, with no conclusion made about the subject
   - A subject central to the story, explored from many points of view, with a conclusion finally made about the subject

   Clarifications, instructions, and examples of how to do this were covered in Chapter 2.17, "Plot Deepening Techniques," and Chapter 2.21, "First-Person Deepening Techniques."

2. I know that the TV series is off the air. Hopefully, you'll have caught at least an episode or two in syndication. I pick her for this example because the show, during its history, explored a wealth of themes.

Combining this idea with the concept of Karma from the previous chapter—when Buffy gains power in terms of special abilities (by doing evil for a short period), she loses power (influence) over her friends, who desert her, and whom she needs on her side to defeat whatever or whoever is the game's dangerous boss. So, when she gains one kind of power in gameplay (heightened abilities), she loses power in other forms of game-play (her friends no longer fight alongside her).[3]

Relationships Between People or Groups That Take A While to Decipher, But Eventually Form Their Own Coherent World

As discussed in Chapter 2.10, "NPC Rooting Interest Techniques," some Emotioneering techniques are multi-functional, in that they serve more than one purpose. This technique is also a Motivation Technique, explored in the previous chapter.

One way to provide Cohesiveness is to take the various characters, locations, and events that at first seem disconnected and let the player gradually discover that there are larger relationships and possibly plot-lines tying them all together.

Before addressing games, let's see how the challenge has been handled in film and television. An example would be the hip, darkly funny (and very worth seeing) film, *Go*. It presents us with a number of teens in a variety of weird adventures. Gradually we see that their different plot-lines, which at first seem unrelated, eventually all tie together. *Pulp Fiction*, which seems to have been one of the inspirations behind *Go*, did the same thing. Shifting to television, the show *Seinfeld* also consistently interwove seem-ingly disparate plot-lines in a funny way. The film *L.A. Confidential* struck a serious tone as it tied together a number of characters and plots that at first seemed disconnected.

Here's an example from a hypothetical game: Let's say that, in the game, you've been collecting shards of colored meteors that have been splinter-ing and falling to earth. These colored rocks, especially when they're collected in quantities, give you unique abilities.

---

3. Would this exploration of power be Idea Mapping or Multiple Viewpoints? If it's an interesting intellectual exercise, it's Idea Mapping and it's a Plot Deepening Technique. If it causes the player to wrestle with moral and emotional issues, it's Multiple Viewpoints and it's a First-Person Deepening Technique. For an extensive discussion of these issues, see Chapter 2.21, "First-Person Deepening Techniques."

Meanwhile, there have been sightings of alien craft that have been appearing in your vicinity with increasing frequency.

The rocks and the alien craft seem unrelated. Later, however, you find out the larger pattern: These meteors have been sent by aliens, who want you to develop your powers so you can help them in their approaching hour of need.

Abilities You Learn in One Part of the Game Are Useful Later in the Game

Continuity doesn't only have to come from external sources. In life, we provide our own continuities by applying skills learned in one part of our life to situations we find in another.

If you learn to swim underwater in one part of the game, and you need this skill in an emergency situation later in the game, this also creates Cohesiveness.

This, of course, is a technique already used frequently in many games.

Remind Us of the Stakes

Here's an example of this technique: You're trying to free the castle, which has been held hostage by a family of dragons.

You've got to go out and learn to slay other mythical beasts, improving your skills and knowledge until you're ready to assault the bionic flame-throwers themselves.

If, every once in awhile, you get news of the increasingly dire situation within the castle, that reminds you of the stakes and gives the game some Cohesiveness—especially if you care about one or more of the characters who are endangered.

Final Thoughts

If you're playing a *Star Wars* game and fighting the Empire, you've got a lot of Cohesiveness built right in. You've got a persistent enemy, persistent allies, you live in a universe where people in one part are aware of those in another, and so on.

But this isn't always the case in every game. If, in the game you design, you've got the player's character going on an adventure, particularly if it's an adventure that takes the player from one location to another on a kind of "road trip," then sometimes you need to work to ensure that it all hangs together—i.e., that it stays Cohesive.

If the game offers you the chance to play different characters, even characters who don't "know" each other, and these characters go through very different types of missions, then the need for Cohesiveness becomes paramount.

Your life, no doubt, has continuity. That's because it utilizes many Cohesiveness Techniques. Although the number of Cohesiveness Techniques is quite vast, hopefully the ones mentioned in this chapter will serve as a strong foundation.

Emotioneering Techniques Category #27

"True-to-Life" Techniques

Techniques

A realistic talk about realism.

Adding a sense
of realism to the NPCs' emotional actions and reactions helps create emotional immersion.

Certainly, in the past, one of the primary ways of making a game immersive has been to make it look, sound, and feel realistic.

This effort has prompted successive innovations in creating software that emulates the refraction of light, the textures of buildings, and the semi-random animation of fire, or of waves on the ocean. It's this effort that has prompted games to include changing weather, or to make day in a game turn into night.

The bottom line: Realism creates emotional immersion.

In *Star Trek Voyager: Elite Force,* you go on a variety of dangerous missions as part of a small squad. There are a few places in the game where you can overhear some of the other team members talking among themselves before a mission.

In one of these situations, you hear a character named Chell expressing his terror at the upcoming mission. Hearing him express his fear actually ups the fearfulness of the mission itself.

The moral of the story is that having NPCs undergo appropriate emotions can make the game much more realistic. This means, for instance, having an NPC express such things as:

- ◆ Fear before or during a frightening situation or event
- ◆ Relief after it's over
- ◆ Sorrow for a wounded or killed comrade
- ◆ Exhilaration after a difficult mission or piece of a mission is over

Remember, however, that when a character expresses fear, sorrow, or some other powerful emotion, quite often the way it's best expressed isn't by the character stating his feelings directly. For instance, having an NPC say "I'm afraid" is usually weak writing and, thus, can undo efforts to create emotional immersion.

The same emotion can often be expressed much more powerfully by such techniques as:

- ◆ Having the NPC feign that he isn't afraid, yet have something about his tone of voice, his wording, or his actions contradict his statement.

- ◆ Having the NPC's pent-up emotion erupt inappropriately toward someone else. For example, before the big, looming battle, which your squad expects to lose, NPC "A" erupts angrily toward his best friend NPC "B," as a result of his inner tension.

- Learning that the NPC, despite his cool demeanor, is actually terrified—from a report by another NPC who saw evidence of the first character's terror.

- If the NPC does express his fear, "less is more" (having the NPC say few words) almost always communicates strong emotion more realistically and more powerfully than having the NPC go on and on.

Remember that your NPCs should have different Character Diamonds and, thus, would show fear in very different ways. (For more on making NPCs sound unique, see Chapters 2.1 through 2.4.)

Final Thoughts

When characters go through emotional situations but don't react with appropriate emotional responses (or react with no emotional responses at all), it causes the game to have a cartoony feeling. That's okay if that's the effect you want, but most of the time I've seen cartoony reactions by NPCs in games, it's a result of poor writing or design.

Once you decide on the emotional response you want, then you've got to find an artful way to communicate it.

Emotioneering Techniques Category #28

Cross-Demographic Techniques

What teens and adults
have in common:
    Hopefully, your game.

This chapter

focuses on techniques to make games appeal to both kids (or young teens) and adults.

At one of the game conventions I attended, a talk on how to make a hit game really caught my attention.

The speaker was the president of one of the most successful game development studios in the world, specializing in platformers. His company had just released a high-budget platformer whose sales, while significant, hadn't measured up to the very high expectations that had been set for it.

The company head's postmortem was that his game needed more violence. He pointed out that *Grand Theft Auto III*, which had debuted four months earlier to massive numbers, had a lot of violence and was selling quite well. He said that his next game would have more violence, so that his games once again would be in sync with popular tastes.

I thought there was one thing right with his analysis, and three things wrong.

The right item is that, as this book is being written, platformers are indeed not performing well. Whether this will change in the future is hard to predict.

But I also had a couple problems with his analysis:

- There is no shortage of violent games on the market. Many sell well, but many sell poorly. So violence in and of itself isn't enough to, in any way, guarantee game sales.

- *Grand Theft Auto III* and its sequel *Vice City* use tons of Emotioneering techniques. It's the artful blending of great gameplay and Emotioneering that has resulted in these games' success, not violence in and of itself. To take another example, there are many games more violent than *Max Payne*, but it sold very well.

- I'd seen such attempts to find "magic pills" (easy solutions) in the film business, and they always fail. Various executives, in substitution for their lack of knowledge about story, characters, suspense, and the creation of emotional experiences, have tried relying on simple formulas. Or they'll become obsessed with one genre as the way to guarantee success. One year they might think it's big action pictures, the next year it's feel-good movies, or teen comedies, or films based on comic books, or romantic comedies, or whatever their idea of a sure-fire hit is.

Yes, there are trends, and it's great when you can ride one. But these magic pills rarely work. It turns out that films also need (what do you know) good writing.[1] This lesson applies to games as well, in that a search for a single formula to make a great game won't work.

Cross-Demographic Techniques

If I thought there was a magic pill, I wouldn't have written this book, for it would mean that everything you'd need to know about making games that were emotionally immersive could be summed up in a single technique.

Certainly one way to try to increase game sales is, when appropriate (and it's not always appropriate), to reach a range of demographics. Various films and TV shows have succeeded in appealing to both kids or teens, and adults as well, such as:

- The *Lord of the Rings* films
- The *Terminator* films
- *Pirates of the Caribbean*
- *Star Wars—Episodes IV, V*, and *VI*
- *The Matrix* (At the time this book is being completed, it's too early to say whether the sequels will have the same cross-demographic appeal as did the first film.)
- The *Austin Powers* films
- *The Simpsons*
- The *Toy Story* films
- The *Men in Black* films
- *Shrek*
- *Buffy the Vampire Slayer*
- *Angel*

These films and TV shows appeal to multiple demographics, and they do so because they use what I call *Cross-Demographic Techniques*.

---

1. The exception might be sequels. Sometimes, if the first film is incredibly popular, people will flock to the sequel even if it's far inferior.

The General Idea

The general idea to making a game with an appeal that crosses demographics is, first of all, to figure out a game that would appeal to the younger demographic you want, whether that's kids (as in *Toy Story*) or teens (as in *The Matrix*). Then layer in those elements that would also make the game appeal to adults. There are many such elements. Let's look at a few.

Self-Deconstructing Humor

This is humor that, with an implicit "wink-wink," makes fun of itself. Kids laugh and adults laugh. *The Simpsons* uses this technique quite frequently.

For instance, in one episode, a friend of Bart's begins using dirty language. His parents recount the list of dirty words he's been using to Marge, Bart's mother, and declare that their son must have picked the words up from Bart. It's the only possible answer, they conclude, for their son couldn't have learned these words from TV. The joke, of course, is that we just saw the words used on TV. *The Simpsons* has always been filled with this kind of humor.

Another example from the same episode: Bart and his class are about to go on a field trip to a boring box factory. Bart deals with it by escaping into a daydream. But the only image he can conjure up is the fantasy of himself going to a box factory. He wakes up from his reverie, angry at television for destroying his imagination.

Giving NPCs Character Arcs

Giving the character you play in the game a First-Person Character Arc (see Chapter 2.20) or giving a Character Arc to a major NPC (see Chapter 2.9) won't turn away a younger player, but might help grab an older one. Adults enjoy the emotional sophistication of a character growing emotionally.

Trendy Comedy

Adults and kids like trendy comedy. I say trendy comedy because comedy, by its nature, tends to be trendy. Many TV shows of the past that seemed hilarious, witty, or cutting-edge when new no longer seem quite as funny. These include *I Love Lucy*, *Remington Steel*, *M*A*S*H*, *Cheers*, *Northern Exposure*, and even *Seinfeld*. Comedy tends to date.

It's to the credit of the writers and other creative talent behind *The Simpsons* that they managed to keep it alive for so many years.

Grand Theft Auto III used a style of comedy popularized in such films as *Pulp Fiction*.

How can you predict the next trend in comedy? There's no formula. But one thing you can do is pay attention to the trends, and watch which trends seem to have the most staying power.[2]

A Game That Takes Place in a Rich World

A rich world is something that, layered into a game, will also increase its appeal to an older demographic.

The richness of Tolkien's world couldn't possibly be captured in a film. Most people agree, however, that the *Lord of the Rings* films did as good a job as was possible. It helped make the movie much more than just a kids' film.

To learn how to construct a rich world, take a look at Chapter 2.18, "World Induction Techniques;" Chapter 2.5, "Group Interesting Techniques;" and Chapter 2.6, "Group Deepening Techniques."

Have Characters Who Undergo Either Adult or Complicated Emotions

One could say that the *Lord of the Rings* films have a heroic struggle that adults can relate to. However, you can see equally titanic struggles and quests on many Saturday morning cartoons. So a "hero journey" or a titanic struggle isn't enough to make a story appeal to an adult.

In *Lord of the Rings*, we also see adult or complicated emotions. For instance, Aragorn (also known as Strider) feels compelled to aid in the destruction of the ring out of guilt. His ancestor was responsible for the failure to destroy the ring the first time around.

---

2. People often say that humor is hard to weave into a game. There are quite a few types of comedy that would work in games. I suspect that one of the reasons we haven't seen more hysterically funny games is because very few A-list comedy writers have worked in games. Of course, even if one was to try, he or she would still need to surmount all problems delineated in Chapter 1.4, "17 Things Screenwriters Don't Know About Games," and would need to figure out how all the various game structures discussed in Chapter 2.16, "Plot Interesting Techniques," could become tools for comedy.

And in *The Two Towers*, the elves have the difficult decision whether to help rescue mankind for a fate that mankind brought upon itself by failing to destroy Sauron's ring when it had the chance.

Also in *The Two Towers*, Gollum is torn between thinking and acting like the degraded creature he has become, or the human (Smiegel) he used to be.

In both films, there's an elf woman, Arwen, in love with Aragorn. She maintains her love, even though she knows she's immortal and he's mortal, and it will bring her sorrow in the end when time takes him away from her.

All of these issues are ones that have the kind of complexity that can appeal to an adult.

The Use of Deepening Techniques

As you might recall from Chapter 1.8, "Where Screenwriting Leaves Off and Emotioneering Begins," Deepening Techniques fall into many categories. And in this book we've looked at many ways that dialogue, individual characters, and groups can be given depth.

Adding depth into a game (or film) can help gain an older demographic without losing a younger one.

By way of a case study, let's take a look at 15 of the Deepening Techniques that were woven into the first two *Lord of the Rings* films (the only ones out at the time of this book was completed), helping them become such huge cross-demographic hits.[3]

- **Character Deepening**: Strider's (Aragorn's) guilt.

- **Character Deepening**: Gandalf's mysterious abilities.

- **Character Deepening**: The Elves' mysterious abilities.

- **Character Deepening**: Any time a character puts aside selfish desires to fulfill a grander duty. This happens repeatedly, with many characters and groups, such as the Ents and the Elves, and even, at times, Gollum.

---

3. Remember, Deepening Techniques are usually designed to operate outside the audience's or game player's conscious awareness. How many of these Deepening Techniques did you spot in the films? If you missed many or all of them, don't worry—most were intentionally designed to affect the audience without being consciously noticed.

- **Character Deepening**: Internal conflict in many characters, such as in Gollum, as discussed earlier. Gollum is torn apart by his self interest, conflicting with a tenuous sense of what's right. He's torn between what he once was and what he has become. He's torn between being human and being an animal. And he's torn between sanity and insanity.

- **Character Deepening**: Many characters have Character Arcs. For instance, Frodo and Sam learn to be heroes. The Ents learn to take responsibility for their world. The Elves overcome their insular self-interest. Gandalf evolves spiritually.

- **Scene Deepening**: An example is the moment of utter desolation when Gandalf and the Fellowship are almost destroyed on a snowy mountain ledge in *Fellowship of the Ring*. There are many other such moments of desolation, such as when all seems lost at the battle that ends *The Two Towers*.

- **Relationship Deepening**: The relationship between Gandalf and Frodo is complex. On one hand, Gandalf feels protective, almost fatherly, toward Frodo. On the other hand, in some ways Frodo is his superior, in that he has the purity to carry the ring.

- **Plot Deepening**: The ring is a symbol that takes on increasing emotional associations as the film goes on (see Chapter 2.23, "Enhancing Emotional Depth Through Symbols").

- **Plot Deepening**: The use of symbols for good and evil. The symbols of good are light, trees, and water. The symbols of evil are dark, machinery, and fire. I call any symbol like this a *symbol of a concept*.

- **Plot Deepening**: Another symbol of a concept is the pendant Arwen gives Aragorn, which symbolizes her love.

- **Plot Deepening**: The rich world of the film, discussed earlier.

- **Plot Deepening**: Parallel plot-lines. Frodo, who is small, turns out to be incredibly powerful. The ring, which is small, turns out to be incredibly powerful.

- **Plot Deepening**: Opposite plot-lines. Gandalf and Saruman are both wizards. However, Gandalf chooses good, and Saruman chooses evil.

- **Plot Deepening**: A theme is woven into the *Fellowship of the Rings*. The theme is "power." We see power explored from many different angles:

- The power of evil to corrupt the good, such as Gandalf's teacher, Sauranon.

- The power of a team working in concert (the Fellowship).

- The power of innocence (Frodo).

- The power of magic (Gandalf).

- The power of an army (Sauron's and Saruman's forces).

    In the second film, the theme changes to duty.

The films use many, many other Deepening Techniques (such as Dialogue Deepening Techniques) in addition to the 15 mentioned here. Together they contributed to the film's emotional depth, and they're a big part of why the film appealed to adults as well as kids.

Final Thoughts

In this chapter, we've glanced at a few ways to make games appeal to a variety of ages. There are no easy solutions to making a game with broad demographic appeal...but there are ways to hedge your bets.

Although this chapter has discussed many techniques used in films and television, they'll work in games as well. For instance, if you take another look at the list of techniques from *Lord of the Rings*, you'd find that every single one would also be appropriate for a game.

Emotioneering Techniques Category #29

Injecting Emotion into a Game's Story Elements

Some people like to keep things simple.
How boring.

What constitutes

a story? Each element opens up possibilities for emotion.

Almost every element or component of a game's story (assuming it has one) offers an opportunity to evoke emotion. But to understand how to use story elements to brainstorm emotional game experiences, we first need to define what a "story element" is.

Dissecting a Story

Not long ago I was addressing the collective faculty at a large arts college in San Francisco. The subject of discussion was, "What creates a feeling of 'story' in a two-dimensional image, even an abstract one?"

I gave my theory, explaining that more than 150 elements are commonly found in stories. Some of these elements are necessary, and many, if not most, are optional—but not uncommon. Some occur in a story just once, some several times, and some recurrently.

If you were to take a slice of a story at any of the points where these elements exist, and made an image of that cross-section, you'd have an image that implies or evokes a "story" in progress.

For instance, *opposition* is common in many stories. A picture that portrays two opposing people or forces—even an abstract image that conveys this feeling—will feel like it "has story" and will be emotionally engaging.

Story Elements in Types of Games That We Normally Don't Think of as Possessing "Stories"

Competition is another common story element. You could have such a element in a football game, even though there's no story in the traditional sense.

Indeed, when sports announcers sum up a football game or even an Olympic ski jumping event, their summaries sound like exciting stories.

Simple and Complex Emotion

Each story element can be scrutinized to see if it can be made more emotionally engrossing or more emotionally complex. "Engrossing" and "complex" may seem to be unrelated terms, but more often than not, they're strongly tied.

Let's take a look at an example: In *Star Wars—Episode IV*, Luke's final struggle to shoot a missile through a small hole to blow up the Death Star seems to be both engrossing and simple. A young man in a spaceship blows up the Death Star. Not very complex, right?

But, upon closer inspection, we can see that this event isn't simple at all. Here are some of the layers of complexity that make that scene of Luke making his final run more emotional:

- **We identify with Luke because of various Rooting Interest Techniques.** For instance, when his family is killed near the beginning, that's Undeserved Misfortune, which is a Rooting Interest Technique. We identify with the climactic Death Star scene because he's in Jeopardy (a Rooting Interest Technique), as are countless others who depend on him.

- **This scene completes Luke's Character Arc: From not knowing who he is at the start of *Episode IV*, to knowing he is a Jedi knight.** In fact, he makes that shot in the end by relying on his Jedi intuition of The Force, not by using his targeting scanners.

- **He's able to make that shot because he's got back-up in the form of Han Solo, who is busy completing his own Character Arc.** He has gone from being a loner to being willing to be part of an ethical group.

- **Luke is not there by himself.** Not only does he have R2-D2 and Han Solo helping out, but even the disembodied Obi-Wan plays a role. So there's a statement being made about the power of a group to combat evil.

- **Luke uses The Force to aid in aiming his missile, while Darth Vader, on the Death Star, uses The Force for evil.** And so the moment is the culmination of a story full of spiritual undertones—which is a Plot Deepening Technique—and opposing plot-lines, which is another Plot Deepening Technique.

- **Luke, using his Jedi powers to aim that missile, represents the rebirth of the Jedi.** At the beginning of the film, the Jedi had suppos-edly all died out, with Darth Vader being their one relic-gone-bad. Obi-Wan had thrown in the towel and was in seclusion. With one shot, Luke revives the Jedi and revives hope.

In summary, we have numerous story-lines converging in this one scene. They belong to:

+ Luke
+ Obi-Wan
+ Han Solo
+ The Jedi
+ The Empire

The convergence of these factors makes Luke's final run to blow up the Death Star anything but simple.

If game designers aren't aware of how such factors work together to create emotionally gripping moments, or aren't able to create such complex and impactful emotionally layered situations, then their games will lose out on countless opportunities to be more emotionally engrossing.

Using Story Elements to Brainstorm Emotional Complexity

Let's take a look at a few of the many possible story elements, and see how they can be used to brainstorm emotionally complex and engaging game experiences. Then we'll ask, "What can be done to make these story elements more emotionally complex?" I call this process *Complexification*.

To demonstrate this technique, I chose a strange assortment of story elements, picking some that occur in many stories (like "danger") and some that would appear in a much smaller selection (like "racing"). The example story elements are:

+ An enemy
+ Danger
+ Racing
+ A mystery
+ Tension
+ Spying
+ Good guys/bad guys

Let's see how emotional complexity can be injected into these elements.

An Enemy

What if it's an espionage game, and the top enemy spy you've got to kill was a close friend of yours earlier in the game?

The illustration provides another example: Our hero fights another version of himself, who has returned from the future. His future self says his younger self has to die, for the good of humanity.

If you're playing the younger character in the game, this would be a very emotionally complex moment, especially if you believe that your future self is both sane, and sincere, and possibly accurate.

Danger

You're a soldier in World War II, and your commander is your uncle—a man who has already saved your life on two occasions. You volunteer for a dangerous mission, but he doesn't want you to go. You go anyway, but upset him in the process. You've hurt someone you care about, in order to do the right thing.

Racing

In a street racing game, what if the guy who fixes up your car—your mechanic and ad hoc pit boss—is the best in the business, but he has a disgusting personality, at least some of the time. He's only helping you build and maintain your car because you both share an enemy—the other great street racer in the city. So you feel different layers of feelings toward him (Admiration and Loathing), either at different times, or perhaps even or simultaneously. (This topic was discussed in Chapter 2.13, "Player Toward NPC Relationship Deepening Techniques.")

Here's another example: You race a crazy street course a number of times, splitting whenever the cops show up. The game itself tracks your score. You have two friends who help keep your car in top shape with all the latest upgrades.

Your two friends are kidnapped by your rival. The kidnapper will kill them all if you don't beat your own best score by 10 percent.

In effect, you're now competing against yourself, and the lives of your crew hang on the outcome. This is an Emotionally Complex Situation (see Chapter 2.15).

It's also a Plot Deepening Technique (see Chapter 2.17), in that the plot doubles back on itself in an interesting way. That is, your own high scores now come back to haunt you in an unexpected manner. However, there won't be much feeling of depth here unless:

- You care about those two friends who've been kidnapped, and

- When you made that earlier high score, it was an exciting, big deal— a big deal to you, and to your (now kidnapped) friends, who helped you celebrate the triumph.

Thus, we have now have the irony that the victory they helped you celebrate may now cause their deaths. The plot has circled back on itself in an interesting (and emotional) way.

A Mystery

You begin a game by walking down a street in Chicago. Suddenly, with no warning, you find that you're in an office on a large, fully operational space station. And everyone seems to know you. Indeed, you look around your office and find evidence that you've spent considerable time here.

Rochelle, a young woman who's a technician on the station, quietly approaches and asks you to help her. She says she's in danger—the same danger you're in. And she's sorry for wiping out your memory. Suddenly guards are firing at her.

Do you help her or not? This tough decision is a First-Person Deepening Experience (see Chapter 2.21).

(I develop a similar plot-line to a much greater degree in Chapter 3.2, "Chasm.")

Tension

This example is a kid's game: You defend a weird animal realm from its enemies.

You've built a large machine that spews out (funny) magic wands. Each wand performs a different function. One reverses gravity and makes your enemies fly up into space. Another one makes an enemy laugh (literally) to death. Another turns an enemy into a large carrot.

Each wand can only be used twice, so you need to keep your machine producing new ones. But 1 out of every 20 weapons is defective and blows up as soon as it's ejected from the machine, all but eliminating your health points.

You could have built a machine that created only perfect wands with no defective ones, but that would have taken much more time to assemble and would have left you vulnerable to your enemy, whom you need to fight with these wands.

As you wait by the machine, you don't know if you're about to get blown up and injured by the next weapon that emerges, which in turn would put you out of commission for a while.

The fear that you'll get a defective wand creates tension as you wait to see what comes out of the machine, but still, there's nothing emotionally complex about it. So how could we add emotional complexity?

Let's say various other life-forms have come to depend on you—turtle-bears (bears with shells); cowraffes (cows with long necks like giraffes); and rabbicats (rabbits with cat heads and paws). These animals will die if you get injured and can't protect them from your mutual enemy. Suddenly, we've added some emotional complexity to the situation.

Spying

A new game: By boat, you've hunted your enemy and pursued him to a small but thickly wooded island. On the way here, you got caught in a storm and barely survived. Your boat was damaged. There are many dangerous creatures on the island.

Now you spy on your enemy, and, oddly, he's carefully repairing the small boat you took to get here, allowing you to escape from danger. There's no trick; he's not secretly sabotaging you. Why *is* he helping you? Is he secretly on your side?

This makes your enemy more complex, of course, but it also takes a story element like spying and adds to it emotional complexity.

Good Guys and Bad Guys (or Good and Evil)

We looked at the illustration on the preceding page and its accompanying hypothetical game in Chapter 2.25, "Motivation Techniques." You play the detective who has just discovered your police chief paying off a mobster. If anything, you had expected to find the mobster paying off someone in the police department, not vice versa.

In that chapter, we discussed this kind of mystery as something that can motivate a player to continue on through the game. Let's go further and see how we can take some of the story elements here and Complexify them.

In this example, we've Complexified not just "spying," but also "good guys and bad guys."

For as the game goes on, things will only get more complex regarding these two characters you're observing. You'll learn, in the following order:

1. That the city government had lost a fortune by purposely overpaying contractors on some city construction projects—with kickbacks going to the top government officials who hired the contractors.

2. Because of that corruption, now the city is broke. So the mayor and city council intend to save money by cutting the size of the police force—which would be a disaster for the citizens. Another reason they're doing this is to punish the police chief (the one you're spying on), because he was investigating the corruption in city government.

3. To keep the police force at its current size, the police chief has decided to manufacture an "emergency" that will make his force seem obviously needed so that the public will rally behind him. So he's paying this mob boss to engineer a riot that the police force will then come in and quell.

4. The chief feels terrible about this, but he's doing it for the greater good—that is, for the citizens.

5. The mobster who is taking the money has made a trade. For helping engineer the riot, the cops will leave his group alone for three years.

6. However, even with that arrangement, the mobster is disgusted by this deal. He has always taken pride that, in all his thefts, control of unions, and fights with other crime organizations, the citizens of the city haven't been physically harmed. But, in starting this riot, innocents stand a chance of being injured. This goes against everything he stands for.

This is our unfolding list of *Reveals*. By the time you, the player, have learned all of them, you'd see that the situation here is anything but black and white. Who are the good guys? The bad guys? You might, at the end of the day, put all the characters in the game somewhere on a scale from good to bad, but certainly the people and the situations are emotionally and morally complex.

Who would you fight in the game? At different times you might fight some friends of the police chief—the mobster and his men—and the mayor and his bodyguards. Alliances will continue to shift as you gain information and continually reassess who is good and who is bad.

Final Thoughts

The point here isn't that games are improved by seeing if there's a way to make every story element more emotionally or morally complex.

This chapter merely suggests a way to brainstorm methods of making a game more emotionally engaging: You can examine all of the game's story elements and decide if you can Complexify them in a way that enhances the game.

Emotioneering Techniques Category #30

Tying Story to Gameplay and Mechanics

What the player does should enhance the story, and vice versa.

In some games,

the story and the gameplay seem to be unrelated. Even if the story is compelling and the gameplay is fun, the ideal is to link the two. This chapter addresses this issue.

A failure to mesh game design and mechanics may not be a fatal flaw, but it's a waste of a good opportunity to further emotional engagement by the player.

Many games don't need to worry about this problem. The game *Spider-Man* is about a guy who turns into a human spider. Naturally, the principal game mechanic has you rapidly flinging your character on a string between skyscrapers like a yo-yo amped up on steroids. So story and game mechanics tie together nicely.

Thus, in some games, this potential problem is a non-issue, while in other games it deserves serious thought.

Final Fantasy X

Please note: If you intend to play *Final Fantasy X*, please skip this sidebar. I'll be giving away key plot twists and character revelations.

Final Fantasy X is a game that elicits strong reactions, both pro and con. Most fans of fantasy found the game wonderfully inventive and evocative, and felt that the world the game puts forward is intriguing and unique, and the plot is nothing short of amazing. But it's a mixed picture....

In an earlier chapter (Chapter 2.24, "Self-Created Story Techniques (a.k.a. Agency Techniques)"), we discussed the fact that the game limits the player's agency. It suffers from an additional weakness as well:

The biggest recurring story element in the game is dreams. In fact, the very character you play turns out to be someone else's dream. The subject of dreams weaves itself into the story in many additional ways. And yet, there are no dream mechanics. In the game, you should have been able to do things such as:

- Dream up weapons
- Go into some kind of dream mode where you receive special information
- Be able to escape into a dream world where you can receive some kind of power-up when you're overwhelmed in battle
- Go into a dream mode where you can leave your body and go into the mind of your opponents to see their weaknesses
- Project a dream image of yourself so that your enemy temporarily sees two of you and gets confused as to who to fight (making the wrong choice about half the time)
- Do *something* that involved a dream mechanic!

But you can't, which is a missed opportunity for tying the gameplay to the story.

Contrasting Examples

I'll further illustrate the importance meshing game design and mechanics with two contrasting fantasy/sci-fi examples.

The Obvious Example

Let's say you're designing a children's game with a *Hitchhiker's Guide to the Universe* kind of offbeat goofiness.

In this game, set in London, you play "Tyrone Camden McMead, ever so posh yet relaxed in his tweed." He's a man who hates cats. After Tyrone punishes the Grand Cat (the cat who rules all other cats), the Grand Cat turns him (*you*) into a cat. At this point, the game begins.

Your goal is to stop a group of adorable wiener dogs from spreading through the city. You know they're really the forward flank of an invading alien force.

This group of wiener dogs are spreading a secret odor that makes Brits love wiener dogs so much that they'll acquire more and more of them until the entire country is literally overrun by millions of wiener dogs.

The streets become a mass of writhing wiener dogs. In certain sectors of the city, wiener dogs are piled high in every house and shop. There's no more food for people to eat, and they get crushed below the towering carpet of wiener dogs. Big Ben is silenced, and becomes Big Has-Been. Soon the aliens will swoop in. Britain will be theirs for the taking.

What are the mechanics we'll use here? Obviously, because you play a cat, they involve such things as leaping, scratching, squeezing through tight spaces, landing on your feet, attracting by purring, repelling by hissing, and many other skills my college girlfriend had mastered.

The moral of the story: Because you're a cat, the mechanics are pretty obvious, and they'll fit in perfectly with the story.

The Not-So-Obvious Example

Now let's take a more challenging example.

Let's say that there's a game where you're an explorer on Mars, and you find that the planet is inhabited by ghosts—*human* ghosts. In fact, you learn that an evil, alien race brings people's souls here between lives. (In this game, reincarnation is real.) Once the human souls are here, the aliens erase their memories and implant new identities and purposes into the souls, and then send them back to Earth.

The goal of the aliens is to ensure that Earthlings are so alienated from their innate personalities, with wrong goals, altered identities, and needless worries, that they will undermine themselves and their world. It's all a way to keep them screwed up, ineffective, and self-destructive. Earth is thus a prison planet that needs no guards.

In the game, at first you need to deal with (fight) some tormented ghosts. Later, you'll need to take on the aliens. Finally, you'll need to go back to Earth and deal with some highly placed political leaders who are in collusion with the aliens.

What kind of mechanics suggest themselves to mesh with the game? It's not nearly so clear as with the cat example.

There are two approaches, and I'd probably apply them both.

One would be to make a list of necessary—almost obvious—mechanics and weapons, such as:

+ A weapon to deflect ghost attacks

+ A way of capturing ghosts

+ A weapon to "kill" a ghost (a strange concept)

+ A special, very cool weapon that can injure or kill the aliens, who have defenses against routine weapons

I'd try to make these items as imaginative, fun, and interesting to use as I could. Of course, all this is the obvious route any game designer would take.

The second approach would be more of a thematic one. This is the approach I suggested for *Final Fantasy X*.

Just as *Final Fantasy X* revolved around dreams, this game revolves around life, death, and identity. Therefore, I'd want some gameplay mechanics or weapons that reflect these themes.

For instance, I might create some kind of ray or device (the "Lazarus Ray") that can bring dead or dying people, animals, and plants back to life, although perhaps I could only use it on rare occasions. Or maybe the device is powered by my own life force—I get drained of life as I give life to others.

As the game is about people passing into a ghost state, I'd want some kind of method whereby *I* could temporarily die, or at least turn myself into a ghost. Maybe, once I turn into a ghost, I have new abilities, such as moving through walls, spying on the aliens without easily being seen, or changing into a frightening appearance.

I would need to use these mechanics—bringing things to life and being able to become a ghost for periods of time—to win the game.

Because the aliens reprogram the identities of the ghosts before they reincarnate, then I'd want some way to awaken them from this programming.

It could be a device or form of gameplay such as:

- A special kind of mirror that showed them their real soul.

- A way of fighting with the dark being—their implanted personality—that rides piggy-back on their soul. Once defeated, it leaves them free to be themselves.

- Maybe another tool could be a pair of questions asked to them: What were your deepest dreams? When did you give them up? The ghosts wouldn't need to answer—just being asked would be enough to snap them out of their programming.[1] Of course, something much more active, dangerous, and difficult than a pair of questions would be more fun.

In short, I'd want mechanics and gameplay that related to the themes of life and death, as well as identity.

Just the Other Day

Just the other day I was talking to the Creative Director at a successful development studio. He was telling me about a rough idea for a game. Although the details of the game were still a long way from coming together, nonetheless his company was committed to making the game. They already had a publisher.

Now, to tell this story, I've got to change a lot of details about the game's story, locations, weapons, and so on, but I'll give an analogous example. He bounced his game off me, and I spent ten minutes giving him some ideas.

---

1. And if I was very clever indeed, I would put the player through a First-Person Character Arc so that, by the end of the game, he or she might be sincerely asking himself or herself the same two questions. See Chapter 2.20, "First-Person Character Arc Techniques."

His game (let's say) involves evil, giant, intelligent crab-like creatures who live under the surface of the ocean's floor.[2] Although not human in appearance, they are as smart as men and have evolved a sophisticated culture. A volcanic eruption has broken through the ocean's crust, and now these are swarming into the ocean, preparing for a land invasion.

You play an oceanographic researcher who stumbles upon this emerging danger. Using what you know, you fashion weapons based on some of the offensive and defensive systems used by sting rays, jellyfish, and octopi.

You capture one of the weapons[3] of the enemy at one point and use it in an emergency situation. It's not the only weapon you could use at that point, but it's the best one for the job.

You don't realize that the weapon itself is *alive. For these creatures, weapons are part of their family and have responsibilities to the family.* The weapon you stole actually *spies on your weapons*—and transmits what it learns to the enemy.

As a result, one of your own weapons is compromised, for the enemy can now build a defense. (The weapon you lose is your poisonous tentacle weapon, based on jellyfish.) So, for a short-term advantage (stealing one of their weapons), you now pay a long-term penalty.

This was my first round of ideas. They handled one issue regarding tying the story to gameplay: I merged the undersea story with sea-related weapons.

I also added some emotional complexity to the plot by having the original advantage poised by the creature's weapon turn into a disadvantage.

However, the story and gameplay still weren't merged nearly enough in my mind. So I suggested that the character you play is the kind of guy who got into oceanographic research because he likes isolation; he doesn't have a very high regard for people. And now that he's fighting these undersea creatures, he's inclined to do it alone.

We'd incentivize this behavior by having a couple people, at the start of the game, act rudely to him by mocking his research. We'd learn that your

---

2. As opposed to your more common *friendly* giant, intelligent crab-like creatures who live under the surface of the ocean's floor.

3. Weapons are a Story Element; here, I Complexified the enemy's weapon. See Chapter 2.29, "Injecting Emotion into a Game's Story Elements."

character has endured a lifetime of this kind of abuse. This way you, the player, don't break your bond with your character when you learn he prefers isolation. After all, when these NPCs mock him, they're in effect mocking you too. (See Chapter 2.19, "Role Induction Techniques.")

Much of the game takes place under water, where there are fish. Fish swim in schools. I suggested that there should be schools of fish we see periodically throughout the game—and they will be the symbol of what your character (and you, the player) need to learn—to act willingly as part of a group. (See Chapter 2.23, "Enhancing Emotional Depth Through Symbols.") They'd appear whenever you had a decision to make regarding whether to go it alone or work with others.

Ultimately, to fight the invaders from under the seabed, you'll need to work with some allies. Like fish, you'll need to leave your isolation behind and, metaphorically, swim with your school. (See Chapter 2.20, "First-Person Character Arc Techniques.") Some of your new allies will be humans, one will be an enemy who has changed sides, and even some sea creatures will lend a hand. The more you work with others, the more success you'll have.

Each ally helps in their own way—either by assisting in battle (an octopus helps you escape behind an ink shield, or a stingray lets you ride on his back as you attack). The humans help in more traditional ways.

In the end, you will have found your own school of fish, so to speak. That is, you will no longer be an isolationist.

So now the story and gameplay are integrated in a number of ways:

- **You have weapons modeled after those of sea creatures for use in an undersea war.** So these weapons tie into the story and offer related gameplay mechanics.

- **To fight, you must work with others who bring their own skills to help you in battle.** This involves not just game mechanics, but teaches a lesson that is part of the story: to work in a group the way that fish do.

- **Some of those who help you in battle are underwater creatures.** So riding on a stingray or being helped by an octopus feed into gameplay mechanics, are integrated into the story, and contribute to your First-Person Character Arc.

- **Even your enemy's weapon—the one that spied on you—is related to both gameplay and the story.** Regarding gameplay, it ruined your ability to use one of your own weapons. Regarding the story, your enemy's weapons acted as part of a family—the exact thing you'll need to learn to do. So using that weapon feeds into gameplay mechanics. It's integrated into the story, and contributes to your First-Person Character Arc.

◆ **Someone you knew and didn't like (at that point in the game) advised you against using that enemy's weapon.** Had you followed that advice, you would have been better off. This story twist also impacts gameplay, but relates to your First-Person Character Arc, too.

In my conversation with the Creative Director, I focused on a number of areas, but primarily on creating a story, a First-Person Character Arc, and gameplay mechanics that all tied together.[4]

My friend, the Creative Director, was delighted with the direction of these suggestions. He thanked me in what perhaps might be the nicest way possible—he hired me on the spot to work on the game. I've already begun.[5]

Final Thoughts

Do the mechanics and gameplay in your game feel like they're an extension of your characters or story? Do they echo the theme or themes of your story? That's the ideal.

Just to make your life more complex, however, I'll toss something into the mix that seems to contradict the ideas in this chapter.

I've worked on many games that started not with a character, nor a story, nor with an overall vision of a game, but began with a group of gameplay ideas and mechanics that someone wanted to see in a game. Those having been decided upon, a story and game were built around them.

Even when working under such an approach, I still strive to take those gameplay ideas and mechanics and weave them into a story for which they have particular relevancy.

---

4. Of course, I also did some Technique Stacking. The techniques used were referenced elsewhere in this section.

5. By the way, the game doesn't take place under water or involve fish or intelligent crabs. The example is an analogy. An NDA (non-disclosure agreement) prevents me from discussing the details of the game. Also, I was biologically altered on a cellular level so that if I was to describe the actual game, I'd explode.

So whether I'm beginning with story or beginning with game mechanics, my approach is the same.

Still left undecided is this question: Is it possible that I've actually been granted the ability to see the future, and, knowing that a wiener dog invasion is at hand, have used this chapter to warn you so you can prepare for the end?

Emotioneering Techniques Category #31

Writing Powerful

Pre-Rendered and In-Game Cinematics

Stacking emotional layers in short cinematics.

This chapter shows

ways to make both in-game and pre-rendered cinematics more artful and,
thereby, more emotionally complex and powerful.

When you talk about writing in games, some designers think you're speaking only about cinematics.[1]

Of all the ways to evoke emotion, however, cinematics are the least game-like portion of any game. That's not a criticism, just a fact. Still, they play a role in many games and probably will for some time to come.

In some games, they serve powerful functions:

+ To set the tone of the game in the beginning or to establish the story itself

+ To establish a particular character

+ To establish the game's world and its backstory

+ To bridge the story from the last game, if the game is a sequel

+ To bridge one section of the game to the next

+ To reward a player for making it to a certain point in the game

Two categories of Emotioneering deal with cinematics. We'll examine one here and the other in Chapter 2.32, "Opening Cinematic Techniques."

Learning from Film

Because cinematics are, in effect, short films, every single technique that factors into writing great films also applies to cinematics. This includes creating unique characters, riveting dialogue, compelling scenes, and so on.

Poorly written cinematics can be:

+ Wooden

+ Corny

---

1. A *cinematic* is a section in a game that is like a very short movie. The player loses control of the game and watches passively. Cinematics can range from a few seconds to a few minutes.

There are currently no consistent terms for these cinematics. Cinematics animated or filmed separately from the game and then later integrated into the game are called *pre-rendered cinematics*, *FMV (full-motion video)*, *cut scenes*, or *CG cinematics (computer graphics cinematics)*. Cinematics created with the game engine are called *in-game cinematics*, *in-engine cinematics*, *in-game-engine cinematics*, or *real-time cinematics*. Some in-game cinematics permit the player to control the camera angle.

To say that an in-game cinematic is created with the game engine necessitates that we define *game engine* as well. A game engine is code that makes a game run, renders what you see in the game, renders the audio, governs the use of the controller, and operates all other systems that make the game function. Some (but by no means all) in the game industry also use either the term *rendering engine* or *renderer* for the code that renders what you see in a game, and say that the *rendering engine* or the *renderer* is a subset (or part) of the *game engine*.

- "On the nose" (people saying their feelings directly instead of hinting at them)

- Amateurish due to many other factors, described next

Here are a few guidelines for writing riveting cinematics.

Few or No "Blocks"

When one is writing in screenplay format, with the dialogue in a column in the middle of the page, I call a *block* any time there are three or more lines (not sentences) in a character's dialogue. Minimize these blocks or your characters will sound like they're making speeches, not conversing. An exception might be in a formal or informal debate.

Give Major Characters Interesting Diamonds

Characters should possess a colorful grouping of personality Traits that determine their dialogue and their actions (a Character Diamond). To learn about creating colorful Character Diamonds, see Chapter 2.1, "NPC Interesting Techniques."

Ambivalence Between Characters Can Make a Cinematic More Interesting

It's okay, in a cinematic, for a character to have mixed feelings about another character. For instance, a character could feel, simultaneously, both appreciation and annoyance toward a second character.

Or, instead of simple ambivalence, you can make the relationships between characters even more complex with this next technique:

Use Layer Cakes Between Characters to Give Their Relationships Complexity Beyond Simple Ambivalence

Layer Cakes mean that Character A has various layers of feelings toward Character B. These varied feelings can present themselves either simultaneously or sequentially. For a full description of how to create Layer Cakes, take a look at Chapter 2.8, "NPC Toward NPC Relationship Deepening Techniques."

Watch Out for the Cliché and Bland Lines

"You won't get away with this!" is cliché and bland. "How's it going?" is bland. Such lines are fine for the first draft or two. But try to avoid any such lines in a cinematic.

Can It Be Said or Told Better with Actions Rather Than Words?

This one in particular will become more and more important as our ability to animate facial expressions in games improves.

Time Permitting, It's Okay to Briefly Stray from the Topic at Hand

Conversations rarely stick to a single topic. Instead, they tend to weave in other strands, some of which never go anywhere. However, with cinematics currently being so expensive to produce and players' eagerness to get on to gameplaying always present, your cinematics might not be able to benefit from this writing technique.

No Predictabilty

Either have the player be unable to predict the outcome of the cinematic, or else be unable predict the way that outcome is achieved.

Obstacles and Interruptions Can Make a Cinematic More Interesting

This is especially true if the obstacle or interruption comes at a seemingly inappropriate time, such as when two people are arguing.

Use Dialogue Devices to Make the Dialogue Sound Natural

There are many techniques you can employ to make dialogue capture the natural sound of spoken speech. I call these *Dialogue Devices*. Many are used and explained in the example that follows.

Summary

The previous sections explain a few techniques you can use to make your cinematics more interesting. They're easier to understand if you see them applied in an example, so let's look at one.

The Example

The first example scene was written by one of my students (a beginner at the time, who asked me to rewrite it). It deals with the first women to join the Navy, which occurred in WWII. It's reprinted here with her permission. (She has, by the way, gone on to become quite an accomplished screenwriter.)

note

Although neither version of the scene in this chapter would necessarily end up as a cinematic in a game, the techniques used in the rewritten version are applicable to almost all cinematics.

The original scene lacks many of the specific techniques that could enrich the scene's flow, the characters, their relationship to one another, and their dialogue.

I then rewrote the scene, using not just the techniques listed previously in this chapter, but many additional ones as well.

The third version is the same as the second, but points out every single technique I used. You'll find there are quite a few. It's dissected with many drawings and explanations as to exactly why certain artistic choices were made, and which writing technique or techniques have been employed.

Writing riveting cinematics requires a wealth of screenwriting techniques, far too extensive to enumerate. However, you'll be introduced to a minor cornucopia of techniques in the third version.

note

There are many terms used in the third (deconstructed) version of the scene to describe the screenwriting techniques that have been used. These terms aren't used anywhere else in the book. Therefore, the last portion of this chapter contains a glossary of these terms. Most of them are only defined here, and not in the glossary at the end of the book.

You'll find that the rewritten scene is longer than the original. Because I rewrote the scene for the purposes of demonstration, I crammed into it tons of techniques. In a real cinematic, you might want to use only a portion of the techniques that are used here.

The Student's Scene

The following is the original scene, written by one of my students.

```
INT. ADMIRAL COLBY'S INNER OFFICE - DAY

Plush oak, immense. At his desk, ADMIRAL JASON
COLBY calmly continues writing. VICE ADMIRAL
MADISON DALTON stands.

                    COLBY
        I'm not backing down, Maddy.

                    DALTON
        Women do NOT belong in MY navy.

                    COLBY
        Your job is to recruit 900 potential
        women officers in the next 90 days.

                    DALTON
        We're in the middle of a war for
        God's sake.

                    COLBY
        Admiral James Madison Dalton,
        are you contradicting a superior
        officer?

                    DALTON
        No, Sir, but...

                    COLBY
        But, nothing, Maddy. You know
        how to recruit and train better
        than anyone and we're in a hurry
        with this thing. Surely someone
        named for a president can handle
        training a few women.

                    DALTON
        Give this to McNary. They can all
        fail together.
```

>   COLBY
> I'm a patient man, but...
>   (booming voice)
> Get the hell out of here and
> that's an order!
>
>   DALTON
> This is an invasion.

This version of the scene conveys information, but neither the characters, their relationships, their dialogue, nor the scene itself are sufficiently compelling nor emotionally layered.

David's Scene

Consider the same scene after my rewrite:

> INT. ADMIRAL COLBY'S INNER OFFICE - DAY
>
> Plush oak, immense. At his desk, ADMIRAL JASON
> COLBY calmly continues writing. VICE ADMIRAL
> MADISON DALTON stands.
>
>   COLBY
> I'm not backing down, Maddy.
>
>   DALTON
> Ed, what do you like most about
> the Navy?
>
>   COLBY
> Like?
>
> He thinks for a few seconds.
>
>   COLBY
> Gotta be the grub.
>
> Both he and Dalton smile.
>
>   DALTON
> See? And I always thought those
> stripes drained a man of his
> humor.

```
                    COLBY
               (smiles)
          Love to chat, but Bertrand's
          due here at three.
               (pulls out a cigarette)
          Match?

                    DALTON
               (tosses him some matches
               from his pocket)
          Four years I've never seen you
          carry your own matches.

                    COLBY
               (lighting up)
          Basis of our friendship.
               (reflecting, wistful)
          Four years. Seems like four
          hundred...

                    DALTON
          War it...compresses time...
               (Colby nods at him)
          Ed, sticking women in blue...
          We're going to put the fear of
          God in the Krauts with our sailors
          wearing lipstick? For Christ's
          sake.

                    COLBY
               (takes a drag;
               seriously considers)
          Got a point.

                    DALTON
          Good.

     He turns to leave.

                    COLBY
          But I'm still doing it.

     Dalton spins to face him, disbelieving.

                    DALTON
          Exactly what do you have against
          the Navy...
               (derisively)
          "Sir?"
```

The door opens, Colby's secretary LORETTA
sticks her head in. She's 67 and frail-looking,
but with the spirit of a 16-year-old.

>
>   LORETTA
>   (rapid-fire)
>   Mimi, Eric's wife? she just had
>   a baby girl, 10 pounds 2 ounces
>   can you imagine? Jeez Louise --
>   (as the men stare)
>   Oh right, the knocking thing.
>   But I know how much you like her
>   and Eric so I thought you'd want
>   the skinny.

A quick smile, her head disappears, and the
door closes.

>   COLBY
>   Betty, she...likes coffee.

A long pause.

>   DALTON
>   War is half honor, half horror.
>   Put women in the middle --

>   COLBY
>   Maddy --

>   DALTON
>   -- they destroy the honor, and
>   I sure as hell don't want
>   to shove them into the horror.

>   COLBY
>   For once, Maddy, you've gotta
>   pretend to be a bigger man than
>   you are. Can't see the future?
>   That's your problem --

>   DALTON
>   Oh, I see it just fine.

>   COLBY
>   -- not the Navy's.

>   COLBY
> They want in and we want them
> in. And the day will come when
> we need them in.

Beat.

>   DALTON
> When that fiasco occurred on
> the Wichita --

>   COLBY
> That was different --

>   DALTON
> -- because of your policy of
> expedited training, I took the
> fall.

>   COLBY
> And I cleared you.

>   DALTON
> Now you're setting me up again.
> You're setting us both up.

>   COLBY
> Clean the wax out. You're
> dismissed, sailor. Now.

Dalton is momentarily stung by the pejorative
"sailor" comment, but then cuts into Colby with
his eyes. He turns and leaves.

Colby's face falls.

Deconstructed Scene

The following is the same scene, deconstructed to highlight the Emotioneering techniques I used. Please refer to the chapter's glossary for any words or terms that aren't self-explanatory.

```
INT. ADMIRAL COLBY'S INNER OFFICE - DAY

Plush oak, immense. At his desk, ADMIRAL JASON
COLBY calmly continues writing. VICE ADMIRAL
MADISON DALTON stands.
```

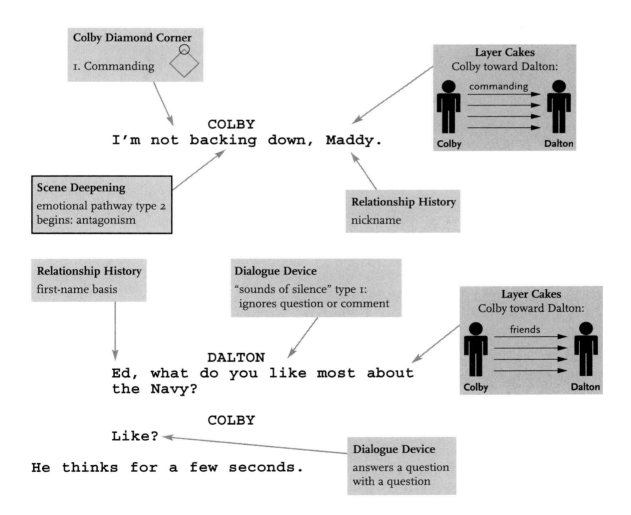

```
                        COLBY
          I'm not backing down, Maddy.
```

```
                      DALTON
          Ed, what do you like most about
          the Navy?
```

```
                    COLBY
              Like?

He thinks for a few seconds.
```

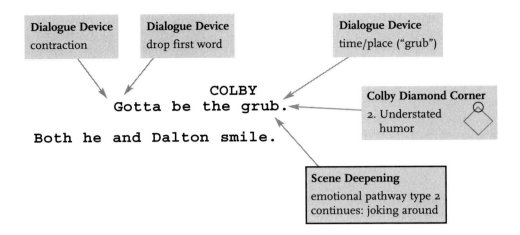

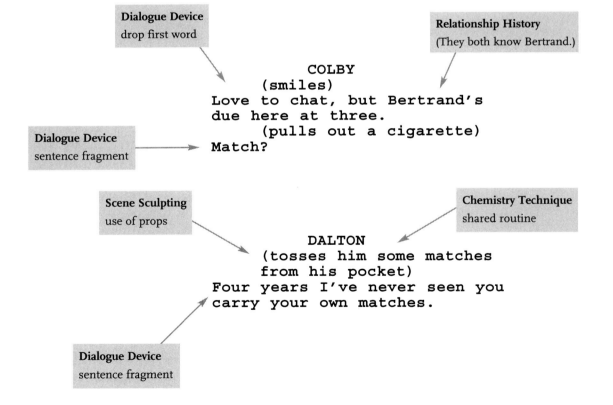

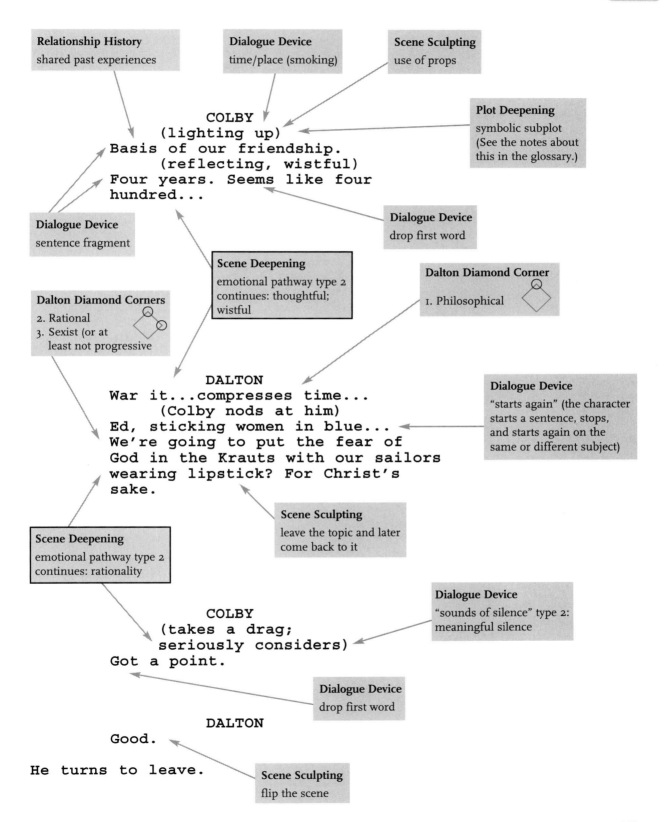

Relationship History
shared past experiences

Dialogue Device
time/place (smoking)

Scene Sculpting
use of props

Plot Deepening
symbolic subplot
(See the notes about
this in the glossary.)

COLBY
(lighting up)
Basis of our friendship.
(reflecting, wistful)
Four years. Seems like four
hundred...

Dialogue Device
sentence fragment

Dialogue Device
drop first word

Scene Deepening
emotional pathway type 2
continues: thoughtful;
wistful

Dalton Diamond Corner

1. Philosophical

Dalton Diamond Corners

2. Rational
3. Sexist (or at
   least not progressive

DALTON
War it...compresses time...
(Colby nods at him)
Ed, sticking women in blue...
We're going to put the fear of
God in the Krauts with our sailors
wearing lipstick? For Christ's
sake.

Dialogue Device
"starts again" (the character
starts a sentence, stops,
and starts again on the
same or different subject)

Scene Sculpting
leave the topic and later
come back to it

Scene Deepening
emotional pathway type 2
continues: rationality

Dialogue Device
"sounds of silence" type 2:
meaningful silence

COLBY
(takes a drag;
seriously considers)
Got a point.

Dialogue Device
drop first word

DALTON
Good.

He turns to leave.

Scene Sculpting
flip the scene

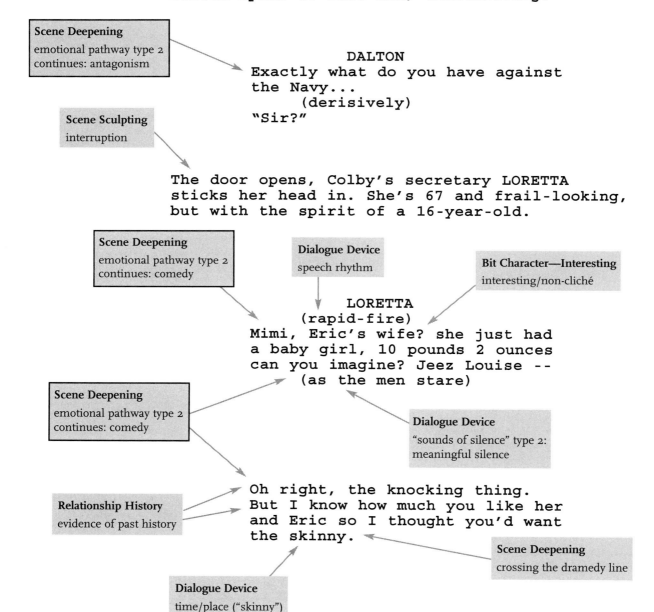

Scene Sculpting
twist

COLBY
But I'm still doing it.

Scene Sculpting
flip the scene back

Dalton spins to face him, disbelieving.

Scene Deepening
emotional pathway type 2
continues: antagonism

DALTON
Exactly what do you have against
the Navy...
        (derisively)
"Sir?"

Scene Sculpting
interruption

The door opens, Colby's secretary LORETTA
sticks her head in. She's 67 and frail-looking,
but with the spirit of a 16-year-old.

Scene Deepening
emotional pathway type 2
continues: comedy

Dialogue Device
speech rhythm

Bit Character—Interesting
interesting/non-cliché

LORETTA
(rapid-fire)
Mimi, Eric's wife? she just had
a baby girl, 10 pounds 2 ounces
can you imagine? Jeez Louise --
        (as the men stare)

Dialogue Device
"sounds of silence" type 2:
meaningful silence

Scene Deepening
emotional pathway type 2
continues: comedy

Relationship History
evidence of past history

Oh right, the knocking thing.
But I know how much you like her
and Eric so I thought you'd want
the skinny.

Scene Deepening
crossing the dramedy line

Dialogue Device
time/place ("skinny")

A quick smile, her head disappears, and the
door closes.

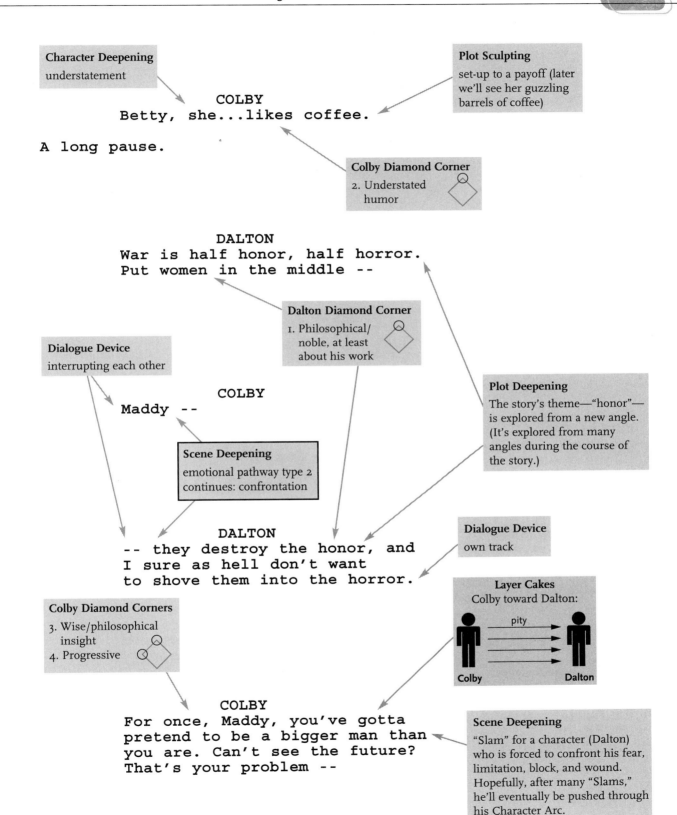

Character Deepening
understatement

Plot Sculpting
set-up to a payoff (later we'll see her guzzling barrels of coffee)

COLBY
Betty, she...likes coffee.

A long pause.

Colby Diamond Corner
2. Understated humor

DALTON
War is half honor, half horror.
Put women in the middle --

Dalton Diamond Corner
1. Philosophical/ noble, at least about his work

Dialogue Device
interrupting each other

COLBY
Maddy --

Plot Deepening
The story's theme—"honor"— is explored from a new angle. (It's explored from many angles during the course of the story.)

Scene Deepening
emotional pathway type 2 continues: confrontation

DALTON
-- they destroy the honor, and
I sure as hell don't want
to shove them into the horror.

Dialogue Device
own track

Layer Cakes
Colby toward Dalton:
pity
Colby   Dalton

Colby Diamond Corners
3. Wise/philosophical insight
4. Progressive

COLBY
For once, Maddy, you've gotta
pretend to be a bigger man than
you are. Can't see the future?
That's your problem --

Scene Deepening
"Slam" for a character (Dalton) who is forced to confront his fear, limitation, block, and wound. Hopefully, after many "Slams," he'll eventually be pushed through his Character Arc.

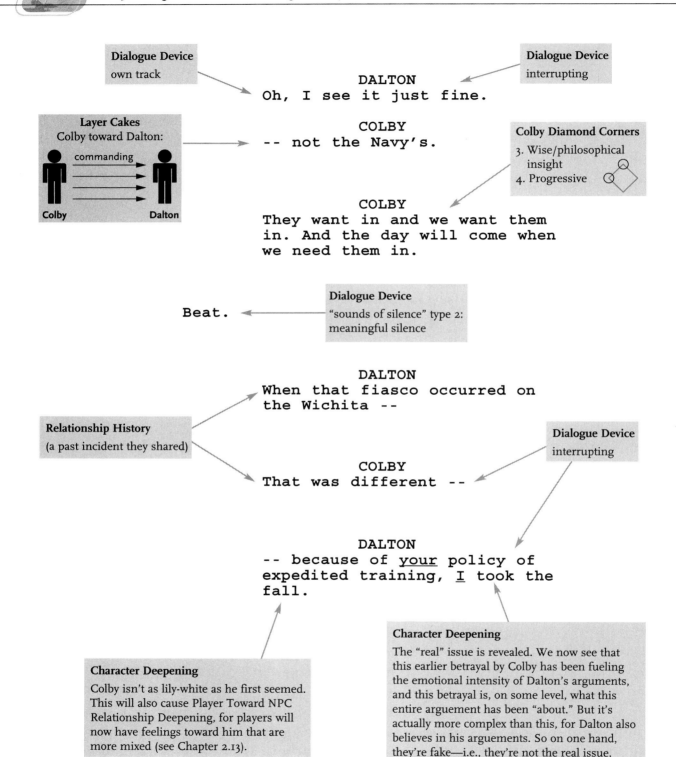

Dialogue Device
own track

DALTON
Oh, I see it just fine.

Dialogue Device
interrupting

Layer Cakes
Colby toward Dalton:

commanding

Colby   Dalton

COLBY
-- not the Navy's.

Colby Diamond Corners
3. Wise/philosophical
   insight
4. Progressive

COLBY
They want in and we want them
in. And the day will come when
we need them in.

Beat.

Dialogue Device
"sounds of silence" type 2:
meaningful silence

DALTON
When that fiasco occurred on
the Wichita --

Relationship History
(a past incident they shared)

COLBY
That was different --

Dialogue Device
interrupting

DALTON
-- because of <u>your</u> policy of
expedited training, <u>I</u> took the
fall.

Character Deepening
Colby isn't as lily-white as he first seemed.
This will also cause Player Toward NPC
Relationship Deepening, for players will
now have feelings toward him that are
more mixed (see Chapter 2.13).

Character Deepening
The "real" issue is revealed. We now see that
this earlier betrayal by Colby has been fueling
the emotional intensity of Dalton's arguments,
and this betrayal is, on some level, what this
entire arguement has been "about." But it's
actually more complex than this, for Dalton also
believes in his arguements. So on one hand,
they're fake—i.e., they're not the real issue,
which, in fact, is Colby's earlier betrayal. It's
another **Character Deepening** technique: "A
character simultaneously expresses a truth—and
a deeper truth." The use here is just one of
many variations of this technique.

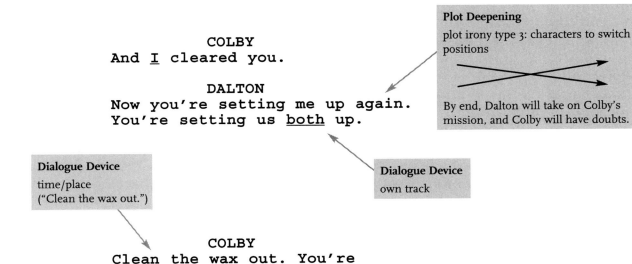

COLBY
And <u>I</u> cleared you.

DALTON
Now you're setting me up again.
You're setting us <u>both</u> up.

Plot Deepening
plot irony type 3: characters to switch positions

By end, Dalton will take on Colby's mission, and Colby will have doubts.

Dialogue Device
time/place
("Clean the wax out.")

Dialogue Device
own track

COLBY
Clean the wax out. You're
dismissed, sailor. <u>Now</u>.

Dalton is momentarily stung by the pejorative
"sailor" comment, but then cuts into Colby with
his eyes. He turns and leaves.

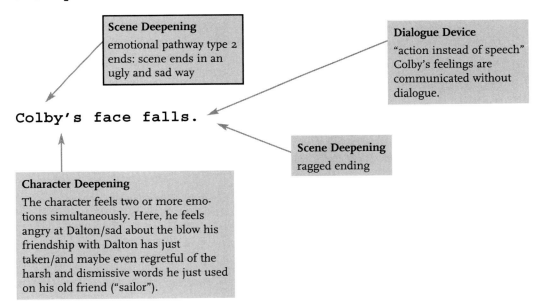

Scene Deepening
emotional pathway type 2 ends: scene ends in an ugly and sad way

Dialogue Device
"action instead of speech" Colby's feelings are communicated without dialogue.

Colby's face falls.

Scene Deepening
ragged ending

Character Deepening
The character feels two or more emotions simultaneously. Here, he feels angry at Dalton/sad about the blow his friendship with Dalton has just taken/and maybe even regretful of the harsh and dismissive words he just used on his old friend ("sailor").

Final Thoughts

As mentioned earlier in the book, some people have a desire to find a "magic pill" that produces masterful writing. This desire for a simple fix doesn't happen just among game designers. I've seen various trends sweep through Hollywood, as executives or writers searched for just such a surefire formula.[2] They'll grasp onto one for a time until they realize it doesn't produce predictable hits, and then abandon it, only to scramble for the next theory.

The solution isn't a formula. The solution is to start with a strong premise, structure the story well, come up with inventive plot twists, and then add techniques that, one by one, steadily enhance the artistry and emotional impact of the writing. The richness of writing comes from *Technique Stacking*.

The first of the three scene samples was weak not because the writer was "bad," but because the writer didn't know and didn't apply all those techniques that were integrated into the next version.

There is no magic pill. As with painting or programming, becoming an accomplished writer takes time and study. And, as in any artform, the day will never come when even the best writer still can't improve.[3]

By the way, remember that the following Glossary explains all the terms used in the "deconstructed version" of the scene.

---

2. Among accomplished writers, this rarely, if ever, happens. They realize all too well the wide array of techniques that they need to integrate into an artful film or television episode.

3. I have a group of friends, all of whom are professional writers (and my former students), that regularly gather to analyze our favorite films and great classics on DVD. We stop the films every few minutes to identify and analyze the techniques being used. There simply is never a time when there's not room for the expansion and deepening of one's craft.

Glossary for This Chapter

As you go through the third version, some of the terms like *Character Diamond Corner* will be familiar to you from reading this book, for you've already learned about the corners (the different Traits) of a Character Diamond. You'll also be familiar with Layer Cakes. (These terms, however, are also defined in the following glossary.)

Other terms will be self-explanatory. But following are a few that you might need to know to make sense of it. They're listed here in alphabetical order.

Beat. Another word for *pause*.

Bit Character. A character who only has several, or maybe even just one, line in the game.

Character Arc. The rocky path of growth a character undergoes in a story, usually unwillingly, during which the character wrestles with and eventually overcomes some or all of a serious emotional fear, limitation, block, or wound (FLBW). Examples: a character who is overcoming a lack of courage or a lack of ethics, or who is learning to love or take responsibility for others, or who is overcoming guilt.

Character Deepening Technique. A technique that gives a character a feeling of emotional or psychological depth or complexity.

Character Diamond. A colorful grouping of personality Traits that determine the character's dialogue and actions. To learn about creating colorful Character Diamonds,[4] see Chapter 2.1, "NPC Interesting Techniques."

Chemistry Technique. A technique to make it feel like two characters have *Chemistry*—i.e., that they belong together as friends or lovers. (For more on Chemistry Techniques, see Chapter 2.7, "NPC Toward NPC Chemistry Techniques," and Chapter 2.11, "Player Toward NPC Chemistry Techniques.")

---

4. The grouping of Traits is called a *Diamond* because, quite frequently, the character has four major Traits, or *corners*, for his or her Diamond. For instance, if a character's main personality Traits are: (1) offbeat humor, (2) badass attitude, (3) protective toward the oppressed, and (4) a philosophical side, these would be the four corners of the character's Character Diamond. Though four corners is common for major characters, three or five can also work for major characters.

Crossing the Dramedy Line. Crossing briefly from drama into comedy, or vice versa.

Diamond Corner. A corner or Trait from a Character Diamond. (See *Character Diamond*.)

Drop First Word. When you drop the first word in a character's line of dialogue.

Emotional Pathway Type 2. When the scene takes us through many different emotions in a quick period of time.

Flipping a Scene. The scene flips and goes the opposite direction it was going earlier. (For instance, the lovers start out by kissing and end by fighting.)

Layer Cakes. When Character A has various layers of feelings toward Character B, and these varied feelings can present themselves either simultaneously or sequentially.

Own Track. When a character completely ignores what the other character is saying, and continues on the same subject he or she was initially speaking about. The character stays on his or her "Own Track."

Plot Deepening Technique. A technique that gives emotional depth to a plot.

Plot Sculpting Technique. A technique that makes plots more interesting.

Ragged Ending. When a scene ends in an unhappy, ugly, or uncomfortable way.

Relationship History. Anything that gives us the feeling that the characters share a common history.

Scene Deepening Technique. A technique that gives emotional depth to a scene.

Scene Sculpting Technique. A technique that makes the scene more interesting. It makes the scene flow in interesting ways, or begin or end or unfold in interesting ways.

Sentence Fragment. When you drop out two or more words from either the beginning, middle, or end of a character's line of dialogue.

Set-Ups and Payoffs. Something—an object, a phrase spoken by a character—is introduced early in the plot. When it's introduced, it's a *set-up*. A set-up is revisited in an interesting way one or more times later in the story. Each of these instances is a *payoff*.

Example: Early in a story, the character puts a child to sleep by reading aloud a story about a sweet little kitten (the "set-up"). Later in the story, the character is attacked by 1,000 rabid cats (a payoff).

Another example: Early in a game, your character (the one you play) learns to throw a Frisbee (the set-up). Later in the game, the character's life will depend on being able to throw a circular, Frisbee-like weapon (the payoff).

Slam. An incident in a scene, which may comprise an entire scene, which forces a character to wrestle with his or her fear, limitation, block, or wound (FLBW).

Example: A gunslinger who is just out for himself (his "limitation") would experience a slam when he suddenly finds that he has to defend an entire community from an enemy (which means he'd have to take responsibility for others).

After enough slams, a character usually grows through his or her Character Arc and overcomes his or her FLBW. In this example, the gun-slinger's Character Arc would be to overcome selfishness and learn to be responsible for others.

Symbolic Subplot. An object or action that represents the character's growth through his or her Character Arc. (See Chapter 2.23, "Enhancing Emotional Depth Through Symbols.")

In the rewritten scene, smoking represents Admiral Colby at his best—he smokes during those parts of the story when he has the vision and courage to bring women into the Navy. As the story progresses, Vice Admiral Dalton, originally so resistant to the idea, will become its champi-on. Colby, originally far-seeing, will become conservative and even reac-tionary. He'll try to stop the plan he put in motion.

As he falls away from his progressive ideals, he gives up smoking. So we set up the symbol that smoking = Colby at his best.

(Most viewers' and gamers' expectation would be that Colby would stop smoking [a healthy act] as his *views evolve*, not as he *loses his progressive ideals*. However, it's often more artful and interesting to go against expectations.)

Of course, some might think a more normal use of smoking at a symbol would be for Colby to be smoking while at his worst, and then stopping when he grows to become visionary.

But since that would be the obvious route, let's "find the cliché and then throw it away," as I tell my screenwriting students.

Time/Place. Something that gives us a sense of the time and place in which the scene or cinematic is set.

Emotioneering Techniques Category #32

Opening Cinematic Techniques

Beginning to master beginnings.

This chapter shows

ways of using an opening, pre-rendered, or in-game cinematic to suck the player into the game.

note

All the guidelines and techniques explained and demonstrated in Chapter 2.31, "Writing Powerful Pre-Rendered and In-Game Cinematics," also apply to a game's opening cinematic.

As was discussed in the previous chapter, because both pre-rendered and in-game cinematics are like movies, many of the techniques that apply to writing films also apply to cinematics.

In films, there's usually a desire to "hook" the audience within the first few minutes. There are many techniques that quickly engage a viewer. They'd work just as well in games.

Let's say your game is about a villain, Hobson, who has learned to control the natural elements. He can imbue them with life and command them to do his bidding.

We'll use this game as a case study and apply some of the different ways to grab a player's attention with opening cinematics.

Begin with a "Fakeout Scene" (Faking Out the Player)

Our hero, Gavin (the character you'll play once gameplay begins), kayaks on a small river. He gets a call on his cell phone from his controller in the CIA, warning him about Hobson's element manipulation. Gavin's controller warns him that he (Gavin) is in particular danger because he once injured Hobson in a firefight and killed Hobson's best friend and right-hand man. Hobson might want revenge.

Suddenly, a torrent of water comes rushing down the river toward Gavin! It's all he can do to stay alive as the racing river threatens to smash him against the rocks.

Just as quickly as the flood had swept upon him, the water abruptly recedes. Once again Gavin finds himself on a placid little stream. He's confused.

CUT TO: Further up the river, two firemen finish tightening down a fire hydrant that had erupted.

The preceding is a *Fakeout Scene*, because we fake out the gamer to think one thing is happening (that Hobson is controlling the water), when it's really something else (a broken hydrant). Fakeout Scenes often have a comic quality to them once they're over and the viewer sees the fakeout.

However, a Fakeout Scene doesn't need to be comic. The film *Total Recall* begins with Arnold Schwarzenegger dying on Mars—but then he wakes up, and both he and we, the audience, realize he was dreaming.

Begin with a Mystery

In the opening cinematic, Gavin is doing some welding on his motorcycle in his garage.

CUT TO: Gavin's kitchen where some water simmers in a pot. The water, seemingly alive, creeps out of the pan, down the side of the counter, along the floor, out the kitchen door, and into the garage—toward Gavin, doing his welding.

We have a definite mystery in progress.

Begin by Introducing Us to a Unique Character

Gavin is welding his motorcycle in his garage. He takes it out for a spin on the freeway—and sees a police chase in progress on the freeway, but going the other direction.

The criminal is firing shots out of the window at the pursuing police car.

Gavin floors the motorcycle, and turns it toward the embankment separating the two halves of the freeway. He shoots up the embankment, jettisons into the air, and lands on the other side of the freeway, but going the wrong direction!

He screeches to a halt as a huge truck barrels down on him. Suddenly, he's driving backward, with the truck still gaining on him even though the driver has hit the breaks. The truck stops just before Gavin is run over.

He whips his bike around and takes off in the direction the police car was heading. Going at an impossible speed, he weaves in and out of traffic, missing cars by inches.

He finally catches up with the astounded police, who shoot him an annoyed look (they know this guy). Gavin throws out a piece of nylon line with a hook at the end, snags the shotgun off the dashboard of the police car, and yanks it right out the window!

Gavin hits the gas and powers toward the car being pursued, as bullets from the criminal's Glock ricochet off his bike. Gavin closes in on the driver, and uses the barrel of his gun to slam the pistol out of the villain's hand!

The criminal veers the car toward Gavin, trying to force him off the road. Gavin adroitly maneuvers his bike out of the way, and fires repeatedly, almost point blank, around the edges of the driver's door. The door falls off!

Gavin points the shotgun right at the criminal and waves goodbye. The criminal gives up, pulls over, stops the car, and jumps to the ground with his hands over his head.

This cinematic, which lasted no more than three minutes, is over. But we've completely established Gavin's character.

Begin by Throwing Us into a Suspenseful Piece of the Plot

This technique means that we start the cinematic with action already in progress.

The illustration here shows a case in point. Gavin snowboards down a mountain, firing at one of the villain's henchman who tries to kill him. Meanwhile, an avalanche has come to life and it chases our hero.

Begin by Entering into a Unique World

We meet Hobson, the mastermind behind the scheme to manipulate elements. He's in a lab in the beautiful Swiss alps.

He and his nine-year-old daughter take a stroll out of the lab. Hobson's got a device with him with a series of antennae and knobs.

As they walk and stroll, he tells his daughter how man's evolution was shaped by the elements in which he found himself. But now it's time for the next stage of evolution, when man shapes the elements. (The conversation, of course, would be enlivened and deepened with all the techniques discussed in the Chapter 2.31.)

As Hobson strolls and talks, he turns knobs and flips switches on the device. Around he and his daughter:

- A river reverses direction and starts flowing up hill.

- Hobson picks a leaf off a tree and turns a knob. A small whirlwind appears and blows the leaf around and around in a lazy circle. It would do that forever, except Hobson's delighted daughter snags it out of the air.

- Hobson turns another switch and a rainbow crosses the sky—and then a second rainbow, a third, a dozen, as his daughter laughs.[1]

In this version, we begin the game by being swept into a very unique world.

Final Thoughts

Although the chapter presents a far from exhaustive list of techniques, it demonstrates that there are many ways to approach an opening cinematic.

When you design an opening cinematic, try to make sure you've found the most captivating way to pull a player into the story behind your game.

I held back the two chapters on cinematics to the very end of this section on Emotioneering for a particular reason: *to de-emphasize their importance.* Far too frequently, when people think of ways to create emotion and story in a game, they think of cinematics.

But creating masterful cinematics in your game, including an opening cinematic if there is one, is the least game-like portion of a game. And, as we've seen so clearly, even the most artful cinematics barely scratch the surface of the techniques available to create a depth and breadth of emotion in a game.

---

1. Although the technology Hobson is using might as yet be a bit mysterious, we still know what he's doing. It's not a mystery on the same level of the water creeping out of a pot, as in the earlier example.

Looking Back

This marks the last chapter of Emotioneering techniques.

You're now equipped with hundreds of specific ways to create emotion in games. A little later in this book (in Chapter 5.2, "Techniques for Creating Fun"), I'll examine methods of creating fun. Fun, of course, is at the core of games' appeal.

The premise of this book, however, is that undergoing rich emotional experiences *is* fun in its own right. I believe we need to expand our definition of "fun" to include experiences that take us up, down, and around the emotional spectrum; that deliver us into new realities; or that give us insight. Fun films and television shows have been using this expanded definition since the inception of their media.

By using the techniques of Emotioneering, hopefully you'll join me in fulfilling the mission that is the slogan of the Game Developers Conference:

"Make Better Games."

part III

An Emotioneering Gallery

Introduction

The richest

emotional experiences in a game are created by layering, or *stacking*, one Emotioneering technique on top of another.

There are a number of color pictures in the center of this book. Of the eight color images, five of them have already been discussed in Part II, "The 32 Categories of Emotioneering Techniques." In this section, we'll continue with the same method and look at the remaining three pages of images, which illustrate case studies of hypothetical games.

As we've seen through numerous past examples, the richest emotional experiences in a game are created by layering, or *stacking*, one Emotioneering technique on top of another. Let's delve further in this direction and explore a few of the countless ways Emotioneering techniques can be woven together to strengthen and deepen a game's emotional impact.

Emotioneering in Reality-Based Games Versus Fantasy and Sci-Fi Games

Since I began brainstorming these three game case studies by mentally springboarding off of pictures containing fantasy elements, the game stories followed in kind. But never believe that Emotioneering techniques apply only to games that involve fantasy or science fiction.

If you comb back through the book, you'll see that it is populated with numerous examples of hypothetical games based in WWII, the American Revolution, a Desert Storm kind of war, a SWAT team, and a present-day police department, as well as with a film noir-style detective.

These choices were intentional, designed to show the wide range of games to which Emotioneering techniques can be applied. My game design and writing consultancy, The Freeman Group, and I are regularly called to work on games that are completely reality-based, as well as fantasy games and sci-fi games.[1]

Let's take a look at ways Emotioneering techniques can be stacked in order to, as the definition of "Emotioneering" states, move the player through an interlocking sequence of emotional experiences.

---

1. Emotioneering is also useful for games of every type. I know this from personal experience. I and my team have applied Emotioneering techniques to RTS (real-time strategy) games, action-adventure games, first-person shooters, platformers, fighting games, driving games, adventure games, and online games.

Chasm

Take a look

at the color painting of a futuristic city with, incongruously, blimps (page 6 in the color section). There's a man on the run.

Hypothetical Game Case Study

Boston Physicist

In this game, we meet the character you play in a brief cinematic set in the present day. You're a scientist with top-secret clearance, researching advanced physics. Your projects, which you pursue in your expansive Boston lab, include work in lucid dreaming, anti-gravity, teleportation, and other cutting-edge research.[1]

Gameplay begins at a futurist convention: You walk through various exhibits about life-extension methodologies, hyper-conductive super-cooled metals, nanotechnologies, and other breakthrough research. You amble up to one exhibit that shows the city pictured in the color-section illustration. Suddenly, a sort of vacuum wind starts pulling you in....

The next thing you know, you're actually *in* this city (still in gameplay). It's the year 2075. Impossibly, you discover that you have a weapon in your hand. (That's you in the picture.)

In this futuristic city, you quickly learn that you're being hunted by the police. They know you came from the past and want to kill you, for they know why you're here—or at least they claim to know—even though you have no idea how or why this time travel took place.

You'll learn that you've been brought here by a small resistance movement trying to overthrow the oppressive government. They wanted you, because your expertise—your anti-gravity work—could help them develop weapons that could make you the critical cornerstone of their resistance activities and turn the tide of their clandestine war.

Of course you—*the player*—don't know anything about anti-gravity, and even the character you play had just begun work in the field back in the time period when the game began. So, your character (i.e., you) tells the members of the resistance you can't help them. Nonetheless, they claim that you're an expert, but the time jump buried that knowledge in your unconscious, so they're working on a way to extract it.

---

1. *Lucid dreaming* means staying awake, or conscious, in a dream and in control of it.

The First Group of Missions

Because the government shock-troops are gunning for you, you have no choice but to fight alongside the resistance fighters to survive. Plus, there's a very attractive woman among the resistance fighters, Katrina, who is falling in love with you. She's unique and special; you develop feelings for her as well.

The Next Group of Missions

Later in the game, you'll be captured by those government troops, but they don't kill you as the resistance fighters had warned. Instead, they desperately plead for your help. They explain, and give you somewhat credible evidence, that the resistance yanked you from the past because they want to make an anti-gravity doomsday weapon and use it to blackmail the world.

All anti-gravity work was banned way back in 2018 because of a horrible disaster that occurred in your lab that killed you, and took out a quarter of the city of Boston.

As strange as this sounds, things are about to become more intriguing and strange.

You'll also meet some people who visit you in secret and who claim that they're friends of yours—and they *insist that neither they, nor you, are actually here!* Instead, they tell you that you have a brain tumor, and that you fell into a coma at the futurist convention. The ensuing operation was successful—but you're still in a coma and dreaming up this world.

Using a method that you yourself helped pioneer in your lucid dreaming research, they've entered your mind in your coma state to try and wake you. They lure you into a high-tech building where they want you to sit in a very scary-looking contraption. They claim it will wake you up from your coma.

All three of these groups—the government troops, the resistance fighters, and those claiming to be your friends—try to kill each other on sight. So you know there's no collusion going on here.

A number of Emotioneering techniques are at work here. Let's take a look at them.

NPC Interesting Techniques (Chapter 2.1)

Katrina will have an interesting Character Diamond. Her Traits are:

1. Bravery; a dedicated and excellent fighter
2. A keen observer of others; an ability to read their moods
3. A warm, sensitive kindness
4. A weird sense of humor, especially when she's drunk
5. A secret sorrow she won't share

Player Toward NPC Chemistry Techniques (Chapter 2.11)

You should feel a lot of chemistry with Katrina, the woman who falls in love with you. The techniques used could include:

- **A shared ordeal:** She fights side by side with you in a ferocious battle.

- **Earning a character's admiration:** If you fight extremely well, she responds with admiration.

- **Taking responsibility for another:** She gets caught and you need to rescue her.

World Induction Techniques (Chapter 2.18)

This game uses a number of techniques to get the player caught up in the world of the game:

- **Mystery:** There is a big mystery here—namely, what's the truth? Are you in the future, or is this all a hallucination because you're in a coma? And if you really are in the future, then who are these people who are trying to convince you that you're not? And if you are indeed in the future, then who is being straight with you—the government or the resistance movement? Solving these mysteries help make you want to stick around.

- **Bonding to another:** Bonding with Katrina also makes you want to immerse yourself in this world.

- ◆ **A rich world**: I won't reprise all the available Rich World Techniques (Chapter 2.18) that could be used in this game, but here are a few:[2]

When you're running missions for the government, you learn their customs. The soldiers pay homage to the sun every morning, the discovery having been made in the year 2056 that there is a spiritual force living inside of every star in the universe, helping animate them. The spiritual forces aren't gods, but they can be communicated with and, if they're happy, they can, to some degree, help control the weather on Earth.

The spirits in suns have symbiotic relationships with planets. Planets need suns to nourish their life forms. But as the life forms evolve, the spirits in the suns are nourished from the life energy of plants and animals, as well as the more evolved emotions of higher life forms.

Information about how a star or sun thinks and feels—a way of thinking and feeling quite alien to a human—will become critical in solving the mysteries around you. Stars and suns think in terms of pictures and symbols, which conjure up feelings (happiness, sadness, and so on) and ideas (truth, bravery, betrayal, and the like).

You must learn this new way of thinking—learn to interpret images and symbols—to figure out what's going on in the world and which of the three groups are telling you the truth. After all, the sun was here long before the birth of the Earth, and knows its entire history. The sun holds the secret answer to the riddles as to whether you're in the present or the past, among other things.

This civilization has mastered space travel. One of the missions will take you inside the sun, which is nothing like what you'd expect. You'll enter right into the sun's memories.

First-Person Deepening Techniques (Chapter 2.21)

At one point you'll have to choose between saving Katrina or saving some other members of the resistance who have saved your skin on many occasions, and whom you've come to care for. That's very tough decision. As such, it's a First-Person Deepening moment.

---

2. This example exists simply to demonstrate various ways of creating a rich world, including complexity and detail. Remember that it's optimal if these details have value in gameplay.

Also, you'll see that the war between the resistance and the government is much more complex than it seems. Both groups have valid points:

- The government feels that the resistance is holding the world back by not participating in the spirituality that has taken root on the planet since the discovery that the sun is alive. In fact, they have proof of this.

- The resistance fighters believe that one's personal beliefs and practices are no business of the government and that the government must be brought down for violating key provisions of the Bill of Rights.

- The government feels that the resistance, because they're using arms, must be crushed.

- The resistance, on the other hand, took up arms only when every peaceful means of enacting change and bringing the country back to its constitutional guarantees of liberty had been stymied.

As you get to taste both sides of this debate and see the validity of both points of view (Multiple Viewpoints), the resulting wisdom that grows in you is a form of First-Person Deepening.

Player Toward NPC Relationship Deepening Techniques (Chapter 2.13)

When you're running missions for the resistance, Brandon, the resistance's leader, is arrogant and thus unlikable. On the other hand, he's brave, inspiring, and risks his own life several times to prevent you from being killed.

You'll have a variety of feelings toward him simultaneously, such as disgust, admiration, and appreciation. Having various layers of feeling toward an NPC is the essence of Player Toward NPC Relationship Deepening.

Emotionally Complex Moments and Situations Techniques (Chapter 2.15)

When, near the start of the game, you're running missions for the resistance, Katrina is captured by government troops. They threaten to harm her unless you do a mission for them, and spy on the resistance. Being forced to violate your integrity like this is an emotionally complex situation.

Later the leader of the government troops will explain that they never were really going to hurt her. You'll be able verify that this is true. And, in fact, whatever you learned on that spy mission does, in fact, plant seeds of doubt in your mind about the motives of the resistance.

Plot Deepening Techniques (Chapter 2.17)

Halfway through the game, you'll find out a shocking secret: Katrina, just like you, was brought here from another time (if that's really what's going on).

She didn't tell you this originally because, like you, she has also met people who act familiar and who claim that she's in a coma. They even show her pictures of her "real" life, including her fiancé, her friends, and more. And, to her, these pictures are somehow emotionally moving. Unlike you, however, she doesn't clearly remember them. Still, she wonders—could she really be in a coma?

On one hand, she's a strong resistance fighter. Secretly, she's confused and lost.[3]

So Katrina's plot-line parallels your own. Parallel plot-lines is one of the many available Plot Deepening Techniques.

Adding Emotional Depth to a Game Through Symbols (Chapter 2.23)

The sun will come to have increasing uses in gameplay:

- As a repository of information

- As a way of teaching you a new language made of pictures

- As a location for you to have an adventure, when you enter the sun and its memories

- As a weapon; after you learn some of the sun's language, you'll be able to use a weapon that channels the far-away sun's force and shoots out fire

But the sun will also work as a symbol, accruing emotional associations as the game progresses.

---

3. This is the source of her secret sorrow she wouldn't share, which is part of her Character Diamond.

On a simple level, it will be a symbol of Katrina. She will have a sunny smile, and, at least in the cinematics, there will always be sunlight on her face.

To discuss other emotional associations that the sun will acquire, I need to share more of the plot:

It will turn out that, just as you were told by the resistance fighters, your anti-gravity research caused a huge explosion in 2018. There were two results:

- The explosion didn't kill you. You were in the center of it, where there was a stillness—a sort of eye-of-the-hurricane effect. You were, however, knocked into a coma.

- The explosion didn't just knock out a piece of Boston. It split the Earth into two Earths—in two separate dimensions. And time runs differently in both dimensions. You're in the future of that second dimension now.

But you're in the other dimension as well, and in that dimension, only three years have passed since the explosion—not the more than 70 years that have transpired in this dimension.

So, strangely, you're in a coma in the 2105 in one dimension, and you really are in 2075 in the second dimension. Both realities are true.

In the 2075 dimension, neither the government nor the resistance are totally good or bad. In the game, you have the ability to bring peace to this world and undo the damage you did in 2018 with the explosion you caused.

When it's all over, and a peace is worked out, you've brought sunlight to this troubled world. Various verbal clues (someone actually saying you've brought sunlight) and visual clues (such as the sun shining down lyrically on the singing of a peace treaty) will bring this home. So the sun will be now be associated with *peace*.

And when you awake from your coma, you'll find yourself in a hospital, looking out a sunny window into a beautiful garden. So the sun will be associated with *rebirth*.

So, in the game, the sun will take on more and more emotional associations. It will be associated with:

- Katrina and your warm feelings for her
- Peace
- Rebirth

Remember that such symbols usually make their most powerful emotional impact when the player *isn't* aware of them consciously.

Final Thoughts

Emotional immersion in a game is created by the artful employment of many Emotioneering techniques in unison.

In this fictional game, I mention 13 different Emotioneering techniques. But, if this were a real game, I'd be more likely to stick in 20 or 30. And that doesn't begin to take into account actual lines of dialogue that would employ many Dialogue Interesting Techniques and Dialogue Deepening Techniques.

Styx[1]

Please take a look

at the two paintings on page 7 in the color section. It's a world of Death
and the setting for this chapter's game.

---

1. In Greek mythology, Styx is the river across which the souls of the dead are ferried into the underworld.

Hypothetical Game Case Study

The Roman Empire

You play a soldier in the Roman empire. You and your best friend Marcus fight a mission together. He's a great guy and a good friend.

But you're fatally injured, and the figure of Death suddenly swoops in toward you. Marcus jumps at him to defend you—and disappears. In effect, he died in your place.

In this fictional game, a number of Emotioneering techniques are at work.

Emotionally Complex Moments and Situations Techniques (Chapter 2.15)

You need to voyage into the realm of Death to try to rescue Marcus. That's the world pictured in these paintings. There you will experience three emotionally complex moments and situations.

1. When you first enter the realm of Death, you'll be powerless to rescue Marcus. Powerlessness to help someone you care about creates an emotionally complex situation.

2. When you enter the world of Death, Marcus, now possessed, tries to kill you. If you slaughter him, he has no chance of coming back to life in your world. So you've got to fight him without destroying him. You can only wound him.

3. Furthermore, the truly emotionally complex portion of this mission is that you'll be torn between being angry at him, as he tries to kill you, and remembering that he's a friend.

NPC Deepening Techniques (Chapter 2.2)

The large eye is Death, but not any form of death character we're familiar with. Death's soul, and his power, is rejuvenated by fear, sorrow, and decomposing flesh.

Death also feels sorrow, however, in that he knows he's missing out on something (life)—but, being Death, he can't really understand what life is. So Death has an unquenchable yearning, but can't even articulate what that yearning is for.

Yearning is an NPC Deepening Technique.

NPC Toward Player Relationship Deepening Techniques (Chapter 2.12)

Once you're in the realm of Death, Death can sense your cares, your passions, your hopes, and your dreams. The dead have none of these. In some ways, Death definitely wants you killed. In other ways, Death doesn't want to kill you, for he longs to possess the kinds of feelings and life force you carry.

You'll battle his henchmen, but he (Death) never quite kills you. (You'll kill many henchmen, though.) Death's goal is to wound you and thus immobilize you, so he can keep you here and "feed" off your emotions.

First-Person Character Arc and First-Person Deepening Techniques (Chapters 2.20 and 2.21)

When you finally face Death in battle, you may have the chance to kill him. (I know that killing death is a strange notion.)

But just as you reach that point, you'll get a glimpse (in a cinematic) of what the world will be like if Death is killed. The world will be totally over-run with people living in abject poverty. It will be a horrible, squalid hell.

Will you kill Death?

Having to take a look at such a "big picture" and take responsibility for all life on Earth is a First-Person Deepening experience. But it also will help you grow in wisdom, which is your Character Arc in this game.

Your First-Person Character Arc After Escaping the Realm

Later, after you rescue Marcus, he'll feel ashamed that he tried to kill you in the realm of Death, even though he was possessed at the time. He'll have a hard time looking you in the face or even being with you.

The only way to restore his feeling that he's worthy of your friendship is to let yourself get in danger, and then let him rescue you.

This is fairly advanced Emotioneering, and I wouldn't make winning the game dependent upon having the player figure this out this difficult "action puzzle" and carry it off. So I'd provide plenty of hints that setting this scheme in motion is a good idea, and let the player get the emotional reward of a friendship reborn with Marcus.

The First-Person Character Arc is the player gaining wisdom. It takes a wise person to solve this emotional puzzle, and when Marcus recovers his feeling of self-worth and the friendship is restored, the player will see the benefit of his or her wise act, reinforcing the wisdom.

Plot Deepening Techniques (Chapter 2.17)

Death had the opportunity to kill you at one point but didn't, because he wanted to vicariously experience your emotions and life force.

You later have the opportunity to kill Death, but you don't, for you come to see that death is necessary.

And so the plot doubles back on itself in an interesting way. A plot that doubles back on itself in an interesting way is a Plot Deepening Technique.

Two More Doubling Backs

In the beginning of the game, your friend Marcus saves your life in battle.

When you bring him back from the realm of Death, you'll be giving him life. So the plot has doubled back on itself in yet another interesting way.

And it will double back one more time when he saves your life near the end. However, because you staged that event, you were really saving his dignity. Without dignity, man is barely alive. In a metaphoric way, you were saving his life.

So once again the plot has doubled back on itself.

Final Thoughts

This game case study derives much of its emotion from staging emotionally complicated situations. It's a technique that is under-utilized in many of today's games.

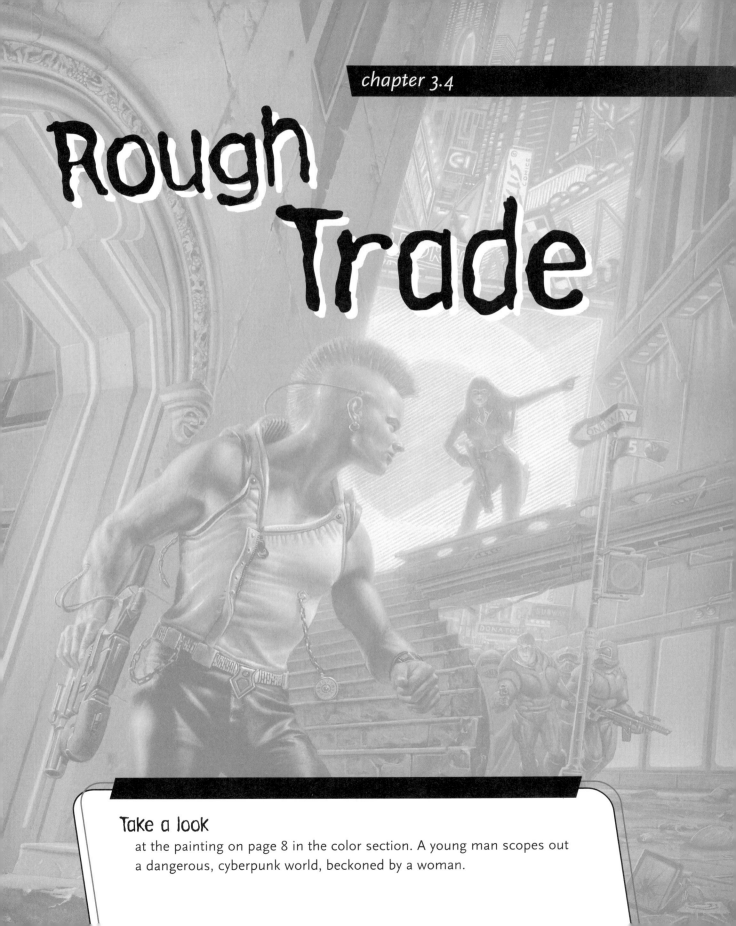

Rough Trade

Take a look

at the painting on page 8 in the color section. A young man scopes out
a dangerous, cyberpunk world, beckoned by a woman.

Hypothetical Game Case Study

Cyberpunk Novelist

You play a young William Gibson type of novelist, writing fictional stories about a cyberpunk world. The world you create is one rife with criminality.

In the opening cinematic, you agree to be a test subject in a research project being carried out at a local university. The research focuses on boosting the creativity of people who are already quite artistic.

You receive a drug...and your creativity soars.

Gameplay begins.

Some of the crimes from your cyberpunk novels actually start coming true in your city. This is strange, because those crimes involve weapons that don't even exist yet.

It couldn't be that someone read your books and is committing crimes based on what you describe, not only because the weapons don't exist yet, but because these crimes are based on a book you're currently writing— one that no one has seen yet.

Are you telepathically causing these crimes?

No. The world in your mind, already quite vivid, actually became "real" as a result of that drug, which unleashed in you powers long dormant in our race: the ability to turn thought into reality. The drug didn't have this effect on anyone else, just you, because of your constitution and level of imagination.

So criminals from the world of your novel have been entering the real world and creating mayhem. You feel responsible for these crimes, and take it upon yourself to try and stop them. However, you're up against truly evil men from that alternative world, who wield superior weaponry.

Still, in gameplay, you fight and kill a number of these vicious visitors from the world of your novel. When you learn you've only been killing henchmen, however, you need to enter the novel world itself.

Once there, you'll find your face, body, and clothing transformed slightly, so you look like the cyberpunk character you created in your fiction (as seen in the painting).

In this world, you'll meet and hook up with Maya, that woman on the stairs. She's neither completely good nor evil. She loves you, but she also runs errands for the top Boss. Maya passes on vital information to you to about the Boss, but also passes on information about you to him as well. She's just trying to survive.

You and the Boss both know Maya's playing both sides but don't mind, because both of you benefit in some ways. She starts getting slowly torn apart emotionally, though, for she's falling in love with you. But she's afraid that if she does, the top Boss will kill her. Her fear is not unfounded.

And what if she puts her faith in you and you abandon her—or are unable to take her back to your world, even if you want to? She'd be dead meat in this world.

You'll finally need to fight your way up to the top Boss. In the end, you'll find that the very top Boss had actually funded the research lab where you received the drug in the real world.

So the game ends with a conundrum:

- Did you mentally create this world, which then came to life after you took the drug?

- Or did this world exist all along, but couldn't break through into our world? Therefore, the top Boss of this world somehow implanted in you the desire to write about it, and your novel opened a slight doorway to this world, and then managed to get some money through to our world and have his agents sponsor the creativity research. And all this was done to get you to take the drug and thus solidly open the connection between the two worlds.

Which one is the truth? The game ends with this question still hanging.

This game scenario employs a number of Emotioneering techniques.

NPC Interesting Techniques (Chapter 2.1)

Maya will have an interesting Character Diamond. She is:

1. Street smart; a survivor.

2. Out only for herself, yet conflicted as she starts having feelings for you.

3. Keenly observant of every detail, and has an incredible memory.

4. Sexy.

She also has an innocent, vulnerable side that she won't show to you until you have proven yourself trustworthy. This is the side she hides behind her street-smart, survivor persona.

NPC Deepening Techniques (Chapter 2.2)

You'll come to see Maya's toughness as a Mask. Masks give an NPC depth.

Player Toward NPC Chemistry Techniques (Chapter 2.11)

You'll bond with Maya because of Player Toward NPC Chemistry Techniques:

- Because Maya helps you survive, you'll feel Chemistry with her.

- Sexual attraction will also play apart.

- Maya understands your feelings. There are numerous ways to apply this Chemistry Technique. For instance, after you return from a ferocious firefight (and your health points are low), she'll see you, quickly assess what's happened to you, and come over to say or do something that shows care and love.

When you protect her from harm (discussed in the section "First-Person Character Deepening"), your Chemistry with her will also increase, for taking responsibility for an NPC has that effect.

Player Toward NPC Relationship Deepening Techniques (Chapter 2.13)

In your relationship with Maya, you'll have several feelings toward her simultaneously:

- Sexual attraction

- Appreciation, for she helps you avoid death several times when you first enter her world

- Suspicion, because you know she also works for the Boss

- Sympathy as you learn that everything she's doing she needs to do in order to survive

- A growing desire to protect her

Layered feelings add depth to a relationship.

Role Induction Techniques (Chapter 2.19)

Your body is different in this world—you've got more stamina, strength, and prowess. Thus you'll be more drawn into your character.

First-Person Character Arc Techniques (Chapter 2.20)

You will grow in your feeling of responsibility for the real world, for the cyberpunk world, and for Maya. To enhance a feeling of responsibility for the cyberpunk world, we'll introduce other characters there, in addition to Maya, whom you'll like and to whom you'll feel indebted for their help.

A sense of growing responsibility can also be enhanced in other ways. For instance, the more sub-bosses you take out in the cyberpunk world, the more the people of that world start treating you as a hero. This positive reinforcement will make you more willing to take responsibility.

First-Person Deepening Techniques (Chapter 2.21)

Will you encourage Maya to rely on you? By helping you, she's already at risk, and the more attached to you she gets (and the more helpful), the more danger she puts herself in. The Boss will want revenge.

If we use enough Player toward NPC Chemistry Techniques, you'll want to look out for her. You'll need to defend her when the Boss, or one of his henchmen, comes gunning to get her.

Taking responsibility for another causes First-Person Character Deepening.

You'll need to decide how much you allow her to fall in love with you, once you learn you won't be able to take her back with you to your realm. We'd set it up in the game that there are small things you can do for her that make her more smitten by you—but the more she's taken by you, the greater her heartbreak will be when you leave.

It might be nice to enjoy her affections, but will you be willing to increase her suffering later on? Wrestling with this decision is another First-Person Deepening experience.

Motivation Techniques (Chapter 2.25)

Responsibility will keep you motivated to move forward, as you try to stop the crimes happening in the real world, and then go to their source in the next world. The need to protect Maya also provides motivation.[1]

Solving the mystery as to the relationship between the two worlds will also keep you motivated.

Plot Deepening Techniques (Chapter 2.17)

The ending is a little open-ended, meaning we're left to speculate as to what really happened. Did the Boss of the cyberpunk world set the chain of events in motion, or did your imagination bring the cyberpunk world to life and thus set the ball rolling? As we saw in Chapter 2.17, leaving a little mystery at the end of a story is a Plot Deepening Technique. (It's certainly not appropriate for every story, but works well with this one.)

---

1. It's worth noting that your feeling of responsibility depends, for it's emotional power, on the designer ensuring that you care about at least one individual hurt in the real world (thus motivating you to enter the cyberworld and stop the crimes at their source), and that you also come to sincerely care about Maya and maybe others in the cyberpunk world.

Final Thoughts

This chapter ends the discussion of Emotioneering techniques. But this book exists in a balanced energy state. Therefore, when you lose something, like Emotioneering, you get something in return, like the next chapter, "Magic."

Among other things, it tells you why I wrote this book.

part IV

Magic

chapter 4

Magic

Why you're needed.

There are
at least four types of magic right at your fingertips.

My publisher originally asked me: Who is the intended audience for this book? I listed the usual suspects: game designers, students, writers, film makers, aliens, forest sprites interested in robotics, talking animals....

But I never told my publisher who my real audience is: magicians and magicians in training. And that's you, my friend.

There are at least four types of magic right at your fingertips.

Are you a magician? Let me tell you a true little story about a woman in white.

Let's Get Real—But in Whose Reality?

It was an autumn night, with rain sprinkling down like cool petals of water. Headlights danced on the pavement.

I was tucked inside a warm, semi-posh restaurant, at an event celebrating a film that a friend of mine had just directed. I was talking to a young woman in white. Her outfit proclaimed "cute," but her world-weary eyes informed me that "cute" was over years ago.

"I hate fantasy movies," she pronounced in a self-congratulatory manner, as if fantasy equaled stuck in adolescence, which equaled, in her mind, living your life in an emotional trailer park.

She punctuated her distaste for fantasy films with a list: *Lord of the Rings, Shrek, Groundhog Day, Toy Story*....

As I listened to her condemn all fantasy, I wished I was a time-cop. I wanted to journey back to the childhood of this woman and arrest whomever had applied a 10,000 watt stun-gun to her ability to dream.

I didn't tell Cute But Weary the truth: That of course she believed in fantasy—just fantasies that had been created by others; fantasies that had been around long enough, and with which enough people agreed, that they had been relabeled as "reality."

Consider a few cases in point.

Our notion of romantic love is a fantasy, a cultural construction. It has its original small seeds in ancient Greece, and then the notion reemerged and was fully created by the Troubadours, who developed it over the course of 200 years, starting at the end of the eleventh century. The idea of love received further elaboration and development in the Renaissance, wrangled a home run out of Shakespeare, and now love is here to stay.

I lived in Ghana (West Africa) for year. There was no notion of romantic love there. Men and women hooked up and married, of course, but it was principally about economic survival, biology, and tradition. Why no romantic love? Because no one had created the fantasy there.

Christmas was a small scratch of a holiday until Charles Dickens wrote *A Christmas Carol* in 1843. His idea of Christmas as a time of charity, of family, of gift-giving, and of celebration swept through England. Audiences there clamored to have Dickens read the story aloud at one gathering after another. Eight stage adaptations were in production within two months of the book's publication.

The book's popularity spread like wildfire across the Atlantic and quickly transformed America as well. Eventually the rest of the world completely embraced Dickens' fantasy as well and enshrined it as the living reality we call Christmas.

Houses skewed toward the dark and claustrophobic until Frank Lloyd Wright had a fantasy of a new kind of open architecture that made music out of space and sunlight. His fantasy became today's reality.

In saying that she liked only "reality," Cute But Weary had simply chickened out, letting others create her fantasies. Actually, the diagnosis was even worse. She was a closet quasi-zombie, living out the fantasies of dead people.

Traipsing through the world with an outward sparkle but a zombified inner core, recycling the faded life-blood of those who are long gone, is no way to forge life into an adventure.

We all live out fantasies. They're either our own, or ones borrowed from or imposed upon us by someone else. Who will create tomorrow's fantasies? What about you, my friend? What visions are you waiting to unfurl?

Time is ticking. As soon as you can, please find a way to splash your universe in front of us all. Maybe the tools in this book will be of help. If not, perhaps you've got a strategy of your own.

I'm being completely sincere here. Do you really think you have the right not to treat me and everyone else who's interested to your imagination and your insights? Don't you think we hunger to have our world replenished, reinvented, expanded, and enriched? For all of us, time on Earth passes too quickly. Please don't deny us your gifts.

And so, the first kind of magic is *creating new worlds for us to inhabit, or expanding or enriching our existing world*. This magic is your ability to paint new worlds for us to live within, or your bringing us new insights into life's breadth, depth, complexity, and sometimes humor.

The politicians aren't going to do these things for us. The newscasters aren't going to do them either. Only artists can. And that means you.

A Secret Land Where Smiles Are Born

There is a secret land where smiles are born. Some call it childhood. Others call it living in the present and future, and not being fixated on the trials of yesterday.

Call it what you will, it's easy to rob someone of their ability to smile. Just toss some problems, losses, betrayals, and fears their way, and the door to that beautiful land can be temporarily or even permanently locked shut.

There are far too many people, in the news business and in politics, who are determined that no one should ever live long in the land of smiles. These people can't wait to assault you with fears and worries that they're eager for you to embrace. It's possible to get an entire population so worked up and anxious that it can be a gorgeous day outside and no one will even notice.

And yet, even when the door is locked to the secret land where smiles are born, that land is always there. It's just a breath away.

It's easy to rob people of their smiles, but so hard to bring them back once their happiness has been torn away. *Bringing people back to smiling and play* is the second kind of magic.

Who possesses the key to lead huge groups of people right back to the land where smiles are born? It's you. You've got the key to the door. And that makes you a magician.

But a magician who doesn't practice his or her magic isn't much of a magician. There are those who've been away from that secret land far too long. Won't you open the door and help them smile?

Creating Life Out of Nothing:
Hard for Scientists, a Cakewalk for You

Have you ever seen someone rebuild, repaint, and polish a classic car until it's "cherry?" People stare, attracted. The person restoring that car literally injected life into it, and people can actually *feel* it.

Have you ever been to someone's house who had decorated it in their own personal way, who kept it clean but not sterile, and who filled the space with life and love? You can actually feel the warm glow when you walk in. That person literally gave the house life.

A large Van Gogh exhibit passed through my town a few years ago. I dutifully stood in the seemingly endless outdoor line of those who waited to become part of the cliché cattle-call of impressionist looky-loos.

The day was sweltering, and an hour and a half passed. By the time the line finally inched forward enough so that I and those around me could actually step foot in the museum, everyone was in a foul mood. I feared I was about to become part of history in the making: the famous Los Angeles Van Gogh riots of the early 21st century.

Well, the riot never happened, but I wouldn't have been surprised if it did. People were so cross with each other that they easily erupted in petty arguments.

But as soon as they stepped into the first room of paintings, a hush fell over everyone. I mean absolute and total silence. Looking at the paintings, this previously irritated group was suddenly speechless with awe. People were moved in a way they never had been before, as they were lifted onto the wings of Van Gogh's rich and layered vision, and as they drank in his symphony of feelings.

Not only did Van Gogh give his paintings life, but now these paintings, just like the beautiful house and the polished vintage hot rod, continued to radiate emotion, radiate insight, radiate energy, and radiate depth. In short, the paintings radiated life.

We can put life into things, and those things can, in turn, continue to give life whenever they're experienced. And that's *real* magic. It's the third kind of magic, and you, my friend, are the magician.

The Ultimate Gift

True art turns those who experience it into artists themselves, for true art solicits participation.

Let's say we're watching a film. Alison enters the apartment she shares with Chloe. Chloe has bought some white orchids and is trying to find the right place to put them.

Alison knows that Chloe had had a date with Zak, a new guy, earlier that day.

> `Alison: How'd it go with Zak?`
>
> `Chloe puts the orchids on an end table, satisfied. She turns to Alison.`
>
> `Chloe (smiles): I usually go for yellow orchids, but I thought, "Hey, why not live dangerously?"`

There's a huge gap here that you have to fill in. You see that Chloe's in a good mood—so good that she's smiling, she bought flowers, and she even overrode her habitual pattern as to what color orchids to buy.

Therefore, *in your mind, you fill in* that the date must have gone very well.

You create the missing portions. Thus, when reading the dialogue, *you co-create* the story. You've been made into an artist yourself.

Or you're playing a console or PC game. You're exploring a destroyed castle. You hear a roar in the other room, and you had earlier been warned that monsters were on the prowl. In your mind, you fill in that there's a monster in the other room, and perhaps you even vaguely picture it. So it's *you, not the game*, who creates the monster at that second. *You* give it life. *You* have been made into *an artist*.

Let's take that game out of the console and insert another—a science fiction example.

You've just gone to Venus—the real Venus, teeming with a thriving civilization. They've projected the image of a deserted planet for thousands of years in order to fool Earth, as self-protection. They do this because they were invaded by Earth in Earth's first epoch, 75,000 years ago. In self-defense, they destroyed Earth's warrior culture then and erased that culture's remnants from our planet. All knowledge of that first epoch have been erased.

Here, on Venus, you find that each of the four directions have a history, and are labeled male or female. North is for warriors and is male. West is for dreamers and is female. South is for sorcerers and is male. East is for freedom bringers and is female.

Each day belongs to one of the four directions, and the days (and the directions they're associated with) rotate in sequence. Depending on which one of the four types of days it is, your weapons behave completely differently. So do your perceptions. The nature of events even change.

For instance, on East (freedom bringer) days, colors are brighter. On North (warrior) days, danger comes. On South (sorcerer) days, you can teleport yourself over miles of land.

Perhaps, as you continue on in the game, you'll learn more. But let's stop right here. I talked of an earlier Earth epoch, when warriors of Earth invaded the civilization on Venus....

There's a huge gap here that you'll start to fill in. What was that earlier culture on Earth like? What was its relationship to and history with Venus? As you begin to imagine and dream up these new elements, you bring them to life. *You co-create them.*

And how about the idea that the different directions on Venus have different histories and different qualities, and that they affect many aspects of this world, depending on which of the four types of days it is? In your mind, you'll assemble all these elements together in a way that starts to make sense. In short, although there are plenty of gaps, you'll fill them in. *You* create this world just as much as the game designer or writer. *You* give this world *life.*

When you see one of the *Lord of the Rings* films and find yourself caught up in the story, you're granting those characters life. When you play *Vice City* and find yourself laughing as your helicopter swoops in on an enemy, you're granting the game life. When you look at a Van Gogh painting and feel moved, that's because you're granting the painting life.

Earlier I said that an artist grants life. But real art solicits co-creation from the viewer or participant. Actually, there is no such thing as a "viewer," for anyone who fills in a painting, or movie characters, or a science fiction world with life is a co-creator and thus a participant. In games, participation is extreme because so much co-creation is elicited.

This book is simply about ways of making that co-creation more emotionally rich and dimensional.

There are those who would like to see a nation full of passive spectators, easily manipulated so they will swallow any news or policy they're force-fed.

But there are those, like you, who turn everyone who experiences your work into co-creators. You energize the most fundamental aspect of their deepest nature: You cause them to grant life.

Putting life into things that, in turn, causes others to also grant them life, is the fourth and, in my opinion, the most wonderful kind of magic. You turn other people into life-givers.

Final Thoughts

And so, magicians, this book of special tools draws to a close. I trust your magician's cabinet is hopefully full of all sorts of new implements you can use to wield your unique gifts.

Remember the four types of magic you create:

- You bring us new worlds. You bring insight. You bring fresh perspectives. You enhance our lives and show us other identities we can be.

- You return people to the secret land where smiles are born.

- You actually create life, and once your job is done, those things you made continue to radiate life forever, whenever they're experienced again.

- You transform those who experience your creations into co-creators, for you cause them to create life too. You turn those people who experience your games into magicians themselves. This is the greatest magic of all.

Hopefully, with the tools in this book, you can do all four of the preceding more artfully, and in a way that's uniquely your own.

I consider myself the luckiest of all men, for day after day, I spend my time either making magic or joining my alchemical talents together with fellow sorcerors to make magic that is more complex and powerful than any one of us could ignite alone.

I'm always surprised and gladdened to find that the world has a way of rolling out a rosy welcoming mat to magicians with honed talents, professional discipline, and a big heart. Are you one? If so, then thanks for pitching in, for the world certainly needs your gifts. And if you're not a practicing magician quite yet, we've got a place saved for you at the table.

I've laid out a few magician's tools in this book. I hope you'll take them for a spin and let me know how it all works out. This world is definitely in need of some additional magic. I'm eager to experience yours.

David Freeman

part V

Addenda

Introduction

After this book

was finished, instead of feeling the satisfaction that usually comes when a large project is finally put to rest, I was left with a disquieting, unsettled yearning.

I then realized it was because I was hungry. I made myself a sandwich and the yearning went away.

Nonetheless, it did strike me that there were a few odds and ends that I thought belonged in the book. You'll find them here.

Chapter 5.2, "Techniques for Creating Fun," is designed to give you a few tools to help power up your own creative warp drive.

Chapter 5.3, "Gatherings," is the strangest chapter in the book. It's where I invite you to eavesdrop on my own twilight thoughts as I abandon my linear shackles and allow my mind to explore the nooks and crannies of some very disconnected creative landscapes. Some of these thoughts have to do with games. Some don't. One has to do with a mouse.

These chapters have one thing in common: I couldn't figure out anywhere else to put them.

A slippery little chapter that first skirted the main body of this book, and then hot-footed it right out of the addendum as well, was one called "Cool Stuff." After all, cool stuff definitely ignites player excitement and engagement in a game. Therefore, it seemed a bit sacrilegious to turn my back on such a powerful immersive tool.

"Coolness" is hard to nail down because it's culturally determined. Whether you're talking about games or sneakers or music, what's cool today is unlikely to be cool tomorrow; what's cool in L.A. might not be cool in New York or Paris. The cultural factors that go into making something cool are countless. Since coolness is so culturally relative, I'm skeptical that there will ever be hard and fast techniques to create "cool stuff."

The chapter called "Cool Stuff" listed what I and a few of my game designer friends thought were some of the coolest features, moments, and gameplay mechanics from scores of games. But since it didn't really offer any specific techniques, at the end of the day it seemed appropriate to kill the chapter, which I did with wistful remorse. I was guided, however, by a Hindu-Buddhist intuition that the chapter would reincarnate on my website. And, in fact, that's just what it did. You're thus invited to **www.freemangames.com**, where you can click on "Participate" and add your own favorite cool game experiences and mechanics to a provocative and steadily growing list.

So following are two bonus chapters, as a thumbs-up for your high-dive into the world of Emotioneering.

If this book is a balmy July, then these final chapters are its farewell Indian summer.

Techniques for Creating Fun

It *is* a book about games, after all.

It's hard to talk

about creating immersion in games without addressing the most primary emotional experience that people seek out through games: a sense of play and fun.

This chapter addresses techniques of creating fun in games, and explores ways game designers might build upon this knowledge, in order to continue to create fun for this and future generations.

In the beginning was the Game, and the Game was good. And the Great Game Designer looked down upon the game and said, "Let There Be Fun."

And lo, from near and far, both the young and the wrinkled timidly put down their school books and their briefcases. Hesitantly, they walked out of the shadows and approached the Great Console, which was the altar of the Great Game Designer.

They moved the joystick, and they felt joy. And lo, they were so elated and so emboldened that they then dared to demand that no one ever used the expression "And lo" again, as it sounded far too corny.

And lo, no one ever did. And fun reigned. But then a new desire swept across the land. With one voice, both the young and wrinkled begged the Great Game Designer, "How can we have even more fun?"

The Great Game designer felt pity for his flock, and also a desire to perfect his creation, as well as a desire to add a multitude of zeros unto the Great Number in his bank account.

So the Great Game Designer sent me an email asking for one last chapter on fun, and I said, "Sure, I'll take a whack at it."

So here goes. But I must admit I had some help.

At one of the GDCs, I had the good fortune to attend a two-day workshop on "Game Tuning." Small groups were given exercises in game design that really challenged long-ossified neural pathways.

To give credit where it's due, the very bright and generous leaders of the workshop were, in alphabetical order, Robert Fermier, Austin Grossman, Robin Hunicke, Frank Lantz, Marc LeBlanc, Andrew Leker, Art Min, Tim Stellmach, and Eric Zimmerman.

I won't reprise all the interesting challenges the workshop leaders set up for the attending group, but I do want to acknowledge them in particular for actually trying to provide a categorization of different ways of having fun, and for doing quite a respectable job. I've expanded somewhat upon their system, and I thank them for their good work.

Types of Fun

Here's a list of types of fun. While the list isn't exhaustive, it does cover a number of the bases. Which of these forms of fun does your game use? Could your game benefit from drawing upon other ways of having fun as well?

- Combat, including:
  - Being part of a squad
  - Melee battles
  - Aiming, targeting, shooting
  - Mixing and matching: spells, weapons, defenses, fighting moves, choice of spirits you can summon, attack strategies, etc.
  - Complicated attacks that include multi-step attacks[1]
  - Multiple ways of accomplishing the same task
  - Turn-based moves with an opponent
  - Simultaneous moves against an opponent
  - Territorial acquisition
  - Capturing an enemy
  - Using scripted sequences to change mission direction and add surprising twists, such as being attacked unexpectedly
  - Sneaking and hiding, including camouflage, stealing hard-to-procure items, and code-breaking
  - Other forms of combat-related gameplay, including making and breaking alliances, negotiations and betrayal, bluffing, or commanding a number of NPCs.
- Different forms of travel:
  - Walking
  - Running
  - Bike riding
  - Driving (in different kinds of vehicles)
  - Flying (in different kinds of vehicles)
  - Traveling over or under the water (in different kinds of vehicles)
  - Swimming

---

1. An example of a *multi-step* attack would be that you (1) leave a rifle on the ground, (2) steal around the corner, (3) see the shadow thrown by an enemy picking up the rifle, and (4) shoot and blow up a gas canister near the corner, which in turn kills the enemy.

- ◆ Snowboarding
- ◆ Skateboarding

- ◆ Kinetic thrills and competitions, including racing, stunts, and other kinds of kinetic excitement (as in the *Spider-Man* game)
- ◆ Sports
- ◆ Being God—building and managing cities, armies, ecologies, including resource management
- ◆ Exploration and discovery
  - ◆ The preceding, in a visually compelling environment, whether pleasant, strange, or frightening
- ◆ Collecting and putting together sets of items
- ◆ Torturing (what you do with your Sims is your business)
- ◆ Asymmetric powers (when different roles have different powers and abilities)
- ◆ Self expression
- ◆ Building a network (like in *Tic Tac Toe*)
- ◆ Taboo thrills—running over pedestrians, barbecuing French poodles, and such[2]
- ◆ Building machines (including cars)
- ◆ Superhuman abilities
- ◆ Narrative/story/drama
- ◆ Humor (many different types)
- ◆ Bartering
- ◆ Changing the actual landscape or buildings in the game you're playing
- ◆ Training an NPC to do what you tell it
- ◆ Balance
- ◆ Solving puzzles
- ◆ Keeping pets, worshipers, or other NPCs alive.
- ◆ Dice, cards, etc. to create semi-randomly generated actions
- ◆ Dancing

---

2. Don't dare write me a nasty email on this one if you ever laughed at *Something About Mary*, any of the *National Lampoon Vacation* films, any of the *Scary Movie* films, or about a hundred other films of that ilk.

- Role playing
- Single paths
- Multi-paths
- Nonlinear structure
- Emergent gameplay
- Choosing what side to play (good or evil, for example)
- Timed missions
- Mini-games (games within a game) of all kinds
- Various forms of online games
  - Socializing

Incongruence

In Chapter 2.15, "Emotionally Complex Moments and Situations Techniques," I discussed incongruence as a way of creating an emotionally complex moment. In Chapter 2.18, "World Induction Techniques," I made reference to some of the powers of incongruence to contribute to creating a rich world, and referred to the painting on page 3 in the color section.

The leaders of the "Game Tuning Workshop" gave an exercise that used, in effect, incongruence. But here incongruence was used as part of a brainstorming process.

The challenge was: What would happen if you took one type of game, and then tried to integrate into it a kind of gameplay that usually applies to a different type of game?

Everyone came up with highly imaginative ideas. Some groups originated ideas that sounded promising. Others came up with game concepts that would undoubtedly be flops. It's hard, for example, to combine "Britney's Dance Moves" (with dance patterns from early 21st-century pop sensation Britney Spears) and a WWII combat game, as much as some people might find the thought to be disturbingly appealing.

But coming up with possible successes or failures wasn't the point. The point was to give a power-up to one's creativity when it came to creating fun.

So, using the idea of incongruence, you might find it a creative challenge to see what would happen if you mixed game types with incongruent game activities.

What's Wrong with This Approach

Some designers have tried to mix and match types of gameplay, and the results have been games that satisfied no one and flopped financially. A very well-founded resistance to mixing modes of gameplay has developed in the game industry.

What's Right with This Approach

What's right is that every once in a while someone mixes types of gameplay and makes a game that is all the more appealing because of it. *Grand Theft Auto III* and *Vice City* are perhaps the most successful of these hybrids, combining foot travel, driving different vehicles (including driving stunts, chases, and combat from within vehicles), flying, and other kinds of fighting. And this isn't the entire list.

As this book is being written, I and the other members of The Freeman Group are currently working on about a dozen games, spread between six publishers. For a fourth of these games, the developers have decided to mix forms of gameplay. I don't know if these experiences are representative, but it does make clear that such experiments persist.

The Exercise

The following examples are by no means intended to be suggestions for great games. Rather, they're here to demonstrate the brainstorming process I've been discussing. Let's mix and match types of gameplay, just to see what happens.

Example #1: A Racing Game with Building, Combat, and Sneaking

You must race across post-apocalyptic America, building cars out of the scraps of debris you find along the way. These cars have been "weaponized" (loaded down with guns, cannons, and so on, as well as defensive armor), so the game includes lots of fighting with your enemies.

Each car only lasts for a limited period of time, so you've got to use your car to find other metal scraps with which to build your next car, before your current car expires. At the end of your car's life, because it's going to die anyway, you load it with explosives and use it as a bomb to destroy an enemy's car or installation.

You can eventually learn how to go into stealth mode and turn you and your car invisible—turning it visible once again, just before you attack your foes.

Example #2: A Fighting Game with Sneaking, Resource Management, and Training of NPCs

Strange, vicious creatures have attacked and conquered parts of Earth.

You've got to build an army of these same creatures, who'll then fight as your warriors, against their own kind. You accomplish this by sneaking into the creatures' habitat and, when they're asleep, stealing one or more of the baby creatures. If the parents wake up, you must fight off the dangerous and cunning beasts.

Once you have the baby creatures, you then need to raise them until they're of fighting age. There's quite a bit of resource management in keeping them alive. There's also extensive fighting that results from defending them both from predators, as well as from their parent's rescue attempts. Once they're grown, they become part of your army, to be called upon at will to do your bidding.

Example #3: An Online Combat Game with Superhuman Abilities and with Making and Breaking Alliances (Betrayal)

There are, in the game, many different superpowers a person can possess, such as:

- You can zoom across the landscape at superhuman speeds.

- For a short period, you can change your appearance to look like an enemy.

- You can command weapons to go off and fight by themselves, although only within a limited radius of where you're located.

In the no man's land that the world has become, you have to make alliances with other superhumans and work as a group.

The problem is that when a group of superbeings work together, and each person in the group has different powers, then the group gives off a "manna ring." It's a ring of power that your group exudes, going out about 30 feet in all directions from where any member of your group stands. As long as the members of your group within eyesight of each other, the manna ring surrounds each person.

Any enemy who comes within your group's spatial manna ring gets a power-up of their own—i.e., they become amped up by tapping your group's power. So, the very thing that makes you strong—your alliance—has the side effect of also empowering any enemies you fight at close range.

Conversely, the best way to fight a group that has more power than your group is to split up the members of the target group so that they can't team up on any of your group members, and then have your group engage them one-on-one, tapping their superior power (their manna ring) to even your own chances.

Here's how alliances and betrayal enters into it: Each alliance can have no more than four people. You may come upon another superhuman whose abilities and powers would be more helpful to your groups' survival than one of your existing members. So there will be incentives to shed your group member and bring the new superbeing into your group. Or perhaps the person shed will be you, in which case, for your own protection, you've got to find or start another alliance.

Some groups may decide they won't betray each other, and will maintain the original group, out of friendship, or for some another reason. That can be done, but the powers of each member of such a group will gradually fade. Thus there's an incentive to continually be swapping out members.

This has, by the way, a social element, in that it always forces players to team up with new players.

Exercise Summary

As mentioned, the point of the exercises wasn't to come up with great game concepts, but merely to demonstrate a certain brainstorming method for creating interesting gameplay, using the taxonomy of types of fun.

Final Thoughts

You could entertain yourself with this creative exercise forever, and it would probably never get tiring. In a way, doing so is like a game in itself—a game centered on creation and building.

You can use the list of Fun Techniques as a checklist to see if any of them might potentially benefit your game. You can also use this list, as I have here, to experiment with incongruence in order to ignite a few creative sparks and break open your thinking in your game's design.

I don't think the world will ever get to the point where it can't benefit from a little more fun. If you're reading this book, my guess is you already are, or soon will be, upping this planet's smile quotient—a very worthwhile endeavor indeed.

Gatherings

The inner workings of an Emotioneer.

This chapter

is a small collection of thoughts, reflections, speculations, and journeys. If you're seeking logic and coherence, look elsewhere in the book. This chapter leaps from stone to stone, across the river of the mind. If, at times, a few points are made, they're accidental.

If the picture on the front of the book was truly representative of a game, there'd be two challenges. The first is, how can you, the man, actually hold the woman's hand? We don't, as in *Ico*, want to create a hand-holding mechanic, for there wouldn't be enough occasions in the game to use it. Therefore, we'd need some kind of pick-things-up mechanic that could be adapted to different uses, and this would be just one of them.

The second, more difficult challenge involves the branching story-line. One branch begins if you let her fall; the other branch begins if you save her. But a branching story-line like this probably costs too much to build. So how can we do it affordably?

The solution would be, if you let her fall, she doesn't die—but you won't know that until later in the game. So you'd feel her loss. The way to minimize expenses would be that, even if you rescue her, the plot would force you and she to part company a few minutes later anyway. This way you only have to build new assets covering those few extra minutes if you save her.

If you let her fall, you think she's dead. The loss could be heightened by the use of a symbol. Let's say that, earlier in the game, she tells you she loves white cats. Later in this mission, after she's dead (so you think), a white cat walks near you and looks at you. You'd think of her—or maybe even believe that, in some ways, it *is* her. (After all, you don't know the extent of her powers—and you did see her spirit almost leave her body on the bridge.)

If the cat is too hard or expensive to model and animate, we could go for a less-expensive symbol. She could have earlier told you that she likes lightning. At the end of this level, when you're victorious, off in the distance, lightning flashes from a large cumulus cloud. You'll think of her—or wonder if perhaps she, in some way, caused it.

The cat or the lightning would be scripted to occur only if you let her fall from the bridge. In the branch where you save her, they wouldn't be seen.

At first, Alex hated the fact that he had been transformed into a field mouse. He envied people and passionately wished he could be one again. With morose envy, he would watch them drive their cars, shop, and go home to their families.

His life was one of terror in the beginning, and adapting was hard. Finally he learned to survive the predators—owls and hawks. Plenty of other animals were friendly, from geese to groundhogs. As he started to ease into his new existence, he realized that he could sense their life forces and those of other animals, just as they could sense his. It was a kind of communication, deeper than words.

One night, he looked into a small, crystalline puddle. He saw the reflection of the full moon. He looked up and saw the stars. Could there possibly be that many? As a man, he had never taken the time to notice. And as he looked at them, he felt the life forces of all the other animals, extending miles away. They too were enthralled by the full moon and the summer night.

He was moved. This was a beauty and connection he never experienced when he was a human. Suddenly his former life was forgotten, and he was glad that he had been transformed into a field mouse.

And that's the exact point where his body began changing once again. Another transformation had begun....

He played flute under the high mountain ridge. It sounded as sweet as vanilla. If I had heard it, I would have listened all day.

Both Judo and Japanese brush painting create great effects with small movements. In the world of language, you find often find this in proverbs. For instance, consider these Arab proverbs:

"The food of a lion causes indigestion to the wolf."

"Live with a singer, and you will sing."

"A tree that affords you shade—do not order it to be cut down."

"I have become like a wick placed in a lamp; it gives light to the people while it itself is burnt."

"Soft words, but open injustice."

"The dog does not bark in his own house."

Perhaps I like these proverbs because, as in the part of Emotioneering called Dialogue Deepening, there's a focus on communicating a tremendous amount with few words.

The method here is interesting. Almost all the proverbs do three, and sometimes even four, things at once:

- They make a point.

- They usually employ a metaphor, so we have to mentally connect the point and the metaphor. This involves us in the proverb.

- The metaphor brings with it all sorts of sensory and emotional associations. This also involves us in it.

- We all apply the proverb personally. This too involves us in it. Two people might, therefore, interpret the same proverb slightly differently.

Let's deconstruct the layers of "A tree that affords you shade—do not order it to be cut down":

- It has a literal meaning: Don't get rid of those people or things that help you.

- It makes us connect the imagery of trees and cutting trees with the message.

- The images of trees, shade, and chopping down something beautiful are rich, both visually and perhaps even synaesthetically, if you smell the leaves, or feel the temperature of the shade. If you like trees, then those emotional associations are also activated.

- Although the statement has a meaning, it is still open to various interpretations as each person makes it their own. One person might think how they got angry with a parent who had protected them during their childhood, now realizing that anger was a mistake. Another person might remember abandoning a business partner who had once been a mentor.

With all these layers going on, no wonder proverbs become wonderful examples of Dialogue Deepening. I think that some people loved the film *Shakespeare in Love* because so much of the dialogue functioned the way these proverbs do.

What if, in a game, you have a player who has made a number of thoughtful decisions based on some kind of moral standards. The game is designed to then route him through a mission exposing him to a greater number of emotional and moral decisions than a player who's been a gung-ho destruction machine up until then.

I suspect few publishers would feel it was worth the money to build the extra assets, but it's an intriguing idea—building up a personality profile of the player and catering the game experience to that personality.

Quite a bit of emotion and intrigue can come from the building or landscape the player explores. For instance, you wander in a pastoral environment...and then find the severed arm of an alien laying among the flowers.

500 million years ago, in the Cambrian era, the world flashed from blackness into visibility. That's because, seemingly spontaneously, animals attained sight for the first time. No one knows the reason; it's shrouded in the secrecy of the spectacular.

In 2084, another evolutionary leap occurred. That's the year that mankind worldwide spontaneously developed another new sense—their first new sense since Homo Erectus took a first, tentative step on a world that someday would obey him.

Across the planet, men and women awoke to discover that they could look at a person, or even a person's image in a photo or on TV, and instantly know that individual's intentions. Did this person secretly intend good or harm?

Now, finally, people across the globe could know the real intentions of their leaders.

Every government across the world fell within the next two weeks.

A First-Person Deepening game experience: You are asked to rescue someone who once tried to kill you, but he did so under the mistaken notion that you were trying to kill him.

Another First-Person Deepening game experience: You love the girl, but her father is the tyrant who rules the land and who has killed many innocents. If you kill him, you lose the girl's love.

Botanist Dr. Simon Knoll was a humble man, getting on in years. He was no use to the university, so they labeled him "Emeritus," honored him at a low-cost farewell dinner, shoved a silver watch in his hands, and showed him the door.

His obsession with vanishing plant species, and his crusade to save them, had grown wearisome to the regents. They were positioning the university to prepare its grads for the technologies of the future, not the plants of the past.

Simon, in his meek way, tried to explain that plants were time-travelers, loaded with vital information. Encoded within their DNA is the secret of how they adapted and survived. You never could know which one held keys we might someday need. And so all species must be saved.

His argument fell on deaf ears. When he left his office of 37 years, a single box of papers in his arms, he took with him, in a jar, the last remaining Adiuvo mushroom known to man. Its ancestors had once been near ground zero when the asteroid that collided with Earth wiped out the dinosaurs, but these mushrooms somehow didn't perish. Simon thought this last little mushroom of their species could teach us how to survive some future calamity.

The university couldn't get rid of Simon and his mushroom fast enough.

The residents of the poor block of apartments and row houses around Simon had a different opinion. They felt that having a man of Simon's intellectual stature living amongst them raised the entire status of the neighborhood. They called him "the Professor" and treated him deferentially, honored that he had spent his life gracing their meager and forgotten corner of the city.

After the nuclear winter was over, and mankind was eliminated from the planet, only Simon and the people of his neighborhood remained behind—saved by lessons stored in a lowly and near-extinct mushroom.

And fifteen thousand years later, when the Earth was repopulated with their descendants, people still fell silent when they walked past the statues of Simon and his mushroom that were erected in every city center.

This book started quite a lively series of discussions with game designers around America and even around the world who read chapters, as they were being written, and sent me their thoughts.

My friend Anand Rajan emailed me:

> In *Deus Ex*, as J.C. Denton (the character you play), you run into Sandra Renton, daughter of Mr. Renton, who owns the "Hilton," referred to as the 'Ton. This is a place (lodge) in Hell's Kitchen, New York, where you stayed with your brother in the early days. When you meet Sandra for the first time, she's in some trouble with a local pimp, and you help her out. The very same night, you fly to Hong Kong to continue your adventures, whereas Sandra runs away from home to go to Eugene, Oregon.
>
> Eventually, you fly to and run missions in Paris—and later execute a complex mission at Vandenburg Air Force Base in California. From there, a mission takes you to an abandoned gas station. Two or possibly three days have passed since you left New York. You run into Sandra at the gas station, huddling around a fire barrel with two bums, trying to keep herself warm. At this time, she reminisces about the "good ol' days, back at the 'Ton.'" In actual fact, however, only two days have passed!
>
> Apparently, the line of dialogue works on the player (and it does work) because, even though only two days' time has passed in-game, the player feels as if considerably more time has elapsed. This is because he has seen and been through so much. And also, to play

through the four-day adventure of *Deus Ex*, it does take a week, playing 4–5 hours per day. This peculiar illusory distortion of time makes the line of dialogue work.

Anand opens up many intriguing possibilities with his comment—or perhaps I should say that the crafty interactive story sorcerers at Ion Storm (who made *Deus Ex*) do. Among other thoughts prompted by this discussion...

The experience of time is related to the quantity of events that have passed, and the differences (in terms of type, location, emotion, etc.) of these events. When many different types of events happen quickly, and they're events in which you're emotionally invested, there can be a sense that a substantial amount of time has passed.

How could you use this to screw around with a player's sense of time? It seems to me that a sci-fi game about time might be a fertile springboard to subvert, distort, and bend a player's time sense through gameplay. Short time periods could be experientially elongated (as with *Deus Ex*), and visa versa.

Ratcheting my mental clutch into a different gear...I've always been interested in the fact that we often operate concurrently in different time frames. In a game, what if, simultaneously:

- *Medium-term time frame (about 15 minutes):* You have to rescue Liam, a good friend (an NPC) who had once rescued you, and who suffered the tragedy of watching his family be killed as a result of his help.[1] He's now imprisoned in a cage, and if you don't get to him in time, he'll be transformed, through some kind of biochemical process, into a frightening enemy creature. (Your emotion about this: *worry*.)

- *Long-term time frame:* A wrong decision by you earlier in the game put Liam in this predicament (being caught and imprisoned), and he's furious at you. Not only do you bear this emotional burden, but you also feel partly responsible for the death of his family, because, as mentioned previously, they died when he had earlier come to your rescue. Thus, your current attempt to rescue him is part of a long-term goal of yours to win back his friendship and make yourself

---

1. Urgency can be increased by having your own successes in battle trigger each increased threat to Liam, giving the illusion that the situation is rapidly becoming more dire. Using this technique, ironically, the more successful you are, the quicker he gets into (apparently) heightened danger.

worthy of the loss that had ravaged him as a result of helping you. (Your emotion about this: *guilt*.)

- *Short-term time frame:* You've got to fend off or destroy enemies who are in your way right now—and they're winning. (Your emotion: *freaked out*.)

Now we've got you, the player, experiencing and operating in three different time frames simultaneously, each with their own emotion.

To truly emotionally deepen the experience, however, these would need to be layered on top of one another simultaneously. (Whenever there are concurrent layers of feeling, a sense of emotional depth is ignited.) Thus, all three time frames, with their different goals and different emotional flavors, would need to be present to you, the player.

However, accomplishing this is much easier said than done, since usually one time frame, with its goal and its attendant emotions, rises to the foreground of experience. In doing so, it partially or completely eclipses any others. Here's an example of how, perhaps, all three time frames could be kept in balance and therefore simultaneously experienced by you, the player:

As you battle the gathered enemy, you can see, from where you fight, Liam imprisoned in his cage, about to be transformed into something hideous (and you'll remember it's your fault he's there). We can increase the guilt you'd feel if the enemies you're fighting are beings who've taken over the bodies of Liam's slain family. Liam, in some kind of delusional denial of what has happened, watches the battle from his cell and plaintively calls out their names.

So you're operating within a short-term time frame (freaked out as you fight the superior enemy); a medium-term time frame (worried if you can save Liam, and worried about his sanity); and a long-term time frame (trying to overcome your guilt by somehow winning his forgiveness).

These three time frames—with their three emotional colorations—are stacked on top of each other as part of a single, layered game experience. If the gameplay is designed correctly, you should feel, simultaneously, freak-out over the battle, worry about Liam, and guilt. In short, three emotionally charged time frames will intersect in this one stretch of gameplay.

Thus, time, in this example, is no longer merely a passage of measurable units of duration. Instead, we seize it and use it as a tool for Emotioneering—that is, for sculpting interlocking, complex emotional experiences.

There is the main road, but that road shows you only the sights that every-one else has already seen.

There are sights to be seen that aren't on the map. There is an entire world under the fallen leaf. Sometimes we're a million miles away, sitting on the edge of a cliff, the cool wind caressing us with the smell of tangerines.

Later, blue flames float down the river under the full moon.

I was brought on board to help with a game based on a well-known ani-mated film. The game was directed at pre-teens and young teens.

The film, filled with off-beat humor, had the message: What matters is who you are inside, not how you look. However, the development team had been given the freedom to introduce new situations and characters into the game—something that makes working on a film franchise game a great deal more fun than if you're just creating a game that allows players to reenact a movie.

The team told me they wanted me on board so I could bring more emo-tion into the game. I said that the essence of what was emotional about the film was its message, so we'd need to convey that message in the game.

The team was skeptical. "How can you put a message in the game?" As the movie was known for its edgy, fantasy humor, I gave them an exam-ple: Our heroes come into a city like a fantasy version of Los Angeles. All the people there are consumed by status symbols, and they all have sun-tans. They deride our band of wandering heroes for not being tanned.

The way you get a suntan in this city is that you go to a tanning salon, and lay down under a hot dog. Now, a hot dog is literally that: a wiener dog with electricity surging through him until he crackles with energy, UV light, and heat.

When our heroes won't leave town, some of the townspeople go to war with them, but only with a variety of (funny) weapons made by high-status companies. (Various status brands of cars, shoes, purses, and neighborhoods would be slightly altered and parodied.) In short, the weapons are status symbols to the people.

And so the fight begins....

However, our heroes discover that the entire tanning trend was created by a conspiracy of the hot dogs themselves, as a ploy to become fabulously wealthy.

The people, realizing they've been had, now join our heroes in doing battle with the hot dogs. The city folk also discover that our heroes' weapons are more effective than the status weapons they'd previously been using.

In the end, they thank our heroes for freeing them from the need for suntans and status weapons.

The preceding type of humor is completely in keeping within the tone of the film. And, while creating new situations and characters who don't appear in the film (which the developer had permission to do), this mission would have carried forth the exact message of the film: Who you are on the outside isn't as important as who you are on the inside.

The development team liked both the idea in specific and the notion of keeping the film's message alive in the game. But the deadlines were too severe, and there was no time to incorporate this type of thinking. In the end, these deadlines limited my role to writing funny dialogue.

An Emotionally Complex Moment in a game: You come upon a small band of nomads who earlier saved you. Now they're starving—and you have no food to give them.

An Emotionally Complex Situation in a game: You need to make a temporary alliance with an evil warlord to rescue someone you care about. He'll use his warriors to ensure you safe passage through another enemy's terrain, but you'll owe him a big favor. To ensure you honor your moral debt, he injects a liquid explosive into your blood that he can detonate any time he wishes. You don't know when, in the game, he'll call upon you for help. Nor do you know what he'll ask you to do. However, it will definitely be something morally questionable or reprehensible to you.

An Emotionally Complex Situation in a game: You're given ESP—and you realize your best friend is a liar.

Another Emotionally Complex Situation in a game: You have to destroy a locket given to you by someone you love, because of a poison that an enemy has put on it.

"We are the technicians of wonder."

Terinne wrote this in log entry in her journal, and also sent it digitally through trans-space. It was to be her last transmission, ever.

The high command on Ramidor, a planet circling Sirus, was not pleased. In their minds, the galaxy was divided into species. Earthlings were just some upstarts that needed to be watched. Thus Terinne's mission: to blend in and observe.

Terinne had begun with their viewpoint, but she had changed her thinking. She no longer divided up higher life forms in terms of species. Instead, she divided them according to their willingness and ability to contribute to their worlds. To her mind, the most creative life forms on Earth, the artists, had much in common with the artists on Ramidor.

She took up violin. She became far beyond good. The human eye, they say, can see more than seven million colors. But with her music, Terinne could evoke emotions that had previously never been experienced. If angels did exist, they would surely bend heaven to hear her play. She had made her heart a landing pad of inspiration. She had, with incalculable work and practice, made her hands those of a master technician. She was a technician of wonder.

The high command was not pleased. But Terinne no longer cared. She had given herself a new mission. If Earth was to be her abode, she would contribute. There was so much to do, and so much fulfillment in the doing.

Night had fallen. Terinne had always enjoyed the fact that this planet rotated, unlike Ramidor, and that the colors of day give way to the secrets of night in endless succession.

She opened her door and walked out upon a river of stars.

An NPC's language, when not a cliché snuggly fit to a situation, can create both a deepened character and an emotionally complex moment. For instance, in a game set in Roman times, a towering gladiator enters the Coliseum to slaughter the two prisoners. One of the prisoners says to the other, "I knew him as a child. He had a small dog. It was the color of sand."

It's a use of incongruence between an emotionally resonant image (the prisoners' impending deaths) and words (about the warrior's childhood dog) to create an Emotionally Complex Moment.

Regarding art direction: A pond will convey one feeling if it contains a single white swan. It will evoke a different feeling if an old soda can is floating in it. Its feeling will be altered yet again if it contains a mother duck followed by five cute ducklings. When it comes to creating moods in game environments, this has many implications. One is that there's just about nothing that isn't changed by the introduction of a duck.

> Listen, reader, and you shall know
> The strange tale of Quinn the Eskimo...

In high school, one of my best friends was named Quinn. We used to call him "Quinn the Eskimo," from a song by Bob Dylan, but popularized in a rendition laden with fun, off-beat sincerity by Manfred Mann.[2]

---

2. When it comes to Eskimo names, for guys, I'm partial to Nanuk and Juat. And for girls, it's hard to beat Kirima, Naqui, and, of course, Apilut. While it's true that, if you're named Nanuk, no one will refer to you as "Quinn the Eskimo," you can still be called "Nanuk of the North," which is almost as good.

Although we ended up at the same university, we drifted apart. While I studied cultural anthropology and spent a year in Ghana, Quinn the Eskimo majored in physics, heading for a Ph.D., a job with DuPont, and eventually, making major contributions to the creation of stain-resistant carpet.

A few years ago we reestablished our friendship, and Quinn the Eskimo read, with interest, much of this book as it was being written.[3] While it's far afield from his own specialty—covering the living rooms of America with synthetic fur—he enjoyed the logical approach to creativity the book embodies.

But he had one major problem with Chapter 1.5 ("Why Game Designers Often Find Writing to Be So Challenging"). That's where I said that the game industry needs a new kind of hybrid game designer/writer, just the way an alpaca is a hybrid, or cross, between a camel and a llama.

This comment distressed Quinn the Eskimo. He emailed me that, though these animals belong to the same family, alpacas aren't part camel. In fact, he informed me, some experts in the field have come to the conclusion that alpacas might just be long-domesticated llamas, living amongst us in disguise and masquerading as a distinct species. His email went on, full of scientific detail, as he tried to narrow in on exactly what constituted the true essence of an alpaca.

These observations by Quinn the Eskimo pry open the door to many difficult issues involving alpacas, science, and the role of the artist.

Sure, my comment that alpacas are a cross between a camel and a llama might slash and burn its way through animal taxonomy, and declare a scorched-earth policy on science in general, but that isn't the point.

I was working in the area of metaphorically stated insights and emotional truth, which is what artists do: reveal emotional truths. If scientific truth needs to bleed a little bit, so be it. Emotional truths are much harder won, and are much more valuable when it comes to enriching the human spirit and making life worth living.

---

3. While it's possible to be a great game designer if you've never heard the song "The Mighty Quinn," or if you've never studied the amazing Eskimos, it's very hard to imagine designing games if you've never done either. To hear a small clip of the song, go to **www.freemangames.com**, and click on "Participate."

It's my opinion that science should be used to uplift mankind by engineering such marvels as bicycles, Christmas lights, and pockets. Science should never use the bulldozer of logic to flatten all the wonder, depth, and humor out of our world. If you see a scientist coming your way without Christmas lights in his pockets, run.

There were so many things I wanted to tell Quinn the Eskimo, but I dared not share with him the ancient secrets that had been entrusted to me. I feared his entire world-view would shatter, and he'd end up wandering the desolate streets at night, broken and insane, with twisted voices swirling like a tempest in his head.

But you, dear reader, I trust to be made of stouter stuff and, I believe, can take the truth head on:

An alpaca is indeed a cross between a camel and a llama. A hamburger is a cross between a cow and a flying saucer. Ping-Pong is a cross between tennis and fly-swatting. Geometry is a cross between algebra and doodling. A zucchini is a cross between a cucumber and wood. Shaving is a cross between skin care and lawn-mowing. Peanut butter is a cross between peanuts and adhesive. And kissing? Kissing is a cross between artificial respiration and non-artificial exhilaration.

My friend Jason doesn't believe in atheists.

Better to be an outlaw than an in-law.

Look what we found
in the park
in the dark.
We will take him home.
We will call him Clark.

—Dr. Seuss

NPC dialogue and action can be used to:

- **Convey the overall mood of the game.** For instance, a bomb accidentally fell on a civilian apartment building that just happened to be in a war zone. You walk in and see dead bodies. The mood is enhanced considerably if there's a woman in the corner sobbing uncontrollably.

- **Add to gameplay by controlling information flow.** For example, you overhear a password for a door when the guards change their shift.

- **Define a setting and dictate gameplay by their mere presence and behavior.** For example, you begin the game in a huge but populated airport lobby with a chase scene—people are screaming and running away.

An Emotionally Complex Situation in a game: You play a cop—and discover that your partner, who just saved your life, is dirty. You've got to bring him down. You know, though, that in doing so, you'll shatter the lives of his wife and two kids, whom you've met and like.

An Emotionally Complex Situation in a WWII game: You play an American soldier of German ancestry and with a German last name. On the battlefield, you find yourself squared off against a German soldier with a last name identical to your own. Between gunshots, this information comes to you through a brief conversation you have with a captured German. In fact, you learn that you and the soldier you've been firing at might even be related.

When you kill the soldier you've been fighting and thus can finally get close, you see that his face looks almost identical to yours.

An Emotionally Complex Situation in a WWII game: You've got to retrieve a German soldier who has gotten a secret communication to American HQ that he wants to defect. HQ plans to have him infiltrate the German army, and then assassinate a high-ranking German general.

You rendezvous with the German soldier. However, as you escort him back through the battle zone, it turns out that there's been a breakdown in communication on the American side. The American soldiers haven't been briefed, and they believe you've defected and have joined the Germans. They begin firing on you, including a soldier named Nate (an NPC) who has been your best buddy.

You've got a strange task on your hands: You need to blow up ammo stockpiles and take other actions that cause the American soldiers to fall back, but without killing any of them.

Later, when you rejoin your side and the confusion is straightened out, Nate is consumed with guilt for having tried to kill you.

On your next mission, you and Nate, who's still depressed and evidences self-loathing, are teamed up to rescue an American pilot who has been taken prisoner. When you finally locate and reach the prisoner, he's being guarded by a German soldier who's a superlative, mean fighter.

Here you have a choice (a First-Person Deepening Experience): If you hold back and let Nate kill the German, his self-hatred and depression will lift. He'll feel that once again he has worth. On the other hand, if you make the kill, you'll feel the emotional surge that comes from victory.

However, in this scenario, the game will end with Nate feeling despondent and going AWOL, leaving a note behind that he's no good to anyone and that your squad is better off without him. His departure will weave a bittersweet overtone into the thrilling and triumphant finale.

Beneath the silver cloud cover of Venus, a civilization grew. The transdimensional mineral Korenth in the rocks and soil put all life forms on the planet out of phase with Earth. And so the cultures of Earth and Venus evolved unaware of each other, as it was meant to be, free to create or stumble into their own separate destinies.

Boredom and a lazy addiction to superficiality eventually slow the river of time of all worlds, and so it was on Venus. They eventually dug for themselves deep and stagnant grooves of behavior and thought.

Some Venusians, dissatisfied with their lives, moved to the Plains of Turan—a zone that was commonly thought to exist only in fables. Here the settlers witnessed many strange things. The following are excerpts from some of their diaries.

Dulak (a man)—Age 37

I met a band of 43 travelers who called themselves "The Measurers." One measured everything in terms of beauty. Another measured everything in terms of size. Another measured everything in terms of how essential it was for living. Each one had a different system of measuring. I asked them if measuring everything gave them happiness. They were intrigued—they had no measurement for happiness, but they quickly devised one. The first thing they measured was themselves, and they learned they weren't happy at all being Measurers. The band broke up and never reunited again.

Isala (a woman)—Age 24

I was walking along the lip of the Deneyb Plateau and the wind wrapped around me. I realized it was alive. I asked it what it wanted. It said it wanted to have a body, like mine. It asked me what I wanted. I said I wanted to be free, like it. This is the last thing I will ever write, for at sunset we're making the trade.

Rinelle (a woman)—Age 31

I met a paranoid woman. She'd point to a cloud and said that its shape was a sign there was a baby in the town of Ulik and it would fall gravely ill. She'd point to some stones on the ground and say that their configuration was a sign that there would be flood in Vekoran. Suddenly she gripped her chest, sunk to her knees, and died. I felt sad, but I wasn't surprised. Earlier that day I had seen, in the shape of a tree limb, a sign that this was going to happen.

Pako (a boy)—Age 12

My parents liked the open desert and we lived far away from civilization. I couldn't stand it, so one day I secretly packed some things and ran away. I'm a good runner so I ran fast and far. I passed another boy my age running in the other direction. We both stopped and I asked him where he was going. He told me that he was an orphan and that he never had a real family. Living by his instincts had made him develop his telepathic abilities. He sensed some parents grieving because they had just lost their son. He hoped that maybe they'd want him. And with that, he took off. I stood there a long time and watched him as he ran in the direction of my house, until he became just a small speck on the horizon.

In the Plains of Turan, all signs have been banned. Signs only help you find those places you're already seeking. All those who settle in Turan are seeking places that they can't even envision.

Some NPC behavior in games is just weird. You walk up to someone, and they start talking to you. I'll tell you, that doesn't always happen to me in real life. Sometimes *I* have to start talking first. When NPCs always turn toward me and start talking when I approach, I get a case of the surrealistic heebie-jeebies. And surrealistic heebie-jeebies are only one step below dental heebie-jeebies.

Why, in a game, can't you walk into an office where a clerk works behind the desk—he looks up from his work, takes note of you—and then goes back to his job. Or why, using Self Auto-Talk, why can't you ask him a question first? Why does your approach always have to turn him into an instant, talking robot?

Places I've touched, and, to my amazement, they touched me back....

Greece, where my feet walked on warm alabaster stones down to the Mediterranean, and she knew my name.

Ghana, where the summer night sweats music.

Scotland, where Druids, long forgotten, still cry, hiding in their secret chamber the beating heart of all Europe was meant to be.

Tibet. After the flute Buddha played was silenced, the pure notes settled there, like a dove landing on a pearl.

Consider the following statements:

> His mercy is an unshakable mountain.

> His mercy is a soft, green valley.

> His mercy is as big as the sky.

> His mercy is a secret that none suspect.

> His mercy is in his eyes, which always know you.

> Winds slow to pay tribute to his mercy.

How can the word "mercy" be used in so many ways, and yet all of them, on some level, make sense?

It brings up the most fundamental questions of art. Do artists:

1. Describe and communicate aspects of reality?

2. Or, does their art actually create reality?

The answer is #2. By using language like the above set of statements about mercy, new ways of seeing and experiencing—new realities to inhabit—are created.

We live on an island comprised of what's real to us, and we can experience only what's on the island. But the artist expands the island, or even creates new islands for us to inhabit. The artist literally creates realities for us to dwell in. Art provides the most important function for making life livable, but is consistently under-appreciated in our culture.

In high school I had a book entitled, *If We Know Where Poems Come From, Why Don't We Just Go There?*. To me, it's the most basic question we can ask.

Near the beginning of this book, I mentioned a friend of mine who said he would never play games because he wanted his entertainment experiences to have meaning. But what is the meaning of "meaning?"

I think by an "experience with meaning," he was implying that:

- The experience takes him through a sequence of emotions that have breadth and depth.

- The experience allows him to explore an issue or issues from different sides, and perhaps, without preaching, leads him to an impactful conclusion.

- The experience gives him new insights.

- That emotions and ideas in the experience are packed together in dense layers (Technique Stacking).

- That, on some level, he feels changed in some way by the experience after it's over.

If games are to have meaning and lure people like my friend, then they'll need to do most or all of the preceding.

And here is the miracle of miracle, friends:

That you can use logical tools (like the ones in this book) to create something that is wondrous, moving, and wise—something that can never be fully explained or understood with logic. For an aesthetic experience operates on a different wavelength than logic, and therefore logic can't touch it. You can use building blocks forged by logic to create something that can only be apprehended by the heart and spirit.

When I was young, I was given the impression that maturity had some relationship to being serious. This is, by far, the biggest sham ever foisted onto children, and the most destructive.

Maturity has nothing at all to do with seriousness. It has to do with:

- Wisdom
- Responsibility
- Being able to get things done
- The willingness and ability to see through the eyes of others

Not included is seriousness. Of course there are times where seriousness might be appropriate, but they comprise only about a tenth or twentieth of the times when most people are serious.

Perhaps what I like most about people in both game publishing and development is that so many know the difference between maturity and seriousness. Many are wise, responsible, capable, and empathetic—but not serious.

And, because I get to work around such people, I have the best of all possible jobs.

Art Credits

This part of the book lists the creators of the book's art, referenced by page number. The next chapter supplies these artists' bios and contact information—useful if you'd like to know more about them, visit their websites, email them, or hire them.

In the book, all black and white art pieces used to illustrate Emotioneering techniques and hypothetical games were art directed by David Freeman, as was the color painting on the cover. All other black and white images (used at the front of each part and chapter), and the color images in the book's center, were art directed by the artists. All images are copyright of the artists, except where otherwise noted.

Many of the black and white images were created in color. Also, many pieces in the book were cropped to fit the book's page size. I strongly encourage you to visit the websites of these wonderful artists to experience the expansiveness and depth of their vision and talent, and to view their art the way it is meant to be seen.

Cover

Art by Jason Manley

Design by Aren Howell

Color Section

Page 1: Art by Jon Foster

Page 2: Art by Andrew Peter Jones

Page 3: Art by Margaret Nielsen

Page 4: Art by Luis Royo

Page 5: Art by Steve Roberts

Page 6: Art by Stephan Martiniere

Page 7: Art by Michael Whelan

Page 8: Art by Donato Giancola

Interior

Front Matter

Page i: Art by Jason Manley

Pages ii-iii: Art by Steve Roberts

Pages iv-v: Art by Youngsang Kim (dodowa)

Pages vi-vii: Art courtesy of Remedy Entertainment

Page viii: David Freeman's picture by Ryan Benjamin

Pages viii-ix: Art by Donato Giancola

Page x: Art by Andrew Peter Jones

Page xi: Art by Donato Giancola

Page xii: Art courtesy of Shiny Entertainment

Page xiii: Art by Andrew Peter Jones

Page xiv: Art by Luis Royo

Page xv: Art by Donato Giancola

Page xvi: Art by Jeff Carlisle

Page xvii: Art by Durwin Talon. "Iguana" character (from "Wasted Lands") © David Dorman.

Page xviii: Art by Steve Roberts

Page xix: Art by Mitchell Cotie

Page xx: Art by Stephan Martiniere

Page xxi: Art by Dan Parsons

Page xxii: Art by Sean McNally

Page xxiii: Art by Aleksi Briclot

Page xxiv: Art courtesy of Remedy Entertainment

Page xxv: Art by Stephan Martiniere

Page xxvi: Art courtesy of Shiny Entertainment

Page xxvii: Art by Jordan Raskin

Page xxviii: Art by Aleksi Briclot

Page xxix: Art by Donato Giancola

Pages xxx-xxxi: Art by Jason Manley

Part I

Page 1: Art by Luis Royo

Chapter 1.1

Page 3: Art by Aleksi Briclot

Chapter 1.2

Page 7: Art by Jeff Carlisle

Chapter 1.3

Page 13: Art by Dan Parsons

Chapter 1.4

Page 17: Art by Durwin Talon. "Iguana" character (from "Wasted Lands") © David Dorman.

Page 19: Pencils by Jason Hall; inking by Chuck Gibson

Page 25: Art by Don Anderson

Page 27: Pencils by Jason Hall; inking by Chuck Gibson

Chapter 1.5

Page 31: Art by Aleksi Briclot, courtesy of the Terminator3.com Featured Artist Project

Chapter 1.6

Page 35: Art by Sean McNally

Chapter 1.7

Page 37: Art by Stephan Martiniere

Chapter 1.8

Page 39: Art by Mitchell Cotie

Artists' Bios

and

Contact Information

As mentioned in the preceding chapter, almost all these artists work on a freelance basis, and welcome your inquiries and feedback. Their contact information is supplied here.

❖ ❖ ❖

Jason S. Alexander currently resides in North Carolina. He's worked, for the last six years, in the comics industry on series like *Queen and Country* for Oni Press and his own title, *Empty Zone,* for Sirius Ent. He's completed illustrations and covers for Harris Comics, Image Comics, and other independents. His illustrations have been seen in adaptations of *Alice and Wonderland, Alice—Through the Looking Glass,* and *The Time Machine* for Dalmatian Press. He's also completed many illustrations for White Wolf Inc. and Wizards of the Coast. He's currently working on a series of paintings and drawings for an upcoming art book, a series of self-published illustrated prose works, and writing and directing independent films with close friend and studio-mate, Kent Williams.

www.studiosection8.com
jason@studiosection8.com

❖   ❖   ❖

In a diverse career spanning more than a decade as a freelance artist, **Don Anderson** has developed and created a staggering body of work from interactive television to children's books. From the inception of the Internet, Don has worked on high-profile sites such as Willy Wonka Candy, where he was lead illustrator on all the main pages and created many of the games and activities. Sought out by many prominent ad agencies, Don did sketch work for movie posters and POP materials. A few of his credits in this arena include *Anastasia*, *Lethal Weapon 4*, *Sinbad*, *The Hulk*, and *Daredevil*. As a creative visionary, storyboards have played a lead role in Don's career. A few of those he did include *The Journey of Allen Strange*, *The Jersey* TV shows, and spots for *Lilo & Stitch*, Burger King, and Honda. In the game industry, he has comped for print ads and box cover art for game titles such as *Wolverine's Revenge, Age of Empires*, and *Tron 2.0*. Don's most recent hat was that of Art Director for the "Artrageous Adventure tour," a bus tour celebrating Crayola's 100th year birthday, where he designed everything from the outside wrap to the tables and shelves, delighting children and adults across the nation.

www.thedonandersonstudio.com

❖   ❖   ❖

Cheryl Austin has been creating computer-generated artwork for 11 years. Using Photoshop, Painter, 3D Studio Max, LightWave, and Maya, she has conceptualized characters for many games, including *Joust, Skins Game, Grey Dawn, Gladiator—the Crimson Reign*, and *10th Degree*. She is currently working on *Return of the King* for Electronic Arts. Cheryl is entirely self-taught and is proficient in traditional artist tools such as pen and ink, pastels, and sculpture, as well as computer art. Following her passion led her to work in the gaming industry. Working on games for *Interplay* during the day and going to the arcade at night, she fell in love with the characters. Working at Electronic Arts has allowed her to put her talent and creativity to work. Cheryl has developed a number of characters of her own.

www.studiodink.com

❖   ❖   ❖

Shawn Barber's signature brushwork has appeared in advertising, book, magazine, entertainment, music, and newspapers. He has exhibited in both solo and group shows throughout the U.S. and has been commissioned by The Butler Institute for their permanent collection. Shawn's work has been featured by The Society of Illustrators, American Illustration, Step By Step Graphics, *American Artist* magazine, *CMYK Magazine*, and *Juxtapoz Magazine*. Shawn also teaches painting, illustration, and drawing at the Ringling School of Art & Design, in Sarasota, Florida.

www.sdbarber.com
www.magnetreps.com

❖   ❖   ❖

Dell Barras has more than 10 years of experience working for various animation studios on the west coast and excelling in every aspect of the productions, such as character designs, storyboard, layouts, and animating on paper with the added ability of animating with Macromedia Flash software. He works with others as a board supervisor, maintaining flow of quality on assumed deadlines. Dell has worked on live-action films; the latest was as illustrator and board artist for *Dude, Where's My Car?*. Currently, he is the storyboard director for Warner Bros. *Ozzy & Drix* (*Osmosis Jones*) second season.

www.barrasandclark.net
Javlin47@yahoo.com

❖   ❖   ❖

Ryan Benjamin
Comic Book Artist/3D Modeler/Animator

After Ryan completed college in 1993, he began to work as a comic book penciler/artist for Image comics. He then freelanced other comic book work for Marvel and Dark Horse comics. In 1998, Ryan began a comic book/design company with other co-artists called Digital Broome. He has worked on an extensive list of books during the years: *Uncanny X-Men, WildCATS, Grifter, StormWatch, Union, Gen13, IronMan, CaptainAmerica, Turok, Gambit, Cable, Ghost, Batgirl, Vagabond, StarWars*...the list goes on. In 1998, Ryan began to study 3D art. Since then, he's done cover art, in-game models, and character and set designs for Xbox and Playstation games. Ryan is presently freelancing in the animated film field and still doing as much design/ad/video game and comic book work as he can.

www.ryanbenjamin.com
rbnjmn@msn.com

❖ ❖ ❖

Aleksi Briclot works in the video-game industry as a concept artist and art director. He's also illustrator for books, RPG books, and magazines, and a comic-book artist. He recently won the conceptart.org Terminator 3 Art Contest and appears on the Terminator3 website. Some of his works will also appear in Spectrum 10th, the biggest annual anthology of fantastic art. He's currently working on a *Spawn* comic for Todd MacFarlane Production.

www.aneyeoni.com

❖ ❖ ❖

Jeff Carlisle is a freelance concept designer and illustrator from Columbus, OH. He was a Concept and Level Designer for Presto Studios *Whacked!* game for the Microsoft X-Box Video Game System. His clients have included Alderac Entertainment Group (AEG), Lucasfilm Ltd., Paizo Publishing, Presto Studios, The Scarefactory Inc., and Wizards of the Coast. His work has appeared in *Dragon, Dungeon/Polyhedron, Star Wars Gamer,* and *Star Wars Insider* magazines, as well as the *Star Wars: New Jedi Order Sourcebook* and *Star Wars: Power of the Jedi Sourcebook* for the *Star Wars Role-Playing Game.* Jeff is currently doing freelance concept and illustration work, as well as writing his first illustrated fantasy novel for children.

www.jeffcarlisle.com
jeff6273@aol.com

❖ ❖ ❖

Justin Cherry

www.nivbed.com
nivbed@hotmail.com

504

❖   ❖   ❖

After 14 years in the military, **Mitchell Cotie** decided to make his art his career—a lifelong dream became reality. Now, after two years in art school, he is a freelance illustrator and a fulltime 2D/3D artist for Raven Software.

mitch@mcotie.com
www.mcotie.com

❖   ❖   ❖

Youngsang Kim (dodowa) is a 3D animation "Thirst" concept designer. He is also the recipient of the Japan Animation planning award (Anime Planning Award, Second Rank, 2003), the Fukuoka Asia Digital Award for Excellence (2001), and the FAN Animation Festival Final List (2001). His art has appeared in an exhibition for concept art called "Final Evolution" (Kwan-Hoon Gallery, Seoul, Korea, 2002).

www.orbiterdesigner.com/bronzeage/
arcaive@hanmail.net

❖   ❖   ❖

Jon Foster. You can view his work at:

www.jonfoster.com

❖   ❖   ❖

Gez Fry is a freelance artist based in London, England. He was born in 1978 in Tokyo, Japan, and since then has been lucky enough to live in several countries. This varied upbringing, and being half-Japanese, has exposed him to many styles of art, and he counts among his influences artists from Japan, Korea, and France, as well as the U.K. and the U.S. Gez's work is comprised of paintings, sequential, and concept art. The two images included here were produced entirely on a computer, with a graphics tablet.

www.gezfry.com

❖   ❖   ❖

Recognizing the significant cultural role played by visual art, **Donato Giancola** makes personal efforts to contribute to the expansion and appreciation of the science fiction and fantasy genre that extend beyond the commercial commissions of his clients. Patrons of his work include companies such as LucasArts, National Geographic, DC Comics, HarperCollins Publishers, Sony, Hasbro, Milton-Bradley, Tor Books, and Playboy Enterprises. His illustrations have won numerous awards, including Gold and Silver Awards from *Spectrum: The Best in Contemporary Fantastic Art*, five nominations for the Artist Hugo Award, and seven Chesley Awards from the Association of Science Fiction and Fantasy Artists. Donato appears as a guest at various colleges, institutions, tournaments, and science fiction conventions around the world, where he demonstrates his techniques, lectures on his aesthetics, interacts with fans, and displays original works of art. Donato's studio is located in Brooklyn, New York.

www.donatoart.com

❖ ❖ ❖

Chuck Gibson. You can view his work at:

http://albums.photo.epson.com/j/AlbumList?u=4036610
inxrus@hotmail.com

❖ ❖ ❖

Atom Gray was born in the cultural limbo of the midwest in 1970. He dropped out of high school, became a paid writer, and self-published his own magazine by the age of 17. Then, dropping out of art school in 1991, he began a 10-year tattoo saga that netted him 40 international awards and a world-famous studio started with only a $500 loan. He soon married, dropped tattooing, and moved to Los Angeles, where he has just completed his first full-length screenplay and has come to suspect he is the reincarnation of Captain James Cook. Atom is also currently executing a series of visionary paintings, album covers, and odd squealing noises from a turntable.

www.voodooplex.com
atomizer@voodooplex.com

❖ ❖ ❖

Matt Haley has been toiling away in the comic-book industry for the past ten years, producing some of the most realistic and meticulously detailed work for the four-color medium. After working on licensed *Star Trek* books for DC Comics, he gained a solid fan base by working on Dark Horse's *Ghost*, which invigorated his love of pulp adventure themes, and his fan base ballooned with his work on *Birds of Prey*, *Supergirl*, and *Batgirl* for DC Comics. He has also provided illustrations for Ubisoft Games, Adidas, Infogrames (Atari), Showtime Networks, Premiere Magazine, KenzerCo, Wizards of The Coast, TSR, and many more. Matt has been quietly developing comic book and film properties with Spyglass Production's MAGE producer Andrew Cosby, including their creator-owned project, *Jack Hunter: G.I. SPY.*

www.matthaley.com

❖ ❖ ❖

Jason Hall was born on September 17, 1974. He began his career doing work in comics on various titles for Wildstorm/DC and Marvel, as well as pencilling the four-issue bad-girl limited series from Spilled Milk, Inc. He has also done interactive design, storyboards, and illustration for various high-profile clients such as Hewlett-Packard, Garnier, Whirlpool, and others, including the internationally acclaimed advertising agency, Publicis Dialog. At 28 years of age, he now works out of his home-based studio in San Francisco, a couple blocks up the street from Ocean Beach.

jason.hall@mindspring.com
http://vanian.home.mindspring.com

❖ ❖ ❖

Andrew Peter Jones is a concept artist and international portrait artist. He began pulling images out of the void and into the world at age five and has continued ever since. His work experience includes Industrial Light and Magic's art department, Interplay's Black Isle Studios, and Nintendo first-party developer Retro Studios, where he worked as the principal concept Artist for "Metroid Prime." Andrew's film credits include concept artist for Jason Wen's world-recognized and award-winning short film, F8. In his free time, Andrew travels the globe with an easel on his back, drawing portraits on street corners from Venice Beach to Venice, Italy. Andrew has created thousands of portraits that hang in homes in almost every country on the planet.

Andrew's latest work can be seen at www.conceptart.org; his saga of art takes him on a journey into the depths of creativity, stamina, and narcissism with his "self-portrait of the day" section, where a new self-portrait is created and displayed each and every day. His influence can be seen in the guest portrait gallery, where he has acquired a cult following of artists across the world to join him in the adventure of artistic expression and self-discovery.

Andrew currently lives and works in Austin, Texas. His work is a personal pursuit of beauty, horror, and imagination, which he shares with the world to inspire the dreams and the art of the next generation.

www.conceptart.org
ajones@spectrum.net

❖   ❖   ❖

Jason Manley is a founder of www.conceptart.org, a not-for-profit web-site devoted to helping artists develop their skills and showcasing their concept work. He is presently Lead Concept Artist for Vivendi Universal Games. Jason has contributed to and been a core artist on many games for both PC and console titles. His website group is a current authority on conceptual idea development and visual development for games and enter-tainment. He has more than 4,000 students and top professionals posting work and teaching on conceptart.org. He is originally from Minnesota and studied traditional fine art with Jim Garrison and Ringling School of Art and Design.

www.massiveblack.com
www.conceptart.org
jasonmanley@onebox.com

❖   ❖   ❖

Smoothly morphing his considerable skill and experience, **Stephan Martiniere** shapeshifts from whimsical to hard-core science fiction, car-toon to realistic, concept illustrator to director. In the last 20 years,

Stephan has become known for his versatility, talent, and imagination, gaining constant recognition and praise through his work in a growing range of clients and projects, including *Star Wars* (Episode 2 and 3), *The Time Machine, Red Planet, Virus,* and *Titan A.E.* During his career as an animation director, he received numerous awards, including in 1991, The Children's Hall of Fame Award, the Humanitas Award, the Parent's Choice Award, the ACT Award, and an Emmy nomination for the five animated musical adaptation specials, "Madeline." As an illustrator, he is the recipient of the 1997 Spectrum Award and the 2001 Thea Award. From 1994 to 1997, he was also the illustrator for the worldwide syndicated comic strip, "Where's Waldo," which became the fastest growing Sunday only ever. Stephan most recently was the creative visual director at Cyan for its upcoming real-time online game, *URU: Ages Beyond Myst.*

www.martiniere.com

❖   ❖   ❖

Sean McNally works as a concept artist at Blur studio in Venice CA, working on a variety of projects including video-game cinematics, television commercials, and in-house feature development. He graduated from the Columbus College of Art and Design in 2002 with a major in illustration. During art school, Sean interned as an illustrator at the American Legion Magazine and as a texture artist at the LucasArts Entertainment Company.

srmcnally@yahoo.com

❖   ❖   ❖

Leslie Minnis creates fantastical imagery. She has worked as head concept artist for the innovative maverick internet video game company, Hypernova. Working for the industrial design firm LFX as well, Leslie conceived, designed, and fabricated the haunting of a house in the project titled "Sanitarium." The project included numerous life-size puppets with costumes, demented toys, and futuristic headdresses. Leslie is a graduate of the Colorado Institute of Art.

plofales@yahoo.com

❖   ❖   ❖

Margaret Nielsen is a fine artist and educator whose paintings have been exhibited in galleries and museums nationally and internationally. She has completed several large-scale public art projects, as well as receiving awards such as the National Endowment for the Arts. A graduate of California Institute of the Arts, she has taught painting at the college level and conducts workshops that focus on the development of a personal artistic vocabulary. Her paintings are an ongoing exploration of psychological and emotional realities. She lives and works in the Los Angeles area.

Nielsen97@aol.com

❖ ❖ ❖

As an artist, illustrator, and writer, **Dan Parsons** is best known for work on his creator-owned *Harpy* comic book series. He has also done cover paintings and interior pen and ink art for other comic book series like *Battlestar Galactica* and Sci-Fi channel's *First Wave*. More recently, Dan has been working on a variety of trading card projects, including "WitchBlade: Disciples of the Blade," "Top Cow Universe," "Lexx," "Battle of the Planets," and "The Crow." Dan is currently a regular inker on the *Star Wars* comic-book line from Dark Horse/Lucasfilm and continues to work on various creator-owned projects.

www.amryl.com
parsonstudio@earthlink.net

❖ ❖ ❖

Puddnhead is a freelance concept development artist located in Hollywood, California, who creates highly developed conceptual drawings and paintings for the entertainment industry. Areas of specialty include creature and character design, game environment concepts, matte paintings, and storyboards. Some of his clients include Lucasfilm, Sony Pictures Entertainment, Columbia Pictures, and Hasbro.

www.puddnhead.com
kev@puddnhead.com

❖ ❖ ❖

Drawing since before he could hold a pencil, **David Pursley** specializes in traditional arts, digital painting, and 3D modeling and animating. Mainly a video-game artist, having worked with Blizzard Entertainment, Black Isle Studios, and Electronic Arts, David has been lucky enough to receive the opportunity to work on *Starcraft, Diablo, Icewind Dale, BG: Dark Alliance, Command and Conquer: Generals, EAs Lord of the Rings*, and many other games, some books, band posters, and websites.

DPursley@artistemail.com

❖ ❖ ❖

Jordan Raskin started his career in the early 1990s working as an artist for just about every major comic-book publisher in the industry including Marvel, DC, Image, and Darkhorse comics. In the mid-1990s, Jordan left comics to expand his art career in advertising, creating both presentation and shooting boards for various clientèle. From there he moved into animation, working as a background designer on such productions as *Courage the Cowardly Dog* and the new *Teenage Mutant Ninja Turtles*. Currently Jordan is hard at work bringing his own merchandising property to fruition. He has written and developed a full-length screenplay entitled "Industry of War," which he is currently illustrating as a cinematic comic book mini-series.

www.jordanraskin.com
www.industryofwar.com

❖ ❖ ❖

Kevin "RAZ" Razel is a diverse illustrator comfortable in various genres and fields of art and media production, having contributed to various fantasy art and comic-book projects, as well as storyboard and development work for film/video/TV and video-game productions (both live action and animation). Previous credits are varied from such clients as Power On Software, American Heart Association and Red Cross, Time Warner, Carnegie Mellon, and FPG to comic and fantasy projects for S.Q.Productions (Gallery Girls series, Demonlust art Portfolio), Sirius Comics (Primal Rage), CFD (Sensual Mystique portfolios 1 and 2), and Savage Planet from Basement Comics/Amryl Entertainment. Currently freelancing for various professional clients, Kevin also enjoys doing many private commissions for comic/fantasy/sci-fi fans and art collectors. Other projects and interests include being the associate producer for a Frank Frazetta film documentary (www.cinemachine.net) and a session vocalist/musician for several band/studio projects (www.stronghold-metal.com). His very latest project is a graphic novel/art book featuring Frazetta's Death Dealer character to be published by the Frazettas.

www.razuniverse.com

❖   ❖   ❖

Steve Roberts is a freelance illustrator with versatile experience in traditional media, design, and computers. He has brought to life many creatures, mythological figures, and role-playing characters. A talented artist of vision and technique, Steve is entirely self-taught in his skills. This he did by studying the works of his childhood heroes—legendary fantasy artists like Frank Frazetta and The Brothers Hildebrandt. Steve received his only formal training when he sat in on classes at the Ringling School of Art. He was born in central Florida, in a little town called Palmetto, a stone's throw from the Gulf of Mexico. He began drawing as a young child like most artists. Recently Steve has been working with book and game publishers such as Palladium Books. He did a number of projects for their "Rifts" series. Other publishers Steve has done work for include Tyranny Games LLC for their *Sack Armies* RPG game. He has also completed the cover for book two of the popular "Of Honor and Treason" series, *Of Death and Duty* by C.J. Merle, published by "Speculation Press." Another recent book cover just completed is *Dragon Reborn*, published by Dragon Moon Press.

www.fantasy-graphic.com
steve@fantasy-graphic.com

❖   ❖   ❖

Luis Royo was born in 1954 in Olalla, Teruel (Spain). He studied technical drawing, painting, decoration, and interior design in the Industrial Mastery School and the Applied Arts School in Zaragoza. Luis works for clients in the U.S., England, Sweden, etc., creating covers for books from all the major U.S. publishers. He also creates covers for American magazines, such as Heavy Metal, and also European ones, such as Cimoc,

Comic Art, Ere Comprimée, Total Metal, and others; he also makes video and video-game sleeves for different countries. Luis is the author/illustrator for several books: *Women, Malefic, Secrets, III Millennium, Black Tarot, Dreams, Prohibited Book* series, and *Conceptions*. He also created or contributed to several card collections, such as From Fantasy to Reality, The Art of Heavy Metal, The Best Of Royo, III Millennium, and Royo Secret Desires, all published by Comic Images. Luis currently had his 12th book published by NBM, titled *VISIONS*. He is represented worldwide by Norma Editorial S. A. and can be contacted through Alan Lynch at their U.S. office:

(607) 257-0330
alartists@aol.com

❖   ❖   ❖

Aaron Sowd is the award-winning art director of Stan Lee Media, where he designed *The Stone Man* with Stan himself. Adept at storytelling in all its many forms, Aaron has done storyboards for *Austin Powers in Goldmember* and *Freddy vs. Jason*. As a conceptual designer, Aaron has worked on Steven Soderbergh and James Cameron's film *Solaris*, as well as *Human Nature* and *Virus*. Aaron's work has appeared in the *New York Times, People, Time,* the *Hollywood Reporter, Gear,* and *Playstation* magazines. His latest creation, the animated show *Masterminds,* can be seen at www.masterminds.us. He lives by the beach in Venice, California, and resents the fact that he has no free time to enjoy it.

www.aaronsowd.com
aaron@aaronsowd.com

❖   ❖   ❖

Durwin Talon has created covers for *Batman: Officer Down for DC,* as well as *Skinwalker* and *Queen and Country* for Oni Press. He has also written *Panel Discussions: Design in Sequential Art Storytelling* for TwoMorrows Publishing. An Associate Professor, he currently teaches sequential art, video game, and multimedia classes for Indiana University Purdue University, Indianapolis, School of Informatics, New Media.

dtalon@iupui.edu

❖   ❖   ❖

Top Cow Productions (TCP) is a comic-book publishing company founded by top comic-book creator and artist, Marc Silvestri. TCP currently publishes its line of comic books in 21 languages in more than 55 different countries. The company has launched 21 original franchises in the industry's Top 10, with seven at #1, a feat accomplished by no other publisher in the last two decades. With retail sales topping $250 million and more than 100 million units published, TCP is the most aggressive and innovative comic-book company created since the founding of industry titan Marvel Comics in 1963.

TCP's flagship franchise, *Witchblade*, was TNT's #1 original film of 2000 and is now in its second season as a television series for the network, already posting stronger ratings than the first season. Virtually all of Top Cow's other properties, including *Inferno*, *The Darkness*, *Rising Stars*, *No Honor*, *The Cleaner*, *Fathom*, and *Felon* are in development as feature films, live-action television, or animation.

TCP spearheaded the now industry-standard of using computers for color and FX production. By bringing this part of the comic process in-house and training artists to use modern computer equipment and technology, TCP revolutionized the comic industry.

www.topcow.com

❖   ❖   ❖

Michael Turner's love for illustration led him to the discovery of comic books, and he eventually landed a job at Top Cow Productions. Turner began his career doing backgrounds for artist Marc Silvestri on the popular comic-book title, *Cyberforce*. Turner's first solo assignment was the *Ballistic* mini-series, which led to his biggest challenge to date, *Witchblade*. Helping to create and launch *Witchblade* in October of 1995, Turner was an integral part of its success, and the title quickly grew to become one of the most popular around. Turner then turned his focus to *Fathom*, his first creator-owned title. *Fathom* was an instant success, becoming the number-one selling comic book of 1998, and was soon optioned as a major motion picture by director James Cameron. In November of 2002, Michael left Top Cow Productions to found his own company, eventually naming it

Aspen MLT Inc. after Fathom's main heroine, Aspen Matthews. Settled in at his new company, Michael is now concentrating his efforts on releasing his newest properties, *Soulfire* and *Ekos*, as well as the long-awaited return of *Fathom*.

www.aspencomics.com

In the last 24 years, **Michael Whelan** has created hundreds of paintings for book covers, calendars, magazines, and record albums. During that time, he has garnered virtually all available illustration or art awards in the international fields of fantasy and science fiction. Michael is a 15-time HUGO (World Science Fiction Award) winner—11 times for Best Professional Artist—and has won the HOWARD (World Fantasy) Award for Best Artist three times. In 1992, he won a HUGO in the new category of Best Original Artwork, and he was awarded the "SuperHugo" for Best Professional Artist of the last 50 years. The readers of *LOCUS* magazine have awarded him "Best Artist" for 22 years running. In 1994, Michael won the Grumbacher Gold Medal and most recently, he was awarded a Gold Medal from the Society of Illustrators, an Award for Excellence in the 1997 Communication Arts Annual, and the SPECTRUM Gold Medal.

www.michaelwhelan.com

Glossary

The secret of understanding and
application is knowing the meaning
of the words.
(A ton of practice helps too.)

Action Puzzles. *Action puzzles* is my term for puzzles that take place in the middle of action. Furthermore, they're puzzles that take *doing something active* to solve the puzzle (i.e., achieve the desired result). They're not puzzles that merely require *thinking*.

Agency. Making the player feel like he or she is impacting, if not shaping, the story is sometimes called "giving the player a sense of agency," or simply "giving the player agency." Chapter 2.24, "Self-Created Story Techniques (a.k.a. Agency Techniques)," focuses on ways to accomplish this—ways to help the player feel that he or she is playing the game, rather than simply being taken along on a ride.

Ambivalence. Feeling simultaneously both positive and negative about a person or situation.

Beyond Structure. (www.beyondstructure.com). The name of David Freeman's screenwriting and fiction workshop, the most popular of its kind in Los Angeles and New York. The workshop is also occasionally offered in other cities around the world, like London and Sydney.

Boss. In games, a villainous or monstrous person or beast of some importance that you fight.

Character Arc. The rocky path of growth a character undergoes in a story, usually unwillingly, during which the character wrestles with and eventually overcomes some or all of a serious emotional fear, limitation, block, or wound. Some examples: a character overcoming a lack of courage, overcoming a lack of ethics, learning to love, learning to take responsibility for others, or overcoming guilt.

Character Diamond. The group of Traits (personality aspects)—usually four, but sometimes three or five—that determine how a major character sees the world, thinks, speaks, and acts. Having a Character Diamond of three to five Traits makes characters dimensional. Character Diamonds make characters interesting, but not deep—unless some of the character's Traits are also Deepening Techniques. (See *Deepening Techniques.*) Major NPCs, as well as the character played by the gamer, can have Character Diamonds. Sometimes the Traits of a character's Character Diamond are referred to *Corners* or *Diamond Corners*. Sometimes a Character Diamond is referred to simply as a character's *Diamond*.

Chemistry Techniques. Techniques to make it feel like two characters have *Chemistry*—i.e., that they belong together as friends or lovers.

Cinematic. A section in a game that is like a very short movie. The player loses control of the game and watches passively. Cinematics can range from a few seconds to a few minutes. There are currently no consistent terms for cinematics. Cinematics animated or filmed separately from the game and then later integrated into the game are called *pre-rendered cinematics*, *FMV* (*full-motion video*), *cut scenes*, or *CG* cinematics (*computer graphics cinematics*). Cinematics created in real time with the game engine are called *in-game cinematics, in-engine cinematics, in-game-engine cinematics*, or *real-time cinematics*. Some in-game cinematics permit the player to control the camera angle.

Cohesiveness Techniques. Techniques to make various parts of the game that are distant in (apparent) space and time feel connected.

Complexification. Adding emotional and/or psychological complexity to any character in or aspect of a game's story. The verb form is "to Complexify."

Cross-Demographic Techniques. Techniques to make games appeal to both kids (or young teens) and adults.

Deepening Techniques. Techniques that, in traditional, linear storytelling, add the feeling of (or the actuality of) emotional or psychological depth or complexity to:

- Characters
- Dialogue
- Relationships between characters
- Scenes
- Plots

In games, many other elements can be "Deepened," such as a moment of gameplay, or even the person who is playing the game. Other words for "deep": making things emotionally layered, poignant, soulful, emotionally complex, psychologically complex, and so on.

Dialogue Deepening Techniques. Techniques that make single lines of dialogue by minor NPCs convey a sense that the NPC has emotional and/or psychological depth.

Dialogue Interesting Techniques. Techniques that make single lines of dialogue by minor NPCs interesting, and thus they make the NPC speaking the line interesting.

Diamond. Another term for Character Diamond. See *Character Diamond.*

Diamond Corner. Another term for Trait. See *Character Diamond.*

Eavesdrop Mode. When you overhear two or more NPCs talking to each other. Some games use this as a way to get information to the player, or to enhance the emotion of the moment. In *Star Trek Voyager: Elite Force*, for instance, you overhear an NPC express his fear about the upcoming mission to another NPC. It has the effect of making that mission seem much more frightening.

Emergent Gameplay. Gameplay such as in the highly popular game *The Sims*. Instead of the game supplying a narrative or a staging a contest (such as with many driving games or sports games), emergent games provide advanced building blocks that the player can use to create his or her own story. Did you ever play with Lego as a child? It's the same basic concept.

Unlike Lego, however, in emergent games, there's usually some kind of instability built into the system. Either you constantly need elements you don't have but are required to get, or the system needs to constantly be attended to so that entropy doesn't destroy it. Thus, the player is continually prompted to take action to maintain or expand whatever world or system the player has created using the building blocks.

Because there could be an almost (or perhaps actual) infinite number of ways a game of *The Sims* could end, and it could perhaps go on without end indefinitely, emergent games such as this are called *Open-Ended*.

Emotioneer™. David Freeman or any member of his game design and writing consultancy, The Freeman Group, when applying Emotioneering techniques to a game or other interactive experience. As a verb, "to Emotioneer" means for David or one of the members of The Freeman Group to apply Emotioneering techniques to a game or other interactive experience. *Emotioneer*™ is trademarked by David Freeman.

Emotioneering™. The vast body of techniques created and/or distilled by David Freeman, which can create, for a player or participant, a breadth and depth of emotions in a game or other interactive experience, or which can immerse a game player or interactive participant in a world or a role. It also means the application of these techniques by David or his game design and writing consultancy, The Freeman Group, to a game or other interactive experience. The goal of Emotioneering is to move the player through an interlocking sequence of emotional experiences. *Emotioneering*™ is trademarked by David Freeman.[1]

Engine. See *game engine*.

First-Person Character Arc Techniques. Techniques that make the player go through an emotional transformation by the end of the game.

First-Person Deepening Techniques. Techniques that give the player more emotional depth by the end of the game.

FLBW. A character's fear, limitation, block, or wound. It's something emotionally wrong with the character, such as a lack of self-esteem, a lack of ethics, blaming the world, being afraid of love, and so on.

---

1. Emotioneering™, drawing from a wide palette of language, visuals, sound, and action, creates emotional special effects in games and other interactive experiences. It's a multifaceted, creative technology that enhances the immersive power and scope of a player's or participant's involvement.

Game Engine. Code that makes a game run, renders what you see in the game, renders the audio, governs the use of the controller, and operates all other systems that make the game function. Some people (but by no means all) in the game industry also use either the term *rendering engine* or *renderer* for the code that renders what you see in a game, and say that the *rendering engine* or the *renderer* is a subset (or part) of the *game engine.*

GDC. The Game Developers Conference, the largest convention in the world of game designers and others intimately involved with the creation of games. (See **www.gdconf.org**.) It's held annually in March, traditionally in San Jose, California. Besides lectures, workshops, and exhibits, it provides opportunities for game designers to mainline Colombian coffee and expand their minds by hobnobbing with their peers late into the night.

Group Bonding Techniques. Techniques that make a group (such as a squad) feel bonded. If the player is part of that group, the player will feel bonded to the group as well.

Group Deepening Techniques. Techniques that make groups—as small as a squad or as large as a race or culture—embody a feeling of emotional depth.

Group Interesting Techniques. Techniques for making groups—as small as a squad or as large as a culture or race—fascinating and intriguing to the player. A group, however, is not simply a few friends who might know each other, but instead is any collection of people who have, to some degree, their own distinct, collective identity—for example, the Celts or the Marines.

Idle. The movement or movements performed by a character you play when you've stopped moving the character about. Idles are used so that the character doesn't seem stiff and lacking life. In some games, funny idles are occasionally used to provide humor.

Incongruence. Putting things together that normally one wouldn't think of as belonging together. Some examples: a white dove settling on the slaughtered body of a war hero—or a small child, alone and laughing in a dark, scary alley at night. There are many types and many uses for Incongruence.

In-Game Cinematic. See *Cinematic.*

Interesting Techniques. Techniques that make one of the following five elements of linear storytelling interesting:

+ Characters
+ Dialogue
+ Relationships between characters
+ Scenes, moments, or situations within a game
+ Plots

Other words for *interesting*: making things unique, imaginative, or original. In games, *interesting* can apply to other categories than those listed in the preceding list, such as a player's relationship to one or more of the NPCs. Another example: a group, culture, or even a race can be interesting.

Layer Cakes. A situation in which Character A has various layers of feelings toward Character B. These various feelings (Character A's Layer Cakes toward Character B's) can present themselves either simultaneously or sequentially.

Mask. A false front, and sometimes an entire false personality, that covers up who the person really is. A character's Mask makes life more manageable and keeps pain repressed. In the great majority of cases, the character is unaware that he or she has a Mask, and would deny it if you brought it to his or her attention. In the provocative film *American Beauty*, Ricky Fitts, a troubled teen played by Wes Bentley, puts on a Mask that he's serene and even enlightened, when in fact he's almost numb (which is his FLBW). That numbness stems from his once having been wrongfully committed to a mental institution and drugged. In the same film, Annette Bening plays Carolyn Burnham, a woman who wears the Mask of a cheerful, successful businesswoman and housewife whose life is storybook example of perfection. In truth, however, her life is hollow, and she's full of loathing for herself and others (her FLBW). There are many varieties of Masks. When used artfully, they give depth to a character, and thus are a subset of NPC Deepening Techniques.

Meaningful Nonlinear Re-Sequencing (MNR). This means that the player in a game can undergo a variety of experiences, or pursue a variety of tasks, in any order he or she pleases (thus, they can be "re-sequenced" in any number of ways, and so are "nonlinear"). These experiences and tasks, which can be re-sequenced nonlinearly, have *meaning*. By meaning, it's implied that the experiences and/or tasks have *emotional content*, and they feel like *they hang together coherently as an emotionally engaging story or as part of a story.*

Mechanics. Actions that can be performed by the character or characters being controlled by the player.

NPC. A non-player character, meaning any character in a game that is not controlled by the player.

NPC Character Arc Techniques. Techniques that give an NPC a Character Arc.

NPC Deepening Techniques. Techniques that give major NPCs emotional depth and/or complexity.

NPC Interesting Techniques. Techniques that make major NPCs dimensional and fresh, and thus interesting.

NPC Toward NPC Chemistry Techniques. Techniques that, with very little reliance on dialogue, make it feel like two NPCs have chemistry—that is, that they belong together as friends or lovers.

NPC Toward NPC Relationship Deepening Techniques. Techniques that, with very little reliance on dialogue, make it feel like two NPCs have a rich and complex relationship.

NPC Toward Player Relationship Deepening Techniques. Ways to make it feel as if major NPCs have emotionally complex relationships with the player.

Open-Ended. Sometimes a game (or film/TV) story has a bit of mystery at the end, leaving the player (or viewer) to speculate as to what really happened in the story. Sometimes the ending leaves a player (or viewer) to wonder or what will happen to the characters in the story, or to the world of the story, after the part of the story the player (or viewer) has experienced is over. I call these types of finales *open-ended* endings. The greater the mystery or the speculation at the end, the more open-ended the story is.

Open-Ended Game. See *Emergent Gameplay*.

Plot Deepening Techniques. Ways to give game stories emotional depth and resonance, the way some films do, such as *Crouching Tiger, Hidden Dragon, The Matrix, Lord of the Rings, American Beauty, Casablanca*, or *Blade Runner*.

Plot Interesting Techniques. Ways of making game plots interesting, taking into account many different kinds of story structures—linear, nonlinear, and multi-path (among others)—unique to games.

Player Toward NPC Chemistry Techniques. Techniques that make the player feel Chemistry with an NPC—that is, make the player feel close to an NPC, either romantically or non-romantically.

Player Toward NPC Relationship Deepening Techniques. Ways to give the player emotionally complex relationships with major NPCs.

Pre-Rendered Cinematic. See *Cinematic*.

Reveal. A piece of information given during a game. It can be information about the story, the backstory, a character, an event, an object, and so on. In a game, some Reveals are necessary for the player to experience in order to make sense of the story. Usually some are optional, meaning that they give information which, though interesting, informative, and/or potentially adding to the game's emotion or context, aren't necessary to experience for the player to make sense of the game's story.

Role Induction Techniques. Techniques that make a player willing to identify with the character he or she is playing.

Rooting Interesting Techniques. Techniques that make players root for or, more precisely, identify with (empathize with) a character. The term sounds like it means players cheer on the character who has Rooting Interest. That's just a byproduct of players identifying with the character. Thus a character with Rooting Interest is one with whom we empathize. (This term, and "Character Arc," are the only two phrases in the book that come from the film industry.)

Scripted Sequence. A small or large sequence of actions that would occur identically if the game was played the same way every time. Usually the scripted sequence is triggered by the player's character taking a certain action or hitting a certain point in the game. An example: when the player's character A, in health condition B, carrying weapon C, who has taken previous action D, hits position E, then the enemy F steps out from behind the tree, and takes a certain action.

Consider a more concrete example from a hypothetical game: The player's character Darius (A), his health points almost gone (B), carrying the Sword of Eden that he has taken from Vladamir (C), which Darius had earlier used to kill Vladamir's father (D), steps into the clearing (E). If these phenomena are all in place, then Vladamir will step out from behind the trees, vow to Darius that he will now avenge his father, and take aim at Darius with his bow.

Vladamir stepping out and saying he's going to avenge his father is the scripted sequence. If any of (A) through (D) above didn't happen (in this fairly sophisticated example), then Vladamir wouldn't step out from behind the tree at that point, or would step out but say or do something different. A Scripted Sequence doesn't require all the components of this complex example. The *key feature* of a Scripted Sequence is that something occurs in a game, triggered by something done by the player—but while it occurs, the player can still control his or her character. (This contrasts to a cinematic, where the player loses control of the character.)

Self Auto-Talk. When you hear the character you're playing speak.

Self Auto-Thought. When you hear the thoughts of the character you're playing.

Set-Ups and Payoffs. Something—an object, a phrase spoken by a character—is introduced early in the plot. When it's introduced, it's a *set-up*. A set-up is revisited in an interesting way one or more times later in the story. Each of these instances is a *payoff*.

Story Element. There are more than 150 elements frequently found in stories, such as opposing sides, quests, obstacles, and so on. Each of these is a Story Element.

Symbolic Subplot. An object or action that represents (symbolizes) the character's growth through his or her Character Arc.

Technique Stacking. Layering one Emotioneering technique on top of another simultaneously, or utilizing them very close to each other in time, to create complex emotional impacts.

Theme. As used in this book, a subject central to the story, explored from many points of view, with no conclusion made about the subject. Or, a subject central to the story, explored from many points of view, with a conclusion finally made about the subject.

Trait. A major facet of the character's personality—part of his or her Character Diamond. As such, a Trait (in combination with all of the other Traits in a character's Character Diamond) governs how the character sees the world, thinks, speaks, and acts.

World Induction Techniques. Techniques other than realism that cause a player to become emotionally immersed in the world of the game. It doesn't mean the teaching of skills and weapons. It refers instead to techniques for making a player want to spend time in the world of the game.

Index

www.informit.com

YOUR GUIDE TO IT REFERENCE

New Riders has partnered with **InformIT.com** to bring technical information to your desktop. Drawing from New Riders authors and reviewers to provide additional information on topics of interest to you, **InformIT.com** provides free, in-depth information you won't find anywhere else.

Articles

Keep your edge with thousands of free articles, in-depth features, interviews, and IT reference recommendations—all written by experts you know and trust.

Online Books

Answers in an instant from **InformIT Online Books'** 600+ fully searchable online books.

POWERED BY

Catalog

Review online sample chapters, author biographies, and customer rankings and choose exactly the right book from a selection of over 5,000 titles.

www.newriders.com

VOICES THAT MATTER

HOW TO CONTACT US

VISIT OUR WEB SITE

WWW.NEWRIDERS.COM

On our Web site you'll find information about our other books, authors, tables of contents, indexes, and book errata. You will also find information about book registration and how to purchase our books.

EMAIL US

Contact us at this address: **nrfeedback@newriders.com**

- If you have comments or questions about this book
- To report errors that you have found in this book
- If you have a book proposal to submit or are interested in writing for New Riders
- If you would like to have an author kit sent to you
- If you are an expert in a computer topic or technology and are interested in being a technical editor who reviews manuscripts for technical accuracy
- To find a distributor in your area, please contact our international department at this address. **nrmedia@newriders.com**

- For instructors from educational institutions who want to preview New Riders books for classroom use. Email should include your name, title, school, department, address, phone number, office days/hours, text in use, and enrollment, along with your request for desk/examination copies and/or additional information.
- For members of the media who are interested in reviewing copies of New Riders books. Send your name, mailing address, and email address, along with the name of the publication or Web site you work for.

BULK PURCHASES/CORPORATE SALES

The publisher offers discounts on this book when ordered in quantity for bulk purchases and special sales. For sales within the U.S., please contact: Corporate and Government Sales (800) 382-3419 or **corpsales@pearsontechgroup.com**. Outside of the U.S., please contact: International Sales (317) 428-3341 or **international@pearsontechgroup.com**.

WRITE TO US

New Riders Publishing
800 East 96th Street, 3rd Floor
Indianapolis, IN 46240

CALL US

Toll-free (800) 571-5840. Ask for New Riders.
If outside U.S. (317) 428-3000. Ask for New Riders.

FAX US

(317) 428-3280

WWW.NEWRIDERS.COM

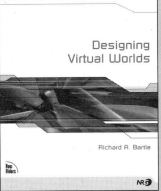
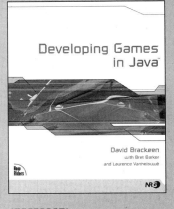